Logistics Management

Logistics Management

David B. Grant

PEARSON

Harlow, England • London • New York • Boston • San Francisco • Toronto • Sydney
Auckland • Singapore • Hong Kong • Tokyo • Seoul • Taipei • New Delhi
Cape Town • São Paulo • Mexico City • Madrid • Amsterdam • Munich • Paris • Milan

Pearson Education Limited
Edinburgh Gate
Harlow
Essex CM20 2JE
England

and Associated Companies around the world

Visit us on the World Wide Web at:
www.pearson.com/uk

First published 2012

© Pearson Education Limited 2012

ISBN 978-0-273-73135-1

British Library Cataloguing-in-Publication Data
A catalogue record for this book is available from the British Library

Library of Congress Cataloguing-in-Publication Data
A catalog record for this book is available from the Library of Congress

10 9 8 7 6 5 4 3 2 1
16 15 14 13 12

Typeset in 9.5/12.5 pt ITC Charter by
Printed by Ashford Colour Press Ltd, Gosport

In memory of my parents,
Donald Bruce Grant (August 1930–April 2009) and Betty Jean Grant
(February 1929–August 2009)

Contents

Supporting resources

Visit www.pearsoned.co.uk/grant to find valuable online resources

For instructors
- Customisable PowerPoint slides which are downloadable and available to use for teaching
- Complete downloadable Instructor's Manual

For more information please contact your local Pearson Education sales representative or visit www.pearsoned.co.uk/grant

Preface

The year 2011 represents a personal milestone as I have now entered my third decade of teaching and researching the subject of logistics. There has been much change in the subject since 1990; however, the basic premises of 'Stop' and 'Go' still very much apply to logistical activities. That is, products are moved through the supply chain and are either waiting for the next step in a process or are in transit. The impetus for change has come from the importance of logistics in a shrinking global market; ongoing advances in computer and information technology; a continuing emphasis on quality and customer satisfaction; and a wider appreciation of logistics' impact on the natural environment. This new book, *Logistics Management,* blends traditional logistics activities with these other developments that have made logistics a critical element for business success.

The pragmatic, applied nature of the text and its managerial orientation make it a useful reference book for present and future logistics professionals. The logistics examples and end-of-chapter questions are structured to challenge readers' managerial skills. They are integrative in nature and examine issues that are important to today's logistics executive. Finally, there is suggested reading in each chapter and a glossary at the end of the book.

This book contains thirteen chapters and the first two set the scene and scope for the rest of the book. The subject of supply chain management has been incorporated into the introductory chapter. Supply chain management is a strategic management concept encompassing collaboration with other supply chain stakeholders to provide products and services to customers. Logistical activities comprise the functional processes that move such products and services through a firm's supply chain. This chapter integrates these two concepts. The second chapter on customer service incorporates material related to service performance measurement such as key performance indicators and service quality of logistics customer service.

The next six chapters discuss the functional activities of logistics, starting with purchasing and procurement in Chapter 3, which encompasses all phases of the purchasing process and introduces advances in electronic purchasing of products and services. Following are discussions of transportation in Chapter 4, warehousing in Chapter 5 and inventory management in Chapter 6. The seventh chapter, on operations and materials management, considers this topic in the context of a chapter-integrative case analysis of Harley-Davidson, Inc., while Chapter 8 discusses logistics information systems and advancements such as efficient consumer response, quick response and radio frequency identification.

The final five chapters turn to more general management and strategic considerations. The ninth chapter, on logistics financial performance, reflects customer and product profitability linking to discussions of performance measurement in Chapter 2. Chapter 10, on human resources and logistics, extends the scope of logistics organisational structure to issues of human resources, including knowledge workers and gender.

The eleventh chapter considers global aspects of logistics. While the focus of this book is European, this chapter encompasses material on global logistics issues facing firms doing business around the globe. Chapter 12 discusses the increasingly important topics of reverse and sustainable logistics. Finally, Chapter 13 discusses implementing logistics strategy in a firm's overall corporate strategy to achieve customer satisfaction, i.e. a strategic approach, and operational objectives for functional logistics activities, i.e. a tactical approach.

The aim of this book is to present instructors and students with the best textbook of this type on the market. I believe this edition provides a nice mix of current academic thought and logistics practice, focusing on issues unique to Europe and North America but which are also very relevant in a global setting. This book is being written during the depth of the global economic recession that began in 2008; this situation is taken into account wherever possible in the text.

David B. Grant
March 2012

About the author

Professor David B. Grant is Director of the Logistics Institute in the Business School at the University of Hull in the UK and has held appointments at Heriot-Watt University and the Universities of Edinburgh, Calgary and Lethbridge. His doctoral thesis investigated customer service, satisfaction and service quality in UK food-processing logistics and received the *James Cooper Memorial Cup PhD Award* from the Chartered Institute of Logistics and Transport (UK) in 2003.

Professor Grant holds BComm and MBA degrees from the University of Calgary and MSc by Research (with Distinction) and PhD degrees from the University of Edinburgh. He also holds a Professional Certificate in University Teaching from the University of Edinburgh and is a Fellow of the UK's Higher Education Academy.

Professor Grant's business experience includes retail, corporate banking, technical design, and financial and marketing consulting and seminar facilitation for clients in Canada and the United States. His recent applied research has investigated on-shelf availability and out-of-stocks, total loss and waste in food retailing, forecasting and obsolete inventory, service quality of internet retailers, and consumer logistics and shopping convenience in both grocery and non-grocery contexts.

Professor Grant has over 125 publications in various refereed journals, books and conference proceedings, regularly referees articles for many academic journals and conferences, and is on the editorial board of six international academic journals. He is a member of the Council of Supply Chain Management Professionals (CSCMP) and its Education Strategies Committee, the UK Logistics Research Network (LRN), the Nordic NOFOMA logistics research group, and the British Retail Consortium's Storage and Distribution Technical Advisory Committee.

Acknowledgements

I want to acknowledge and thank my many colleagues not only at the Logistics Institute and Business School at the University of Hull but also at many other universities, companies and associations around the world for their ongoing intellectual stimulation on logistics theory and practice. There are too many to name individually, but I want to mention particularly the Council of Supply Chain Management Professionals for their cooperation in allowing me to use their materials throughout the book, especially the glossary. I also want to thank Rufus Curnow, Senior Acquisitions Editor, and his colleagues at Pearson Education for their guidance and support during the writing and production process.

Publisher's Acknowledgements

We are grateful to the following for permission to reproduce copyright material:

Figures

Figure 2.8 adapted from A Conceptual Model of Service Quality and Its Implications for Future Research, *Journal of Marketing,* Vol. 49, No. 4, pp.41–50. (Parasuraman, A., Zeithaml, V. and . Berry, L. 1985), reprinted with permission from Journal of Marketing, published by the American Marketing Association; Figure 3.1 reprinted from Purchasing myopia – revisited, Journal of Purchasing and Supply Management, Vol. 3, No. 1, p. 5 (Farmer, D. 1997) with permission from Elsevier; Figure 3.4 from Total cost of ownership: An analysis approach for purchasing, *The International Journal of Physical Distribution & Logistics Management,* Vol. 25, No. 8, p. 12 (Ellram, L. 1995), reproduced with permission of Emerald Group Publishing Limited in the format Journal via Copyright Clearance Center. © Emerald Group Publishing Limited all rights reserved; Figure 4.6 from Langley, C. John and Capgemini Consulting (2010) "15th Annual Third-Party Logistics Study" http://www.3plstudy.com p. 11, fig. 5; Figure 4.7 from Langley, C. John and Capgemini Consulting (2010) "15th Annual Third-Party Logistics Study" http://www.3plstudy.com p. 9, fig. 3; Figure 4.8 from Langley, C. John and Capgemini Consulting (2010) "15th Annual Third-Party Logistics Study" http://www.3plstudy.com p. 13, fig. 8; Figure 5.10 from Methodological Choices in Depot Location Studies, *Operational Research Quarterly,* Vol. 27, No. 1, ii, p. 242 (Rand, G.K. 1976); Figure 6.6 from Information Distortion in a Supply Chain: The Bullwhip Effect, *Management Science,* Vol. 43, No. 4, p. 547 (Lee, H.L., Padmanabhan, V. and Whang, S. 1997); Figure 8.2 from A Model for Structuring Efficient Consumer Response Measures, *International Journal of Retail & Distribution Management,* Vol. 36, No. 8, p. 593 (Aastrup, J., Kotzab, H., Grant, D.B., Teller, C. and Bjerre, M. 2008), reproduced with permission of Emerald Group Publishing Limited in the format Journal via Copyright Clearance Center. © Emerald Group Publishing Limited all rights reserved; Figure 9.1 from A Review and Evaluation of Logistics Metrics, *International Journal of*

Logistics Management, Vol. 5, No. 2, p. 20 (Caplice, C. and Sheffi, Y. 1994), reproduced with permission of Emerald Group Publishing Limited in the format Journal via Copyright Clearance Center. © Emerald Group Publishing Limited all rights reserved; Figure 9.2 from www.supply-chain.org; Figure 9.3 from The Performance Prism in Practice, *Measuring Business Excellence,* Vol. 5, No. 2, p. 12 (Neely, A., Adams, C. and Crowe, P. 2001), reproduced with permission of Emerald Group Publishing Limited in the format Journal via Copyright Clearance Center. © Emerald Group Publishing Limited all rights reserved; Figure 9.7 adapted from Implementing Activity-Based Costing (ABC) in Logistics, *Journal of Business Logistics,* Vol. 15, No. 2, pp. 1-23 (Pohlen, T.L. and La Londe, B.J. 1994); Figure 9.9 from Cash-to-cash: the new supply chain management metric, *International Journal of Physical Distribution & Logistics Management,* Vol. 32, No. 4, p. 290 (Farris, M.T. and Hutchinson, P.D. 2002), reproduced with permission of Emerald Group Publishing Limited in the format Journal via Copyright Clearance Center. © Emerald Group Publishing Limited all rights reserved; Figure 10.6 from Management development and the supply chain manager of the future, *International Journal of Logistics Management,* Vol. 16, No. 2, p. 181 (Mangan, J. and Christopher, M. 2005), reproduced with permission of Emerald Group Publishing Limited in the format Journal via Copyright Clearance Center. © Emerald Group Publishing Limited all rights reserved; Figure 10.8 from *Management of In-store Replenishment Systems: An exploratory study of European retailers being a Thesis submitted for the Degree of Doctor in Philosophy (PhD) at the University of Hull* p. 270 (Trautrims, A. 2011); Figures 11.5, 12.7 from Challenges and Opportunities, *Presentation at the 25th German Logistics Congress,* October (Kolding, E. 2008); Figure 12.1 from Design of Closed-Loop Supply Chain and Product Recovery Management for Fast-Moving Consumer Goods: The Case of a Single-Use Camera, *Asia Pacific Journal of Marketing & Logistics,* Vol. 22, No. 2, p. 234 (Grant, D.B. and Banomyong, R. 2010), reproduced with permission of Emerald Group Publishing Limited in the format Journal via Copyright Clearance Center. © Emerald Group Publishing Limited all rights reserved; Figure 12.2a from *Transport and Climate Change: Advice to Government from the Commission for Integrated Transport* (Commission for Integrated Transport 2007); Figure 12.2b from *The Guardian,* 01/12/2008, http://image.guardian.co.uk/sys-files/Guardian/documents/2008/12/01/CO2_EMISSIONS_0212.pdf, Copyright Guardian News & Media Ltd 2008; Figure 12.5 adapted from *Transport and Climate Change: Advice to Government from the Commission for Integrated Transport* (Committee for Integrated Transport 2007) pp. 20-22; Figure 13.6 from Logistics, strategy and structure: a conceptual framework, *International Journal of Physical Distribution & Logistics Management,* Vol. 29, No. 4, p. 39 (Stock, G.N., Greis, N.P. and Kasarda, J.D. 1999), reproduced with permission of Emerald Group Publishing Limited in the format Journal via Copyright Clearance Center. © Emerald Group Publishing Limited all rights reserved

Tables

Table 3.1 from Total cost of ownership: An analysis approach for purchasing, *The International Journal of Physical Distribution & Logistics Management,* Vol. 25, No. 8, p. 13 (Ellram, L. 1995), reproduced with permission of Emerald Group Publishing Limited in the format Journal via Copyright Clearance Center. © Emerald Group Publishing Limited all rights reserved; Table 3.2 reprinted from Environmental supply chain dynamics, Journal of Cleaner Production, Vol. 8, p.461 (Hall, J. 2000) reproduced with permission of ELSEVIER BV in the format Journal via Copyright Clearance Center; Table 9.1 from

Logistics performance measurement in the supply chain: a benchmark, *Benchmarking: An International Journal*, Vol. 16, No. 6, pp. 785-798 (Keebler, J.S. and Plank, R.E. 2009), reproduced with permission of Emerald Group Publishing Limited in the format Journal via Copyright Clearance Center. © Emerald Group Publishing Limited all rights reserved; Table 9.2 from A Review and Evaluation of Logistics Metrics, *International Journal of Logistics Management*, Vol. 5, No. 2, p. 14 (Caplice, C. and Sheffi, Y. 1994), reproduced with permission of Emerald Group Publishing Limited in the format Journal via Copyright Clearance Center. © Emerald Group Publishing Limited all rights reserved; Table 10.1 from Management development and the supply chain manager of the future, *International Journal of Logistics Management*, Vol. 16, No. 2, p. 181 (Mangan, J. and Christopher, M. 2005), reproduced with permission of Emerald Group Publishing Limited in the format Journal via Copyright Clearance Center. © Emerald Group Publishing Limited all rights reserved; Table 12.1 from Eyewitness: An atlas of pollution; the world in carbon dioxide emissions, *The Guardian*, 31/01/2011, p. 18 (Harvey, F.), Fiona Harvey Copyright Guardian News & Media Ltd 2011

Text

Extract 2.2 adapted from All homeward bound, *Logistics Business Magazine* November/December pp.10–4 (2004); Extract 7.3 adapted from Lean Manufacturing Solutions Inc., http://www.lmsi.ca/cs.htm (accessed 5 August 2011); Extract 11.01 adapted from *CSCMP Global Perspectives: Japan,* http://cscmp.org (Kitamura, T. 2006) Council of Supply Chain Management Professionals; Extract 11.02 adapted from *CSCMP Global Perspectives: India,* http://cscmp.org (Shah, J. and Suresh D.N. 2009) Council of Supply Chain Management Professionals; Extract 11.03 adapted from *CSCMP Global Perspectives: Brazil,* http://cscmp.org (Centro de Estudos em Logística of COPPEAD Management Institute, Federal University of Rio de Janeiro 2007) Council of Supply Chain Management Professionals

Picture Credits

The publisher would like to thank the following for their kind permission to reproduce their photographs:

(Key: b-bottom; c-centre; l-left; r-right; t-top)

Dexion Comino Ltd part of the Constructor Group AS: 86c, 86cr, 86bl, 86bc, 86br, 88b, 88bc, 88br; **Fotolia.com:** Andreas Krutzler 86cl; **Linde Material Handling (UK) Ltd.:** 88bl

All other images © Pearson Education

Chapter 1

Introduction to logistics and supply chain management

> ## Key objectives
>
> - To define concepts of logistics and supply chain management and the 'Stop' and 'Go' nature of logistics.
> - To explore the evolution of logistics.
> - To show the importance of logistics to the economy.
> - To introduce the functional activities of logistics and systems approach between logistics and the firm.
> - To consider briefly important trends in logistics.

Introduction

Business logistics permeates almost all aspects of our daily lives and without it we would not have many of the goods, products and services that we take for granted in our normal existence. For example, electronic products such as flat-screen televisions, computers or mobile telephones are usually not manufactured locally or in national markets – they are now manufactured in a few Asian countries and shipped all around the world. As another example, most seasonal fresh food such as fruit and vegetables is available all year round due to sourcing from foreign markets or sophisticated chilled storage that helps prevent the stored food from spoiling or aging.

This book presents and discusses the fundamental concepts underlying logistics and applications of logistical activities or functions in a business context. This chapter provides an introduction and overview to logistics by considering various important definitions required to set the scope of this topic, concepts of logistics representing movement and storage and meeting customers' requirements as an output, the evolution of logistics and its economic impact, various logistics activities and a systems approach to logistics in the firm, and a discussion of trends affecting logistics. These latter two sections will also provide an outline of how this book is structured by noting where succeeding chapters will go into topics in more depth.

Definitions of logistics and supply chain management

A first step is to define the word 'logistics' in the context of business and this book. The Council of Supply Chain Management Professionals (CSCMP), a worldwide professional association of logistics and supply chain professionals, defines logistics management as:

> that part of supply chain management that plans, implements, and controls the efficient, effective forward and reverses flow and storage of goods, services and related information between the point of origin and the point of consumption in order to meet customers' requirements.[1]

Two key concepts inherent in this definition are those of movement or '*GO*' and storage or '*STOP*'. 'Go' in this context refers to goods being moved or transported to customers or back in a reverse logistics flow; this is a *temporal* or *time* concept. 'Stop' in this context includes the storage of goods for processing and other operations or to await further movement to customers at a later time; this is a *place* or *location* concept. These ideas reflect the time and place *utility* that logistics provides for customers and which comes from utility theory in the economics discipline.

The other key concept is the objective of meeting customers' requirements, which is the primary output of logistics activities and which ties into the 'Go' and 'Stop' ideas; goods that are required by customers are provided in the right place at the right time. This objective is akin to the marketing objective and thus logistics has a relationship to marketing and customer service, which is further explored in Chapter 2.

Logistics activities are considered by many to be part of a firm's business activities and only within the context of that firm. Five primary logistics activities are the management of transportation, inventory, warehousing or storage, information technology, and production or operations management. These logistics mix variables, which are shown in Figure 1.1, have a number of elements related to each of them. For example, inventory management will have to consider volumes for initial order processing based on customer and operations demand, the purchasing and procurement function to obtain raw materials and other goods for stock, and the reduction of inventory records through the returned goods or waste-disposal processes.

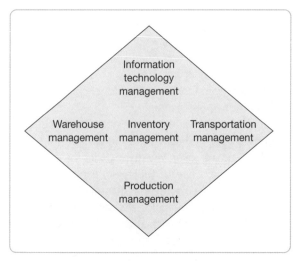

Figure 1.1 Logistics mix variables

However, once a firm actively engages with its suppliers, customers and other stake-holders, its logistical activities go beyond its own doors into the wider supply chain. Such engagement contemplates additional management, known as supply chain management (SCM), and another definition is required to set the scope of this concept. The CSCMP defines SCM as encompassing:

> the planning and management of all activities involved in sourcing and procurement, conversion, and all logistics management activities. Importantly, it also includes coordination and collaboration with channel partners, which can be suppliers, intermediaries, third party service providers, and customers. In essence, supply chain management integrates supply and demand management within and across companies.[2]

The concept of SCM first appeared in the 1980s to address wider logistical activities in an increasingly global economy. Much academic and practitioner discussion has taken, and continues to take, place to set the scope for SCM and its relationships to already established concepts of logistics. Figure 1.2 shows the consideration of one such debate.[3]

The three concepts presented in this figure represent views of various authors published in the academic literature regarding the relationship between logistics and SCM. Some consider SCM is merely a *re-labelling* of logistics due to a lack of understanding by academics and practitioners of what supply chains are and what supply chain managers do. This view is declining due to developments in SCM in both academia and practice. Others consider there is an *intersection* between logistics and SCM as SCM represents a broad strategy across all business processes in the firm and the supply chain. However, the integration and implementation of this concept is currently quite theoretical and there are few empirical studies to support it.[4]

The *unionist* concept considers that logistics is a sub-set of SCM due to a wider supply chain and business process perspective of SCM. Indeed, the CSCMP definition above represents a unionist view. The debate will continue as academics and practitioners alike develop the SCM concept, which at about 30 years is a young theoretical concept in chronological terms. However, for the purposes of this book the unionist concept and the CSCMP definition are adopted as they intuitively make sense given the wider perspective they represent.[5]

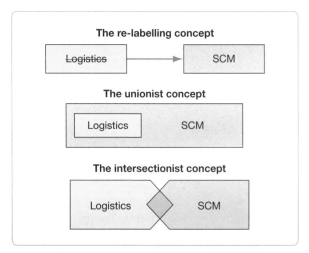

Figure 1.2 Logistics versus supply chain management

Source: adapted from Larson and Halldórsson (2004).

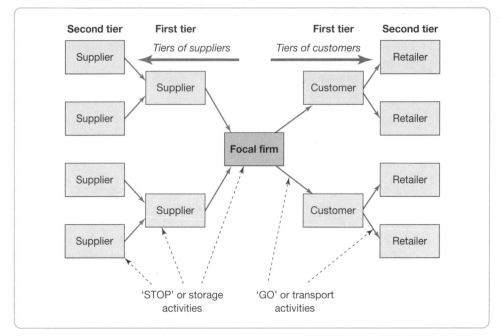

Figure 1.3 A simplified supply chain

A simplified supply chain and its relevant features are shown in Figure 1.3. The firm under consideration is known as the focal firm. Its immediate customers or wholesalers in this case are known as Tier 1 customers; that is, they are the first tier away from the focal firm. The wholesalers' Tier 1 customers or retailers in this case are the focal firm's Tier 2 customers, and so on. Similarly, the focal firm's Tier 1 suppliers are Tier 1 suppliers to their suppliers while the focal firm is a Tier 2 supplier, and so on.

This idea of 'tiering' allows the focal firm to establish where it is in the supply chain and to determine those supply chain relationships that impact its business. This notion of relationships and collaboration is at the heart of SCM – the focal firm has to work with its many SCM stakeholders in order to achieve an effective and efficient supply chain. At each supply chain node – that is the focal firm, supplier or customer – the 'Stop' or storage function takes place. Further, the transport or 'Go' function takes place between these nodes. While this book is about logistics management and activities, it will delve into supply chain and SCM activities where they interact with or influence logistics activities.

The evolution of logistics

The practice of logistics has been in existence for centuries, particularly in a military context, and history is replete with stories of how logistical supply lines, or lack of them, have shaped campaigns by Alexander the Great, Genghis Khan and Napoleon. Armies usually pillaged the lands they conquered for the supplies that they needed; however, in the 19th century, the increased scale of battles meant that armies on the march required more substantial and reliable sources of supply.

In the American Civil War, the southern Confederates developed a strong army after secession as the bulk of their officers came from the existing Union Army and took many provisions and stores with them. President Lincoln appointed Montgomery C. Meigs as Quartermaster General, or logistics manager, of the Union army at the beginning of hostilities in 1861 and Meigs literally had to create from scratch the various stocks required, including uniforms, tents, blankets, rations and animals, to outfit the army.

It seems strange in the 21st century to consider the necessity of animals until one remembers that in the 19th century mules were used to transport goods (rather than trucks), horses were used for cavalry (instead of armoured vehicles and tanks) and cattle were needed for food as long-life tinned food was not yet available. Further, roads were not paved and railroad networks were underdeveloped and thus rain and winter conditions made movement of goods difficult.

Meigs' task was monumental: there were just 30,000 troops in the Union army before the war but almost 670,000 by the end of 1862. Meigs essentially invented a very effective and modern logistics infrastructure to manufacture, procure and distribute the supplies that were required. This infrastructure was very effective. For example, when General Sherman reached Savannah, Georgia in December 1864 on his famous 'March to the Sea' he found 60,000 shirts, trousers and pairs of socks, 10,000 greatcoats, 10,000 waterproof ponchos, 20,000 blankets and three days' food rations for each man waiting in secure storage on Hilton Head Island.[6]

While military logistics has occupied much endeavour in centuries past, its scholarly study in a business context really began in agricultural or farm-to-market economics and physical distribution at the beginning of the last century after the industrial revolution saw an exodus of people from rural areas and farms to cities. One of the early authors of such 'market distribution' was Louis Weld, who noted the dichotomy between large lots of goods that could be efficiently delivered and the inability of small retailers to accept and store such large lots, differences between demand and availability of products at certain times of the year, and difficult relations between country shippers and retail stores.[7] These issues remain today, as we will discuss in other chapters of this book.

An examination of the evolution of logistics thought from that time provides a chronology of major contributions through six different 'eras' or time periods in the 20th century. This chronology is primarily a North American perspective but is nevertheless representative of the changes in logistics thinking over the last century:

Era 1: Farm to market (1916–1940)

Era 2: Segmented functions (1940 through to early 1960s)

Era 3: Integrated functions (early 1960s to early 1970s)

Era 4: Customer focus (early 1970s to mid-1980s)

Era 5: Logistics as differentiator (mid-1980s to the present)

Era 6: Behavioural and boundary spanning (the future).[8]

During Era 1: Farm to market and Era 2: Segmented functions, logistics was integrated with marketing and both were influenced by agricultural economics until the Second World War. The war saw concepts in logistics migrate into two sectors: military and business. Military needs focused on logistics activities pertaining to materials while business logistics remained a sub-set of marketing.

Business logistics received an increased impetus after the war as technological and product innovation, together with the booming economy of the 1950s, provided many new goods for consumers. Authors such as management guru Peter Drucker compared business logistics to Africa as the last unknown and undiscovered continent.[9] Other academics such as Wroe Alderson, Bob Bartels, Donald Bowersox and Bernard LaLonde began to focus research on physical distribution activities and the role they played in the marketing and business functions. Eras 3–6 represent the output of work that has gone on over the past 50 years in the discipline of 'business logistics'.

In particular, Era 5: Logistics as differentiator has stressed the strategic importance of logistics in giving firms a competitive advantage by allowing them to compete by providing the 'right quantities of the right goods in the right place at the right time and in the right condition' – an often-repeated adage in business logistics for several decades. There have been other factors and trends responsible for the evolution and growth of business logistics, including historical factors such as transportation deregulation in North America and Europe, the development of containerised shipping, the increased use of computing and information technology, and changes in supply chain power from manufacturers towards retailers. A discussion of various current trends follows later in this chapter.

The importance of logistics to the economy

Logistics activities have a major economic impact on countries and their societies. In terms of size, logistics accounted for 8.3 per cent of the United States' gross domestic product (GDP) in 2010, or about $1.2 trillion. In Europe, logistics activities accounted for 7.2 per cent of European GDP across the EU-27 countries, or about €850 billion ($1.2 trillion) in 2009.[10]

A breakdown of the cost allocations for the United States and Europe of the four major logistics activities – transportation management, warehousing or storage management, inventory management, and information technology and administrative management – is shown in Figure 1.4. By far the largest cost for firms is transportation (the 'Go' activity) at 63 per cent in the US and 48 per cent in Europe, with inventory and warehousing management (the 'Stop' activity) comprising 32 per cent of costs in the US and 41 per cent in Europe.

Although logistics costs today represents about 8 per cent of GDP in the US and Europe, they were in the order of 15–20 per cent of GDP in both regions during the 1970s and 1980s. To further illustrate this point, Figure 1.5 shows the decrease in inventory costs in the US and days of inventory coverage in Europe over the last 20 years.[11]

The various trends discussed below and throughout this book illustrate how such cost savings have been achieved through economies of scale, better use of technology and expanding markets. And yet economies in other parts of the world still have logistics costs around 20–25 per cent of GDP. Further, firms in the United States and Europe are still somewhat inefficient in terms of their costs and cash-to-cash cycles, so there is room for improvement everywhere. An example of such improvement is discussed in Logistics Example 1.1. Logistics financial performance and issues will be addressed further in Chapter 9 as well as in Chapter 13 on logistics strategy.

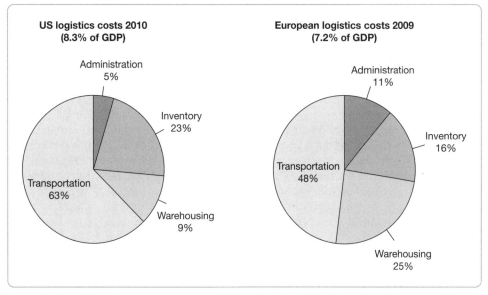

Figure 1.4 Logistics costs by activity
Source: Wilson (2011).

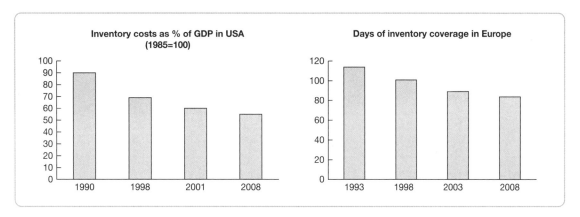

Figure 1.5 Inventory profiles
Source: Wilson (2011).

LOGISTICS EXAMPLE 1.1

Transforming logistics infrastructure at Procter & Gamble

Procter & Gamble (P&G) manufactures and markets nearly 300 brands of consumer products, including Ariel, Pampers, Sunny Delight and Pringles. With a workforce of nearly 100,000, P&G operates in around 80 countries and in 2003 generated net sales of almost £24.5 billion. However, its supply chain was inefficient. One underperforming measure was missed cases – availability was 96 per cent and the number of missed cases was 4 per cent – and they were delivering only about two-thirds of orders on time. The 4 per cent of missed cases amounted to seven or eight million cases a year and cost P&G an estimated £40 million.

Logistics example 1.1 (*cont.*)

The company has since been transforming its UK supply chain into a more efficient and collaborative operation. This process has involved implementing a range of innovative schemes to help optimise and consolidate the supply chain. P&G invested almost £23 million to upgrade its logistics infrastructure, including focusing on supplier relationship management and improving the speed and accuracy of information flow up the supply chain; creating two distribution centres in the north and south to deliver the full range of P&G's ambient products on one truck; introducing cross-docking so that products bypass storage, saving time and resources by going straight onto store shelves; and using IT solutions such as GPS tracking and electronic proof of delivery. P&G also built an automated distribution centre (DC) at its London plant and upgraded its existing DC at Skelmersdale, Lancashire.

In the 15 months since implementation, P&G's 'first-time fill rate' for customers now stands at 99 per cent and the percentage of missed cases has reduced from 4 per cent to less than 0.5 per cent. Losses – reduced inventory and fewer truck miles – have been cut out of the supply chain. P&G is already working on further innovative schemes, including joint forecasting with customers on data synchronisation, and is implementing trials with customers. One trial concerns cross-docking where some of its products arrive at a customer's warehouse but rather than being put away in racking, are picked and sorted immediately. Two other trials with Tesco include using wheeled dollies for promotions and wheeled half pallets for laundry cleaning products. The company is also developing a 'satellite pen' for signatures and is considering providing 24/7 deliveries.

Question

Discuss the cost tradeoffs involved in P&G's decision to invest in its information systems.

Source: adapted from 'The innovative trailblazer', *Logistics Manager,* Vol. 11, No. 5, June 2004, pp. 11–13.

Logistics activities

The five major logistics activities have already been identified as transportation, warehousing or storage, inventory, information technology, and production or operations management. Within these activities there are also elements of inbound and outbound transportation, in-house fleet management or management of outsourced third-party logistics services providers, materials handling and order fulfilment, logistics network design, packaging and assembly, supply and demand planning, and international sourcing and procurement.

Regarding the location of these five major activities in this book, transportation management issues such as modes, carrier choice and third-party or outsourced transportation are addressed in Chapter 4 as well as in Chapter 11 on international and global logistics. Warehousing management issues such as site location, the numbers of warehouses needed and their size are discussed in Chapter 5. Inventory management issues such as the inventory conundrum of maintaining sufficient stocks to satisfy demand while keeping costs low are covered in Chapter 6.

Logistics information systems and technology such as radio frequency identification (RFID) and electronic commerce are addressed in Chapter 8 but also appear in other chapters. Finally, the purchasing and procurement function that underlies all of the logistical activities is considered in Chapter 3, while production and operations management issues such as just-in-time, quality and lean and agile systems are discussed in Chapter 7.

An integrated and systems approach in the firm

Logistics management is an integrating function within the firm – logistics activities must be coordinated and optimised and must be integrated with other functional areas of the firm, including marketing, sales, manufacturing, finance, human resources and information technology. SCM, meanwhile, is an integrating function beyond the firm linking major business functions and processes within and across many firms into a holistic and high-performing business model.

Such integrating functions suggest that logistics management and SCM are essentially 'systems' and as such elements of 'systems thinking' would be relevant and useful in these contexts.[12] A systems perspective allows a firm to look beneath the surface of events to the underlying structures of behaviour and attitudes in order to gain leverage for constructive change and competitive advantage not accessible through a concentration on specific events.

A systems thinking approach enables a firm to consider 'archetypes' through which structural dilemmas are identified at their root and which in turn can solicit appropriate responses by firm members. Further, the advent of reverse logistics and SCM suggests that the system can be closed-loop and self-containing.

Trends in logistics

There are many aspects of logistics in this second decade of the 21st century that are affected by various trends. Following is a discussion of some of the most important trends that have developed since the turn of the millennium.[13]

Globalisation

Globalisation has increased tremendously since the 1960s and 1970s and there is no doubt that it will continue well into the future as developing countries in Asia, Africa and South America contribute more to the world's economy. As noted above, this growth was spurred by the development and widespread adoption of the standard shipping container but is also being facilitated by liberalisation of international trade, the expansion of international transport infrastructure such as ports, roadways and railroads, and cost differentials between countries. This trend will be further discussed in Chapter 11. A logistics example related to global sports entertainment features in Logistics Example 1.2.

LOGISTICS EXAMPLE 1.2

Integrated global logistics for motorcycle racing teams

The World Superbike (WSB) Championship has 11 motorcycle races each years, ten at various European racing circuits and one at Phillip Island in Australia. WSB organisers have developed a unique logistics strategy to enable the 13 race teams competing in the series to ship their entire operations to and from the event.

Teams prepare up to 25 shipping crates, including motorcycles, spare parts, tools and riders' equipment, two weeks before the race date. Each team has a weight allowance paid for by WSB organisers dependent on the status of their riders, from 900 kg per rider for a top team reducing to 500 kg per rider. Teams can ship as much freight as they wish – for example, the Fila Ducati team ships 9,600 kg while the Foggy Petronas team ships 5,810 kg – but they must pay for weight above the allowance. Ten days before the race date 30 articulated lorries are sent throughout Europe to pick up each team's cargo as well as 4,300 tyres weighing 25 tonnes from Pirelli and a total of 5,000 litres of fuel from Shell, Agip, Petronas and Elf.

Two days later a Boeing 747 cargo freighter is loaded at Turin, Italy and departs for Melbourne 24 hours later. Two fuel stops are required during the 11,000-mile journey, in Dubai and Kuala Lumpur. Six days before the race date 17 lorries ferry the cargo to the Phillip Island racing circuit and the race teams unpack and begin their usual race routines. The packing up for the return journey begins in the evening of the race date, and while there is no fuel to return, used tyres are recovered by Pirelli for analysis.

The 747 cargo freighter is hired from Malaysian airlines at a cost of US $550,000. The cargo is insured for €50 million at a premium cost of €15,000. While the operation is complicated, Pierluigi Matta, who is in charge for WSB, told *Motorcycle News* it is not as difficult as it sounds as WSB has been handling the logistics for 11 years and knows each team's needs. This integrated and global approach to logistics allows WSB organisers to effectively and efficiently transport participating teams to Phillip Island and thus gives Australian motorcycle racing fans an opportunity to be part of the WSB championship.

Question

What other types of sporting or entertainment events would face similar logistics issues as WSB?

Source: adapted from 'Shifting the WSB circus down under', *Motorcycle News*, Vol. 34, No. 4, 31 March 2004, pp. 58–59.

Technological innovations

Technology has also increased remarkably during the last few decades due to the advent of computing that has seen the invention of the personal computer, laptop computers and increases in processing speed and memory storage. These innovations enable firms to develop faster and longer supply chains due to their ability to trace and track goods in production or storage or in transit. The application of newer technologies such as RFID and wider adoption of electronic commerce will add to a firm's competence in its logistics activities. This aspect is explored further in Chapter 8.

Corporate social responsibility and the environment

These two topics are linked in that a socially responsible firm will ensure that its environmental impact is reduced or negated. While consideration of the environment is not new, we have seen increased emphasis during the last decade due to the widespread recognition of climate change from carbon emissions and greenhouse gases and various environmental disasters such as oil spills in oceans and on land. Firms nowadays need to consider their carbon footprint from all sources, including transportation and warehousing.

However, corporate social responsibility (CSR) goes beyond the environment to include aspects of fair trade, good employment practices, and appropriate relationships with not only customers and suppliers but shareholders, governments, the public and any other stakeholders. Logistics Example 1.3 presents a debate about such practices. A full discourse of all these issues is beyond the scope of this book; however, Chapter 12 on reverse and sustainable logistics and Chapter 13 on logistics strategy will address many of them.

LOGISTICS EXAMPLE 1.3

Food store wars

In 2001, Levi Strauss & Company won a landmark case in the European Court of Justice to force Britain's dominant food retailer, Tesco, to stop selling its 501 brand of jeans at £30, well below Levi's £45 recommended retail price. The decision was hailed by 'brand owners' as a victory in their battle to protect expensive franchises against the increasingly powerful and aggressive mega-retailers. However, by April 2004, and with the manufacturer's full support, Levi's new 'Signature' brand jeans began appearing in a dozen Tesco stores in Britain, priced at just £25 (€37) a pair. Levi's may have won the legal battle, but Tesco – and other big retailers – have won the wider marketing war.

While the move by Levi Strauss to sell a cheaper range was seen by many as inevitable, it also demonstrated vividly a power shift that has occurred over the last few years, particularly in Europe. The giant food retailers have, to a large extent, turned the tables on the brand owners, controlling customer information through new technology, developing their stores as strong brands in their own right, dictating price terms to suppliers and forcing profound strategic changes right through the supply chain. What's more, with relentless downward pressure on prices in Europe's largest industry, it is the finance chiefs of both the retailers and the manufacturers who are driving much of that change.

Levi's also realised that this would mean a change in its manufacturing strategy. It had to cut its worldwide workforce by a fifth, close plants in western Europe (Belgium, France and Scotland) and North America (the last plants in the US and Canada were shut earlier in 2004), and contract out production to places such as Turkey, Hungary, Poland, Mexico and low-cost Asian countries. It is still dealing with the cost of the restructuring, which is already running into the hundreds of millions of dollars.

Retailers are the flip-side of this coin – wresting control of consumer behaviour is a key objective. At Tesco, aggressive price competition has been at the core of that strategy. Over the past decade the price pressure in UK food retailing has been intense, coming first from the German discounters, Aldi and Lidl, and then from Wal-Mart's acquisition of Asda. And price pressure is just as acute in Europe's other large markets, where sales growth has

---

Logistics example 1.3 (*cont.*)

been weaker. Slim profit margins are maintained by putting relentless pressure on the cost base. Tesco has been absolutely tireless in taking out costs: building stores for less than half what we did ten years ago, £120 a square foot, versus £275 a square foot, and constantly re-engineering its supply chain. This has also meant using its growing power to push its suppliers hard on price and payment terms.

But wielding that power has its consequences. In early 2004, the UK's Office of Fair Trading (OFT) said it would investigate whether supermarkets were complying with the Supermarket Code of Practice, introduced in 2002 after the big retailers were found to be abusing their powerful positions. One public complaint came from a small family-run retailing chain in the north of England, Proudfoot, whose owner argued Tesco was using 'bully-boy tactics' and 'predatory' pricing. It is just such small local retailers and food suppliers that the 1996 Galland law in France is meant to protect. This law stipulates that the large retailers cannot sell goods at 'below cost', as they can in Britain (as long as it's not deemed to be predatory pricing).

The challenge for those trying to raise the alarm about the growing power of the retailers is that it is hard to drum up public outrage over continually declining grocery prices. But Professor Paul Dobson, of Britain's Loughborough University, says a distinction has to be made between the short- and long-term effects of the price pressure.

> Consumers benefit from price pressure. The problem comes if suppliers end up pricing at variable cost without taking the total cost into account. You price at the margin rather than average costs, never covering fixed costs. This leads to under-investing and could lead suppliers to try to get around contract terms by not meeting quality aspects.

The complaints of buyer power may be a relatively recent phenomenon, but retailers and their suppliers have always had an uneasy relationship. When he founded his first store in London in 1919, Jack Cohen (motto: 'Pile them high, sell them cheap') chose the name Tesco to brand his new line of tea. The name was derived from the name of the tea supplier, TE Stockwell, and Cohen to reflect their partnership. Needless to say, the tea supplier has long since faded away.

Question

In a situation driven by a demand for financial performance – i.e. short-term profits – and retailer power, how can small suppliers or small and medium enterprises (SMEs) effectively compete on a logistics basis, smooth out product flows, and meet retailers' needs without seriously compromising profitability?

Source: adapted from Tony McAuley, 'The food chain', www.cfoeurope.com, June 2004.

Relationships, collaboration and cooperation

As noted above, establishing and maintaining mutually beneficial relationships with customers, suppliers and other stakeholders is an increasingly important aspect of logistics management and SCM in an inter-connected and global environment. For example, collaborative and horizontal distribution where two competitors share transportation and possibly warehousing facilities is becoming a way for retailers to avoid 'empty running' of trucks and provide return or 'backhaul' opportunities. Relationships with customers are discussed in Chapter 2, while relationships with suppliers are discussed in Chapter 3.

○ Human resources

People are a necessity in logistics activities: trucks do not drive themselves and goods do not locate themselves on appropriate warehouse racking, despite advances in automation. The fact that you are reading this book indicates you have an interest in this topic and suggests you may possibly want to go further within this industrial sector.

The notion of logistics workers being knowledge workers to lead and make decisions in a team environment is fast becoming a feature in this decade as there is a skills shortage in many markets for logistics and supply chain staff. The interface between logistics workers and technology is also important – for example, 'pick-to-voice' or 'pick-to-light' systems in warehouses – and these issues are considered in Chapter 10.

Summary

Business logistics is an exciting and complex business function that has a fairly young history; it is about half a century old. Despite its youth, logistics has undergone many changes during that time and the pace of change has not abated – in fact, it has increased with developments in technology and globalisation. Such change presents many challenges for firms and logistics service providers.

However, as this book is being written, economies around the world are still suffering from the recession that began in 2008 and which does not appear to be subsiding. Global trade has decreased by about 20 per cent since then and GDP growth in the US and most European nations hovers around the 1–2 per cent mark. This externality to the world's economy also poses fresh challenges and these will be addressed where relevant in this book, particularly in Chapter 11.

This chapter has presented an introduction to the fascinating world of logistics by first defining what it is, together with supply chain management, before reviewing its history and evolution as well as its importance in a modern industrialised and globalised world. This chapter has also highlighted some of the issues surrounding this topic and has briefly identified major trends affecting logistics, including globalisation, the environment, changes in technology, and the need for corporate collaboration and consideration of human resources.

We now turn to the various activities and issues highlighted in this chapter, beginning with customer service as the important output of logistical and supply chain activities.

DISCUSSION QUESTIONS

1 How do you define logistics in terms of your own contexts of country, culture and lifestyle?

2 Do you agree that logistics is a sub-set of supply chain management, i.e. the unionist view, and if not why do you prefer either the re-labelling or the intersectionist view?

3 How might the history of military logistics inform business logistics in the 21st century?

4 Based on the ongoing recession in this second decade of the new millennium, what do you believe will happen to logistics costs around the globe in the next few years and why?

5 Where do you see areas of opportunity for logistics given the key trends affecting logistics today?

Suggested reading

Alvarado, Ursula Y. and Herbert Kotzab 'Supply chain management: The integration of logistics in marketing,' *Industrial Marketing Management,* 2001, Vol. 30, pp.183–198.

Bowersox, Donald J., David J. Closs and Theodore P. Stank 'Ten mega-trends that will revolutionize supply chain logistics,' *Journal of Business Logistics*, 2000, Vol. 21, No. 2, pp.1–16.

Christopher, Martin *Logistics and Supply Chain Management*, 4th ed. Harlow: FT Prentice Hall, 2011.

Drucker, Peter 'Economy's dark continent,' *Fortune*, 1962, Vol. 64, April, pp.103–104.

Fabbe-Costes, Nathalie and Marianne Jahre 'Supply chain integration gives better performance – the emperor's new suit?' *International Journal of Physical Distribution & Logistics Management*, 2007, Vol. 37, No. 10, pp.835–855.

Fabbe-Costes, Nathalie and Marianne Jahre 'Supply chain integration and performance: A review of the evidence,' *International Journal of Logistics Management*, 2008, Vol. 19, No. 2, pp.130–154.

Fernie, John, Frances Pfab and Clive Marchant 'Retail grocery logistics in the UK,' *The International Journal of Logistics Management,* 2000, Vol. 11, No. 2, pp.83–90.

Kent, John L. and Daniel J. Flint 'Perspectives on the evolution of logistics thought,' *Journal of Business Logistics*, 1997, Vol. 18, No. 2, pp.15–29.

Larson, Paul D. and Árni Halldórsson 'Logistics versus supply chain management: An international survey,' *International Journal of Logistics: Research and Applications*, 2004, Vol. 7, No. 1, pp.17–31.

New, Steve and Roy Westbrook (eds.) *Understanding Supply Chains: Concepts, Critiques, and Futures*, Oxford University Press, 2004.

Porter, Michael E. *Competitive Advantage: Creating and Sustaining Superior Performance*, New York: Free Press, 1985.

Schama, Simon *The American Future: A History from the Founding Fathers to Barack Obama*, London: Vintage, 2009.

Senge, Peter M. *The Fifth Discipline: The Art & Practice of the Learning Organization*, New York: Doubleday, 1990.

Skjøtt-Larsen, Tage 'European logistics beyond 2000,' *International Journal of Physical Distribution & Logistics Management,* 2000, Vol. 30, No. 5, pp.377–387.

Stock, James R. 'Logistics Thought and Practice: A Perspective,' *International Journal of Physical Distribution & Logistics Management,* 1990, Vol. 20, No. 1, pp.3–6.

Stock, James R. *Development and Implementation of Reverse Logistics Programs*, Oak Brook, IL: Council of Logistics Management, 1998.

Notes

1 Definition on the CSCMP's website: http://cscmp.org/.
2 Ibid.
3 Paul D. Larson and Árni Halldórsson, 'Logistics versus supply chain management: An international survey,' *International Journal of Logistics: Research and Applications*, 2004, Vol. 7, No. 1, pp.17–31.

4   For example, see Nathalie Fabbe-Costes and Marianne Jahre 'Supply chain integration gives better performance – the emperor's new suit?' *International Journal of Physical Distribution & Logistics Management*, 2007, Vol. 37, No. 10, pp.835-855 and 'Supply chain integration and performance: A review of the evidence,' *International Journal of Logistics Management*, 2008, Vol. 19, No. 2, pp.130–154.

5   For further discussion about SCM see Martin Christopher, *Logistics and Supply Chain Management: Creating Value-adding Networks*, 3rd ed. (Harlow: FT Prentice Hall, 2005) and Steve New and Roy Westbrook (eds.) *Understanding Supply Chains: Concepts, Critiques, and Futures* (Oxford University Press, 2004).

6   For further details of this logistics feat see Simon Schama, *The American Future: A History from the Founding Fathers to Barack Obama* (London: Vintage, 2009), particularly Chapters 6 and 7.

7   Louis D.H. Weld, 'Market distribution,' *The American Economic Review*, 1915, Vol. 5, No. 1, pp.125–139.

8   John L. Kent and Daniel J. Flint, 'Perspectives on the evolution of logistics thought,' *Journal of Business Logistics*, 1997, Vol. 18, No. 2, pp.15–29.

9   Peter Drucker, 'Economy's dark continent,' *Fortune*, 1962, Vol. 64, April, pp.103–104.

10 Rosalyn Wilson 'CSCMP's 22nd Annual State of Logistics Report: Navigating through the recovery' http://cscmp.org/, 2011.

11 Ibid.

12 Peter M. Senge, *The Fifth Discipline: The Art & Practice of the Learning Organization* (New York: Doubleday, 1990).

13 Sources: Donald J. Bowersox, David J. Closs and Theodore P. Stank 'Ten mega-trends that will revolution-ize supply chain logistics,' *Journal of Business Logistics*, 2000, Vol. 21, No. 2, pp.1-16; Tage Skjøtt-Larsen 'European logistics beyond 2000,' *International Journal of Physical Distribution & Logistics Management*, 2000, Vol. 30, No. 5, pp.377–387; and Frank Straube and Hans-Christian Pfohl, *Trends and Strategies in Logistics – Global Networks in an Era of Change* (Berlin: Bundesvereinigung Logistik, 2008).

Chapter 2

Logistics customer service

Key objectives

- To define concepts of logistics customer service.
- To consider elements of logistics customer service.
- To show the relationship between logistics and marketing.
- To explore satisfaction and service equality as outputs of logistics customer service.
- To illustrate approaches to logistics customer service strategy.

Introduction

Customer service is a crucial business element for any firm. The late management guru Peter Drucker observed that a firm has one only purpose: to create a customer. He argued that it is the customer who determines what a firm is and that what the customer considers value is decisive as it determines what a firm produces and whether or not the firm will prosper.[1]

A firm can use customer service to differentiate itself from its rivals and thus obtain a competitive advantage and enhance its profitability. Customer profitability has been shown to increase over time due to increased purchases and reduced costs from economies of service to the customer. Also, a reduction in customer defections by 5 per cent may increase a firm's profits anywhere from 25 per cent to 85 per cent over their tenure with them.[2]

This chapter begins by considering the concept of customer service and its importance in logistics activities and the relationship between logistics and marketing. It then goes on to present the nature of logistics activities as services that allow firms and researchers to make use of various marketing and service quality tools and techniques to enhance logistical service opportunities. Following on is a discussion of the natural extension from service to satisfaction and service quality which lead to long-term relationships. Finally, several techniques for developing and using customer service strategies are explored to provide a view of the options available to firms to improve and enhance their logistics service offerings.

The concept of customer service

Customer service may mean different things to different people and firms. Indeed, differing expectations of customer service between suppliers and customers can often lead to conflicts and affect relationships. What, then, is an appropriate definition of customer service, especially as it relates to logistics? Customer service has been researched in the logistics discipline for more than 40 years.[3] One useful definition that reflects the 'Stop' and 'Go' nature of logistics states that customer service is:

> ... a process which takes place between the buyer, seller, and third party. The process results in a value added to the product or service exchanged. This value added in the exchange process might be short term as in a single transaction or longer term as in a contractual relationship. The value added is also shared, in that each of the parties to the transaction or contract is better off at the completion of the transaction than it was before the transaction took place. Thus, in a process view: customer service is a process for providing significant value-added benefits to the supply chain in a cost-effective way.[4]

This definition ties in with Drucker's thesis that value is the key feature of customer service. But what is value in the eyes of the customer? Most marketing and logistics professionals consider that customer value is created when the customer's perceived benefits derived from a purchase are greater than the customer's perceived costs to purchase. Perceived benefits include all product and service attributes for the use and enjoyment of the product, while perceived costs include transaction costs, disposal or product life-cycle costs, and risk costs, either personal risk or the 'psychic risk' cost of ownership.

As examples, major companies such as Marriott Hotels, KLM and Nokia have gained significant advantage in the marketplace by meeting a customer's needs and providing value as follows:

- Marriott Hotels' core *values* for customers include using a hands-on management style, i.e. management by walking around; being open to innovation and creativity in serving customers; and possessing a pride in the knowledge that customers can count on Marriott's unique blend of quality, consistency, personalised service and recognition almost anywhere they travel in the world or whichever Marriott brand they choose.[5]

- The Royal Dutch Airlines, KLM, is a signatory to the European Airline Passenger Service Commitment of 2002. KLM's *commitments* are based on four concepts: responsibility to deliver what it promises; transparency to make flight information understandable and accessible; efficiency of ticketing, check-in and baggage services; and prompt and clear care and assistance if service is disrupted.[6]

- Nokia, as a high-technology manufacturer, focuses on quality for its customer service. Its *quality* programme is continuous and has three main aspects: quality in processes for better productivity and innovation; quality in products which is equated to customer experiences and perceptions; and quality in management to balance values-based leadership and fact-based management.[7]

Thus, value, commitment and quality are three customer service elements set out by these firms. However, the number and types of customer service elements can vary across industry sectors and it is important to consider which ones are appropriate for logistics.

Elements of logistics customer service

Research has found that the elements of logistics customer service fall into one of three categories: *pre-order* or *pre-transaction*, *order service and quality* or *transaction*, and *post-transaction*, which has two distinct element groupings of relationship service and relationship quality.[8] These categories and their associated elements are shown in Figure 2.1. These elements are by no means exhaustive of all possible logistics customer service elements but are those that appear most frequently as the most important in research and practice.

Pre-order or *pre-transaction* elements are those sought by firms before they place an order. They are sometimes referred to as 'order qualifiers' or 'hygiene factors' in that they must be provided by every supplier to the firm. Availability is the ability of firms to fulfil orders from existing inventory, i.e. the product is in stock. Products that are out of stock will need to be delivered at a future date and thus an order will be 'short-shipped' and have a 'back order' to fulfil. Fulfilment is very important in an online shopping context as it is the only aspect of the purchase process that customers actually experience. The use of technology to assist with fulfilment activities such as tracking and tracing is discussed in Logistics Example 2.1.

Availability is important to customers as recent research has found that an average out-of-stock (OOS) rate for fast-moving consumer goods (FMCG) retailers across the world is 8 per cent, or an average on-shelf availability (OSA) of 92 per cent. Five consumer responses

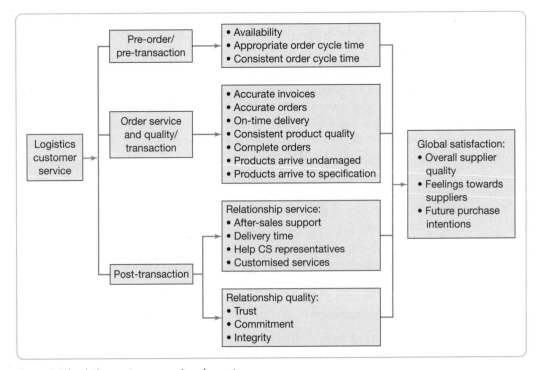

Figure 2.1 Logistics customer service elements

Source: adapted from Grant (2004).

LOGISTICS EXAMPLE 2.1

Technology assisting home delivery customer service

Home delivery, and the specialist urban logistics services it uses, is a burgeoning business, with annual market growth of 7.3 per cent or a total annual value of almost €45 billion. Therefore, the need to get it right is more urgent than ever before if those involved are keen to take a share of this buoyant market and meet growing customer demand.

Technology is at the forefront when it comes to getting urban delivery right. For instance, track-and-trace systems are being used increasingly to enable customers to log on to the retailer's/carrier's website to find out the status of their orders. Customers are provided with a number of points of reference, including order received and being processed, order being picked and packed in the warehouse, order despatched, and with the carrier for delivery. Thanks to this information, customers receive an improved service and the number of enquiries made to the call centre as to the whereabouts of orders are reduced. Track-and-trace technology, such as topograph systems and satellite technology (General Packet Radio Service, better known as GPRS), are also beneficial from an operations point of view as monitoring the carriers' progress allows for a more efficient and effective delivery service.

Often carriers will be away from the warehouse for a week, delivering products to customers over a large geographical area, so without the use of some form of tracking technology, head office is blind to which products have been delivered and to whom. By having electronic information consistently fed back, head office is made aware of which customers have or have not received their goods, which customers were not at home to receive the goods, as well as other issues, such as damaged goods. This allows head office to work immediately to rectify any problems and the call centre can be ready should a customer call up with a query or complaint.

Cost-effective telecommunications devices, such as portable Bluetooth units, allow automatic, efficient transmissions back to the head office computer system from a cradle in the carrier's vehicle. Personal digital assistants (PDAs) are also being used increasingly by carriers so that on delivering goods, customer signatures can be obtained electronically with the use of a pen-like device. The signature and date and time stamp are then uploaded to head office as confirmation that the job has been completed and so that head office knows where the carrier is up to in their delivery schedule.

However, in order to make a success of home delivery, a number of factors need to be considered, including identifying the proposition from the outset, using technology to support home delivery, ensuring staff reflect the brand and taking into account returns. Yet all of these are unlikely to result in success if the home delivery service is not integrated with the rest of the business – an integrated approach to multi-channel retail is the key to getting home delivery right. One company employing that sort of expertise is Amtrak Express parcels. The company recently took on a new client, major UK electrical consumer goods retailer Comet.

Amtrak delivers electrical items, working alongside existing carrier Parcelforce and Comet's own fleets that handle larger goods. Comet makes 13 million sales a year and with home deliveries increasing, peak volumes reach 7,000 parcels a night. To enable this service Amtrak has made significant investment in core IT systems and new technology, utilising wireless barcode scanning systems and the web. The automation has helped in reducing overheads, but is primarily aimed at giving Amtrak class-leading service levels. With the new 'DayTrak' courier service and established 'Collections Service', customers can track their bookings using real-time information via the web.

Logistics example 2.1 (*cont.*)

Comet stocks much of its one-man delivery items such as phones, PDAs and small vacuum cleaners at its central England distribution centre. Evening collections are arranged by the nearby Amtrak office in Nottingham, with trunking direct to the Amtrak hub near Birmingham. Amtrak then delivers the next morning through its 100-strong depot network. Amtrak has become the first UK parcel carrier to offer evening deliveries as part of a standard service, adding to Saturday and unattended delivery services geared for the urban delivery sector. The sort of service offered to Comet has boosted Amtrak's reputation and in 2004 the company achieved a 4 per cent growth in turnover to £70 million and an increase of £6 million in operating profit.

Question

What other applications would benefit from Amtrak's technology?

Source: adapted from 'All homeward bound', *Logistics Business Magazine*, November/December 2004, pp. 10–14.

---

to OOS were found to be buy the item at another store (31 per cent), substitute a different brand (26 per cent), substitute the same brand (19 per cent), delay their purchase until the item became available (15 per cent), and do not purchase any item (9 per cent). The implications of these findings is that 55 per cent of consumers will not purchase an item at the retail store, while 50 per cent of consumers will substitute or not purchase the manufacturer's item.[9]

Appropriate order cycle or lead time is what the supplier can offer in terms of delivery dates, i.e. three weeks or three days. The product type, whether or not it is perishable, and final demand from the customer's customers will be important factors in determining the appropriate order cycle. Consistent order cycle or lead time is the variance around the appropriate order cycle time, i.e. three weeks plus or minus four days. Customers are also concerned with this element as too great a variance can affect their own scheduling and planning.

Order service and quality or *transaction* elements are those elements that occur during the order fulfilment stage from supplier to customer. These elements can differentiate suppliers and are sometimes referred to as 'order winners' as they may represent decision criteria for customers. Accurate invoices and accurate orders measure how well the supplier can fulfil the order and then bill the customer. On-time delivery relates to whether an order received by the customer is on the date promised. Consistent product quality means the products meet the customer's quality requirements for every order, i.e. the product quality for a current order is the same as the last order. Complete orders indicate that there is no shortage in an order that requires back-order fulfilment. Products arriving undamaged means that all products are able to be used or re-sold immediately without any re-ordering or compensation. Products arriving to specification reflect the supplier's ability to produce to an agreed set of standards and conditions.

Post-transaction elements are those elements that come into play after the order has been received and relate to ongoing relations between the supplier and the customer. As noted above there are two sub-groupings for these elements: *relationship service* and *relationship quality*. *Relationship service* is concerned with actual post-transaction service elements of after-sales support that is provided by the supplier, the actual delivery time offered for orders on an ongoing basis, and whether the supplier has helpful customer service representatives and can offer customised services. *Relationship quality* is about the nature of the relationship between the parties and whether there is trust, commitment and integrity exhibited by them.

A satisfied customer is thus the output of a successful customer service strategy. The key indicators of satisfaction in Figure 2.1 are a positive view of a supplier's overall quality, a good feeling towards the supplier, and an intention to repurchase from the supplier in future. A customer who is satisfied over many orders or transactions will develop a relationship with the supplier and loyalty towards them.

This concept of satisfaction and the customer service definition in the last section, which also considers *exchange* between related parties in a customer service context, are fundamental features of the marketing concept. Thus, there is a symbiotic relationship between logistics and marketing.

The relationship between logistics and marketing

A key point emerging from the definition of logistics in Chapter 1 and the definition of customer service is that logistics activities represent a process undertaken by a firm to achieve an outcome of meeting customer requirements or needs; hence customer service is the output of logistical activities in this process view. The logistics functions affecting the physical distribution of both a firm's inbound and outbound goods include the management of transportation, warehousing, inventory, information technology and production. These functions may be considered the logistics mix variables. However, meeting a customer's needs is also a key element in the marketing concept and it is important to consider the relationship between logistics and marketing, particularly as it affects customer service.

The marketing concept is defined as a

> ... process in a society by which the demand structure for economic goods and services is anticipated or enlarged and satisfied through the conception, promotion, exchange, and physical distribution of such goods and services.[10]

The last element in this definition, physical distribution, relates to those logistical functions that are required to meet a customer's needs. Thus, customer service and any resulting satisfaction or dissatisfaction represent outputs of both logistical processes and the marketing concept.

The marketing concept presented in this text is based on ten characteristics, known as the marketing mix variables or '10 Ps', which are product, price, promotion, precedents, positioning, power, people, planning and control, processes and place of sale or distribution.[11] *Product* is the tangible good provided to a customer and which adds value for them. *Price* is the monetary exchange provided for the product and is a function of the added value. *Promotion* represents all activities required to communicate to the customer to make them aware of the product and its attributes. *Precedents* refer to the strategies and tactics that can be learned by the firm through its market or environmental scanning. *Positioning* is the firm's place in the market in terms of both market share and size and where the customer perceives the firm's position relative to its competition. These five marketing mix variables mostly pertain to the marketing domain of a firm.

However, the remaining five marketing mix variables are also important for logistical activities. *Power* relates to the market power of the firm providing the product: is the firm a

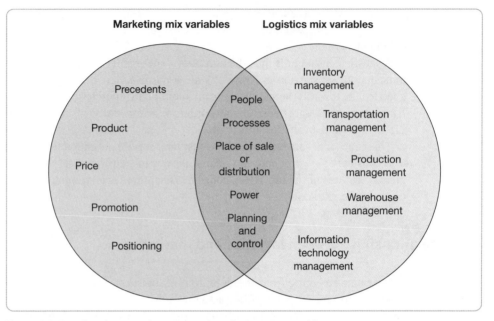

Figure 2.2 Interface between logistics and marketing mix variables

market leader or a market follower and how much influence does it have with various stake-holders such as suppliers and customers? *People* are the firm's various stakeholders, including suppliers, customers, employees and shareholders. *Planning and control* refers to the firm's ability to engage with its stakeholders in order to carry out its business objectives and strategies. *Processes* are those activities required to successfully bring a product to market, including the other marketing and logistics mix variables. Lastly, *place of sale or distribution* relates to the physical distribution of products and is the direct link with logistics activities. Figure 2.2 shows the interface between the various logistics and marketing mix variables and the overlapping five variables described above.

Logistics activities as services

The activities represented by the logistics mix variables do not include any form of tangible product as in the case of the marketing mix variables. Hence, logistics activities essentially may be considered services as they exhibit the fundamental characteristics of services as opposed to products. There are five characteristics of services that distinguish them from products or goods. Services are generally *intangible*; service provision can be *inconsistent* or heterogeneous; services are *perishable* and cannot be inventoried; the production and consumption of a service are *inseparable*; and services cannot be *owned* in the same manner as a physical product.[12] Logistics activities are thus services relative to the products and goods they act upon in their respective roles.

For example, DVD players or flat-screen televisions manufactured in Asia to be sold in North America or Europe need to be packed together in bulk with similar products, shipped, received and stored at various locations along the supply chain before reaching the final retail destination. However, the tertiary packaging, i.e. for shipping, transportation and storage functions undertaken, does not physically alter the products in any way.

Logistics activities therefore impact customer service through providing high-quality service in order to ensure customer satisfaction.

Logistics satisfaction and service quality

Few things are as fundamental to customers, the firm, and the logistics and marketing concepts as the notion of satisfaction. Satisfied customers represent the outcome of a firm's successful customer service policy. Satisfaction has been defined as a customer's fulfilment response to an order or transaction and is based on a judgement that a product or service feature, or the product or service itself, has provided (or is providing) a pleasurable level of consumption-related fulfilment, including levels of under- or overfulfilment.[13]

The dominant paradigm in satisfaction theory is the *expectancy-disconfirmation paradigm* that has its roots in social and applied psychology. This paradigm presents satisfaction judgements as a function of two constructs: (1) a preliminary or baseline expectation of a product or service's performance, and (2) a comparison of the product or service's performance afterwards that yields a perceived confirmation or a perceived positive or negative 'disconfirmation' of expectations. That is, if perceptions equal expectations, e.g. P=E, then expectations are *confirmed*. If perceptions exceed expectations, e.g. P>E, then expectations are *positively disconfirmed*. However, if perceptions do not exceed expectations, e.g. P<E, then expectations are *negatively disconfirmed*.

A confirmation of expectations, or zero disconfirmation, is considered a state of satisfaction. A negative disconfirmation indicates that expectations were not met and yields a state of dissatisfaction. Alternatively, a positive disconfirmation indicates that expectations were exceeded and yields a state of excessive satisfaction. Disconfirmation may indicate that preliminary expectations are incorrect; however, it may also be that a firm providing the product or service did not perform as it had in the past, suggesting a change in product or service quality. For example, the level of products damaged in a delivery may be 15 per cent in one event whereas it is usually no more than 5 per cent during other events.

Customers will accept some variation in service quality due to external environmental conditions; for example, restaurants at lunch and dinner time will be busier than at other times in the day and thus customers may have to wait longer than expected to be served. Customers will then moderate their short-term expectations in line with this situation. Long-term expectations may also be modified depending on the cause; for example, ash clouds from the eruption of the Eyjafjallajökull volcano in Iceland during 2010 disrupted passenger and cargo aircraft flights across many parts of Europe for about a week and thus customers either had to wait for service to resume or seek alternatives for travel or shipping goods. Such moderation of expectations leads to customers having a *zone of tolerance* between what service level they expect and what is adequate or feasible given these external environmental conditions.

A firm that uses suppliers and logistics service providers on a regular basis over time will generate a 'set of expectations' for the respective services based on the firm's overall perceptions of the many service encounters it has experienced. Positive perceptions over time will likely lead to the firm developing long-term relationships with suppliers and logistics service providers.

Logistics relationships

It has been argued that channel relations will hold an ever-increasing importance in the study and practice of logistics in this century and will evolve beyond descriptive and anecdotal considerations. Important dimensions of relationship management will include concepts of service quality, value and customer satisfaction that would require more work between logistics, marketing channels and buyer behaviour.[14] It is therefore appropriate to consider and possibly adopt existing relationship practice in the marketing discipline.

Marketing relationships developed as extensions to the concept of exchange that characterises the marketing concept and can be purely transactional or relational exchanges. Transactional exchanges are considered discrete dyadic exchanges between firms and suppliers with minimal personal relationships and no anticipation or obligation of future exchanges, while relational exchanges contain elements of cooperation, sharing and planning between both sides of the dyad. However, there is also a range of exchanges in between and a continuum representing these additional exchanges between transactional and relational has been developed and is shown in Figure 2.3.[15]

Transactional exchanges will tend to be anonymous and automatic, and probably driven by technology. Making transactions routine is most applicable in commodity markets with certain or known demand patterns and limited product variation, for example basic food products such as vegetables and fruit. At the other end of the continuum collaborative exchanges will tend to require very close information, social, and process linkages and mutual commitments made in expectation of long-term benefits, for example the use of vendor-managed inventory (VMI), which we will discuss further in Chapter 6.

This type of exchange relationship is close to vertical integration where a firm controls all aspects of its channel of distribution or supply chain from raw material extraction to sales to final consumers. Although vertical integration is less prevalent than in the last century, a good example of an industrial sector that is vertically integrated is oil and gas. Large multinational firms such as Exxon and Shell explore for oil and gas, extract and refine the raw materials into petroleum products, and sell the products to end users at petrol forecourts or to industrial users from the refinery gate.

Relationships are built upon trust and commitment from shared values and information, mutual dependence, communication and relationship benefits. Benefits that should accrue to both sides in a relationship include cost reductions, risk sharing, shared creativity, understanding of customer defections and the potential for new business.

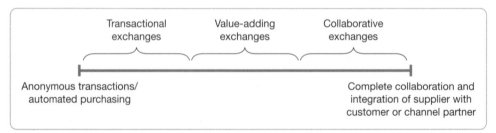

Figure 2.3 Relationship continuum
Source: Day (2000, p.25).

Appropriate conditions for establishing relationships include an asymmetry in power or influence by one actor in the dyad, a desire for business stability, a requirement to establish some form of business legitimacy, a necessity due to government regulation, the usefulness of reciprocal benefits, and the ability to achieve efficiencies. However, environmental factors affecting relationships include increased competition, more sophisticated and fragmented customers, advancing technology and the commoditisation of products.

A partnership is an enhancement of a relationship where relational actors may invest in each other's business, undertake joint research and development, or share strategic planning. A partnership may also take the form of an alliance between a firm, its suppliers and a third-party logistics (3PL) service provider to develop a better competitive advantage than by having a simple cooperative business arrangement.[16]

The types of logistics relationships practised in Europe between logistics suppliers and customers have been documented as shown in Figure 2.4.[17] There is an almost equal split of respondents among 'traditional', i.e. transactional, 'collaborative' and 'partnership' relationships, and the trend is for relationships and partnerships to increase as we enter the second decade of this century.

However, while cooperation and collaboration are necessary in relationships, conflict between those engaged in a relationship may arise due to incompatible goals and differing ideas of roles, functions and perceptions of reality. Individual relationship members often exert power to manage conflict and maintain order. This balance of power is further discussed in Logistics Example 2.2.

Relationships towards the relational exchange end of the continuum will develop as a result of a changing business environment, emerging techniques for logistics and SCM and the development of distribution technology. Grocery retailers have been the progenitors of such integration in the grocery supply chain. Organisations such as Efficient Consumer Response (ECR) Europe and the Institute for Grocery Distribution (IGD) in the UK have promoted the benefits of closer supplier–retailer integration, technological advancements and relationships

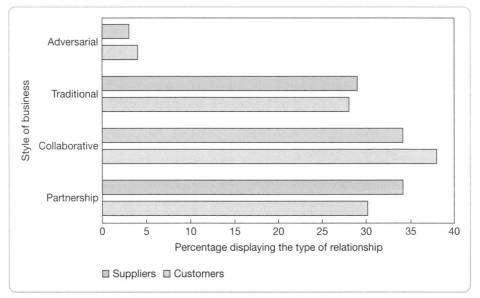

Figure 2.4 Types of logistics relationships in Europe
Source: McIlraith (2000, p.38).

LOGISTICS EXAMPLE 2.2

UK grocery retailer and supplier relationships

Customer service effectiveness by online grocery retailers has recently been challenged. Research by Tim Laseter *et al.* uncovered four fundamental difficulties in online retailing: limited online sales potential; high cost of delivery; a selection–variety tradeoff; and existing, entrenched competition. In UK online grocery retailing, the selection-variety tradeoff is the only major difficulty in this marketplace.

However, the UK's biggest supermarkets were under investigation in late 2004 after claims that they overcharged online customers and failed to deliver the requested goods. The UK Office of Fair Trading (OFT) scrutinised British retailers, including Sainsbury's, Tesco and Asda, after customers complained that they received an inferior service from supermarket websites.

One of the most common grievances was the delivery of substitute items. Shoppers reported that groceries ordered were often out of stock and supermarkets sent a replacement, which was often inadequate. Shoppers also complained that they were sometimes overcharged. The actual price of an item could be higher than the advertised 'guide price' and based on what the local shop was charging, it was alleged.

In addition, items were missed off delivery orders because they were not available, but consumers were still required to pay the full delivery costs, which can be up to £5.99. Customers also complained that supermarkets used their websites to offload food close to its sell-by or expiry date. Non-food items, such as books, DVDs, clothes and electrical goods, could cost more online than in shops.

A spokeswoman for the OFT said: 'We have held confidential discussions with supermarkets, but this is an ongoing investigation.' The OFT refused to name the supermarkets but has been in touch with Tesco, Sainsbury's and Asda.

A spokesman for Asda said: 'We have had one meeting with the OFT, but unlike other online stores we sell our goods at one price.'

Lucy Neville Rolfe, group corporate affairs director and company secretary at Tesco, said: 'With a Tesco.com grocery shop your food is picked off the shelves of your local store, so whether it is a book you are buying or a carton of milk you will be paying the same price as you would in store. The OFT contacted the industry several weeks ago on a confidential basis on a fairly technical issue and we will be responding to them.'

A survey for *Which?* magazine in the UK found that of 1,500 online shoppers, nearly nine out of ten of those using the Sainsbury's website said that their orders 'generally' contained replacement items. A spokeswoman for Sainsbury's said: 'We are in consultation with the OFT. . . It would be inappropriate to comment further.'

Part of the problem may be the way online customer distribution is structured. It is usually store-based. Orders are taken centrally, but then passed on to individual stores, where they are met from the shop's own shelves. Inevitably, not all 30,000 or so lines are available, especially in smaller stores.

By contrast, the Ocado system used for Waitrose's online grocery shoppers is warehouse-based. All orders are fulfilled from a single large warehouse in Hatfield, Hertfordshire, near London. Product availability is much higher and customers get the products they order. The scope for abuse is also reduced. Other supermarkets could consider following the Ocado approach. However, based on the experiences of failed online grocery retailers who had warehouse-based fulfilment, such as Webvan in the US, the Ocado approach is not a perfect solution either.

Logistics example 2.2 (*cont.*)

Question

How can supermarkets improve online customer service and their image by adopting one of the five methods for customer service for establishing customer service strategies discussed in the chapter? Which one(s) would you recommend and why?

Sources: adapted from Helen Nugent, 'Online shoppers complain of second-rate service,' *The Times*, 13 December, 2004, p.7; Robert Cole, 'Hard cheese not acceptable,' *The Times*, 14 December 2004, p.33.

---

in the UK grocery supply chain that have resulted from increased retailer concentration. This concentration is subject to criticism on the grounds of coercive power and retailer motives; the UK government's Competition Commission has investigated the large UK grocery retailers several times during the last decade but has not found significant evidence of abuse of power.

Nevertheless, the development of an appropriate logistics service strategy is an important factor in meeting customers' needs and enhancing long-term relationships with them.

Approaches to logistics customer service strategy

A logistics customer service strategy must be developed from the customer's perspective to ensure their needs are met and that they are satisfied. Figure 2.5 presents a framework for developing such a strategy.[18]

The first step in the framework is to identify a customer's requirements or needs related to the firm's logistics service offering and their relative importance to the customer. This may be accomplished by auditing the firm's existing customer service policies and customer demand. Such an approach requires the firm to have a customer focus as advocated in the marketing

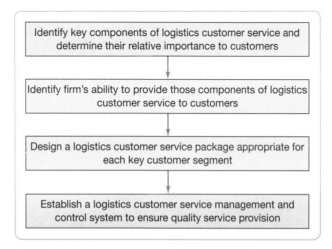

Figure 2.5 Framework for logistics customer service
Source: adapted from Christopher (1986).

concept. The third stage entails a comparison with competitors to determine where the firm fits, and finally the fourth stage is to determine the product-service profile for the firm.

The second step in the framework is to identify how well the firm can provide the service offerings demanded. This step can be determined by examining customer records and complaints and includes determining the tradeoff between customer service and cost, which could include a Pareto or 80–20 analysis of the firm's service offerings versus the percentage of sales revenue generated. This cost tradeoff issue is discussed further in Chapter 9.

The third step introduces the concept of segmenting the market by service requirements by identifying 'clusters' of customers according to similarity of service preferences. Lastly, the fourth step requires the firm to establish a customer service control and management system to ensure service consistency and quality.

A firm's approach to implementing and refining a logistics customer service strategy may be either reactive or proactive. Figure 2.6 shows these two approaches together with a sample of techniques that can be used with each.

Firms will act reactively if they respond to a service failure. The trigger for this response may come from negative media coverage, for example continually late aircraft or railroad arrival times, analysis of customer complaints which tend to be unsolicited and by the critical incident technique (CIT) which stems from psychology.[19] CIT was developed as a set of procedures for collecting direct observations of human behaviour in such a way as to facilitate their practical usefulness in solving practical problems and developing broad psychological principles. Marketers, particularly in service quality, have adopted CIT and consider it to be essential to understand the concept of service encounters. In this context a critical incident is a 'moment of truth' that becomes representative in the mind of a customer.

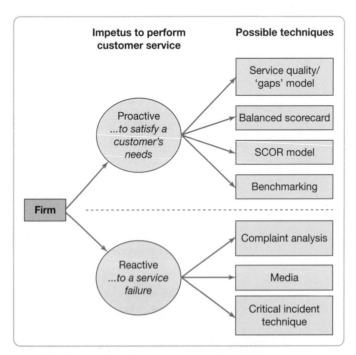

Figure 2.6 Possible logistics customer service techniques

However, when firms choose to adopt the framework in Figure 2.5 and seek to meet customers' needs, they are usually acting proactively. One popular technique for doing so is benchmarking a competitor's customer service performance. However, major issues for a firm to consider are who and what to benchmark. There are several concerns about the effectiveness of benchmarking – for example it may promote imitation rather than innovation, best-practice operators may refuse to participate in any benchmarking exercise, it may focus on particular activities only and thus there will be a failure to allow for interactivity tradeoffs, and there is difficulty in finding well-matched comparators.

Further, while it may be interesting to see what the competition is doing, this information has limited usefulness. For example, how does the firm know whether the competition is focusing on the right customer service elements in terms of what the customer requires? Therefore, competitive benchmarking alone is insufficient. Competitive benchmarking should be performed in conjunction with customer surveys that measure the importance of various customer service elements.

Another popular technique to develop a proactive strategy is the supply chain operations reference (SCOR) model from the Supply Chain Council (SCC), an independent, not-for-profit corporation interested in applying and advancing the state of the art in supply chain management systems and practices.[20] The SCOR model provides a unique framework that links business process, metrics, best practices and technology features into a unified structure to analyse internal processes according to five elements – plan, source, make, deliver and return. While the SCOR model is a useful tool to understand a firm's abilities to provide customer service, the SCC notes that it does not attempt to describe every business process or activity, including sales and marketing or demand generation and some elements of post-delivery customer support that are also important in a firm's customer service strategy portfolio.

The balanced scorecard shown in Figure 2.7 is another strategic planning and management system that is used by firms, governments and not-for-profit organisations to align business activities to the strategy of the organisation, improve internal and external communications, and monitor organisation performance against strategic goals.[21] It originated as a performance measurement framework that added non-financial performance measures such as customer service to traditional financial metrics to give managers and executives a more 'balanced' view of organisational performance; indeed, one of the four elements of the scorecard focuses on customers. While the balanced scorecard has evolved from its early use as a simple performance measurement framework to a full strategic planning and management system, it is now more than 15 years old and some criticisms of the scorecard and its applications include the exclusion of people, competitive environments, environmental and social aspects of business.

Lastly, customers evaluate services differently to products due to their unique characteristics. One method to examine such evaluations is the service quality or 'gaps' model as shown in Figure 2.8.[22] In this model, customers develop expectations of a service based on several criteria, such as previous experience, word-of-mouth recommendations or advertising and communication by the service provider. Once the customers 'experience' the service they compare their perceptions of that experience to their expectations according to the expectancy-disconfirmation paradigm discussed earlier. If their perceptions meet or exceed their expectations then they are satisfied; conversely, if perceptions do not meet expectations then they are dissatisfied. The difference between expectations and perceptions forms the major 'gap' that is of concern to firms.

Figure 2.8 shows the service quality model that includes the customer's and firm's positions. The expectations and perceptions gap is affected by four other gaps related to the

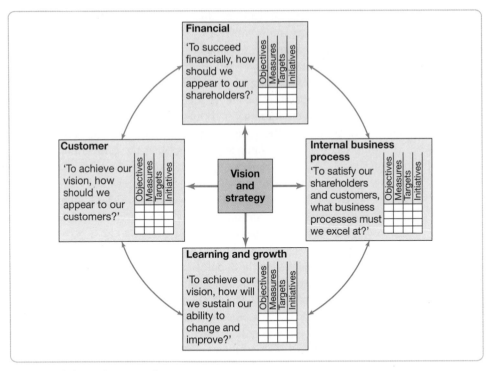

Figure 2.7 Balanced scorecard

Source: adapted from Robert S. Kaplan and David P. Norton, "Using the Balanced Scorecard as a Strategic Management System," Harvard Business Review (January-February 1996): 76, the Balanced Scorecard Institute, www.balancedscorecard.org (2010).

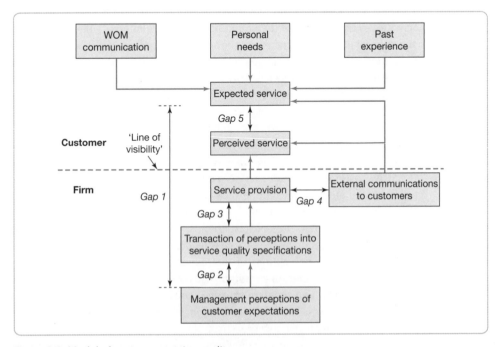

Figure 2.8 Model of customer service quality

Source: adapted from Parasuraman *et al.* (1985).

firm's customer service and service quality activities that are for the most part invisible to the customer. First, the firm must understand the customer's expectations for the service. Second, the firm must then turn the customer's expectations into tangible service specifications. Third, the firm must actually provide the service according to those specifications. Lastly, the firm must communicate its intentions and actions to the customer. Using the service quality model forces a firm to examine what service and service quality they provide to customers in a customer-centric framework. As an example, the Spanish-based retailer Zara focuses on service through its operations as outlined in Logistics Example 2.3.

LOGISTICS EXAMPLE 2.3

Responsiveness at Zara to meet customer desires

In the last 30 years fashion has changed from an elite accessory of the super-rich to a mass-market product. Since the mid-1990s the department stores that traditionally dominated this broader market have started to lose ground to specialist clothing chains offering the latest designs at competitive prices.

One of the most successful specialist players is Zara, a subsidiary of the Spanish Inditex Group. Since 1975 Inditex has become an international fashion business, with 5,221 stores in 77 countries; with more than 4,000 stores located in Europe. Its turnover in 2010 was just over €12.5 billion, with more than €8 billion generated by Zara. The fact that this pre-eminent position has been achieved without a formal marketing department and with minimal advertising expenditure has prompted reams of journalistic commentary and academic study.

Zara's success is based on its unique customer focus or what theorists term 'market orientation'. The customer and whole-market focus permeates every level of the Zara operation. Typical company statements include 'Our customers are the basis and the reason of our group's existence'; 'The customer is our inspiration'; and 'Our own and our suppliers' production will be able to focus on trend changes happening inside each season'. It is this last statement that reveals what market orientation really means for day-to-day working.

The traditional view of fashion products is that they are durable articles with a seasonal sell-by period. The Zara concept views fashion products as disposable, with a maximum 3–4-week sell-by period. Zara's efforts are therefore focused on reducing the time between design and sale, which means that its production cycle is entirely different from fashion-sector norms. The fashion sector traditionally moves along a clearly segmented time line from trade fairs through design and shows to production and sale. For example, goods sold in quarter 4 will have been designed in quarter 1 and produced in quarter 2. In contrast, Zara views design and production as processes that are 'live' throughout the entire seasonal cycle as the company responds to market information. At the same time, the focus on market changes means that 85 per cent of products are manufactured in the season they are sold.

The Zara concept means that the company is able to work to incredibly short lead times. The average time from design to delivery is just two weeks and new stock is delivered to all Zara's stores at least twice a week; Zara's mantra is to take less than 48 hours to go from distribution centre to store. Products responding to changing market trends are brought into stores in a continuous stream. The stores are therefore always fully stocked with successful lines and there is little chance of Zara being left with large stocks of failed lines. Buying and producing lines late in the traditional cycle is also cost effective because suppliers will offer low prices to clear materials before the season ends. The Zara concept also means that customers behave differently in its stores. The continuous stream of new

> **Logistics example 2.3 (*cont.*)**
>
> products means that customers will keep coming back throughout the season to see what's new. At the same time, the short shelf life of Zara products means that customers know they will have to buy them straight away or never see them again.
>
> Zara brings an average of 10,000 products to market each year. Information gathering drives this phenomenal offering. The design team works throughout the season studying everything from what clothes are worn in hit TV series to how clubbers dress. 'Product-shop teams' check product sales and store trends every day and this information is cross-checked against stores' twice-weekly orders. The information is fed to purchasing, design and production functions. Unsuccessful products are immediately taken off the market and stores can place only small orders to avoid building up stocks.
>
> Zara has repeated its resounding success in country after country and has never closed a single store. Industry insiders say that wherever Zara is located, its sales are the leading sales per square metre. The secret of Zara's success has been to ignore traditional fashion-sector behaviours yet be customer and market responsive with its service and logistics activities.
>
> **Question**
>
> *Discuss Zara's efforts and success in the context of the 'Stop' and 'Go' concepts introduced in Chapter 1.*
>
> *Source*: adapted from 'Zara creates a ready to wear business', *Strategic Direction* 2003, Vol. 19, No. 11, pp.24–26; and 'Inditex Annual Report 2010', www.inditex.com (September 2011).

Summary

This chapter began by defining generic customer service, which also provided an introduction to concepts of value and quality. The important elements of logistics customer service were discussed and found to be important at three different times in the service encounter: before, during and after a purchase. These elements are similar to elements in services marketing and thus the relationship between logistics and marketing was explored and many areas of overlap were found. It therefore makes sense to utilise tools and techniques from the marketing discipline in a logistics context.

The characteristics of logistics activities were found to be the same as those of services and this finding led to the consideration of customer service outcomes, namely satisfaction from proper service quality. Satisfactory service encounters over time will lead to long-term relationships that are beneficial for both customer and supplier. Finally, various approaches to developing a successful logistics customer service strategy were presented. Since customer service is concerned with and related to a customer's satisfactory product purchase, the next chapter discusses purchasing and the extended concept of procurement.

DISCUSSION QUESTIONS

1 How would you define logistics customer service and what elements of it do you consider most important?

2 Do you agree that logistics is related to marketing and if so, why? If not, why not?

3 Discuss the four characteristics of services as they apply to an outsourced transportation activity.

4 What do you consider are the most important aspects of longer-term business relationships?

5 Outline the service quality model as it would apply to a freight railroad service.

Suggested reading

Bowersox, Donald J. 'The strategic benefits of logistics alliances,' *Harvard Business Review*, 1990, Vol. 68, July–August, pp.36–45.

Christopher, Martin *The Strategy of Distribution Management,* Oxford: Butterworth-Heinemann, 1986.

Christopher, Martin *Logistics and Supply Chain Management,* 4th ed. Harlow: FT Prentice Hall, 2011.

Drucker, Peter *Management: Tasks, Responsibilities, Practices*, London: Butterworth-Heinemann, 1999.

Flanagan, John C. 'The critical incident technique,' *Psychological Bulletin*, 1955, Vol. 51, July, pp.327–358.

Grant, David B. 'UK and US management styles in logistics: Different strokes for different folks?' *International Journal of Logistics: Research and Applications*, 2004, Vol. 7, No. 3, pp.181–197.

Grant, David B. 'The transaction–relationship dichotomy in logistics and supply chain management,' *Supply Chain Forum: An International Journal*, 2005, Vol. 6, No. 2, pp.38–48.

Kotler, Philip *Marketing Management: The Millennium Edition,* 20th ed. Upper Saddle River, NJ: Prentice Hall, 2000.

Marketing Staff of the Ohio State University 'A statement of marketing philosophy,' *Journal of Marketing*, 1965, Vol. 20, No. 1, pp.43–44.

Mentzer, J. Tom 'Managing channel relations in the 21st century,' *Journal of Business Logistics*, 1993, Vol. 18, No. 1, pp.199–216.

Oliver, Richard L. *Satisfaction: A Behavioral Perspective on the Consumer,* New York: McGraw-Hill, 1997.

Paliwoda, Stanley J. *The Essence of International Marketing,* Hemel Hempstead: Prentice Hall, 1994.

Parasuraman, Ari, Valarie A. Zeithaml and Leonard L. Berry 'A conceptual model of service quality and its implications for future research,' *Journal of Marketing*, 1985, Vol. 49, No. 4, pp.41–50.

Trautrims, Alexander, David B. Grant, John Fernie and Tim Harrison 'Optimizing on-shelf availability for customer service and profit,' *Journal of Business Logistics*, 2009, Vol. 30, No. 2, pp.231–247.

Xing, Yuan, David B. Grant, Alan C. McKinnon and John Fernie 'Physical distribution service quality in online retailing,' *International Journal of Physical Distribution & Logistics Management*, 2010, Vol. 40, No. 5, pp.415–432.

Notes

1   This philosophy is outlined in Peter Drucker's book *Management: Tasks, Responsibilities, Practices* (London: Butterworth-Heinemann, 1999).

2   Frederick F. Reichheld and W. Earl Sasser, 'Zero defections: Quality comes to services,' *Harvard Business Review*, 1990, Vol. 68, September–October, pp.105–111.

3   For an overview of how customer service has developed over the previous 40 years see 'A compendium of research in customer service,' *International Journal of Physical Distribution & Logistics Management*, 1994, Vol. 24, No. 4, pp.1–68; and David B. Grant, 'A quarter-century of logistics customer service research: Where are we now?' in Edward Sweeney, John Mee, Bernd Huber, Brian Fynes and Pietro Evangelista (eds.) *Proceedings of the 9th Annual Logistics Research Network Conference* (Dublin: National Institute for Transport and Logistics, 2004), pp.201–213.

4   Bernard J. La Londe, Martha C. Cooper and Thomas G. Noordewier, *Customer Service: A Management Perspective* (Chicago: Council of Logistics Management, 1988), p.5.

5   Marriott International, Inc., www.marriott.com/ (2010).

6   KLM's Airline Passenger Service Commitment, www.klm.com/ (2010).

7   Nokia, www.nokia.com/ (2010).

8   Bernard J. La Londe and Paul H. Zinszer, *Customer Service: Meaning and Measurement* (Chicago: National Council of Physical Distribution Management, 1976); and David B. Grant, 'UK and US management styles in logistics: Different strokes for different folks?' *International Journal of Logistics: Research and Applications*, 2004, Vol. 7, No. 3, pp.181–197.

9   Alexander Trautrims, David B. Grant, John Fernie and Tim Harrison, 'Optimizing on-shelf availability for customer service and profit,' *Journal of Business Logistics*, 2009, Vol. 30, No 2, pp.231–247.

10 Marketing Staff of the Ohio State University, 'A statement of marketing philosophy,' *Journal of Marketing*, 1965, Vol. 20, No. 1, pp.43–44.

11 For further discussion about the 10 Ps of marketing and the marketing concept see Stanley J. Paliwoda, *The Essence of International Marketing* (Hemel Hempstead: Prentice Hall, 1994); and Stanley J. Paliwoda and John K. Ryans, Jr., 'Landmarks in the mapping of international marketing,' in P. Kitchen (ed.) *Marketing Mind Prints* (London: Kogan Page, 2004), pp.77–95.

12 Philip Kotler, *Marketing Management: The Millennium Edition, 20th ed.* (Upper Saddle River, NJ: Prentice Hall, 2000), pp.428–454.

13 Richard L. Oliver, *Satisfaction: A Behavioral Perspective on the Consumer* (New York: McGraw-Hill, 1997), p.13.

14 J. Tom Mentzer, 'Managing channel relations in the 21st century,' *Journal of Business Logistics*, 1993, Vol. 18, No. 1, pp.199–216.

15 George S. Day, 'Managing marketing relationships,' *Journal of the Academy of Marketing Science*, 2000, Vol. 28, No. 1, pp.24–30.

16 Donald J. Bowersox, 'The strategic benefits of logistics alliances,' *Harvard Business Review*, 1990, Vol. 68, July–August, pp.36–45.

17 Gordon McIlraith, 'Routes to best practice,' *Logistics Europe*, 2000, Vol. 6, No. 2, pp.36–41.

18 Martin Christopher, *The Strategy of Distribution Management* (Oxford: Butterworth-Heinemann, 1986).

19 John C. Flanagan, 'The critical incident technique,' *Psychological Bulletin*, 1955, Vol. 51, July, pp.327–358.

20 See the Supply Chain Council's website at http://supply-chain.org/resources/scor for further details.

21 See www.balancedscorecard.org/BSCResources/AbouttheBalancedScorecard/tabid/55/Default.aspx for further details.

22 Ari Parasuraman, Valarie A. Zeithaml and Leonard L. Berry, 'A conceptual model of service quality and its implications for future research,' *Journal of Marketing*, 1985, Vol. 49, No. 4, pp.41–50.

Chapter 3

Purchasing and procurement

Key objectives

- To define the nature of both purchasing and procurement.
- To consider the strategic role of purchasing for in-bound logistics and the wider supply chain.
- To describe the purchasing process and the total cost of ownership of products.
- To illustrate supplier appraisal, development and relationships.
- To explore trends of global and ethical sourcing and e-procurement.

Introduction

Chapter 1 noted that logistics comprise 'Stop' and 'Go' activities along the supply chain. However, what go and stop are are actually products or goods that must be acquired for re-sale or processing. Purchasing and procurement are the functions that allow such acquisition by firms. Implicit within these functions are many issues such as what to buy, how much as a function of demand, where from in terms of supplier and location, delivery terms and conditions and, of course, price. In fact, logistics decisions concerning transportation and storage cannot be made until these issues are addressed and resolved. This chapter considers the nature of purchasing and procurement from both the buyer's perspective, i.e. industrial buying behaviour, and the supplier's perspective, i.e. supplier development and involvement, relationships between buyers and suppliers, and issues of global and ethical sourcing in a modern business environment and new techniques of vendor-managed inventory and e-procurement.

The nature of purchasing and the development of procurement

Purchasing may be defined as the function associated with buying the goods and services required by the firm. It has traditionally been thought of as simply an administrative activity to negotiate price, order and expedite the goods, and solve any delivery or quality problems as they occur. In fact, as discussed in Chapter 13, it was still considered a secondary or support activity in business by Michael Porter in his value chain discussions in the mid-1980s.[1]

However, the term procurement was developed around that period, as discussed below, to denote an extension to the purchasing function towards a more strategic and process-oriented level that includes selection of supply source locations, determination of the form in which the material is to be acquired, timing of purchase, price determination on a total life product cost basis, and supplier strategies. Some organisations and firms now consider these terms to be synonymous and this book adopts that view for clarity and convenience.

As noted above, the purchasing function was generally regarded as being a service activity to production in the late 1960s.[2] However, external events in the 1970s began to change views about the role and importance of the purchasing function. The OPEC oil crisis of 1973 saw material shortages on a large scale and demonstrated that corporate strategies that did not consider a supply market input were flawed. Also, the impact of Japanese business on Western economies was beginning to be felt at this time. The Japanese approach of *keiretsu*, or cooperation and coordination among buyers and suppliers to, for example, deliver on time and to the agreed specification, introduced the notion that firms should look to manage their supply markets as opposed to reacting to them. Total quality management (TQM) and just-in-time (JIT) delivery techniques that had their origins in Japan also fed into this management style. These changes describe a move towards two different facets of purchasing: procurement strategy and purchasing operations where the former becomes a strategic resource of the firm and not simply a purveyor of services.

Thus, firms in the US and Europe began to change and consider how they could influence suppliers in terms of costs, performance and relationships with their customers. Figure 3.1 shows how the percentage of a buyer's time changed under their new procurement-oriented roles, with almost 80 per cent of the tasks delineated under a 'traditional' role compressed

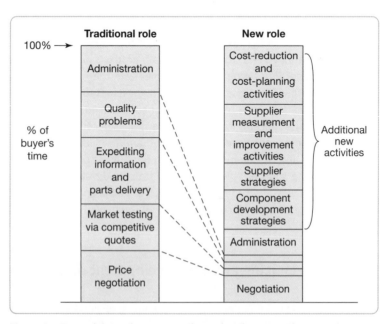

Figure 3.1 Time changes between traditional and new purchasing roles
Source: Farmer (1997, p.5).

into less than 30 per cent of the 'new' role.[3] Also, the principal tasks listed under the 'new' role are far more strategic in their nature than those that are shown as 'traditional'. An example of how a major drinks manufacturer has developed strategic purchasing is shown in Logistics Example 3.1.

Peter Kraljic introduced the first comprehensive portfolio approach for purchasing and supply management in 1983.[4] Kraljic constructed a matrix that classifies products on the basis of two dimensions, from 'low' to 'high': profit impact and supply risk, i.e. fewer suppliers as risk increases. The matrix contains four categories, classified as non-critical

---

LOGISTICS EXAMPLE 3.1

Diageo Scotland uses 12 enablers for world-class procurement

Diageo is the world's leading premium drinks business with an outstanding collection of beverage alcohol brands including Smirnoff vodka, Dom Perignon champagne, Johnnie Walker whisky and Captain Morgan rum. Diageo's corporate goal for growth is that every adult adores at least one of its brands. One of the company's strategic imperatives to accomplish this goal is to 'maximise value through ruthless focus' by aligning resources and capability building with value creation and transforming the value chain and supply costs.

This latter transformation is driven by key procurement deliverables: risk management; quality service; growth support innovation, costs, cash, capital and overheads; and resourcing development and progressions succession. Diageo Scotland uses 12 enabling statements to measure its procurement activities to meet the company's global procurement deliverables. Supply is the largest part of Diageo Scotland's business, providing materials for 120 brands in 180 markets, mostly whisky and white spirits. The group has 3,800 employees across three packaging sites, 27 malt distilleries, two grain distilleries, four cooperages, eight main warehouses, three office sites and one technical centre.

Approximately 80 per cent of total production is undertaken in Diageo production areas located in Australia, Canada, Cameroon, Ghana, Ireland, Jamaica, Kenya, Nigeria, Uganda, the UK (most importantly Scotland), and the US. The remaining 20 per cent of output is produced in many countries by joint-venture businesses or under contract with commercial partners.

Diageo Scotland spends about £350 million annually on packaging (£146 million), cereals, spirits and ingredients (£60 million), support services such as energy, maintenance and human resources (£95 million), and logistics (£49 million).

The 12 enabling statements are Diageo's own selections; they are not exhaustive but fit Diageo's needs and capabilities.

1 Sponsorship and Support, i.e. where does the real drive and support for improving Procurement's capability, contribution, standing and rewards come from?

2 Total Expenditures Impacted, i.e. what is the real organisation reach of Procurement within Diageo?

3 Consistent Processes, i.e. what is the level of routine application of codified processes to drive source selection, supplier management and capability development?

4 Aggregation of Expenditures, i.e. to what extent are purchases being aggregated across business unit and geographic boundaries wherever justified?

5 Supplier Selection Criteria, i.e. what key criteria determine sourcing and which functions actively input to decision making?

Logistics example 3.1 (*cont.*)

6 Supplier Relationship, i.e. what is the nature of prevailing supplier relationships, how and by whom are they managed?

7 Size of the Supply Base, i.e. what concerted effort has gone into consolidation of the total supply base?

8 Business and Strategic Planning Processes, i.e. what direct linkages are there between Procurement and overall company budgeting, annual and strategic plans?

9 People Capability, i.e. what is the principal source of talent and what is the depth and breadth of functional, organisational and leadership capability contained within Procurement?

10 Procurement Information Systems and e-Technology Systems, i.e. what is the level of e-enablement supporting sourcing strategy, supplier selection decisions, supplier relationship management and capability development?

11 Measurement and Reporting, i.e. what key performance indicators measure Procurement's contribution against imperative, and when and by whom are they monitored and reviewed?

12 Communications, i.e. how effective are Procurement's communications of key internal and external stakeholders?

The Procurement Leadership team uses these enabling statements in a framework as a diagnostics tool to measure progress. Current priority areas of focus for Diageo Scotland are the organisational impact of expenditures, the leverage of expenditures, e-technology and human resources.

Question

How could these 12 steps be successfully implemented in small and medium-sized enterprises?

Sources: interview with Procurement Director Diageo Scotland (2005) and Diageo website, www.diageo.com (accessed 10 January 2011).

(low impact and risk), leverage (high impact and low risk), bottleneck (low impact, high risk) and strategic items (high impact and risk). Each of the four categories requires a distinctive approach towards suppliers and plotting the buying strengths against the strengths of the supply market, three basic power positions are identified and associated with three different supplier strategies: balance, exploit and diversify, as shown in Figure 3.2.[5]

- *Non-critical* items require efficient processing, product standardisation, order volume and inventory optimisation.

- *Leverage* items allow the buying company to exploit its full purchasing power, for instance through tendering, target pricing and product substitution.

- *Bottleneck* items cause significant problems and risks which should be handled by volume insurance or stocking up, vendor control, security of inventories and backup plans; and

- *Strategic* items require further analysis to exploit any power available to the firm, i.e. if it is a significant buyer for one of a few suppliers, diversify away from the supplier if

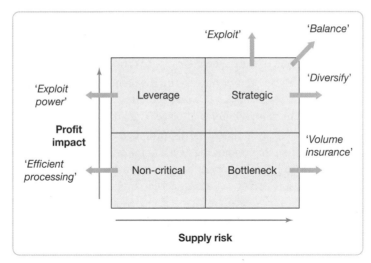

Figure 3.2 Strategic directions for categories of Kraljic's model

Source: adapted from Gelderman and van Weele (2003).

risk increases, or strike a balance establishing long-term relationships or partnerships to ensure continuance of critical supplies.

The general idea behind Kraljic's model is to *minimise supply risk* by avoiding suppliers who could prove troublesome, and *maximise the firm's buying power* by reducing costs. However, it has also been said that

> if a firm adopts a cost focused approach to its competitive position it will be unlikely to consider supply as a strategic process, because its competitive priority is to reduce cost … [However,] if a firm sees itself as a differentiator in the market place, it is likely to take a more strategic view of supply; supply will be seen as a source of competitive advantage through inter-organisation collaboration management.[6]

In addition to issues of purchasing such as business-to-business (B2B) or industrial buyer behaviour and the purchasing process, which are discussed next, the strategic issues of developing strategic supplies, power, exploitation or management of suppliers and diversification from one supplier to another have informed much of purchasing research and practice over the last 30 or so years and will be discussed further below.

The purchasing process

Purchasing industrial products and services is performed on a group basis or what Arjan van Weele calls a decision-making unit (DMU) and what others call a buying centre. A DMU consists of all the individuals or groups who participate in the purchasing decision-making process and who share some common goals and risks arising from such decisions.[7] The roles of those individuals in the DMU are contained in essentially five categories, as follows:

- *Users* – these are the people who will work with the product, either on an individual basis or in a group context. It is obvious that the user has an important say when it concerns the specification and selection of the product.

- *Influencers* – they are able to affect the outcome of the purchasing process by means of solicited or unsolicited advice. In the construction business, for example, architects have an important say in the choice of materials. Software specialists can exert influence on the selection of the hardware supplier (and vice versa).

- *Buyers* – these are not necessarily the same individuals as the users. In large organisations, it is often the buyer who negotiates with the supplier about the terms and conditions of the contract and who places the order.

- *Decision makers* – these are the professionals who actually determine the selection of the supplier. Sometimes the decision maker is a designer who writes their specifications 'towards' a specific supplier because of positive experiences with this supplier's products in the past. In other cases the decision maker is the person who controls the budget.

- *Gatekeepers* – these are the people who control the flow of information from the supplier towards the other members of the DMU (and vice versa). In some cases the gatekeeper may be the technical director's secretary, who screens contacts with (particular) suppliers. In other cases the buyer is the gatekeeper, who has the power to decide whether or not to circulate specific supplier documentation within the organisation.[8]

The actual purchasing process is shown in Figure 3.3. Firms will first recognise a need for a product or service; this need may come about from making a new product, entering a new market or in response to a request from a customer or the firm's salespeople. The firm will then define the purchase specifications for the product or service and if in a manufacturing situation will determine whether to make or buy the item. Next will be a supplier pre-qualification exercise to determine who to solicit quotations from. Once the quotations are received, and this process can be a tendering process where all bids are due on the same day and at the same time, the firm will select the supplier or suppliers they would like to engage. A period of negotiation then follows to determine the terms and conditions of the contract, often known as a purchase order (PO), or the service level agreement (SLA). Once the contract or SLA is settled, the order is placed and the firm then expedites the order where necessary, i.e. following up on completion date of manufacture, shipping delays, failure to show on a scheduled service date, etc. When an order is received it is evaluated for completeness, damage, specification, etc. and then payment is made in accordance with the contract.

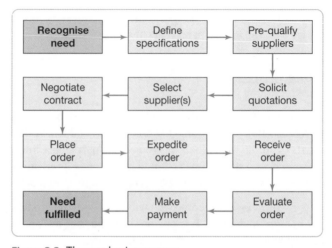

Figure 3.3 The purchasing process

Payment is usually required 30 days after receipt of the goods, but some firms offer discounts if the invoice is paid earlier. For example, a 2 per cent discount may be applied if an invoice is paid within ten days of receipt, otherwise the full amount would be due in 30 days; this feature would be specified '2/10, net 30' on the supplier's invoice that accompanies the shipment. However, some firms that have cash flow problems or look to exploit their purchasing power may 'stretch the trade' by delaying payment for another 30 or 60 days. The UK retailer Tesco did just that at the depth of the recession in late 2008 by separately extending credit terms from 30 to 60 days for some of its non-food suppliers.[9]

The above purchasing process takes place for each and every item but may be reduced in effort depending on the item being purchased. For example, commodities such as office supplies or light bulbs are considered routine or straight re-buy types of products and may be subject to a simple re-order under a 'blanket PO' that is set up for a certain period such as a year. At the other end of the spectrum, an order for new products or a major piece of equipment such as a passenger aircraft will be considered a new task and every aspect of the purchasing process will be followed together with many of the strategic considerations discussed in the following sections.

The European Commission has defined a framework agreement for blanket POs with public-sector suppliers, the purpose of which is to establish the terms governing contracts to be awarded during a given period with regard to price and quantity. In other words, a framework agreement is a general term for agreements with suppliers which set out terms and conditions under which specific purchases or call-offs can be made throughout the term of the agreement. Framework agreements can be concluded with a single supplier or with several suppliers, for the same goods, works or services. The length of call-offs is not specifically limited by the EC, for example call-offs might be for three, six or twelve months, or longer.

Purchasing costs and total cost of ownership (TCO)

The purchasing cost of a product is often considered the unit price that is paid by the buying firm. Other costs such as transportation and warehousing may be considered logistics costs and a percentage allocation applied to the product cost for selling purposes. However, this is simplistic and ignores the cost impact of a product in other areas of the firm. The strategic concept of total cost of ownership recognises the total cost of a product to the firm over its total life cycle. TCO is a complex approach which requires that the buying firm determines which costs it considers most important or significant in the acquisition, possession, use and subsequent disposition of a good or service.[10] In addition to the price paid for the item, TCO may include such elements as order placement, research and qualification of suppliers, transportation, receiving, inspection, rejection, replacement, downtime caused by failure, disposal costs, etc.

The benefits of adopting a TCO approach are that it helps clarify and define supplier performance expectations both in the firm and for the supplier; improves the buyer's understanding of supplier performance issues and cost structure; and provides a consistent supplier evaluation tool to improve the value of supplier performance, a focus and prioritisation of the areas in which supplier performance would be most beneficial, excellent data for negotiations, an opportunity to justify higher initial prices based on better quality/lower total costs in the long run, and a long-term purchasing orientation by emphasising the TCO rather than just price. However, barriers to adopting TCO include complexity, a lack of readily available accounting and costing data, and a lack of a standard TCO analysis or methodology.

Two major approaches in applying TCO are cost based and value based. A cost-based approach relies on gathering or allocating actual cost data for each of the relevant TCO elements. An example of a cost-based approach is shown in Figure 3.4. While determining which cost elements to include and gathering the data to determine the TCO may be complicated, explaining the results of a cost-based approach is relatively straightforward.

A value-based TCO model combines cost data with other performance data that are often difficult to monetise. These models have a tendency to become rather complex, as qualitative data are transformed to quantitative data. They often require lengthy explanations of each cost category. An abbreviated illustration of this method is shown in Table 3.1 for four categories, including examples for delivery. The total cost derived from value-based models is not directly traceable to funds spent in the past, spent currently or estimated to be spent in the future, as are the cost-based TCO results. However, the way in which a supplier's performance is scored within categories and points allocated among categories reflects the buying organisation's estimate of the cost of various performance discrepancies. In summary, TCO analysis, whether cost or value based, represents a good way to improve supplier selection and evaluation.

Price paid, F.O.B origin (12.632/unit)		$12,000.00
Delivery charge		500.00
Quality:		
Cost to return defects	$100.00	
Inspection (in-house)	300.00	
Delay costs (downtime)	–	
Rework parts	–	
Rework finished goods	200.00	
Subtotal quality costs		$600.00
Technology		
Our engineers at their facility	$1,500.00	
<credit> Their engineers at our facility	<300.00>	
<credit> Their design change to improve yield		
Subtotal technology		$1,200.00
Support/service		
Cost of delivery delays	$104.00	
Charge for not using EDI ($50.00/order)	150.00	
Subtotal support/service		$254.00
Total costs		$14,554.00
Units shipped		950
TCO per unit (total costs/units shipped)		$15.32

Figure 3.4 Cost-based TCO illustration

Source: Total cost of ownership: An analysis approach for purchasing, *The International Journal of Physical Distribution & Logistics Management*, Vol. 25, No. 8, p. 12 (Ellram, L. 1995), International Journal of Physical Distribution and Logistics Management by Emerald Group Publishing Limited. Reproduced with permission of Emerald Group Publishing Limited in the format Journal via Copyright Clearance Center.

Table 3.1 Value-based TCO illustration

Total cost of item per dollar purchased = [(100 − score)/100] + 1	
Category	Maximum points
Quality	30
Delivery	20
Technology	30
Support	20
	100

Example: Delivery '% of line items delivered on time' (A)	Percentage of maximum points allotted (B)	Score (A × B)
100%	100% of maximum	20
99%	95%	19
95–98%	85%	17
90–94%	70%	14
85–89%	45%	9
80–84%	25%	5
<80%	0%	0

Supplier appraisal, development and relationships

The pre-qualification of suppliers during the purchasing process was discussed above and may simply mean that a supplier has the specified product in stock for a straight re-buy. However, in a strategic sense and for more involved procurement a firm may undertake a supplier appraisal to objectively examine a supplier's capability and performance. The appraisal also provides a risk assessment for the buyer.

There are many factors that could be taken into account. However, the normal range of information sought includes the status and type of organisation, its finances, litigation and insurance standing, number of employees, experience in providing similar goods and services, recorded performance and track record, quality including accreditations, training and continuous professional development, and sustainability policy. This last factor will be discussed below as regards ethical sourcing. A rating can be applied for the supplier on all these factors which can then be compared with appraisals for other suppliers.

TCO analysis and supplier appraisal are aimed at improving the performance of suppliers. However, a further enhancement is supplier development, which Andrew Cox defines as a buyer and supplier jointly making 'dedicated investments in the relationship and [creating] technical bonds … in order to create new product and service offerings [and where] the buyer takes the lead in setting 'stretch' [improvement] targets on functionality and costs'.[11] For example, suppliers may be invited to participate with buyers in the design and development of a new product; this is known as early involvement.

The next level for supplier and buyer is to establish long-term relationships. As discussed in Chapter 2, buyer–supplier dyadic exchanges and relationship marketing are well established in the marketing discipline. Relationships or partnerships in logistics and supply chain management have also developed since the late 1980s, particularly in the outsourcing of 3PL service providers discussed in Chapter 4. Such relationships can be undertaken with many suppliers in a supply network. The concepts of networks and how they operate has been a feature of work by the Industrial Marketing and Purchasing (IMP) Group since the mid-1970s.[12] An example of a network strategy is given in Logistics Example 3.2.

Relationships in logistics are considered a source of competitive advantage for firms to determine their future with buyers and suppliers in an increasingly complex world.

LOGISTICS EXAMPLE 3.2

Network innovations at Lufthansa

Global commercial aviation markets have seen an unprecedented dynamic in growth during the past 20 years after deregulation and liberalisation activities. Dynamic markets have led to strong competition among the established carriers and numerous newcomers, resulting in tremendous cost pressure for all airlines and consequently for technical aftermarkets. These technical aftermarkets embrace the maintenance, repair and overhaul (MRO) business providing services such as scheduled checks of airframes, engines, landing gears, components and cabin interiors, and repair and modification programmes including engineering services. In the MRO industry, the market structure is highly competitive – Lufthansa Technik AG (LTAG) is the global market leader with a market share of approximately 10 per cent.

The aircraft fleet is by far the most important asset for an airline, and punctuality of flights is of highest importance for the customers. As a result, the priority in the MRO industry is to provide both safe and reliable aircraft in order to fulfil the airlines' preconditions. Therefore, all spare parts have to be available immediately whenever and wherever they are needed to make the aircraft fly. In the past, this has often led to excessive safety stocks, no matter what costs were implied. High stock values are not only a result of limited cost awareness but also a consequence of a significant portion of non-routine work included within major MRO tasks, with only limited predictability of parts needed to be replaced during a specific event. In combination with partly excessive lead times for aircraft parts of up to one year, MRO shops have a wide range of parts available, many of them being slow movers. For example, LTAG keeps detailed information on 775,000 parts within its enterprise resource planning system.

In addition, for safety reasons, each of these aircraft-related parts needs to be certified by the aviation authorities and requires full traceability back to origin. These high standards for production and approval of parts, as well as other quality regulations for suppliers, in combination with high investment costs, generate an overall highly oligopolistic – and, for key parts, even monopolistic – market structure for the supply of aircraft parts and services.

However, the aviation industry has suffered from an ongoing decline of average yield per passenger due to the downturn after 11 September 2001, the recent global recession and increasing competition by new market entrants such as low-fare carriers Ryanair and easyJet in Europe. The combination of these factors has massively increased economic pressure in the new millennium.

LTAG has used a four-phase model to overcome this pressure, optimise processes and find innovative ways to increase efficiency and therefore improve airline profitability under strong competition in the long term.

Logistics example 3.2 (*cont.*)

Phase 1: Cost-cutting programme

After market deregulation in the late 1980s and early 1990s, newly privatised inefficient flag carriers were forced to significantly cut costs and reduce inefficiencies. In 1996, Deutsche Lufthansa AG set up a programme to decrease its total cost base. This included massive negotiations on big supplier contracts for aircraft and aircraft-related parts and services.

Phase 2: Cost–benefit approaches to purchasing processes

A second step was to increase overall efficiency and work on essential processes. This was based on a net present value analysis for each project process and a total-cost-of-ownership approach for all long-term investments such as contracting the parts supply and the customer support for new aircraft for more than a decade. During this phase, major original equipment manufacturers (OEMs) started offering parts pools and on-site support services for the aftersales market of engine parts, components, expendables and consumables in order to contribute to common cost-saving initiatives, and also to secure aftermarket service. Innovative tools for purchasing enabled LTAG to head in this direction, especially the invention of a state-of-the-art vendor monitoring/purchasing controlling system, as well as the use of internet-based platforms for reverse auctions such as the international aviation e-marketplace Aeroxchange.

Phase 3: Supply chain development

New tools – together with the ongoing economic pressure that could not be absorbed by MRO providers themselves but needed combined efforts of both MRO providers and suppliers – led to strategic projects that not only considered purchasing but included the supplier base as well as selected airline customers. This required a new level of frankness with key suppliers concerning information exchange and openness in mind, resulting in long-term reciprocal agreements, improving demand predictability and reducing 'bullwhip effects'. Consequently, making use of online, on-time availability of information has lowered stock levels drastically. To support ongoing supply chain initiatives, LTAG also promotes the extension of already existing, and the invention of new, electronic communication and purchasing tools. Currently, supplier communication via the internet is introduced in cooperation with Aeroxchange. As a result, all participating parties will save costs in ordering and accounting processes as well as finding intelligent supply chain solutions such as just-in-time ordering/delivery.

Phase 4: Integrated supply chain solutions

The next step in evolving purchasing and SCM will be a systematic cross-functional collaboration within the complete MRO organisation including all affiliates; cross-border to the supplier base including their sub-suppliers; and with the airline/alliance customers worldwide. LTAG is working on establishing a network with its more than 30 different affiliates and also with selected customers. Airlines and MRO providers are also looking for global cooperation, for example within the Star Alliance Network or by using cooperative e-auctions.

Question

What potential problems do you foresee with these types of networks?

Source: adapted from Dr Jörg Rissiek and Joachim Kressel, 'New developments in purchasing and supply chain strategies for the aviation industry,' *Business Briefing: Global Purchasing & Supply Chain Strategies,* London: World Markets Research Centre plc, 2004, pp.52–55.

Conditions for establishing such relationships include an asymmetry in power or influence by one firm, a desire for business stability, a requirement to establish legitimacy, regulatory necessity, the usefulness of reciprocity, and an ability to achieve efficiencies. Relationships are built upon trust and commitment from shared values and information, mutual dependence, communication and relationship benefits.

A key feature in establishing permanent relationships is a supplier's and a buyer's understanding of, and willingness to sacrifice, short-term advantages for long-term gains. Such gains accruing to logistics suppliers and buyers include cost reductions, risk sharing, shared creativity, understanding of buyer defections and the potential for new business. Table 3.2 details the advantages and disadvantages of closer buyer–supplier relationships for both sides of the dyad.[13]

The dimension of power has been much discussed regarding relationships. While cooperation and collaboration are necessary in relationships, conflict between buyers and suppliers will arise due to incompatible goals and differing ideas of roles, functions and perceptions of reality. The use of power by individual channel members is often used to manage conflict and maintain order. Andrew Cox has also argued that 'the concept of power is rarely discussed in supply chain writing – except to deny it is important or to argue that power should not be used because "lean" approaches should be based on equity, trust and openness'.[14] In reality, however, the abuse of power has been found to play an important role in supply chain integration and relationships.

Table 3.2 Advantages and disadvantages of closer buyer–supplier relationships

Buyers	Suppliers
Advantages	*Advantages*
● Reduced manufacturing and labour costs	● Contract predictability
● Improved quality	● Workforce and production more stable
● Reduced complexity and cost of assembly and buying	● Increased R&D effectiveness
● Supplier insurance	● Buyer allies with supporting firm's status
● Cooperative relationships with suppliers	● Buyer assistance
● Contract predictability	● Influence on buyer's future decision making
● Fair pricing assurance	● Insider information on buying decisions
● Fair pricing assurance (open books)	● Firm becomes gatekeeper for competitors' innovations
● Negotiated price reductions during contract life	● Information about competition
● Avoidance of bad press caused by reduction in personnel	
Disadvantages	*Disadvantages*
● Increased dependence on supplier	● Cost information shared (loss of proprietary information)
● New negotiating style	● Pressures to assume burden of all phases from design to warranty while improving quality and reducing costs
● Less supplier competition	
● Increased management skills	● Decreased autonomy
● Reduced personnel mobility	● Increased communication and coordination costs
● Increased communication and coordination costs	● Reduced personnel mobility
● Increased support for supplier	● Potential pendulum reversal (i.e. no buyer–supplier trend is written in stone)
● New reward structures	
● Loss of direct contacts with secondary suppliers	

Source: Hall (2000, p.461).

Further, firms and managers who are evaluated on short-term performance measures, such as quarterly or annual profitability, might lack the ability or desire to embrace long-term relationships if the purpose of doing so is not clear. Managers may also engage in selfish and individualistic behaviour that has significant economic benefits over cooperative relationships but is not conducive to relationship building. Such behaviour contradicts a 'humanist' interpretation of relationship building that considers individuals to be stable, identifiable and autonomous, and moral due to encompassing wholesome and beneficial values shared by everyone.

Finally, evidence from several empirical B2B research studies suggests buyers in exchange situations might be of 'two minds' and not ready or able to fully embrace relationship concepts. Buyers appear to focus on transactional issues in customer service while promoting the value and importance of relationships. The concept of supplier–buyer relationships is still relatively new in Western business settings, and old habits of using supplier competition to maintain low prices and releasing those suppliers who do not do so are slow to change. For example, a survey of more than 100 UK firms by A.T. Kearney and the Manchester School of Management revealed that 39 per cent of them admitted they threatened suppliers with withdrawal of business to obtain lower prices, while 64 per cent said customers used that threat against them.[15]

Global and ethical sourcing

In today's globalised economy many firms are sourcing products offshore in other countries, particularly Asia, as discussed in Chapter 11. There are two forms of such sourcing: international sourcing and global sourcing. International sourcing or purchasing initially emerged in the 1980s as a reactive approach designed to reduce production costs in an effort to neutralise the threat of foreign competition and to also take advantage of better-quality international products at that time, particularly from Japan. Products were purchased for processing or straight re-sale in the home market. Strategic global sourcing, meanwhile, is a much more intense process and refers to the integration and coordination of procurement requirements across worldwide business units, looking at common items, processes, technologies and suppliers.[16] For example, the Ford Motor Company bought about $3 billion (€2.4 billion) worth of parts in China in 2006 and shipped them to Ford assembly plants worldwide, double the total in 2005.

The benefits of global sourcing include:

- cost reduction through lower labour and material costs;
- ensuring availability and improved delivery performance;
- access to high-quality goods in other markets;
- access to worldwide technologies;
- access to new markets;
- developing a competitive advantage.

However, there are risks involved in global sourcing, including:

- longer lead time, delays, and supply shortages or disruption;
- possible poorer quality control;

- political turbulence and instability;
- changes in regulations such as quotas, tariffs, duties and taxes;
- fluctuation of currency exchange rates;
- higher shipping risks;
- corporate and social responsibility issues such as child labour, social responsibility and pollution;
- protection of intellectual property.

The process for global sourcing is the same as the purchasing process; however, extra elements are added to it, including doing more upfront planning, obtaining a deeper appreciation of costs including taxes, tariffs, duties, transportation and inventory carrying costs, and so forth – TCO is particularly useful here, establishing long-term relationships with suppliers and other stakeholders in the global markets, and undertaking closer monitoring and control.

Products that are suitable for global sourcing include:

- products with a high proportion of labour cost;
- products with high procurement volumes;
- products of average technological and qualitative requirements;
- products with low complexity of materials;
- products that attract low import duties;
- products with a small proportion of transportation costs relative to total costs;
- products with a high shelf life and transportability.

Global sourcing is complex and as a result intermediaries called international procurement offices (IPOs) have sprung up to assist firms in their global endeavours. IPOs are offshore buying offices or buying houses set up to procure components, parts, materials and other industrial input to be used globally by manufacturing plants. IPOs can offer firms assurance on quality control, know-how and technology transfer, search for new suppliers, recruit and train local personnel, negotiate with suppliers, offer information exchange, and other business functions such as managerial, legal, organisational and administrative.

An example of an IPO is Li & Fung Ltd, part of the Li & Fung Group based in Hong Kong. Li & Fung Ltd was established in 2005 and in 2011 had a network of over 15,000 suppliers in more than 40 countries to find quality-conscious, cost-effective manufacturers to match the production needs of more than 2,000 customers around the world. This framework enables Li & Fung to tailor sourcing options to meet customers' specific requirements across a wide range of consumer products, from soft goods (garments and apparel) to hard goods (toys, home furnishings, sporting goods, footwear, and health and beauty products). Li & Fung also has comprehensive product design and development capabilities to assist its customers by taking an initial design idea all the way through to finished products.[17]

Ethical sourcing

Corporate and social responsibility (CSR) has become an important issue for firms in the second decade of the 21st century. After ten years of price deflation, 2010 saw the culmination of many adverse factors which increased costs and uncertainty of global sourcing.

The evolution of China from a production economy to a consumption economy has led to a reduction in factory capacity and a displacement for domestic consumption. Thus, price and quality factors have now been overtaken by buyers' concerns for capacity. Further, concern over global sourcing ethics and negative publicity surrounding a spate of suicides at the consumer electronics original equipment manufacturer (OEM) Foxconn in 2010 led to the doubling of the basic wage in China, which has affected Chinese industry as well as pushing up prices in neighbouring countries. Thus, it is possible that a shift in global sourcing to closer geographic markets by US and European firms will occur in a process known as nearshoring.

A focus on CSR presents another dimension for fashion supply chains and supports a wider concept of sustainable development.[18] Environmental or ecological responsibility mainly relates to the textile 'pipeline', with issues of pollution and depletion of natural resources, while social responsibility is pertinent to the garment manufacturing function. The large-scale shift of garment manufacturing activities to lower-labour-cost countries in a quest for profit maximisation has resulted in exploitation of workers in garment manufacturing facilities, in terms of wages, working hours and working conditions. In response to growing concerns among consumers, investors and international organisations, firms must now address issues of CSR in their supply chains and ensure compliance with international conventions on basic human and environmental duties, regardless of whether or not they own the production facilities where the garments are made. Poor CSR practices in global supply chains can result in negative publicity and consumer boycotts in Western markets, while industrial action in supplier countries can result in an increased risk of supply chain delays. However, appropriate management of the supply chain in terms of design and operation can provide solutions to problems of human resource exploitation in Western retail buyers' global supply chains.

Many larger firms are moving towards rationalising their global supply chains by developing closer partnership relationships with a smaller number of suppliers. This increased collaboration and coordination between buyers and suppliers helps to reduce costs as well as improve agility by developing fashion products closer to demand. Additionally, supply chain rationalisation increases visibility within complex global supply chains and thus supports the implementation of CSR throughout the supplier tiers. Large global retailers such as Gap, Nike and Marks & Spencer have faced allegations of supply chain misconduct in the past but have become ethical sourcing pioneers in recent times by building strong relationships with trusted suppliers.

Vendor-managed inventory and supplier-managed inventory

Vendor-managed inventory (VMI) and supplier-managed inventory (SMI) are two initiatives within a broad class of automatic replenishment programmes (ARPs).[19] Other ARPs of continuous replenishment, quick response and efficient consumer response are discussed in Chapters 2 and 8. VMI involves the coordinated management of finished goods inventories outbound from a manufacturer, distributor or reseller to a retailer or other merchandiser, while SMI involves the flow of raw materials and component parts inbound to a manufacturing process.

VMI is the more common of the two replenishment programmes. VMI vendors generate purchase orders on an as-needed basis by closely monitoring customer inventory levels and replenishing supplies based on an established inventory plan. The inventory plan accounts for dynamic changes in demand associated with the product forecast, life cycle and related promotional activity.

SMI employs a similar logic to VMI but on the inbound side to the manufacturing operation. The key difference between SMI and VMI is that rather than replenishing finished goods on a re-order point basis, the manufacturer's production schedule triggers the replenishment of materials in the SMI programme. Suppliers are provided with production schedules in advance, with regular updates as 'takt' time (desired time between output units of production that are synchronised to customer demand), production assortments and total volume adjust to changes in demand.

E-procurement

The widespread use of the internet has created numerous opportunities for improving supply chain performance, particularly in purchasing and procurement. E-procurement is the use of the internet in purchasing and procurement. There are six forms of e-procurement applications: e-sourcing, e-tendering, e-informing, e-reverse auctions, e-MRO and web-based enterprise resource planning (ERP).[20]

E-sourcing consists of identifying new suppliers using internet technology. E-tendering is the process of sending requests for information and proposals to suppliers and receiving responses via the internet. E-informing is the process of gathering and distributing purchasing information among internal and external parties, using internet technology. E-reverse auctioning is the internet-based equivalent of a reverse auction, which enables a supplier to sell surplus goods and services to a number of known or unknown buying organisations. e-MRO and web-based ERP are processes for creating and approving purchasing requisitions, placing purchase orders and receiving goods and services ordered by using internet-based software systems. E-procurement is also useful for the public sector, i.e. government and non-profit organisations, as shown in Logistics Example 3.3.

LOGISTICS EXAMPLE 3.3

e-procurement in public purchasing

Gateshead Council is a local government authority in North East England employing approximately 11,000 people who are involved in providing essential services to a population of around 200,000. Gateshead undertook an e-Procurement project guided by UK e-Government targets designed to make local authorities more electronically efficient. It first set up an e-Commerce Steering Group, comprising its Head of Information and Communications Technology, Head of Corporate Procurement and key users in these sections, whose remit was to examine all council services, and look at what the options were before deciding how to build up electronic-driven systems and stocks.

After considering e-tendering and an e-marketplace, Gateshead realised that an e-marketplace would be the best fit for its plans and put together a pilot focusing on collaboration and local regeneration issues. The goal was to bring local suppliers on board, work with other nearby local authorities to develop a central portal, and develop an e-Procurement toolkit to help demystify the process of doing business electronically.

The portal provides a central hub with up-to-date contact details for key staff at local authorities; all the purchasing organisation's standard documents, such as tender documents, canvassing certificates; and a discussion forum regarding the electronic tendering facility and Request for Quotations. It also enabled suppliers to have the facility of a forward planning tool so they could interrogate what local authority contracts were coming up for renewal and thus express an interest. The portal also includes health and safety documentation, environmental questionnaires, and a calendar and diary of events.

Gateshead was one of five local authorities in the North East that made up the project team in developing the portal, and the overall goal was to make sure the project strands met all their objectives, both business and social, and to ensure that adequate resources and finances were available to enable the project to come to a satisfactory within timescale and budget.

Gateshead determined that taking part in an e-marketplace would provide it with efficiency gains and streamline council procurement processes. Areas of the e-marketplace that were carefully observed in order to distinguish which issues could be resolved with possible solutions included e-tendering, e-sourcing, e-invoicing, purchase cards, and an information sharing website. The council's annual budget is £200 million including staffing costs, half of which is considered addressable spend.

A challenging factor in the introduction of e-Procurement was the initial government targets laden by time and budget constraints. Further, working as a collaborative body meant that the existing processes already in place didn't always facilitate the standardisation of processes. Gateshead understood that the implementation process would mean a re-engineering of procurement processes which in turn would require a great deal of support for the rollout of e-Procurement. Gateshead also had to make sure that it had a good communications plan in place so that people knew why a new system was being introduced and what it meant for them, how it can streamline processes and reduce the amount of time spent on administrative tasks, and how that would allow them to do more interesting and productive work.

The financial benefits from collaboration and e-Procurement and introducing good procurement practices have enabled cost savings in supplier products, lower administrative costs and time-saving benefits. The greater purchasing power of the give local authorities involved has also enabled Gateshead to access high-quality products from dependable suppliers. Monetary benefits include the reduced cost of administration, reduced staffing requirements and more fairly-priced standardised products. Organisational benefits have included a faster, efficient and a more cost effective service.

Another area that has benefited is collaboration with suppliers. Gateshead has been heavily involved in helping suppliers to trade electronically. With great emphasis placed on the harmonisation of processes and, to a certain extent, the harmonisation of mindset and sharing of knowledge, e-Procurement seems certain to produce a long-term win-win situation for all parties involved. This is particularly true for small and medium-sized companies,

> **Logistics example 3.3** (*cont.*)
>
> some of who may feel threatened by e-procurement technology, and may be reluctant to use it.
>
> Gateshead produced a 10-page guide for suppliers called "Delivering e-Procurement – a guide to trading electronically," which explains what electronic trading is, what it means for both the buyer and supplier side, and contrasts how sales orders were done previously versus how they will be done in future. Gateshead found that existing suppliers were the first joiners and now e-tendering has become their normal method of transaction business, with very few orders manually sent.
>
> **Question**
>
> *What are some potential applications of electronic purchasing in other, non-public sectors?*
>
> Source: Adapted from Local Government Improvement and Development (2005) http://www.idea.gov.uk/idk/aio/944841 (accessed 10 April 2012)

Summary

The function of purchasing has expanded from simply buying goods and services to encompass a strategic dimension that can provide competitive advantage for a firm. The wider procurement function considers better and more involved supplier management, issues of globalisation and sourcing, and the use of new techniques such as TCO, VMI and e-procurement to ensure dependable and quality supplies of products in a timely manner and at competitive costs. Thus, purchasing and procurement have indeed moved on from being merely a support or secondary activity to an important function in a firm's modern supply chain. The next chapter begins the book's discussion of the traditional logistical activities with transportation, the 'Go' activity in logistics.

DISCUSSION QUESTIONS

1 Do you agree that purchasing and procurement are strategic functions, and why?

2 How can a fashion retail firm use the Kraljic purchasing portfolio approach to evaluate its supply strategy?

3 Outline in detail all the steps in the purchasing process for Boeing to purchase jet engines for one of its passenger aircraft.

4 On a consumer level, what would comprise the elements for the total cost of ownership (TCO) of a family automobile?

5 How does corporate and social responsibility (CSR) affect sourcing of fresh food products for the European marketplace?

Suggested reading

Birou, Laura M. and Stanley E. Fawcett 'International purchasing: Benefits, requirements and challenges,' *International Journal of Purchasing and Materials Management*, 1993, Vol. 9, No. 2, pp.27–37.

Christopher, Martin *Logistics and Supply Chain Management,* 4th ed. Harlow: FT Prentice Hall, 2011.

Cousins, Paul 'The alignment of appropriate firm and supply strategies for competitive advantage,' *International Journal of Operations and Production Management*, 2005, Vol. 25, No. 5, pp.403–428.

Cox, Andrew 'Power, value and supply chain management,' *Supply Chain Management: An International Journal*, 1999, Vol. 4, No. 4, pp.167–175.

Cox, Andrew 'The art of the possible: Relationship management in power regimes and supply chains,' *Supply Chain Management: An International Journal*, 2004, Vol. 9, No. 5, pp.346–356.

de Boer, Luitzen, Jeroen Harink and Govert Heijboer 'A conceptual model for assessing the impact of electronic procurement,' *Journal of Purchasing and Supply Management*, 2002, Vol. 8, No. 1, pp.25–33.

Ellram, Lisa 'Total cost of ownership: An analysis approach for purchasing,' *The International Journal of Physical Distribution & Logistics Management,* 1995, Vol. 25, No. 8, pp.4–21.

Farmer, David 'Purchasing myopia – revisited,' *Journal of Purchasing and Supply Management*, 1997, Vol. 3, No. 1, pp.1–8.

Gadde, Lars-Erik and Håkan Håkansson *Supply Network Strategies*, Chichester: John Wiley & Sons, Ltd, 2001.

Gelderman, Cees J. and Arjan J. van Weele 'Handling measurement issues and strategic directions in Kraljic's purchasing portfolio model,' *Journal of Purchasing and Supply Management*, 2003, Vol. 9, pp.207–216.

Kraljic, Peter 'Purchasing must become supply management,' *Harvard Business Review*, 1983, Vol. 61, No. 5, pp.109–117.

Pohlen, Terrance L. and Thomas J. Goldsby 'VMI and SMI programs: How economic value added can help sell the change,' *The International Journal of Physical Distribution & Logistics Management,* 2003, Vol. 33, No. 7, pp.565–581.

Porter, Michael *Competitive Advantage: Creating and Sustaining Superior Performance*, New York: Free Press, 1985.

Trent, Robert J. and Robert M. Monczka 'International purchasing and global sourcing – what are the differences?' *The Journal of Supply Chain Management*, 2003, Vol. 39, No. 4, pp.26–36.

van Weele, Arjan *Purchasing and Supply Chain Management,* 5th ed. Singapore: Cengage Learning, 2010.

Notes

1 See Michael Porter (1985) *Competitive Advantage: Creating and Sustaining Superior Performance*, New York: Free Press.

2 David Farmer (1997) 'Purchasing myopia – revisited,' *Journal of Purchasing and Supply Management* (formerly *European Journal of Purchasing & Supply Management*), Vol. 3, No. 1, pp.1–8.

3 Farmer (1997, p.5).

4 For a complete discussion about the purchasing portfolio model see Peter Kraljic (1983) 'Purchasing must become supply management,' *Harvard Business Review*, Vol. 61, No. 5, pp.109–117.

5 Cees J. Gelderman and Arjan J. van Weele (2003) 'Handling measurement issues and strategic directions in Kraljic's purchasing portfolio model,' *Journal of Purchasing and Supply Management*, Vol. 9, pp.207–216.

6 Paul Cousins (2005) 'The alignment of appropriate firm and supply strategies for competitive advantage,' *International Journal of Operations and Production Management*, Vol. 25, No. 5, pp.403–428.

7 Arjan van Weele (2010) *Purchasing and Supply Chain Management* (5th ed.), Singapore: Cengage Learning.

8 van Weele (2010, p.28).

9 Jenny Davey (2008) 'Tesco faces revolt from suppliers,' *The Sunday Times*, November 2 (available from http://www.thetimes.co.uk/tto/news).

10 This section is adapted from Lisa Ellram (1995) 'Total cost of ownership: An analysis approach for purchasing,' *The International Journal of Physical Distribution & Logistics Management*, Vol. 25, No. 8, pp.4–21.

11 Andrew Cox (2004) 'The art of the possible: Relationship management in power regimes and supply chains,' *Supply Chain Management: An International Journal*, Vol. 9, No. 5, p.349.

12 For further information about the IMP Group see Lars-Erik Gadde and Håkan Håkansson (2001) *Supply Network Strategies*, Chichester: John Wiley & Sons, Ltd; and www.impgroup.org.

13 Jeremy Hall (2000) 'Environmental supply chain dynamics,' *Journal of Cleaner Production*, Vol. 8, pp.455–471.

14 Andrew Cox (1999) 'Power, value and supply chain management,' *Supply Chain Management: An International Journal*, Vol. 4, No. 4, pp.167–175.

15 A.T. Kearney and Manchester School of Management (1994) *Partnership or Power Play?* Manchester: Manchester School of Management.

16 This section draws upon Laura M. Birou and Stanley E. Fawcett (1993) 'International purchasing: Benefits, requirements and challenges,' *International Journal of Purchasing and Materials Management*, Vol. 9, No. 2, pp.27–37; and Robert J. Trent and Robert M. Monczka (2003) 'International purchasing and global sourcing – what are the differences?' *The Journal of Supply Chain Management*, Vol. 39, No. 4, pp.26–36.

17 For further information see www.lifung.com/eng/global/home.php.

18 John Fernie and Patsy Perry (2011) 'The international fashion retail supply chain,' in Joachim Zentes, Bernard Swoboda and Dirk Morschett (eds.) *Fallstudien zum Internationalen Management*, Wiesbaden: Gabler, pp.270–290.

19 Terrance L. Pohlen and Thomas J. Goldsby (2003) 'VMI and SMI programs: How economic value added can help sell the change,' *The International Journal of Physical Distribution & Logistics Management*, Vol. 33, No. 7, pp.565–581.

20 Luitzen de Boer, Jeroen Harink and Govert Heijboer (2002) 'A conceptual model for assessing the impact of electronic procurement,' *Journal of Purchasing and Supply Management* (formerly *European Journal of Purchasing & Supply Management*), Vol. 8, No. 1, pp.25–33.

Chapter 4

Transportation

> ## Key objectives
>
> - To define the nature of the freight transport sector.
> - To describe the various modes of freight transportation.
> - To consider choices regarding mode and carrier selection.
> - To examine the role of third-party logistics in freight transport.
> - To describe the concept of outsourcing.

Introduction

As noted in Chapter 1, the transportation of freight is a key element in the logistics mix and accounted for more than US$760 billion or 60 per cent of average US expenditure on logistics in 2010. Further, road freight transport comprised US$592 billion or 78 per cent of all transport expenditure.[1] The physical movement of goods between locations thus remains a core competency within logistics and supply chain activities. Despite the requirements to serve greater broader geographic markets quicker, more frequently and with highly customised services, freight transport costs have generally fallen over the last few decades due to deregulation and liberalisation of trading practices.

This chapter discusses freight transportation by considering the nature, background and scope of transport activities, the characteristics of the various modes of transport, issues surrounding mode and carrier choice, and outsourcing transport activities to third-party logistics service providers.

The nature of the freight transport sector

Transportation may be defined as the planning and the undertaking of the movement of goods by a carrier between two points in a cost-effective manner that achieves the times and conditions specified by the shipper; i.e. it is the 'Go' activity discussed in Chapter 1. Transportation services play a central role in seamless supply chain operations, moving inbound materials from supply sites to manufacturing facilities, repositioning inventory among different plants and distribution centres, and delivering finished products to customers.

The European Commission considers effective transportation to be essential for the European Union's prosperity and well-being and that the mobility of goods is an essential component of the competitiveness of European industry and services. The EC estimates that when transporting products to fill store shelves and fuels, building materials and other inputs for trade, industry and homes, a tonne of goods travels an average daily distance of 23 kilometres for every one of the 491 million EU-27 citizens, with 11 of these kilometres moved over roads.[2]

Further, the US Department of Transportation's Federal Highway Administration notes that the 117 million households, 7.6 million business establishments and 89,500 governmental units in the US are part of an enormous economy that demands the efficient movement of freight.[3] Transportation is also considered a second-order economic activity which is generated by other economic activities; i.e. demand for transport depends heavily on economic activities and consumption and changes in both of these.[4]

The freight transport sectors in Europe and the US, while still regulated and monitored by their respective governments, have nonetheless enjoyed significant deregulation during the past 30 years. The following sections provide in turn a brief discussion on the status of current transportation systems in the EU and the US.

EU goods transportation system[5]

The transport sector generated €380.1 billion of value-added to the EU-27 economies and employed 8.7 million persons in 2005. Transport services thus accounted for close to 7 per cent of both total value-added and persons employed in the EU-27's non-financial economy. The effect on transportation by the 12 new member nations making up the EU-27 is discussed in Logistics Example 4.1. The total goods transport performance in the EU-27 by road, rail, inland waterways, oil pipeline, domestic and intra-EU sea transport and air

---

LOGISTICS EXAMPLE 4.1

Gearing up transportation in an enlarged European Union

The European Union grew from 15 member states (EU-15) with the addition of ten central and eastern European countries in 2004 and two additional eastern European countries in 2007; all these countries now make up the EU-27. The growth in the EU is regarded as a sensible response to changing economic environments, as competition has become fiercer than ever in the global economy. Consequently, the efficient management of the flow of materials, goods and information between EU countries is fast becoming an important factor for success.

The subsequent growth in trade among the EU-27 countries has created coincident growth for the demand of logistics services. Twenty per cent of respondents to a European Logistics Association (ELA) survey in the mid-2000s had plans to significantly increase business in the new EU countries within one year, while 16 per cent intended to do so in 3–5 years. Many respondents believed local logistics service providers for transport and warehousing would provide cost advantages and thus relatively few (31 per cent) were planning to restructure their logistics infrastructures in the new member countries.

Notwithstanding, firms may still have to redesign their logistics networks, especially the location of distribution centres. Almost 60 per cent of centres responsible for continental Europe distribution are situated in the Netherlands. As a result of EU enlargement, three regions will gain more importance: the Baltic Sea, the continental EU countries adjacent to the former East–West border (Austria, Czech Republic, Germany and Poland) and the Mediterranean Sea.

Companies and logistics service providers expanding their business towards the new EU countries will have to take this shift into consideration and rethink their logistical distribution concepts. A better service level towards the customer at an affordable price can be achieved by adequate centralisation of the system in combination with cross-docking strategies. To achieve this, one possibility is to cooperate with local logistics providers. In this way, companies can benefit from the existing knowledge of local partners and thus enjoy a lower investment risk. The challenge here is to find the right partner, with whom a trustful collaboration is possible, and to design adequate, flexible contracts with them.

A more expensive way would be to re-adapt existing logistical topology and install hubs and distribution centres in the 12 new EU member countries. This would allow for maximum flexibility and control alongside customised solutions. For some companies an alternative might be to establish a production plant on-site, hence profiting from low wages and distribution costs. However, some EU-15 logistics service providers are not concerned about competition from Eastern logistics companies. This is due to the fact that special regulations in the enlargement treaty assure that the new members are integrated gradually. During the first years following enlargement there was no completely liberalised competition between logistics service providers from the new and old EU countries. The main concern was that in a free competition situation EU-15 companies would not be able to compete with wages in the new countries. Another disadvantage for logistics service providers in the new EU countries is their out-of-date transport assets, which will soon have to be replaced by environmentally friendlier carriers.

Another factor is the European Commission's general views on how freight transport should be improved for all EU-27 countries. In a document produced in 2006 the EC noted that Europe's transport policy, which has been characterised by liberalisation and harmonisation, has seen rapid freight transport growth, driven to a large extent by economic and business decisions, that contributes to economic growth and employment but also causes congestion, accidents, noise, pollution, increased reliance on imported fossil fuels, and energy loss. To overcome such problems, the EC believes Europe's transport system needs to be optimised by means of advanced logistics solutions. However, it also notes that while developing freight transport logistics is primarily a business-related activity and a task for industry, government authorities nevertheless have a role to play in creating the appropriate framework conditions and keeping logistics on the political agenda.

Question

If your firm was an EU-15 manufacturer looking to expand into the EU-12 countries, would you choose an alliance with a local logistics service provider or establish your own transport and distribution centres in that region, and why?

Sources: adapted from Lauri Ojala, 'The logistical impact of EU enlargement,' *Economic Trends*, April 2004, pp.29–33; Alfred Angerer, Daniel Corsten, Frank Straube and Philippe Tufinkgi 'The EU enlargement – influence on European logistics,' St Gallen, CH: Kuehne-Institute for Logistics, University of St Gallen, September 2003; and European Commission 'Freight transport logistics in Europe – the key to sustainable mobility,' COM(2006) 336, Brussels.

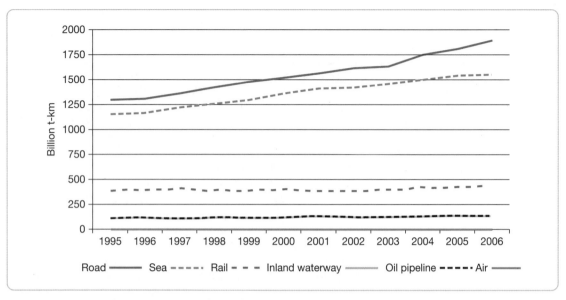

Figure 4.1 EU-27 goods transport growth by mode 1995–2006

Source: European Commission (2009, p.56).

freight and mail transport grew from 3,060 billion tonne-kilometres (t-km) in 1995 to 4,140 billion t-km in 2006, as shown in Figure 4.1.

During that same period all six modes contributed positively to the EU-27's average 2.8 per cent yearly growth in goods transport performance, as shown in Figure 4.2. The modes grew at average yearly rates ranging from 1.1 per cent in rail to 3.8 per cent in inter-EU air. Over half (55 per cent) of the increase in total performance during the period was attributable to road (compared with its 46 per cent share in total in 2006) and to ocean or sea transport (37 per cent of total increase and equal to its share in 2006).

The EU-27's transport network in 2005 was an estimated 4.5 million kilometres comprising 4.2 million kilometres of road (92 per cent), 220,000 of rail (5 per cent), and 40,000 of inland waterways and 30,000 of pipelines (about 1.5 per cent each). Road freight transport accounted for 1.89 trillion t-km in 2007 and carried 17.06 billion tonnes of goods in 2006. The EU-27 countries had an average yearly increase of 3.1 per cent in the number of road goods vehicles from 1990 to 2006, the total stock of these vehicles expanding to 32.2 million in 2006. Close to 60 per cent of this increase was due to growth in fleet size of around 2 million units in Spain, 1.6 million in Italy and around 1 million in both Poland and the United Kingdom. In 2006, the EU-27 fleet of road goods vehicles was made up to nearly 75 per cent by those of France (17 per cent), Spain (16 per cent), Italy (13 per cent), the United Kingdom (11 per cent), Germany (9 per cent) and Poland (7 per cent). Road cabotage, i.e. when national road transport is performed by a vehicle registered in another country, grew at an average yearly rate of 6 per cent and totalled 16.1 billion t-km in 2007. Hauliers from Germany were the most active (16 per cent), followed by the three Benelux countries: Luxembourg (14 per cent), the Netherlands (12 per cent) and Belgium (10 per cent).

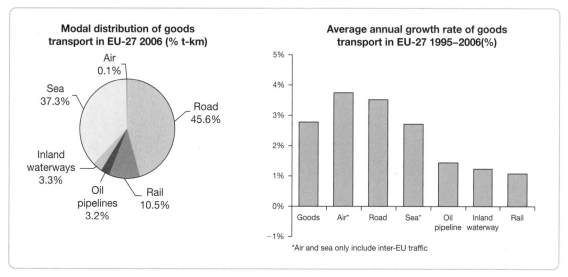

Figure 4.2 EU-27 modal distribution 2006 and growth rate 1995–2006 of goods
Source: European Commission (2009, p.7).

EU-27 rail freight in 2007 comprised 435 billion t-km but carried only 1.63 billion tonnes of primarily bulk goods, with national rail goods transport accounting for about 54 per cent of the latter. Further, goods transport wagons in EU-27 reduced by close to half between 1990 and 2005 from 1.455 million to 741,000 wagons. Of the estimated reduction by 715,000 wagons, more than 80 per cent are explained by decreases in Germany (209,000), Poland (172,000), Romania (101,000), Italy (54,000) and France (52,000). Although the phasing-out of obsolete stock is most probably responsible for a large part of the reduction, the data may also suggest a shift in haulage from rail to road. Domestic and intra-EU-27 sea transport comprised 1.55 trillion t-km. However, while inland waterways comprised only 138 billion t-km, over 503 million tonnes of goods were carried. Oil pipelines accounted for only 135 billion t-km.

US freight transportation system[6]

Goods transportation in the US was 6.27 trillion t-km in 2006, comprised of 1.89 trillion t-km road (30 per cent), 2.71 trillion t-km rail (43 per cent), 854 billion t-km oil pipelines (14 per cent), 486 billion t-km inland waterways (8 per cent) and 332 billion sea and inland waterways (5 per cent). The total weight of shipments was 18.58 billion tons or 16.86 billion tonnes in 2007, as shown in Table 4.1. While total volumes fell due to the recession to 16.12 billion tons or 14.62 billion tonnes in 2009, they are expected to increase to 27.10 billion tons or 25.51 billion tonnes by 2040, with intermodal (see below) and mail seeing the largest increase in share from 8.3 per cent to 11.5 per cent.

The total value of goods shipped in 2007 was US$16.54 trillion, as shown in Table 4.2. Again, due to the recession that value fell to $14.65 trillion in 2009 but is also expected to rise to $39 trillion by 2040, with multiple modes and mail again increasing their share more

Table 4.1 Weight of shipments by transportation mode (millions of tons)

	2007		2009		2040 (estimated)	
Truck	12,766	68.7%	10,868	67.4%	18,445	68.1%
Rail	1,894	10.2%	1,689	10.5%	2,408	8.9%
Water	794	4.3%	734	4.6%	1,143	4.2%
Air, air and truck	13	0.1%	11	0.1%	41	0.2%
Multiple modes and mail	1,531	8.2%	1,336	8.3%	3,119	11.5%
Pipeline	1,270	6.8%	1,220	7.6%	1,509	5.6%
Other and unknown	313	1.7%	265	1.6%	440	1.6%
Total	18,581	100.0%	16,122	100.0%	27,104	100.0%

Source: US Department of Transportation Federal Highway Administration (2010).

Table 4.2 Value of shipments by transportation mode (US$ billions)

	2007		2009		2040 (estimated)	
Truck	10,783	65.2%	9,511	64.9%	21,656	55.1%
Rail	511	3.1%	421	2.9%	733	1.9%
Water	286	1.7%	263	1.8%	412	1.0%
Air, air and truck	1,079	6.5%	884	6.0%	4,347	11.1%
Multiple modes and mail	2,923	17.7%	2.639	18.0%	10,520	26.8%
Pipeline	623	3.8%	595	4.1%	728	1.9%
Other and unknown	331	2.0%	334	2.3%	898	2.3%
Total	16,536	100.0%	14,647	100.0%	39,294	100.0%

Source: US Department of Transportation Federal Highway Administration (2010).

than the other modes. The increase in multiple modes probably reflects more integrated strategies as well as an increase in deliveries by smaller vans and trucks directly to households as the use of the internet to purchase goods continues to increase.

The private sector owns a significant share of assets in the US transportation industry: $1.1 trillion in equipment plus $681.2 billion in private structures, compared with $502 billion in transportation structures and $2.5 trillion in highways owned by public agencies. Freight railroad facilities and services are almost entirely private, while trucks in the private sector operate over public highways, air-cargo services in the private sector operate in public airways and mostly public airports, and ships in the private sector serve public waterways and both public and private port facilities. Pipelines are mostly in the private sector, although significantly controlled by public regulation. In the public sector virtually all truck routes are owned by state or local governments. Airports and harbours are typically owned by public port authorities (although terminals are usually owned or managed by private operators). Air and water navigation is mostly federal, and safety is regulated by all levels of government.

Modes of freight transport[7]

There are six different modes of transport:

● road transport, for example in trucks or vans;
● rail transport, for example on dedicated freight trains;

- pipeline transport for oil, other liquids and slurries;

- inland waterway transport, for example on river barges, tows or canal boats;

- ocean or sea shipping, for example on container ships or crude oil super-tankers;

- air transport, for example in dedicated air-cargo freighters or as belly-hold cargo in passenger airlines.

Transportation of freight may also use multiple modes; this is known as intermodal or multi-modal transport and usually involves a container or other fixed storage unit being transferred from one mode to another, for example road to rail, during its journey.

Road transport

Road freight transport in the EU is subject to some EU regulation as well as national operating controls and fiscal arrangements. For example, in 2005 Germany introduced a new tariff system on 12,000 motorway kilometres for all vehicles with a gross vehicle weight of more than 12 tonnes. This system, called LKW-Maut, is based on the distance in kilometres travelled, the truck's number of axles and its emissions. Otherwise, the EU market is a fairly liberalised, highly competitive, open market with low barriers to entry.

Actors in the market include private-company-operated fleets for their own account and public-company operators that operate for hire and reward, including 3PL service providers and transport companies. There are many small operators, with almost 70 per cent of the UK's truck fleets owning three or fewer trucks.[8] Since there are few large providers this situation generates a high churn in the marketplace and bankruptcies average around 10 per cent per year.

A standard load size in the UK is restricted to 28 tonnes on a 44 tonnes gross weight vehicle that can be only 13.6 metres in length. Shipments transported by trucks are referred to as truckload (TL) or less-than-truckload (LTL). Smaller shipments transported by trucks are LTL, which is any quantity of freight weighing less than the amount required for the application of a truckload rate. Road transport is best suited for door-to-door transport and the widespread distribution of goods over a 24-hour delivery cycle, for example replenishing retail grocery stores at night from distribution centres.

The strengths of road transport include high flexibility for different transport requirements and changed plans, fewer waiting periods for loading and unloading compared with other modes, relatively low transport times for short and medium distances, good economies of scale over a wide distance range from local to international. However, the weaknesses of road transport include limited transport volume, weather effects on travel and congestion, restrictions on the transport of hazardous goods, and poor environmental aspects due to fuel use and emissions.

Rail transport

Rail transport is subject to a broad EU regulatory structure but has a partially liberalised market. However, rail has high entry barriers in the form of capital for equipment, safety requirements and necessity for expertise in operations. The operating network across Europe is complex and there are few train operating companies and service providers.

Rail is restricted to its track infrastructure and due to rail-network inflexibility can provide only terminal-to-terminal operations with limited sidings. Departures are also usually fixed and pre-scheduled given competition with passenger rail transport over the same tracks. However, unlike trucks there are no bans on when trains may run, such as Sundays or holidays. The maximum wagon load size is 55 tonnes and the maximum train size is 1,000 tonnes.

Rail transport is best suited for bulk shipping (several wagonloads) of many types of bulk goods (coal, raw materials) over distances of 300 kilometres or more where it is very economical and can travel at higher consistent speeds than truck. It is also more environmentally friendly per tonne of freight. However, rail's weaknesses are that it is inadequate for short-distance transport or with frequent cargo changes and is subject to the monopolistic power of the main operators and operator-provided and government-incentivised track investment; rail has traditionally been highly subsided in order to compete with road.

Pipeline transport

Pipeline transport is used solely for a limited range of products, including natural gas, crude oil, petroleum products, water, chemicals and liquid products. Natural gas and crude oil are the main products transported by pipeline. Pipeline's strengths are that it is economic, safe and environmentally friendly. However, there is a small pipeline network in Europe and pipelines have high fixed costs.

Inland waterway transport

Inland waterway transport is best suited for large cargo shipments covering longer distances. Such transport is economic, environmentally friendly, and there is a good availability of specialised ships. However, weaknesses include a limited waterway network, high handling and trans-shipment costs and a dependency on weather for water levels in certain waterways.

Ocean or sea shipping

Ocean or sea shipping is best suited for the intercontinental shipment of bulk cargo, bulky goods, containers and dangerous materials such as oil and gas over large distances. Due to the global nature of this mode it is covered in more depth in Chapter 11. Its strengths are that it is very economic, environmentally friendly per tonne of cargo despite bunker fuel being a particularly 'dirty' fuel, can handle very large transport volumes and can operate independent of weather conditions. Its weaknesses include high capital costs and long lead times to construct ships, slow speed of transport, a dependency on specially equipped ports, and less security while at sea, i.e. easily subject to piracy.

Air transport

Air transport is best suited for high-value goods and high-speed shipments. Its strengths include frequency of flights and security, and the cost-efficient transport of light parts.

However, it is very expensive for heavy or bulk goods – for example, flying mechanical equipment into remote areas – it has relatively low transport capacity, the time the cargo spends on the ground time is over 70 per cent of total transport time, and it is very environmentally unfriendly.

Intermodal or multi-modal transport

With logistics becoming more and more a global business it is appropriate to discuss intermodal transport as a mode in its own right. Intermodal or multi-modal transport essentially carries unitised freight, i.e. containers, and the various means of doing so across modes has different terms. When containers are moved by a handling system such as an overhead crane from one type of transport platform to another, i.e. from a rail flat car to a truck flat car, this process is known as 'lift-on/lift-off', i.e. Lo-Lo. When a container on a truck trailer is driven on and off a transport platform, i.e. a rail flat car or a ferry, this process is known as 'roll-on/roll-off', i.e. Ro-Ro.

A trailer or a trailer plus a container travelling on a rail flat car is termed 'piggyback' and 'trailer on flatcar' or TOFC. A container travelling on a rail flat car by itself is termed 'container on flatcar' or COFC. A Ro-Ro on a flat car is termed a 'rolling road' in Europe. In the US there can be several containers in a row on one rail flat car or two stacked together known as a 'double-stack' unit.

As discussed, road transport has tended to displace rail transport in past decades; however, governments and other organisations are making a concerted effort to have more freight moved via rail to reduce road congestion and emissions from diesel truck engines. One such organisation, the International Union of combined Road–Rail transport companies (UIRR), was founded in 1970 with the objective of shifting as much freight transport as possible from road to rail. To achieve this goal, UIRR members offer different products often developed in collaboration with their clients, such as direct or block trains that operate non-stop between destinations with variable capacity and composition of wagon loads all destined for the same location or shuttle trains that have fixed composition of wagon loads. Block trains operate on agreed train paths between specific origin–destination pairs, e.g. Hamburg–Vienna, without intermediate stops and on set days and at set times. Locomotive traction is provided from different railway enterprises. The train is operated at the risk of the service provider, with the wagon mix driven by market requirements.[9]

Ports

The movement of intermodal or multi-modal freight on a global basis requires sea ports to handle container traffic. With its sizeable coastline that makes up 85 per cent of the EU-27's boundaries and is the world's second-longest, and its large number of ports, the maritime sector is considered a valuable alternative to land transport, according to the EU.[10] The 22 EU-27 member states with seaports total 313 'main' ports between them, i.e. ports handling over 1 million tonnes of goods per year.

The greatest number of main seaports can be found in Italy (46) and the United Kingdom (45). Moreover, in these two similarly populated countries, it takes about the same number of main ports to absorb at least 80 per cent of traffic (respectively 18 and

17 ports). However, when looking at similarly populated France, the port structure and concentration are different. France has only 20 main ports and the 80 per cent threshold is reached by only 6 of them. The larger number of main ports in the United Kingdom and Italy can be explained by a number of reasons. In the case of the United Kingdom, maritime routes are important notably for connecting the island with mainland Europe as well as with neighbouring Ireland and more distant Scandinavia. Italy, in addition to being a peninsula, serves as a maritime gateway for EU-27 trade with countries in south-eastern Europe and beyond. A discussion about the largest ports complex in the UK is presented in Logistics Example 4.2.

LOGISTICS EXAMPLE 4.2

The Humber ports

Despite the global recession hitting the UK hard, the Humber ports complex is gearing up for exciting opportunities and growth. The complex consists of four major facilities on the north and south banks of the Humber River in the Humber region, which comprises ports at Kingston-upon-Hull, Immingham, Grimsby and Goole (see map).

The Humber River estuary has the largest port conurbation in the UK in terms of tonnage; the Humber ports account for just over one-third of Britain's sea traffic. Despite the recession, Grimsby and Immingham remain the leading ports in the UK, handling 17 per cent of the country's 86 million tonnes of bulk freight, consisting of freight, coal, forest products and oil. Immingham is the sixteenth largest port in Europe for liquid bulks and the seventh biggest in terms of dry bulks. It also handles considerable volumes of Ro-Ro truck traffic and is Europe's fifth busiest Ro-Ro port, with more than 18 million tonnes of freight.

Relatively few containers come through the Humber ports in comparison with Southampton and Felixstowe, despite many of these containers being delivered to the north of England and Scotland. The Humber River is a shallow estuary, which means that

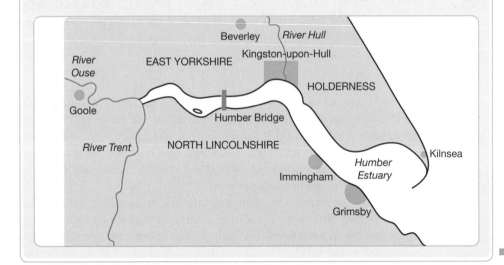

the largest modern container ships are unable to dock. The need to minimise time spent in port with large container ships and the congestion within the southern ports has led to UK ports suffering a significant decline in share of EU container traffic in recent years. However, these issues could lead to the Humber ports and others in the north benefiting from increased feeder volumes trans-shipped from other EU ports such as Rotterdam. The geographical positioning of the Humber River, together with other logistical assets and capabilities in the region, gives it a particular edge, which it could exploit in cooperation with a continental European port.

A road congestion analysis shows that the road network within the Humber region performs significantly better than the south of England. The region also has available land and distribution areas outside of the congested urban areas with good access to major trunk roads such as the M1, A1 and M62 where distribution centres and facilities could be located, reducing problems of urban congestion. Some recent examples of national UK retailers basing facilities in the region, on land which has good access to the motorways but is not part of a major urban area, include B&Q, Asda, IKEA and Tesco.

Changes in the economics of distribution provide further opportunities. For example, the UK imports around 60 per cent of its fruit and vegetables, utilising a combination of airfreight, Ro-Ro and containers, with much of this volume landing at the southern ports, being transferred to the Humber region for processing into other food products and then being transferred to distribution centres in the Midlands e.g. Birmingham, for retail distribution. However, by using a port-centric strategy and transferring these volumes to ports and airports in the Humber region close to the manufacturing and processing sites, total supply chain costs and carbon could be reduced.

The region has three airports – Leeds-Bradford, Robin Hood and Humberside – all of which have freight-carrying capacity. Tonnage volumes in the UK are small, with only 2.2 million tonnes of airfreight moved in 2007; however, this cargo comprised about 40 per cent of total UK freight value. Humberside airport is the closest to the Humber ports and moved 168 tonnes of freight in 2008, while Leeds-Bradford moved 334 tonnes.

The Humber region also has some of the busiest rail freight corridors in the UK, especially tracks on the south bank of the Humber River. The main rail freight products include coal and biomass for the region's power stations, intermodal containers, construction materials such as aggregates, and metals and petroleum. The strength of the region for warehousing has also been recognised by chartered surveyors who examined the most appropriate locations for warehousing based on a variety of factors, including transport connections, labour market issues and the environment. Additionally, the Humber ports are ideally placed to secure significant opportunities in the burgeoning offshore wind industry by providing port-side space to develop manufacturing and maintenance facilities and services.

Yet despite its significant logistical assets, the Humber region is perceived to be too distant and thus remote from the populous south of England, a perception encouraged by geographic distance, which doesn't make it easy to attract companies to the region. However, the region's geographic position is an asset, with it being strategically located between the south and the Midlands on the one hand and Scotland on the other; the Humber ports are also well placed to be part of the European Community as they are ideally placed to trade with the port of Rotterdam.

To take full advantage of all this, ports-based businesses have recognised a need for an effective, unified marketing strategy and in 2011 were looking to establish an initiative to build a unified Humber brand and allow the region to be promoted more effectively

---

Logistics Example 4.2 (*cont.*)

at home and abroad. Such an initiative could give the region significant opportunities in terms of port-centric logistics and short sea transport and, combined with the increasing prosperity of the Midlands and Scotland moving the centre of gravity for UK distribution further north, should enable the region to attract distribution centres and other logistics activities away from the south.

Question

Identify other major ports in the European Union 25 (EU-27) member states and the markets they serve.

Source: adapted from Riverhumber.com (2011) www.riverhumber.com/ (accessed 25 July); and Richard Faint (2010) *The Logistics Sector in the Yorkshire and Humber Region*, University of Hull: Logistics Institute.

The construction of Trans-European Transport Networks (TEN-T) is a major contributory element to the economic competitiveness and the balanced and sustainable development of the EU. TEN-Ts aim to improve economic and social cohesion by linking island, landlocked and peripheral regions with the EU's more central regions, through interconnecting and interoperable national networks by land, air, sea and inland waterways, and including GALILEO, the European satellite navigation system. A specific novelty of the TEN-T networks concerns the development of 'Motorways of the Sea' which has inter-modality at its heart. Its aim is to foster integrated intermodal options, based on short-sea shipping providing frequent, high-quality alternatives to road transport.[11]

The development of such initiatives, and the fact that container ships are growing in size and capacity (see Chapter 11), has led to a concept of port-centric logistics,[12] which is defined as the provision of distribution and other value-adding logistics services at a port. Traditionally, most ports acted as simple trans-shipment hubs where freight passed between ships and landside transport. Ports are increasingly recognising that higher profit margins can be made on non-core port activities and are thus driven to engage in activities beyond simply providing berths for ships and other core port services.

Port-centric logistics represents a new phase in port development that looks beyond a port's physical boundaries via regionalisation where the reach of the port involves market strategies and policies linking it more closely to inland freight distribution centres. In the UK, some ports are actively encouraging companies to locate distribution centres at ports rather than in their traditional locations, which tend to be in geographically central, inland locations. One advantage of establishing a distribution centre at a port is that it cuts down on the number of empty (return) containers on roads by 'stripping' (i.e. emptying) imported containers at the port. This also allows faster repositioning of containers to another port where they are required. Port-centric logistics also allows major ports such as Rotterdam to act as a hub port for large container ships to offload and smaller container ships to then trans-ship containers to feeder ports in other nearby countries.

Different modes of freight transport have strengths and weaknesses and the choice of any mode or modes will depend on various factors, including cost, time and service. Figure 4.3 summarises some of these factors. The next section will discuss additional decision-making factors and criteria for carrier and mode choices.

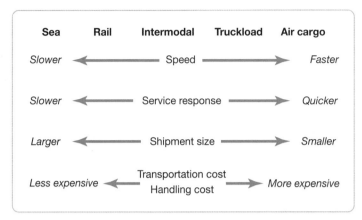

Figure 4.3 Transportation service and economic characteristics

Carrier and mode choices

The motivations of both shippers and carriers as they affect carrier and mode choice decisions must be considered first. Shippers transporting goods are essentially seeking to *maximise service* and *minimise cost* for a given customer when they offer a consignment of goods for transport. They will look to do this by managing direct transport costs, such as inventory costs, including in-transit, safety stocks and transaction costs and the cost of service failure, including the time specified for delivery, the lead time and the condition of the goods upon arrival. Shippers will also evaluate a number of shipping parameters to distinguish modes, which will vary by country, including:

- the geographic coverage of the carrier;
- the volume, weight, value and type of goods the carrier can handle;
- any consignment, load and dimension limits;
- the importance to the carrier of their consignment;
- transit time from door to door;
- the carrier's reliability versus risk;
- the price for throughput, distance, time and the cost per 'unit' moved;
- the service frequency and schedule flexibility;
- the carrier's service range and choice, including the use of technology;
- any intermediate handling and/or alternative routings;
- any environmental externalities.

Carriers, meanwhile, have to balance their transport asset utilisation versus the frequency of service provided to the shipper. Their goal will be to *achieve a satisfactory return on investment* (ROI) through *maximising revenue and minimising costs* by route or customer. They will look to do this by managing fixed terminal costs, access or track costs, intermediate and terminal handling, maximising load sizes through consolidation and return loading, and minimising variable trip costs such as fuel, distance and labour. Capital and operating cost factors a carrier will consider include the following.

Capital

- Fixed assets and facilities such as terminals, hubs, trans-shipment points, offices.
- Mobile assets and equipment such as vehicles, trailers, containers, handling equipment, communications equipment.
- Business costs, including the cost of capital, profit targets, taxes and regulatory costs.

Operating

- Fuel, including taxes.
- Drivers.
- Maintenance and repairs.
- Track cost, tolls and ferries.
- Schedulers.
- Loading.
- Sales, administration, legal and insurance for vehicles and goods, operating licence, permits and fixed taxes.
- Outsourced delivery services, short-term hires and third-party carriers.

In summary, the decision to choose a mode and carrier is multifaceted. However, shippers tend to purchase freight based on service parameters, not modes or routes; they recognise that carriers have the knowledge of infrastructure, routes and modes. Shippers are also looking for a 'one-stop shop' and base their decisions on key service attributes of cost where the carrier can provide the reliability, transit time and efficiency desired at the lowest possible prices and reliability equates to on-time and damage-free shipments and the carrier being financially stable and transit time equates to consistent performance and not necessarily speed. Such service parameters increasingly include the use of various forms of technology such as GPS and RFID, which will be discussed further in Chapter 8. An example of *vehicle telematics systems* is presented in Logistics Example 4.3 to highlight a direct technological application in road transport. For carriers, cost and efficiency drives route and mode choice over the total trip where efficiency equates to load consolidation, utilising equipment and backhauling or return trip opportunities to reduce empty-running.

Third-party transportation

Shippers and companies can use third-party firms to arrange and manage their shipping needs. Traditional types of third party include freight forwarders, brokers and shippers' associations.

Freight forwarders tend to be the most common type of third party used. They purchase transportation services from carriers and then sell on this capacity to shippers. Forwarders

Vehicle telematics systems

Vehicle telematics systems (VTS) can be used as a source of key performance indicator (KPI) data for the measurement of road transport efficiency. However, VTS can also be used for better traffic management, improved road safety, and road user charging through electronic toll collection (ETC).

VTS use GPS satellites to track truck movement through onboard units in the truck cab. Vehicle location data can be updated regularly at one-minute, two-minute or five-minute intervals, while the ignition status is on. The GPS satellites circling the earth rely on line of sight, which means they have to be able to see the vehicle in order to track it. If the vehicle goes into a garage, tunnel or building, the VTS will not allow the server to know what the vehicle is doing. This can also apply when vehicles are in a major built-up area where the signal may be intermittent. To resolve these issues some VTS have both active and passive tracking.

There are actually two distinct types of vehicle tracking. Some products on the market are a hybrid of both automatic vehicle location (AVL) and events-activated tracking system (EATS) technologies. AVL, also known as active tracking technology, is predominantly used when applying vehicle tracking to fleet or driver management solutions. The unit is configured to automatically transmit its location at a set time interval, e.g. every five minutes. The unit is activated when the ignition is switched on/off. EATS or passive tracking is primarily used in connection with vehicle or driver security solutions. For example, if someone breaks into a truck and attempts to steal it the passive tracking system can be triggered by the immobiliser unit or motion sensor being activated. A monitoring bureau will then be automatically notified that the unit has been activated and begin tracking the vehicle.

Vehicle tracking can be used in the following scenarios:

- *Fleet management.* When managing a fleet of vehicles, knowing the real-time location of all drivers allows management to meet customer needs more efficiently. Whether it is delivery, service or other multi-vehicle enterprises, drivers now need only a mobile phone with an internet connection to be inexpensively tracked by and despatched efficiently.

- *Asset tracking.* Companies needing to track valuable assets for insurance or other monitoring purposes can now plot real-time asset locations on a map and closely monitor movement and operating status; for example, alcohol products which may or may not be bonded.

- *Field service management.* Companies with a workforce deployed in the field to deliver services such as repair or maintenance must be able to plan field workers' time, schedule subsequent customer visits and be able to operate these departments efficiently. Vehicle tracking allows companies to quickly locate the closest field engineers and despatch one to meet a new customer request or provide site arrival information.

- *Field sales management.* Sales managers can access real-time locations of staff, thus adding nearby last-minute appointments to itineraries. Benefits include increased productivity, reduced driving time and increased time spent with customers and prospects.

- *Trailer tracking.* Haulage and logistics companies often operate trucks with detachable load-carrying units or trailers. There are different types of trailers used for different applications, e.g. flatbed, refrigerated, curtain-sided, box container, and tracking will allow a company to know which trailer and type is where at any given time for further deployment.

Logistics example 4.3 (*cont.*)

There are many suppliers and users of VTS in the European road freight sector. The main focus appears to be on vehicle time utilisation from the VTS suppliers' point of view, while users understandably focus on the main cost drivers for the operation of the vehicle: fuel consumption and drivers' hours. Governments, meanwhile, are concerned with using VTS to assist their ETC initiatives.

However, currently VTS is unable to monitor vehicle loading either directly through the use of sensors or indirectly through interfacing with other company IT systems, which is a major constraint on the wider adoption of performance measures used in any transport KPI initiative, particularly energy-intensity indices. Further, it has taken ten years for the ETC industry to reach agreement on a European standard, but this standard still has issues of interoperability with other technologies such as GPS. Europe also has a poor record on the interoperability of ETC services between different countries as each nation has developed its own system for toll collection.

Question

Do you believe vehicle telematics have any consumer logistics uses and if so, what are they?

Sources: adapted from David McClelland and Alan C. McKinnon (2004) 'Use of vehicle telematics systems for the collection of key performance indicator data in road freight transport,' Edinburgh: Logistics Research Centre, Heriot-Watt University; Robin Meczes 'Public policy to drive telematics take-up?' *Logistics & Transport Focus*, 2003, Vol. 5, No. 7, pp.38–40; and UK Telematics Online (2011) www.uktelematicsonline.co.uk/ (accessed 25 July 2011).

---

receive their remuneration in the form of costs plus commission from the shipper. Their traditional services include:

- export/import documentation completion and compliance;
- planning and costing of 'through freight' movements;
- booking space from scheduled and charter carriers;
- consolidating payments to transport services, ports, etc.;
- presenting and arranging goods for customs clearance;
- advising clients on trade and financial procedures to permit preparations of export/import quotations;
- arranging insurance, bank letters of credits, etc.

The growth in global logistics has seen the service portfolio of freight forwarders increase to include:

- grouping small consignments, i.e. less-than-container load (LCL), into regular scheduled services in their own name using the shipping company resources for all kinds of freight;
- providing their own cargo collection and delivery vehicles;
- providing their own warehouses to hold shipper inventories either in-bond or in standard domestic conditions;
- preparing export packing and labelling;
- coordinating multiple consignments into single client movements;

- tracking and tracing of consignments;
- providing assured security compliance.

Transportation brokers are often considered the same as freight forwarders; however, they act on behalf of both shippers to purchase transport services and carriers to sell transport capacity. They are thus a true intermediary between both parties and receive their remuneration in the form of fees. Brokers are useful for small companies that do not have transportation or traffic departments. However, as small companies begin to grow it often makes sense to establish their own systems and go from being an 'order taker' to an 'order maker' to achieve efficiencies and cost savings.[13] Shippers' associations are non-profit entities that represent the interests of a number of shippers. Their main focus is to pool cargo volumes of members to leverage the most favourable service contract rate levels and in that way they function similarly to freight forwarders.

A new type of intermediary developed during the 2000s with the advent of widespread, high-speed computerisation and internet services. These intermediaries provide web-based load matching and e-enabled tendering services either over an intra-company network or on the public worldwide web. The idea of e-tendering, which is a derivative of e-sourcing or e-procurement, has been popular in government settings, as shown in the example of Glasgow City Council in Chapter 3. The adoption of these services in the private sector has generated many benefits for shippers, carriers and, of course, the e-intermediary.

Outsourcing and third-party logistics service providers

The use of 3PL service providers is related to the phenomenon of outsourcing. Outsourcing has been an area of growing interest and activity in business since the early 1990s.[14] The origins of outsourcing are in transaction cost analysis developed by the Nobel Laureate Oliver E. Williamson[15] and the concept of core competence, which are those activities unique to a firm and which can achieve definable pre-eminence and provide unique value for customers.[16]

Outsourcing to 3PL service providers increased dramatically in the 2000s and is now a major business segment in the logistics and supply chain domains. The number of European companies that turned to 3PL service providers nearly doubled from 28 per cent in 2000 to 53 per cent in 2004, with more than 35 per cent of European logistics activities being outsourced, representing a volume of business in excess of €70 billion.[17,18]

The volume of business in the US 3PL market increased from $56 billion in 2000 to over $125 billion in 2008.[19] But despite the recession impacting the logistics and 3PL markets, a survey of 3PL chief executive officers (CEOs) in 2010 indicated that average three-year regional 3PL industry growth projections were 7.8 per cent for North America, 5.4 per cent for Europe and 12.9 per cent for the Asia-Pacific region.[20]

Logistics outsourcing often involves many different forms, including transportation, warehousing, forwarding, brokering, reverse logistics services and information technology. Table 4.3 shows the percentage use of outsourced logistics services across the globe from the Langley and Capgemini 2010 3PL study and the former four activities still comprise the majority of use.[21]

Table 4.3 Percentages of outsourced logistics services used

Outsourced logistics service	User percentages				
	All regions	North America	Europe	Asia Pacific	Latin America
Domestic transportation	83%	75%	94%	89%	80%
International transportation	75	62	89	86	74
Warehousing	74	73	82	77	63
Customs brokerage	58	57	54	68	65
Forwarding	53	47	54	70	48
Cross-docking	38	33	47	42	34
Product labelling, packaging, assembly, kitting	36	32	41	41	34
Reverse logistics (defective, repair, return)	35	27	47	46	25
Transportation planning and management	31	32	32	30	26
Freight bill auditing and payment	28	40	22	23	15
Information technology (IT) services	20	20	15	19	25
Supply chain consultancy services provided by 3PLs	18	20	11	25	17
Order entry, processing and fulfilment	16	17	11	21	14
Fleet management	15	15	17	14	20
Customer service	13	9	10	21	15
LLP/4PL services	13	9	13	16	19

Source: Langley and Capgemini Consulting (2010).

The reasons to outsource logistics activities include:

- an ability to concentrate on 'core competencies';
- the avoidance of large capital investments in logistical assets or a release of existing capital;
- converting logistics activities from a capital to current expenditure;
- reducing labour costs;
- improving standards of service;
- enjoying a greater logistical expertise offered by a 3PL and their economies of scale in vehicle acquisition, fuel, etc.;
- a need for wider geographical coverage offered by a 3PL;
- better support for a wider product range;
- the 'groupage' of loads among several 3PL clients that offer lower unit costs and balancing seasonal fluctuations.

These reasons can provide tangible benefits, as shown in Table 4.4 from the Langley and Capgemini 2010 3PL study, where costs, fixed assets and inventory costs were shown to have been reduced 15 per cent, 25 per cent and 11 per cent respectively, together with several improvements in usual service parameters. However, firms considering outsourcing must take into account several critical success factors, including ensuring there is a selective match of 3PLs to the firm, two-way information sharing between the firm and 3PL, proper role specifications for both sides, appropriate 'ground rules' for engagement and an exit provision if the arrangement doesn't work out.

Table 4.4 Benefits of outsourcing logistics services

Results		All regions
Logistics cost reduction		15%
Logistics fixed asset reduction		25%
Inventory cost reduction		11%
Average order cycle length	Changed from	17 days
	Changed to	12 days
Order fill rate	Changed from	73%
	Changed to	81%
Order accuracy	Changed from	83%
	Changed to	89%

Source: Langley and Capgemini Consulting (2010).

There are several disadvantages in outsourcing logistics activities to 3PL service providers, which include:

- the loss of control over logistics operations to the 3PL;
- the subsequent loss of management expertise and experience over time;
- a partial loss of direct contact with customers;
- a tendency to underestimate core activities, i.e. what should be outsourced and what should not;
- disclosing competitively sensitive information to the 3PL;
- undertaking extra effort in searching for and selecting 3PLs;
- possible customer confusion regarding service provision and follow-up;
- an increased risk of customer service failure; and
- an over-dependence on the 3PL which may lead to a loss of bargaining power.

Table 4.5 provides some reasons why respondents to the Langley and Capgemini 2010 3PL study would not outsource their logistics activities. Key themes in this table indicate that relationship propensity, trust, capabilities and commitment are issues in this sector; indeed, these themes are not new and continue to be important to firms.[22] However, techniques to mitigate the disadvantages of using 3PL services and address the reasons and themes above include:

- reducing the number of 3PLs used;
- changing, i.e. shortening, the length of 3PL contracts awarded;
- shifting from dedicated to shared-user services;
- adopting open-book accounting to determine best value;
- adopting tighter monitoring of the 3PL;
- involving the 3PL more closely in the firm's logistics system design;
- developing stronger relationships and partnerships.

Table 4.5 Reasons not to outsource logistics services

Reason	Per cent in agreement
Logistics is a core competency at our firm	19
Cost reductions would not be experienced	15
Control over the outsourced function(s) would diminish	14
Logistics too important to consider outsourcing	13
Service level commitments would not be realised	11
We have more logistics expertise than most 3PL providers	10
Corporate philosophy excludes the use of outsourced logistics providers	9
Too difficult to integrate our IT systems with 3PL's systems	8
Global capabilities of 3PLs need improvement	6
Issues relating to security of shipments	5
We previously outsourced logistics, and chose not to continue	5
Inability of 3PL providers to form meaningful and trusting relationships	3

Source: Langley and Capgemini Consulting (2010).

Reasons for the failure of 3PL relationships include a strategic error in outsourcing, i.e. the firm should have retained operations in-house; a poor choice of a 3PL service provider; poor management of the relationship with the 3PL; and a lack of suitable and appropriate performance measurement tools, notwithstanding the service level agreement between the firm and the 3PL.[23]

An extension to 3PL is the concept of a fourth-party logistics (4PL) service provider. A 4PL differs from a 3PL in the following ways: a 4PL is often a separate entity established as a joint venture or long-term contract between a primary client and one or more partners; a 4PL acts as a single interface between the client and multiple logistics service providers; ideally, all aspects of the client's supply chain are managed by the 4PL; and it is possible for a major 3PL service provider to form a 4PL organisation within its existing structure. In essence, the 4PL aims to establish 'comprehensive supply chain solutions' rather than simply improve efficiency of the physical logistics operation.

The nature of a 4PL is similar to a lead logistics partner (LLP), which is a firm that organises other 3PL partners in outsourcing of logistics functions. However, a 4PL combines a client's in-house resources and capabilities with those of outside agencies and essentially controls the supply chain for the client. A 4PL also takes a lead role in creating value, for example undertaking the assembly of finished goods on behalf of customers.[24] A 4PL operates almost virtually, i.e. it typically doesn't own any assets like a 3PL but does make intense use of technology and software in managing the outsourced and supply chain processes.

Summary

Transportation is an important activity not just in a logistics sense, i.e. the 'Go' activity, but also as an activity for modern economies and societies in terms of providing goods in a timely and efficient manner. The globalisation of business activities has seen the normal modes of road, rail, water and air become more integrated from both an intermodal and an outsourcing perspective. This chapter has considered basic transportation issues, modes, carrier choice and the outsourcing options available to firms to increase their competitive advantages. The next chapter begins a two-chapter discussion of the 'Stop' activity in logistics by first examining issues of warehousing.

DISCUSSION QUESTIONS

1 Assess the strengths and weaknesses of the six transport modes in your country based on the service and economic characteristics in Figure 4.3.

2 What types of intermodal transport would be used in a supply chain for bananas produced in South America and sold in Europe, and why?

3 Prepare a decision matrix for choosing different carriers to transport electronic consumer products based on the service and economic characteristics you consider appropriate.

4 Should all firms outsource their transport activities? Why or why not?

5 Discuss the role, functions and importance of third-party logistics service providers in the retail supply chain.

Suggested reading

Browne, Michael and Julian Allen 'Logistics outsourcing,' in Ann M. Brewer, Kenneth J. Button and David A. Hensher (eds.) *Handbook of Logistics and Supply Chain Management*, London: Pergamon Press (Elsevier), 2001, pp.253–268.

Christopher, Martin *Logistics and Supply Chain Management*, 4th ed. Harlow: FT Prentice Hall, 2011.

Grant, David B. 'The transaction–relationship dichotomy in logistics and supply chain management,' *Supply Chain Forum: An International Journal*, 2005, Vol. 6, No. 2, pp.38–48.

Hamel, Gary and C.K. Prahalad 'The core competence of the corporation,' *Harvard Business Review*, 1990, Vol. 68, No. 3, pp.79–91.

Holter, Andreas, David B. Grant, James Ritchie and Nigel Shaw 'A framework for purchasing transport services in small and medium size enterprises,' *International Journal of Physical Distribution & Logistics Management*, 2008, Vol. 38, No. 1, pp.21–38.

Langley, C. John and Capgemini Consulting '15th Annual Third-party Logistics study,' 2010, www.3plstudy.com/.

Leonardi, Jacques, Allan Woodburn, Julian Allen and Michael Browne 'International road and rail freight transport activity,' in Donald Waters (ed.) *Global Logistics: New Directions in Supply Chain Management*, 6th ed. London: Kogan Page, pp.390–408.

Lieb, Robert C. and Kristin Lieb '2010 3PL CEO surveys,' 2010, www.penskelogistics.com/.

Mangan, John, Chandra Lalwani and Brian Fynes 'Port-centric logistics,' *International Journal of Logistics Management*, 2005, Vol. 19, No. 1, pp.29–41.

McKinnon, Alan 'Optimizing the road freight transport system,' in Donald Waters (ed.) *Global Logistics: New Directions in Supply Chain Management,* 6th ed. London: Kogan Page, pp.284–304.

Quinn, James Brian and Frederick G. Hilmer 'Strategic outsourcing,' *Sloan Management Review*, 1994, Vol. 35, No. 4, pp.43–55.

Ruijgrok, Cees 'European transport: Insights and challenges,' in Ann M. Brewer, Kenneth J. Button and David A. Hensher (eds.) *Handbook of Logistics and Supply Chain Management*, London: Pergamon Press (Elsevier), 2001, pp.29–46.

Rushton, Alan and Steve Walker *International Logistics and Supply Chain Outsourcing: From Local to Global*, London: Kogan Page, 2007.

Williamson, Oliver E. *Markets and Hierarchies: Analysis and Antitrust Implications*, New York: The Free Press, 1975.

Notes

1 Rosalyn Wilson (2011) 'CSCMP's 22nd Annual State of Logistics Report: Navigating through the recovery,' http://cscmp.org/ (accessed 17 June 2011).

2 European Commission (2009) 'Panorama of transport,' *eurostat Statistical books*, Luxembourg: European Commission, p.3.

3 US Department of Transportation Federal Highway Administration Freight Facts and Figures (2010) www.fhwa.dot.gov/ (accessed 25 July 2011).

4 Cees Ruijgrok (2001) 'European transport: Insights and challenges,' in Ann M. Brewer, Kenneth J. Button and David A. Hensher (eds.) *Handbook of Logistics and Supply Chain Management*, London: Pergamon Press (Elsevier), pp.29–46.

5 This section draws upon data from the European Commission (2009) 'Panorama of transport'; and European Commission (2011) 'White Paper: Roadmap to a Single European Transport Area – Towards a competitive and resource efficient transport system,' *COM(2011) 144*, Brussels.

6 This section draws upon data from US Department of Transportation Federal Highway Administration Freight Facts and Figures (2010) www.fhwa.dot.gov/ (accessed 25 July 2011).

7 This section draws upon data from DHL (2011) 'Discover logistics – DHL Logbook,' www.dhl.com (accessed 11 April 2011).

8 UK Department for Transport, www.dft.gov.uk (accessed 28 July 2011).

9 International Union of combined Road-Rail transport companies, www.uirr.com/ (accessed 2011).

10 European Commission (2011).

11 See http://ec.europa.eu/transport/maritime/motorways_sea/motorways_sea_en.htm for more information on Motorways of the Sea.

12 John Mangan, Chandra Lalwani and Brian Fynes (2005) 'Port-centric logistics,' *International Journal of Logistics Management*, Vol. 19, No. 1, pp.29–41.

13 Andreas Holter, David B. Grant, James Ritchie and Nigel Shaw (2008) 'A framework for purchasing transport services in small and medium size enterprises,' *International Journal of Physical Distribution & Logistics Management*, Vol. 38, No. 1, pp.21–38.

14 James Brian Quinn and Frederick G. Hilmer (1994) 'Strategic outsourcing,' *Sloan Management Review*, Vol. 35, No. 4, pp.43–55.

15 Oliver E. Williamson (1975) *Markets and Hierarchies: Analysis and Antitrust Implications*, New York: The Free Press.

16 Gary Hamel and C.K. Prahalad (1990) 'The core competence of the corporation,' *Harvard Business Review*, Vol. 68, No. 3, pp.79–91.

17 Charles Davis (2004) 'Countering the costs,' *Supply Chain Standard* (formerly *Logistics Europe*), Vol. 12, No. 7, p.27.

18 Anon. (2001) 'An industry on the up,' *Supply Chain Standard* (formerly *Logistics Europe*), Vol. 9, No. 7, p.4.

19 Rosalyn Wilson (2009) 'CSCMP's 20th Annual State of Logistics Report: Riding out the recession,' http://cscmp.org/ (accessed 30 June 2009).

20 Robert C. Lieb and Kristin Lieb (2010) '2010 3PL CEO surveys,' www.penskelogistics.com/ (accessed 16 March 2011).

21 C. John Langley and Capgemini Consulting (2010) '15th Annual Third-party Logistics Study,' www.3plstudy.com/ (accessed 23 March 2011).

22 David B. Grant (2005) 'The transaction–relationship dichotomy in logistics and supply chain management,' *Supply Chain Forum: An International Journal*, Vol. 6, No. 2, pp.38–48.

23 Michael Browne and Julian Allen (2001) 'Logistics outsourcing,' in Ann M. Brewer, Kenneth J. Button and David A. Hensher (eds.) *Handbook of Logistics and Supply Chain Management*, London: Pergamon Press (Elsevier), pp.253–268.

24 Cecilia Cabodi (2004) 'The fourth way,' *Supply Chain Standard* (formerly *Logistics Europe*), Vol. 12, No. 3, pp.24–28.

Warehousing

Introduction

Warehousing remains an important function in logistics. Along with inventory management, warehousing represents the 'Stop' activity in the logistics concept. As noted in Chapter 1 these two functions together represent 32 per cent of logistics costs in the US and 41 per cent in Europe. However, warehousing costs alone in the US were $112 billion or 9 per cent while in Europe they were 23 per cent, as shown in Figure 5.1.[1] The primary difference in

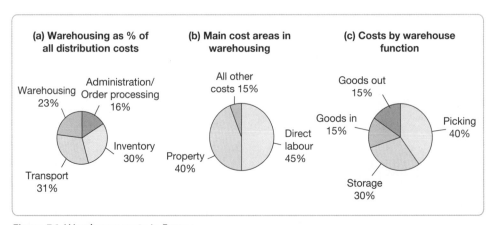

Figure 5.1 Warehouse costs in Europe

Source: A.T. Kearney and European Logistics Association (2009).

these proportions stems from the fact that firms in the US primarily have one national warehouse or national distribution centre (NDC) and several regional distribution centres (RDCs) across all the various states. However, in Europe firms may have European distribution centres (EDCs) as well as NDCs in the 27 member states of the EU and RDCs within those nations.

The role of warehouses has changed as they are increasingly being used in the supply chain as a 'flow-through point' rather than a 'storage point' in order to meet customer demands in fast-paced global supply chains. Thus, warehouses have become 'dynamic systems' in their own right. This chapter discusses the purpose and features of warehouses on a micro-level, including design and materials handling, and also considers issues of warehouse location and number of warehouses on a macro-level.

The nature of warehousing

Warehousing is defined as that part of a company's logistics system that stores products (raw materials, parts, goods in progress, finished goods) at certain nodes in a firm's supply chain, and provides information to the firm on the status, condition and disposition of items being stored. Warehouses can be used to support manufacturing operations on-site, mix or assemble products from multiple production facilities for shipment to a single customer, sub-divide or 'break-bulk' a large shipment of product into many smaller shipments, and combine a number of small shipments into a higher-volume shipment.

Warehouses are necessary to hold stocks that are required in the supply chain to meet customer demand and provide a strategic disconnect between production and consumption. Their general business objectives are to achieve economies by the effective and efficient management of inbound and outbound stocks and distribution services, and to provide an acceptable level of customer service in terms of delivery time and conditions of shipments.

Many levels in the supply chain, including suppliers, producers and distributors, try to hold stocks to meet customer demand. With the changes in distribution that have occurred over the past 30 years firms are now trying to respond to customer requirements rather than 'pushing' products at the customer. Warehouses have had to adapt to these changes and become more flexible and leaner. They have to add value to products while they are in the warehouse and respond to more efficient production schedules, changes in work practices and focus on getting the right product to the right place at the right time. Thus, warehouses today provide more than simple storage; they can provide a facility where a product is assembled, re-assembled, packaged and priced to satisfy the customer.

In today's fast-paced, high-volume warehouse operations, efficient warehouse management depends upon a continuous product flow that necessitates an information system that can locate products and reveal how they should be moved in order to maximise space and labour resources. It is no longer just a matter of storing inventory, but rather getting products into the hands of customers faster, at a better cost and in better condition than the competition.

At the heart of modern warehouses and stock movements is the notion of a stock keeping unit or SKU. Every unique product or item is an SKU and has a unique identification number assigned by the global standards non-profit association GS1. In Europe this number is termed an International Article Number (EAN) and is visible on every product as a 13-digit barcode. Figure 5.2 shows the breakdown of a pallet of one SKU from a pallet load to individual items.

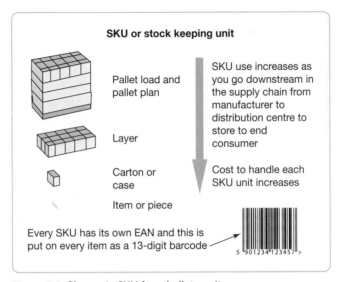

Figure 5.2 Change in SKU from bulk to unit

A pallet plan consists of the number of cases in a layer and the number of layers to make up a tier. The height of a pallet will vary based on an item's weight and density and the pallet's ability to be stacked. What must remain the same are the pallet's horizontal proportions. However, pallet sizes are different in different regions: in the US they are 40 × 40 inches (1016 mm), in continental Europe they are 800 × 1000 mm, and in the UK they are 1200 × 1000 mm. As a pallet load is broken down into layers, cases and finally items, both the use to a customer and the handling cost increase.

The general purpose of a warehouse, as shown in Figure 5.3, is to:

- *receive* inbound shipments of stocks in an orderly manner that includes checking quality and quantity against the order and then disbursing the shipments into bulk or reserve pallet storage or to other points of use. The type of storage depends upon product characteristics, quantity, handling characteristics, and the time and space available;
- undertake *added-value* operations within the warehouse such as cross-docking;
- *assemble* orders for despatch;
- *despatch* outbound shipments of stocks.

Figure 5.4 provides an overview example of a warehouse that shows the various purpose notations as well as the added-value operations undertaken in the warehouse. These operations include:

- *cross docking* inbound shipments to a nearby area for immediate outbound shipment, i.e. the shipments never get prepared and put into storage;
- *pre-packing/unitising* products when they are received in bulk for storage (cages/pallets) or use elsewhere (kitting);
- *order picking* to retrieve and collect bulk or individual items from storage to make up orders for customers according to demand;

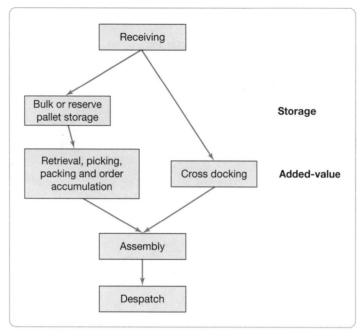

Figure 5.3 General purpose of a warehouse

- *sortation and accumulation* of batch picks into individual orders as well as assorting, aggregating, disaggregating and accumulating these picks in accordance with customer preferences;
- *unitising and shipping* orders and checking them for completeness, weighing them for shipping charge and loading trucks.

The main types of warehouses are:

- *Bonded warehouse* – where goods are held in-bond without having to pay government duties until the product actually leaves the warehouse – for example, alcohol or tobacco products.
- *Distribution centre (DC)* – holds minimum items, performs a high percentage of value-adding and focuses on maximising the profit impact of meeting the customer's delivery requirements.
- *Cross docking warehouse* – where product arrives in bulk and is broken down and mixed in the proper quantity of products for customer shipment.
- *Component hub* – where components are stored prior to final assembly.
- *Special commodity warehouse* – handles one kind of product, usually agricultural.
- *Bulk storage warehouse* – provides tank storage of liquids or open/sheltered storage of dry products such as coal and sand.
- *'Cash and carry' warehouse* – provides storage of bulk products which can be purchased.

Warehouses can take one of three forms. One form is private ownership and operation by the firm; i.e. it is for their 'own account' and they bear all the capital and operating costs.

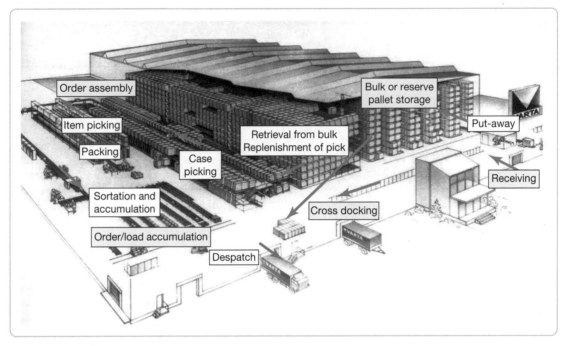

Figure 5.4 Warehouse activities

As shown in Figure 5.1, property costs represent 40 per cent of total warehousing costs, with labour at 45 per cent and all other costs at 15 per cent. Another form is a contracted warehouse, which again is owned and operated by a 3PL but on behalf of only one customer. The final form is a public warehouse, which is owned and operated by 3PL service providers on behalf of multiple customers. Logistics Example 5.1 discusses how the French tyre manufacturer uses 3PL warehouse services for its North American market.

LOGISTICS EXAMPLE 5.1

Warehouse outsourcing at Michelin

TNT Logistics is a division of TPG, a global leader in logistics, mail and express operating in 39 countries, and based in the Netherlands. In 2002, TNT assumed operations of Michelin Group's entire North American network of tyre distribution centres, totalling 650,000 square metres in the United States and Canada. Michelin is a leading global manufacturer of tyres for the automotive, trucking and other industries.

The contract was the latest in TNT's relationship with Michelin that began in 1995 in Europe. Since that time TNT has expanded its relationship by providing a combination of warehousing, inbound and outbound distribution services in Germany, Italy, France, Turkey, Malaysia, Australia and North America.

Michelin turned to TNT's expertise in warehouse management as part of an initiative to reduce annual operational costs by €154 million, as well as to become more cost competitive and improve services to its customers.

TNT assumed the operation of 12 Michelin distribution centres in the United States and 6 in Canada. TNT also transitioned nearly 650 Michelin employees to its operations. In addition, TNT's internal logistics design team redesigned the distribution network and optimised material flow throughout the United States and Canada, resulting in greater efficiencies and cost savings in outbound distribution to Michelin's retail outlets throughout North America. Going forward, the plan calls for the implementation of three 'super distribution centres' to further improve distribution efficiency in North America.

Within the first year of its operation, TNT initiated the phased implementation of a new warehouse management system that allows for more efficient processes and increased visibility to replace Michelin's legacy system. After one year of operation, all Michelin distribution centres were declared 'green', meaning that they were meeting and exceeding operational goals set by Michelin. Efficiency in distribution to retail outlets has also increased by a significant percentage.

Question

What are control versus efficiency tradeoffs in outsourced logistics networks?

Source: adapted from 'Case study: Michelin tyres,' (2005) TNT logistics (now part of CEVA logistics).

The amount of flexibility and customisation for a firm decreases when moving from the first form to the last, i.e. the warehouse goes from being a specialist unit to a generic unit. The role of public warehousing is greater in the US and continental European countries than it is in the UK where own account and contracted warehouses predominate. In the case of public or contracted warehouses customers 'pay for what they use' and the payment could be based on a storage charge such as 'per pallet per week', a throughput charge such as 'per pallet in and out' of the warehouse, or an area charge such as 'per square foot used per week'.

Inside the warehouse

Design and flow

A basic warehouse structure with some of its flows within is depicted in Figure 5.3. The internal layout of the warehouse itself should take into account the need to increase output, improve product flow, reduce costs, improve service to customers and provide acceptable employee working conditions. The optimal warehouse layout and design for a company will vary by the type of product being stored, the company's financial resources, supply chain requirements and the needs of the customer. Thus, warehouse design criteria include:

- achieving a given level of customer service;
- operating at a given level of throughput(s);
- storing a given level of inventory;

- minimising capital investment and operational cost while achieving maximum throughput;
- reducing investment risk while maintaining process flexibility into the future;
- providing a safe and secure environment for people and products.

Since warehouses are expensive to build, same firms such as Unipart are optimising warehouse design and location by using simulation software as discussed in Logistics Example 5.2.

There are five principles in designing a warehouse:

1 *Unitise loads.* Products should be handled in modules or units as large as possible to reduce handling costs by carrying each module as a single unit as far as possible through the logistical system without dividing it for sorting, thereby achieving economies of scale in handling and improving handling efficiency, minimising the number of journeys, and integrating storage and handling systems.

2 *Maximise cubic space utilisation.* Figure 5.1 notes that 40 per cent of total warehouse costs are related to property, therefore it is desirable to utilise as much space in the warehouse

---

LOGISTICS EXAMPLE 5.2

Simulating a warehouse

The high cost of warehouse construction and operations has led to a wide range of logistics software packages being developed to design warehouses and select locations. However, one aspect that is not as prominent is computer modelling and simulation. Modelling allows a company to perform sensitivity analyses or 'what-if' scenarios on various warehouse criteria in order to determine feasible solutions to the problem at hand.

One logistics service company, Unipart, was able to win a tender to provide a warehouse solution for a manufacturer by doing just that. Unipart is one of Europe's leading providers of outsourced, aftermarket logistics and distribution services. It specialises in managing complete supply chains from manufacturers through to retail distributors and seeks to add value at every level of the chain.

Unipart modelled an optimum warehouse design by creating a three-dimensional, animated computer presentation. This use of technology captured important client issues and presented them in dramatic visual scenarios. The client was confident enough in Unipart's abilities to choose it as its warehouse designer. Once the tender was won, Unipart continued to use modelling to develop richer simulations that provided numerous 'what-if' scenarios for testing different options for racking, picking, packing and transportation.

Simulation of warehousing operations can also be used for risk management, as well as investigating proposed changes in the ongoing management and development of existing and new facilities.

Question

Where else in its logistics services systems could Unipart use computer simulation and modelling?

Source: Robin Vega 'Thinking outside the box,' *Logistics & Transport Focus*, 2004, Vol. 6, No. 2 (March), pp.16–21.

as possible. The factors influencing this principle are the tradeoffs between cubic utilisation or warehouse density and accessibility, speed of throughput, and the need to minimise double-handling; and the choice of preferred storage location systems: fixed, hybrid, zone and random.

As a first step the total size requirement for a warehouse needs to be known and that can be calculated based on throughput according to a queuing theory relationship known as Little's Law.[2] Little's Law is stated as $L = \lambda W$, where L is the size of the queue or in this case gross warehouse size, λ is the average rate of arrival into the system, and W is the average waiting time within the system. This relationship can be used to estimate the size of bulk storage required based on how many pallets arrive per day and the average length of time a product stays in the warehouse. For example, given the number of pallets entering a warehouse is on average 200 pallets per day, the warehouse works 300 days per year and the stock turn is 4 times per year, the average length of time a product stays in the warehouse W would be the number of days the warehouse works divided by the stock turn: $300 \div 4$ or 75 days. The size of the queue or gross warehouse size L would then be λW: 200×75 or 15,000 pallets. If the number of pallets arriving per day increased to 250, then L would be λW: 250×75 or 18,750 pallets.

3 *Optimise warehouse height.* Higher warehouse buildings achieve scale economies in warehouse construction using 'clad rack' or 'roof on rack' buildings; use land more intensively; and exploit mechanised and automated storage and handling systems. However, disadvantages include future marketability and flexibility of the facility and planning restrictions.

4 *Minimise internal movements.* Moving inventory less is efficient in terms of cost and time. Techniques to minimise internal movement include the application of popularity storage whereby items with high activity level, i.e. fast movers, are located closest to the storage and retrieval functions; the design of layouts and flow to minimise movement, avoid congestion and separate storage and picking; and the use of technology and information systems and the use of mechanisation.

5 *Provide a safe working environment.* A safe working environment can be achieved by the elimination of hazards, such as separating people from moving equipment, providing a formal risk assessment process and training in using transport, racking systems and machinery, reducing manual handling to avoid cumulative strain through the use of lifting equipment, and adopting ergonomic design principles for reach, height and load.

Warehouse racking[3]

Firms are faced with a wide array of options when choosing a storage racking system for a warehouse. The two operational criteria when choosing a configuration are selectivity and space utilisation. However, the selection of a rack configuration is also done in consideration of both initial cost and ongoing operational costs. The operational cost of a rack system is driven primarily by throughput through the system; however, rack and product damage, product expiration and product pilferage contribute to operational costs. Load characteristics drive the selection of the components, which make up the system. These characteristics include weight, physical dimensions and other factors such as pallet type and condition. Other factors include the type of lift equipment, the design and layout of the building, and inventory practices which dictate its movement.

While the purpose of racking is simple – to store loads vertically and reduce the floor space required – there is some science involved in the selection of the proper configuration and components. Configuration selection most often boils down to economics, either yielding a result with the lowest overall cost, or a result which is defined by the total available capital. Because of the range of available solutions, it is becoming more common to see storage facilities with multiple configurations, in order to accommodate the needs of several groupings of SKUs, each with its different movement pattern. Usage of the equipment is important, with safety being of prime importance. Proper selection of the configuration and components, along with good safety practices and a culture promoting safety, will allow a long service life for any rack system at minimal cost to the user. Figure 5.5 illustrates the major types of racking configurations, which are detailed as follows.

Block stacking refers to unit pellet loads stacked on top of each other and stored on the warehouse floor in lanes or blocks. The pallets are stacked to a specific height based on a number of criteria such as pallet condition, weight of the load, height clearance and the

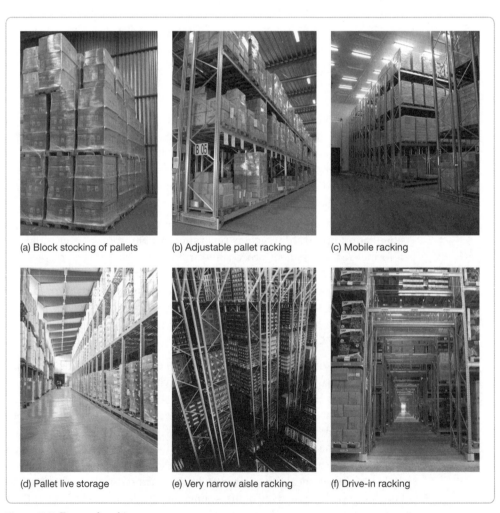

(a) Block stocking of pallets   (b) Adjustable pallet racking   (c) Mobile racking

(d) Pallet live storage   (e) Very narrow aisle racking   (f) Drive-in racking

Figure 5.5 Types of racking

capability of the warehouse forklifts. The pallets are retrieved from the block in a last-in, first-out (LIFO) manner. This does not allow for removing stock based on date basis or on a first-in, first-out (FIFO) manner.

Adjustable pallet racking (APR) is a highly versatile storage option and gives direct access to individual pallets without specialist handling equipment. It is particularly well suited to storing a wide variety of items of different sizes, weights and types, and high turnover operations where fast access to products is needed.

Very narrow aisle (VNA) racking enables high-density storage by making use of the warehouse floor area and roof height. VNA can reduce aisle width by up to 50 per cent compared with standard aisles and is particularly well suited to pallets of a uniform size and warehouses with a high roof and a flat floor. Pallets can be reached only by specialist equipment, which is costly but helps to protect the security of your stock. VNA aisle trucks are guided by rail or wire systems, so the risk of rack damage due to collision is reduced, as are maintenance costs.

Drive-in or *drive-through racking* is a very economical, bulk-storage system. Drive-in racking gives access to just one side of the aisle, so it operates on a first-in, last-out (FILO) basis. Drive-through racking gives access to both aisles using a FIFO stock-rotation system. This is limited, however, by the need to empty lanes at every level. Drive-in and drive-through racking are particularly well suited to low turnover products with a high number of pallets per SKU, cold storage, including chilled and frozen, and high-density storage of easily damaged or fragile items.

Mobile racking is comprised of standard racking mounted on motorised, mobile bases. This enables increased storage capacity by eliminating most aisles and block racking, without restricting access. Mobile racking is particularly well suited to cold storage – both frozen and chilled – space maximisation where order picking isn't a major concern, and batch-storing pallets or other heavy goods that all need to be accessed at the same time.

Pallet live racking allows the loading of stock in one aisle and removing it from the next. A FIFO system allows automatic stock rotation. Each lane is usually dedicated to storing one product variant or for marshalling loads in or out. Pallets are loaded on rollers sloping towards the pick face. When a pallet is removed, gravity and an automatic braking system bring the pallets stacked behind it to the front of the rack at a controlled pace so the picking face is always full. Pallet live racking is particularly well suited to goods with expiration dates that need failsafe stock rotation, a relatively small number of SKUs in a high quantity of pallets, and fast-moving ranges where items need to be retrieved at speed.

Table 5.1 provides a table comparing these racking configurations regarding service characteristics, space utilisation and relative cost.

Table 5.1 Comparison of racking

System	Block stacking	APR	VNA racking	Drive-in	Mobile racking	Pallet live storage
Space utilisation	40–45%	27%	35–37%	39–43%	53–55%	45–48%
Selectivity	4%	100%	100%	20%	100%	10%
Stock rotation	very poor lifo	random	random	poor lifo	random	very good automatic fifo
Order picking	very poor	first 2 levels	very good	poor	poor	fair
Maximum height	3–4 pallets	8 m (25 ft)	12 m (40 ft)	8 m (25 ft)	8 m (25 ft)	8 m (25 ft)
Relative cost	0	1	1.4	2.5	4.2	8.5

Source: NITL (2002b).

Warehouse materials handling equipment[4]

It has been said that the best handling solutions involve the least handling. Handling adds to the cost but not to the value of a product. The choice of the right equipment or system to optimise material flow is broadly a definition of materials handling and includes many different materials-handling equipment (MHE) systems. There are various MHE types and Figure 5.6 illustrates some of the most common varieties.

Hand pallet trucks, suitable for low volumes over small distances, are inexpensive and are suitable for palletised loads. They are often carried on vehicles to help offload palletised trailers. *Power pallet trucks* are available in pedestrian, stand-on or rider versions. They are designed for truck loading/unloading and pallet transfer duties to and from receiving/despatch and storage areas.

Forklift trucks (FLTs) are the most ubiquitous and versatile of mechanical handling equipment. FLTs can have any number of attachments added to their main frame to handle a variety of products. A basic forklift can be used for handling standard pallets and a clamp adaptation for lifting and stacking of bulk products such as fridges. They can also be used with slip mats and there is a teleport machine with extendable boom, typically used in the building industry. *Counterbalance forklifts* can be gas, battery or diesel powered, with a typical lift capacity of 2–3 tonnes up to a height of 4.5–5.5 metres. FLTs are of moderate cost, are versatile and can be container compatible. They are excellent for loading/unloading operations and transporting product over moderate distances. They are able to operate in aisle widths of 3.5–4.5 metres and are adaptable for indoor (electric) and outdoor use.

Narrow aisle reach trucks are used for warehousing duties in narrow aisles from 2.7–2.9 metres and are side-seated operated. The load is retracted for travelling, reached forward for stacking. Narrow aisle reach trucks are typically 1–2 ton capacity with lift heights of 9 metres; however, they are not suitable for outside use and not good for travelling with loads over long distances.

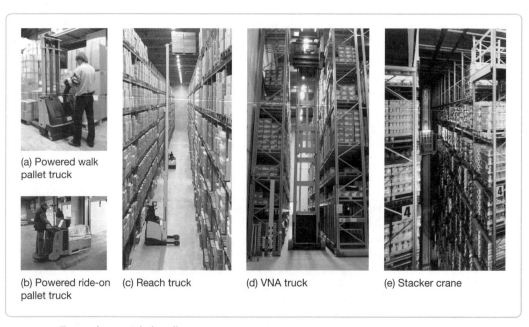

(a) Powered walk pallet truck

(b) Powered ride-on pallet truck

(c) Reach truck

(d) VNA truck

(e) Stacker crane

Figure 5.6 Types of materials-handling equipment

Table 5.2 Comparison of materials-handling equipment

Type/Name	Aisle width	Lift height	Lift capacity - tonnage	Power source	Main use
Hand pallet truck	The width of a pallet	N/A	1 ton	Manual	Low volume, over short distances
Power pallet truck	The width of a pallet	N/A	1–2 ton	Electric	Horizontal transport, good for loading and unloading
Forklift counterbalance truck	3.5–4.5 m aisles (11'6" to 14'9")	4.5–5.5 m (16 ft)	Typically 2–3 ton	Gas, electric, diesel	Loading and unloading, lifting, good for moderate loads over moderate distances
Reach truck	2.7–2.9 m (9–10 ft)	9 m (29 ft)	Typically 1–2 ton	Electric	To load and unload into a racking system
VNA truck	1.85 m 1.5–1.6 m with traversing plattens	12 m	Typically 1–2 ton	Electric	To load and unload into a racking system

Source: NITL (2002a).

VNA systems permit the narrowest working aisles for high-density storage. They enable maximum stack heights on racking while maintaining 100 per cent load access, high work throughput rates, and flexibility. With up to 2 tonnes capacity and lift heights of 12 metres, they typically work in aisle widths of 1.85 metres.

The range and options available in handling equipment are nearly endless. Other specific equipment types include side loaders, stacker cranes, automatic guided vehicles (AGVs) and conveyor systems. Table 5.2 compares various racking configurations regarding their service characteristics and space considerations.

Technology and warehouse management systems

The main objective of any warehouse manager must be ensuring a totally reliable operation but at the most effective operating costs. The concept of a whole life cycle cost (LCC) is recognised as the correct method for calculating the real cost of any equipment. LCC takes into account all capital and operating costs over the anticipated working life of the system, but is annualised to provide a constant basis.

The total LCC of any piece of warehouse equipment consists of three main elements: the acquisition of the equipment, the power required and maintenance costs, and the labour to operate the equipment. The capital equipment cost can often represent only around 10–25 per cent of total costs. The energy and maintenance costs of the equipment can typically represent 5–15 per cent of total LCCs. The final cost – the most significant element in the LCC – is by far the cost of the operator. In most situations, this represents up to 70 per cent of the total. Further, moving goods in and out and order picking represent 70 per cent of costs by warehouse function, as shown in Figure 5.1. Therefore, maximising human efficiency or making greater use of automation is essential in today's warehouse environments.

The adoption of any warehouse automation is dependent on volume throughput and number of SKUs and pallets in order to be economically efficient. Figure 5.7 shows a simple assessment chart for technology adoption.[5] For example, with small volumes of throughput and small numbers of pallets, a simple manual system of block stack pallets, cartons placed in shelves and paper list picking could be the most beneficial. For a larger number of pallets but only marginally higher throughput volumes, a mechanically assisted system of pallets in racking and some straight-line conveyors to assist carton movements could be adopted. If throughput volumes increase further, a simple automation system consisting of full pallet automated storage and automated retrieval (AS/AR) cranes and simple conveyors could be considered. Finally, if the number of pallets increases then a complex automation system of pick to light systems, complex conveyoring, high-speed sortation, AGVs could be used.

Types of automation devices that can be used in various warehouse activities include:

● *input devices:* forklift truck, live bed, conveyors, AGVs, stacker/de-stacker;

● *put-away/retrieval machines:* stacker cranes, driver-less forklift trucks, AGVs;

● *storage systems:* high bay racking, small parts storage racking/shelving;

● *picking and sortation:* horizontal and vertical carousels, pick by light displays, robotic picking, accumulation and sortation conveyors;

● *output devices:* conveyors, AGVs, forklift truck.

Chapters 8 and 10 will further consider devices and technology such as pick by light, pick to voice and radio frequency identification (RFID).

A warehouse management information system (WMS) provides, stores and reports the information necessary to efficiently manage the flow of products from time receipt until time of shipping.[6] WMS benefits include increased productivity, reduction of inventories, better space utilisation, reduced errors, support of customer EDI requirements, and value-added logistics compliance programmes.

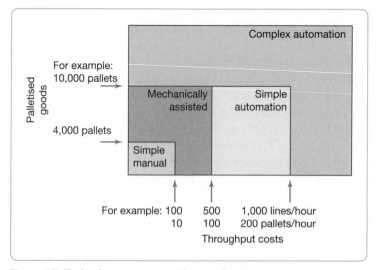

Figure 5.7 Technology assessment for warehousing
Source: adapted from Naish and Baker (2004).

A basic WMS will have a focus on stock and location control, pick sequencing and replenishment, and an information focus on throughput. An advanced WMS will have the features of a basic system but will also plan resources and activities to synchronise the flow; information widens from throughput to stock and capacity analysis. A complex WMS will cover multiple warehouse sites, optimisation of storage, replenishment and order picking. It will use information to plan, execute, control and feed back into warehouse operating parameters and possibly even provide some level of simulation for sensitivity analysis.

However, warehouse technology is not a panacea if development and implementation are incorrect. Mothercare, the UK retailer for mothers and babies, ran into extensive problems in 2001–2003 when implementing an automated warehouse operated by Tibbett & Britten, now part of DHL.[7] It opened the facility in August 2001 when its shares were trading around £3.00 for much of that summer. However, the warehouse was badly run and a lot of stock was put in the wrong locations. Annual distribution costs rose by 50 per cent to £23.2 million to cover the costs of renting and operating from temporary warehouses. In November 2001 the company's share price was around £2.05 when it announced a £4.1 million 'exceptional write-off' on its annual accounts for that facility. Troubles continued and a new CEO was appointed in September 2002; its share price fell to £0.87 in January 2003. Mothercare eventually sorted out its warehouse problems, but by then it had also renegotiated its warehouse contract with Tibbett & Britten from five to two years.

Warehouse location

The location and layout of the warehouse and the stock, within the warehouse, are integral to the warehouse management process. Warehouses should be located where they can best serve their customers. Locating a warehouse will depend on company strategy, but will have to take into account the locations of customers, suppliers and producers, transportation economies, labour availability, site availability, other warehouses in the supply chain, building costs, taxation systems, and where distribution can be effectively carried out from.

Aside from purchasing its own warehouse facility, a business has the option of choosing third-party warehousing, which provides warehousing, inventory management and possibly distribution services. This form of warehousing allows the company to focus on its core competence and avail itself of the expertise of warehouse specialists. However, most decisions will be focused on the cost tradeoffs affecting the various logistical functions, particularly in a global economy where labour rates, a large portion of warehousing costs, may be cheaper in countries far away from markets. Figure 5.8 illustrates the classic logistics cost-tradeoffs curves showing their impact on each other.[8] As the number of warehouses increases, the cost of inventory also increases but the cost of transport decreases, and vice versa. The question then becomes: how can firms determine their optimum strategy?

There are three basic scenarios for warehouse location: locate close to market and customers; locate close to production facilities; and locate close to major modal interchanges such as ports. However, various analytical models exist for locating warehouses and determining the optimal number of warehouses, such as mathematical programming using the centre of gravity, heuristic methods using experience and 'rules of thumbs' in the analysis, and simulation models. From a cost perspective, the square root law of inventory[9] provides a relationship that indicates that a percentage reduction in inventory from reducing the

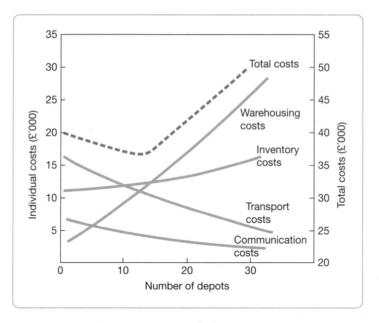

Figure 5.8 Distribution costs and warehousing
Source: Rand (1976, p.242).

number of warehouses will be equal to (1 − √number of warehouses after decentralisation / √number of warehouses before decentralisation) × 100 per cent. For example, if the number of warehouses before is 36 and the number after is 25, there will be a 17 per cent reduction in inventory.

Notwithstanding all the models available for firms, there has been a trend in the UK towards centralisation over the past 20 years due to low transportation costs, retailers wanting to control distribution as tightly as possible, and national boundary issues.[10] Many of these benefits, as well as an efficient WMS, were behind the SPAR Group's choice to establish one national warehouse in Austria, as discussed in Logistics Example 5.3.

LOGISTICS EXAMPLE 5.3

One warehouse, many benefits

The grocery retailer SPAR Group has 1,500 stores of various sizes and types throughout Austria, presenting a variety of large, medium and small orders. At the end of the 1990s SPAR Austria was operating six regional warehouses that were inefficient and outdated. In addition, out-of-stocks at the retail stores were high and unacceptable.

Rather than build new distribution centres or refurbish existing ones for different categories of products, SPAR Austria chose to build a new 13,020 square metre facility in Wels, near good road and rail links. To ensure error-free picking and store sequencing and deal with issues between slow- and fast-moving SKUs, SPAR chose the Witron company's Dynamic Picking System (DPS) as its warehouse management system. DPS is based on the Pareto principle, or 80–20 rule, and is applicable to high picking levels and large numbers

---

of SKUs. The SPAR system has 93,000 bin locations and 12,500 pallet locations in 11 aisles on 18 levels that are served by 5 large cranes. Fast-moving SKUs are placed in bins while slower-moving SKUs are placed in high-bay pallet locations.

The selection of the DPS system has been the key to SPAR's successful implementation of its facility and has brought many benefits for SPAR's retail operations. The WMS is very efficient and accurate – SPAR claims an error rate of only one case in every 27,000. SPAR ships 24,000 bins in 35 trucks each day that are tracked by barcodes and the WMS that ensures proper store sequencing. SPAR is also able to meet last-minute orders. Orders received by 7pm are shipped by noon the following day.

Out-of-stock situations at the company's stores have been reduced by 25 per cent. Thus, by using advanced automated warehouse systems SPAR Austria has been able to improve its warehouse operations and store order fulfilment in one location.

Question

How could SPAR use this type of system for internet or online grocery sales and delivery?

Source: 'Automating for efficiency,' *Logistics Manager*, 2004, Vol. 11, No. 5 (June), pp.16–18.

However, with increasing transportation costs due to increases in fuel costs and investment to reduce engine emissions, a movement back towards decentralisation might occur during the coming decades. Further, other issues affecting warehouse locations include the availability of suitable sites and a move towards port-centric logistics, as discussed in Chapter 4; the use of pristine or greenfield sites versus reclaimed industrial or brownfield sites; planning permission issues related to plot size and shapes and height; traffic congestion on various routes; employment density and labour availability and skills; and the creation of distribution parks and sector 'clusters', for example food or electronics.

Summary

Warehousing is an integral part of every supply chain and is an important link between the producer and the customer. Over the years, warehousing has developed from a relatively minor facet of a firm's logistic system to one of the most important functions within the supply chain. Warehouses store and manage inventory in the supply chain and must be able to react to customer demands and provide, along with inventory management, the 'Stop' activity in logistics, notwithstanding the flow-through nature of their operations. Advances in technology have allowed warehouses to become more efficient, albeit more complex.

This chapter has discussed the nature of warehousing and its functions of receiving, sorting, adding value, assembling and despatching, considering issues inside the warehouse in terms of design, structure and operations, the use of technology, and finally warehouse location. The next chapter moves to the next function in the 'Stop' activity, inventory management.

DISCUSSION QUESTIONS

1 What is the role and purpose of warehousing in modern supply chains?

2 Describe the main types of warehouses. Which types best suit the three forms of private, contracted and public warehouses?

3 How can warehouse design and flow, racking or storage systems and materials handling systems affect warehouse productivity, efficiency and effectiveness?

4 What are the advantages and disadvantages of warehouse management systems?

5 Discuss the differences between the types of warehouse locations.

Suggested reading

Abrahamsson, Mats 'Time-based distribution,' *International Journal of Logistics Management*, 1993, Vol. 4, No. 2, pp.75–83.

Baker, Peter *The Principles of Warehouse Design*, 3rd ed. Corby: The Chartered Institute of Logistics and Transport, 2010.

Baker, Peter and Marco Canessa 'Warehouse design: A structured approach,' *European Journal of Operational Research*, 2009, Vol. 193, No. 2, pp.425–436.

European Logistics Association and Kurt Salmon Associates *Success Factor PEOPLE in Distribution Quality in Logistics*, Brussels: European Logistics Association, 2004.

Faber, Bynke, René B.M. de Koster and Steef L. Van de Velde 'Linking warehouse complexity to warehouse planning and control structure: An exploratory study of the use of warehouse management information systems,' *International Journal of Physical Distribution & Logistics Management*, 2002, Vol. 32, No. 5, pp.381–395.

Frazelle, Edward H. *World-Class Warehousing and Materials Handling*, New York: McGraw-Hill, 2002.

Little, John D.C. 'A proof of the queuing formula: $L = \lambda W$,' *Operations Research*, 1961, Vol. 9, No. 3, pp.383–387.

Maister, D.H. 'Centralisation of inventories and the "square root law",' *International Journal of Physical Distribution & Logistics Management*, 1976, Vol. 6, No. 3, pp.124–134.

McKinnon, Alan 'The advantages and disadvantages of centralised distribution,' in John Fernie (ed.) *Retail Distribution Management: A Strategic Guide*, London: Kogan Page, 1990, pp.75–89.

Naish, Stuart and Peter Baker 'Materials handling: Fulfilling the promises,' *Logistics and Transport Focus*, 2004, Vol. 6, No. 1, pp.18–26.

Quinn, James Brian and Frederick G. Hilmer 'Strategic outsourcing,' *Sloan Management Review*, 1994, Vol. 35, No. 4, pp.43–55.

Rand, Graham K. 'Methodological choices in depot location studies,' *Operational Research Quarterly*, 1976, Vol. 27, No. 1, ii, pp.241–249.

Rushton, Alan, Phil Croucher and Peter Baker *The Handbook of Logistics and Distribution Management*, 3rd ed. London: Kogan Page, 2006.

Notes

1 A.T. Kearney and European Logistics Association (2009) 'Supply chain excellence amidst the global economic crisis,' *6th European A.T. Kearney/ELA Logistics Study 2008/2009*, Brussels: European Logistics Association.

2 John D.C. Little (1961) 'A proof of the queuing formula: L = λW,' *Operations Research*, Vol. 9, No. 3, pp.383–387.

3 Adapted from NITL (2002b) *Supply Chain Management Technical Fact Sheet: Racking*, Vol. 2, Issue 5; and Warehouse Systems Limited (WSL) (2011) www.warehouse-systems.co.uk/ (accessed 31 July 2011).

4 Adapted from National Institute for Transport and Logistics Ireland (NITL) (2002a) *Supply Chain Management Technical Fact Sheet: Materials Handling Equipment*, Vol. 2, Issue 2.

5 Stuart Naish and Peter Baker (2004) 'Materials handling: Fulfilling the promises,' *Logistics and Transport Focus*, Vol. 6, No. 1, pp.18–26.

6 Bynke Faber, René B.M. de Koster and Steef L. Van de Velde (2002) 'Linking warehouse complexity to warehouse planning and control structure: An exploratory study of the use of warehouse management information systems,' *International Journal of Physical Distribution & Logistics Management*, Vol. 32, No. 5, pp.381–395.

7 Laurence Fletcher (2001) 'Mothercare takes £4.1 million warehouse hit,' http://citywire.co.uk/new-model-adviser/mothercare-takes-4-1m-warehouse-hit/a231200 (accessed 31 July 2011).

8 Graham K. Rand (1976) 'Methodological choices in depot location studies,' *Operational Research Quarterly*, Vol. 27, No. 1, ii, pp.241–249.

9 D.H. Maister (1976) 'Centralisation of inventories and the "square root law",' *International Journal of Physical Distribution & Logistics Management*, Vol. 6, No. 3, pp.124–134.

10 Alan McKinnon (1990) 'The advantages and disadvantages of centralised distribution,' in John Fernie (ed.) *Retail Distribution Management: A Strategic Guide*, London: Kogan Page, pp.75–89; and Mats Abrahamsson (1993) 'Time-based distribution,' *International Journal of Logistics Management*, Vol. 4, No. 2, pp.75–83.

Inventory management

Introduction

For most people the everyday 'faces of logistics' relate to either transport or 'Go' and warehousing or 'Stop' activities. However, according to the definition presented in Chapter 1, the purpose of logistics is to make materials, goods or products available for customers. These items moving through the supply chain represent stocks to be sold onwards until they reach the final consumer and thus their composition and levels must also be managed in order to properly meet customer needs while maintaining an effective and efficient supply chain.

This process is referred to as inventory management and is an important factor in most businesses. The average investment in all business inventories in the US, including the agriculture, mining, construction, services, manufacturing, wholesale and retail sectors, was $2.06 trillion in 2010. The cost to carry or hold that level of inventory was $396 billion or 19.1 per cent of the total value. The inventory-to-sales ratio during that year was about 1.25, which means that for every $1 of sales there was $1.25 of inventory waiting to be sold.[1]

This chapter first considers the nature and types of stocks and the purpose of stocks and inventory. Then, the financial impact of inventory is discussed, which leads to the 'inventory conundrum' and the management of inventory. Next, basic inventory management and replenishment models are presented along with a further discussion of inventory costs as they relate to these models.

The nature of inventory

From a definitional perspective and as noted above, stocks are the materials, products and goods that flow through the supply chain until they are needed to either transform or sell onwards to customers and ultimately the final consumer. An inventory is a list of these items kept in stock by the firm.[2] Inventory management is thus a broad term that includes all decisions related to stocks. However, in common use inventory is often used to mean the same thing as stock.

The introduction also noted the high costs of inventory, which will be discussed later in this chapter. However, these costs, together with initiatives such as just-in-time which promote inventories of one item, suggest that high levels of inventories may be considered an unacceptable business practice. So, then, what value and benefits do inventories provide for the firm and its customers? Essentially, inventories provide a buffer between customer *demand* and *supply*. For example, the manufacture and distribution of a DVD player cannot occur immediately. However, if a consumer decides to purchase one at a weekend then the product must be available for the customer to buy and take home at that time. There has been considerable research into consumer behaviour when faced with a stock-out, i.e. the product they seek is not available on the shelf, and aspects of retail logistics to prevent that happening. These aspects will be discussed in Chapter 7.

Generally, though, the major benefits that inventories provide include:

- *time*: having inventories on-hand reduces customer waiting time and thus provides the customer with time and place utility of a product;
- *discontinuity*: having inventories along the supply chain allows interrelated functions to be disconnected and operated more efficiently;
- *uncertainty*: having inventories offers protection against unanticipated and unplanned events such as inclement weather that forces customers to buy extra products;
- *economy*: having inventories permits customers to make bulk purchases at discounted prices – however, customers should beware false economies due to increased inventory carrying costs.

Inventories can be classified according to their *location* in the production process, for example raw materials, supplies and fuel, work in progress or in-process inventory, and finished goods; by the *frequency of replenishment* required for the inventory, for example whether the product or item is intended for single use or sale, such as an automobile, or whether continuous replenishment is required for repeat purchases, such as groceries or fast-moving

LOGISTICS EXAMPLE 6.1

Continuous replenishment programmes to replenish and manage grocery inventory

Continuous replenishment programmes such as efficient consumer response (ECR) began in the early 1990s. ECR was developed by consultants Kurt Salmon Associates for

Logistics example 6.1 (*cont.*)

a working group of grocery industry representatives concerned about losses in market share and declining productivity. Leading European retailers and manufacturers founded ECR-Europe in the mid-1990s to consider ECR for the European business situation. ECR is defined as a grocery industry strategy in which distributors and suppliers are working closely together, i.e. in partnership, to bring better value to the grocery consumer through a seamless delivery of products at a total low cost. This seamless delivery is consumer driven through a paperless information flow initiated by a retailer's electronic point-of-sale (EPOS) that also sets and manages production levels for suppliers. Benefits of ECR include lower total system inventories and costs, enhanced consumer value in terms of choice and quality of products, and more successful development of new consumer-driven products.

However, implementation of ECR, while easy in theory, has proved difficult in practice. An early ECR pilot programme at the UK grocery firm Somerfield saw inventory levels reduced by up to 25 per cent but service levels improved by only about 2.5 per cent. Despite integration difficulties some 'soft' benefits occurred, such as improved management of seasonal events. Stock-outs and availability continue to be a problem in some settings, and product category management that is a feature of some ECR applications has been criticised as being too time and data intensive. ECR is still perceived as a technique suitable only for large manufacturers and retailers.

Collaborative planning, forecasting and replenishment (CPFR) follows from ECR and was developed by the Voluntary Inter-industry Commerce Standards (VICS) group in the United States to minimise out-of-stocks by synchronising forecasting and planning between retailers and manufacturers. This enhancement is therefore a step beyond ECR or other continuous replenishment programmes that rely on inventory restocking triggered by actual needs rather than on long-range forecasts and layers of safety stock just in case.

CPFR, as presently configured between only manufacturers and retailers, is currently unsuitable for every firm as firms require sufficient revenue and product volumes to be economically feasible and real-time information sharing on a common platform such as the internet. This will require collaboration and technological sophistication throughout the entire supply chain. The reported number of active CPFR partnerships in the US is only 20, but a survey published in 2000 indicates that 80 per cent of grocery executives intend to increase collaboration in the future. The uptake in Europe has been slow, with only five pilots reported. This lack of progress in Europe may be a result of the Y2K phenomenon and the 'dot.com' retreat slowing progress, differences in retailers' economic status, cultural issues, existing ECR implementation and supply chain structures, or sustained business consolidations and increased market competition with foreign entrants.

Question

What benefits will initiatives such as ECR and CPFR bring to consumers?

Sources: adapted from Herbert Kotzab 'Improving supply chain performance by efficient consumer response? A critical comparison of existing ECR approaches,' *Journal of Business & Industrial Marketing*, 1999, Vol. 14, No. 5/6, pp.364–377; R. Marzian and E. Garriga, *A Guide to CPFR Implementation*, Brussels: ECR Europe, 2001; Theodore P. Stank, Patricia J. Daugherty and Chad W. Autry 'Collaborative planning: Supporting automatic replenishment programs,' *Supply Chain Management: An International Journal*, 1999, Vol. 4, No. 2, pp.75–85; and R. Younger, *Logistics Trends in European Consumer Goods: Challenges for Suppliers, Retailers and Logistics Companies*, London: Financial Times Management Report, 1997.

consumer goods; and by the inventory or stock's *function*. An example of how the grocery sector has dealt with replenishment issues is discussed in Logistics Example 6.1.

Usual stock functions include:

- *cycle stock*: this is stock required to satisfy the average level of demand during the period between the placing of an order and the arrival of the goods (that is to say, the order lead time or order cycle time);
- *safety stock*: this is stock required to meet variations in demand in excess of the average during the order lead time;
- *anticipatory stock*: this is stock required to accommodate seasonal fluctuations, stabilise levels of production and be prepared for known events;
- *pipeline stock*: this is stock that is required internally as work-in-progress for production or externally as in-transit inventory, that is inventory that is being transported;
- *decoupling stock*: this is stock required to 'de-synchronise' activities and allow them to operate or function at the most efficient rates;
- *psychic stock*: this is stock used for marketing and presentation that may stimulate demand and is therefore revenue generating, for example window and in-store displays in retail stores;
- *value-adding stock*: this is stock held in storage to enhance the product's value, for example whisky being matured, or antiques.

The above stock functions may occur at different points in the supply chain and Figure 6.1 details the various flows of stock or inventory from point of origin to point of consumption. The dotted lines in the figure show various backwards or reverse flows for reworking, recycling, redistribution or waste-disposal purposes. The process for dealing with returned or waste stock is referred to as 'reverse logistics' and is further discussed in Chapter 12.

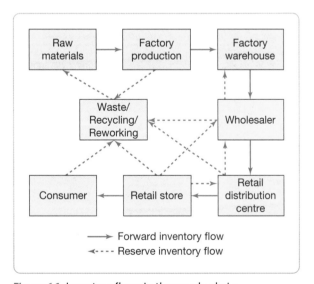

Figure 6.1 Inventory flows in the supply chain

The inventory cycle and replenishment

As inventory is used up, for example either in a factory's production process or by being sold to a retail store's consumers, it will need to be replenished for future production or sales. The classic 'sawtooth' inventory cycle and replenishment diagram is shown in Figure 6.2. The X-axis in the figure is time while the Y-axis is the level of inventory on-hand. The left-to-right sloping line is the demand rate for inventory; the linearity of this line over a single period indicates that the rate is constant. When the inventory runs out at the end of the period and thus cannot meet demand, replenishment occurs and is indicated by the vertical straight line, which means that replenishment is instantaneous at that moment in time. The horizontal dotted line half-way between full replenishment and no inventory is the average level of inventory for the period or for an entire year if demand is constant and replenishment is instantaneous.

However, this diagram may not reflect actual conditions in practice. For example, demand is not usually constant and replenishment may not occur instantaneously. Thus, a firm may keep additional inventory on-hand as safety or buffer stock for such eventualities and this adds to the inventory level on-hand as shown.

Inventory management therefore becomes key for firms, as too little inventory may mean stock-outs where demand is not met and customers become dissatisfied. However, too much inventory may be a significant cost to the firm to buy and keep stocks. A firm therefore has an 'inventory conundrum', as shown in Figure 6.3, where it must manage inventory to achieve a balance between costs of inventory and inventory availability and customer service. If inventory levels are high, so are service levels represented by availability and customer service. However, investment in inventory and inventory carrying costs are also high. Similarly, if inventory levels are low then costs are probably lower, but service levels might also be lower than a firm and its customers would want. It is thus important for firms to first understand the cost and service tradeoffs associated with this conundrum before attempting management.

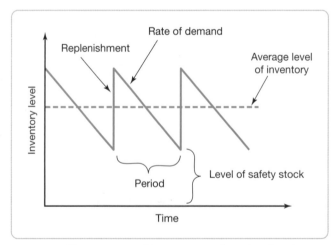

Figure 6.2 Classic 'sawtooth' inventory cycle and replenishment diagram

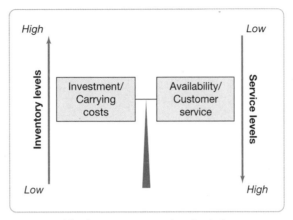

Figure 6.3 The 'inventory conundrum': a balance between cost and service

The cost of inventory

What is the financial impact of inventory on a firm? Inventory appears in two places on a firm's financial statements: it is recorded as a current asset in a firm's balance sheet but it also implicitly appears in the firm's income statement. Figure 6.2 showed the demand and replenishment of inventory over the course of a period of time. This continual flow of inventory through the firm over time represents the cost of inventory purchased or the cost of goods sold for the financial year. Also, the total average level of inventory represents the level of inventory recorded on the firm's balance sheet at the beginning and the end of the financial year.

The financial effect of inventory on a firm's profitability shows up in the return on investment financial ratio. ROI is calculated by dividing a firm's annual profit after tax by the firm's total investment, which are the firm's total assets. Since inventory is a current asset, the smaller the levels of average inventory, the smaller the denominator in this ratio and thus ROI is larger. Further, if firms can reduce their cost of goods sold, which will also have an effect on average inventory levels, the larger the numerator in this ratio and thus ROI is once again larger. So, from a purely financial statement and ratio perspective, it makes sense to keep inventory levels low.

One method of doing so while not affecting availability and customer service is to turn over the inventory at a faster rate, that is increase the number of inventory cycles in a year. The inventory turnover ratio is calculated by dividing the cost of goods sold by average inventory. For example, a turnover ratio of six means that the firm turns over its level of average inventory every two months, while a ratio of two means that average inventory is turned over twice a year. So, what is an appropriate turnover ratio? Arithmetically, there is a point where increasing the turnover ratio provides diminishing returns regarding levels of inventory. For example, if cost of goods sold in a year is £100,000, turnover ratios can be plotted for different levels of average inventory. Table 6.1 numerically shows a few of these ratios from average inventory levels of £5,000 to £100,000. The lower the value of average inventory, the higher the turnover ratio. However, the higher this ratio, the more likely that availability may become a problem and the risk of stock-outs increases.

Table 6.1 Inventory turnover ratios
for cost of goods sold of £100,000

Average level of inventory (£)	Turnover ratio (£100,000 ÷ average level of inventory)
100,000	1
80,000	1.25
60,000	1.67
50,000	2
40,000	2.5
30,000	3.33
20,000	5
10,000	10
5,000	20

Figure 6.4 graphically shows these ratios and the shape of a curve connecting them has an exponentially decreasing slope. That is, at some point the slope starts to flatten or become asymptotic to the X-axis as the number of inventory turns, or the turnover ratio, increases with corresponding less average levels of inventory. Thus, at that point it may not make much sense to turn over inventory levels faster and run the risk of increasing non-availability and detrimentally affecting customer service.

The type of product will also be a factor in determining an appropriate level of turnover. For example, fast-moving consumer goods in a grocery retailer may have a turnover ratio of 24 or perhaps higher as such products typically do not stay on the store shelf for more than two weeks. Perishable food may have a ratio of 52 or higher, i.e. this product turns over completely once a week. Lastly, fashion clothing may have a ratio of 4, or a turnover every three months, reflecting the various clothing seasons.

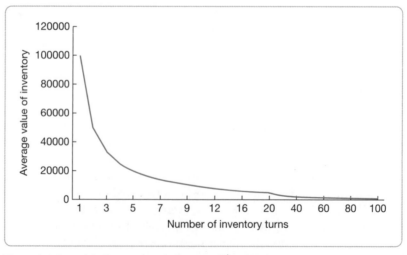

Figure 6.4 Inventory turnover ratio versus value of inventory

The foregoing discussion considers the cost to purchase or invest in inventory. However, the concept of an inventory carrying or holding cost reflects the cost, expressed in percentage terms, to keep or hold on to inventory until it is sold or otherwise dealt with. This concept is also implicit in a firm's income statement as an expense item not included in cost of goods sold. However, inventory carrying costs are made up of several components and thus this cost is usually not shown separately and may therefore be difficult to calculate. The usual components in the inventory carrying cost calculation are:[3]

- *opportunity cost* of capital or the cost of money to the firm for an alternative investment, i.e. what type of return the firm could make by investing money somewhere other than in inventory;
- *storage and material handling* of inventory, particularly if extra amounts are purchased that incur additional handling and storage requirements;
- *loss due to obsolescence, damage and/or pilferage* of existing inventory in the normal course of business activity;
- *insurance and taxes* related to existing inventory, the former to partly cover issues above while the latter may relate to some political jurisdictions taxing inventory.

However, other components may include fixed costs related to new handling equipment such as forklift trucks, racks to deal with additional inventory, additional personnel costs, new computer software required to manage and track increased inventory levels, and increasingly costs related to green purchasing and recycling. The types of components will vary with individual firms and business sectors, and thus make it difficult to develop standard rates and benchmark against other firms. However, the aggregate carrying cost percentage in the US of 19.1 per cent discussed in this chapter's introduction may provide a useful starting point for firms.

Inventory management

There are really three fundamental questions related to inventory management:

- How much inventory should we buy?
- When do we buy it?
- Where do we store it?

The last question relates to the centralisation and decentralisation of inventory and distribution centres or warehouses and was covered in Chapter 5. However, firms considering the first two questions should always keep location of stocks in mind.

There are three types of inventory management methods: *informal methods, statistical methods* and *requirements planning methods*. The first two methods are appropriate for *independent* demand situations, while the last method is appropriate for *dependent* demand situations. Independent demand relates to demand for an item that is independent of demand for items such as health and beauty products purchased at a pharmacy or grocery retailer; the demand for men's shaving gel is independent of the demand for shampoo, deodorant and soap, as is the demand for each of these other three items. Dependent demand relates to those items where demand is linked, such as raw materials, parts and sub-assemblies that are used to manufacture a unique product such as an automobile or computer.

Dependent demand is found further upstream in a supply chain as suppliers rely on actual orders from customers to determine what inventory they need to have on-hand to fulfil an order. Figure 6.5 shows that situation for a tier 1 supplier to a retailer. The retailer's demand profile is the classic sawtooth curve and at a certain and fixed order point before inventory reaches the safety stock level the retailer places an order with the supplier. The supplier will probably serve other retail customers and thus will have much more inventory on-hand. In this example the supplier's order point level is not reached until the third order from the retailer, at which point the supplier orders more inventory.

Information flow and product flow between customers and suppliers all along the supply chain are critical so that upstream suppliers avoid misinterpreting the nature of variable customer orders and build up too much inventory in anticipation of demand that will not materialise. This phenomenon was first considered by Jay Forrester in 1958 and is commonly known as the Forrester or 'bullwhip' effect.[4] Figure 6.6 shows the pattern of orders versus sales when there is lack of proper information flow – the shape of the orders curve has large, sinusoidal amplitude that is the basis for the 'bull-whip' name.

Informal methods rely on 'rules of thumb' or 'gut feel' to determine how much inventory to have on-hand, while statistical methods make use of demand forecasting and costs parameters to determine when to obtain cost-optimal amounts of stock. Requirements planning methods take into account other aspects of a firm's activities in helping to determine inventory requirements for dependent demand. Methods in this context such as material requirements planning (MRP), just-in-time (JIT) and enterprise resource planning (ERP) will be discussed in Chapter 7.

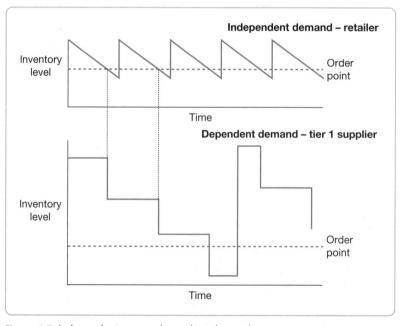

Figure 6.5 Independent versus dependent demand

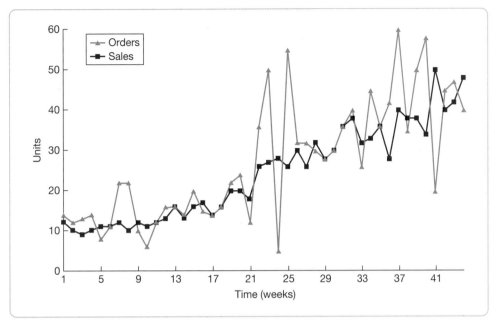

Figure 6.6 Forrester or 'bullwhip' effect
Source: (Lee *et al.* 1997, p.547).

Informal inventory management methods

There are two popular 'rules of thumb' methods for inventory as well as other types of business management, for example customers. One is the 'Pareto Principle' or '80–20' rule. The Italian economist Vilfredo Pareto created a mathematical formula in the early twentieth century to describe the unequal distribution of wealth in Italy, observing that 20 per cent of the people owned 80 per cent of the wealth. In the late 1940s, the quality guru Joseph M. Juran applied this observation concerning economics to a broader body of work and called it Pareto's principle, or the 80–20 rule.

The 80–20 rule posits that in any context a few (20 per cent) are vital and many (80 per cent) are trivial. Juran's work on quality identified 20 per cent of the defects causing 80 per cent of the problems. In inventory terms this means that 80 per cent of a firm's sales are from 20 per cent of its inventory or stock keeping units. For example, modern grocery retailers such as Tesco in the UK, Safeway in the US and Carrefour in France each list 25,000 or more SKUs. However, 80 per cent of their sales will come from 5,000 basic SKUs representing products demanded most by consumers during their weekly shop. Firms wanting to use this method should first determine which 20 per cent of products are demanded most and then focus inventory management on them.

The other popular informal method is ABC analysis, which is an extension of the Pareto principle analysis applied to all SKUs. SKUs are then classed into categories depending on how much they contribute to sales. Figure 6.7 illustrates this use of this method, which relates a percentage category of items to annual sales and is a measure of the item's importance. In this example, 20 per cent of items or SKUs represent 65 per cent of a firm's annual sales and are termed 'A' items, 30 per cent of items termed 'B' items represent

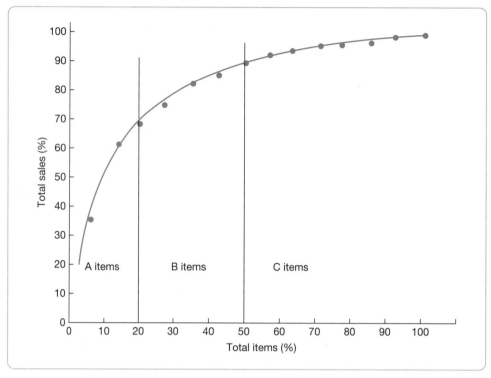

Figure 6.7 ABC analysis of inventory

20 per cent of sales, and the remaining 50 per cent of items, or 'C' items, represent the remaining 15 per cent of sales. Firms can then design inventory management strategies given these categorical importance rankings. For example, 'A' items might be subject to frequent monitoring, sophisticated forecasting and high safety stock levels, and be offered at the best service levels possible to customers. Meanwhile, management of 'C' items might use a simple and automatic system, be minimally monitored and have a zero safety stock policy.

Statistical methods

Usual statistical methods consider three situations:

- continuous review or order quantity at a re-order point or level;
- periodic review at a fixed point in time with a maximum replenishment level;
- hybrid methods of the above two methods.

The continuous review method develops a fixed-order quantity that minimises costs and places an order for this quantity at a certain re-order point in the demand cycle. Thus, critical decision parameters for this method include the quantity to be ordered and the re-order point or level that acts as a signal for replenishment. The basic building block for this method is the economic order quantity (EOQ) model,[5] which was first discussed in 1913 by Ford W. Harris, a production engineer.[6]

The equation for the basic model determines the minimum point between *order costs*, which include operations or production set-up if upstream in the supply chain, the ordering task, packaging, transportation, and other order-related costs, and *inventory carrying* or *holding costs*. This equation is as follows:

$$EOQ = \sqrt{\frac{2 \times OC \times D}{HC \times C}}$$

where:

OC = order cost per order (€)
D = annual demand (units)
HC = annual holding or carrying cost (per cent)
C = purchase cost per unit (€)

To illustrate the use of this equation by an example, assume annual D is 120,000 units, C is €65, OC is €53 per order and HC is 20 per cent. Substituting these values into the equation yields an EOQ value of 989.17; in other words, the most economic quantity to order given these conditions and thus minimise the total cost is 989.17 units. The signal to order the EOQ amount will depend on a supplier's lead time to deliver upon receipt of the firm's order. The total numbers of orders in a year would then be D of 120,000 divided by the EOQ of 989.17; this would result in 121.3 orders per year or 2.3 orders per week. Graphically, Figure 6.8 shows the usual EOQ costs curve based on the two key parameters: order costs and carrying or holding cost. The total cost curve is the sum of the cost curves for these two parameters and the minimum point on the total cost curve represents the EOQ amount.

For the example above, the total EOQ cost would be OC multiplied by EOQ (€53 × 121.3) added to the carrying cost multiplied by one-half EOQ (20 % × 989.17/2), which is the average inventory on-hand at any one time as discussed above, for a total of €6,528. Further, the total value of purchases for the year would be D multiplied by C (120,000 × €65) or €7.8 million. Thus, the total EOQ cost would be only 0.083 per cent of the total purchase cost.

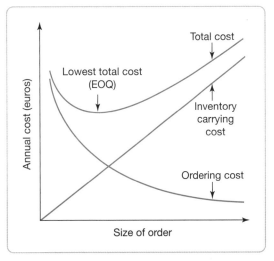

Figure 6.8 EOQ cost curve

In reality, an EOQ value of 989.17 is unrealistic as suppliers would probably want to provide even lots of, say, 1,000 units per order and perhaps deliver only 120 times a year. Substituting 1,000 units and 120 orders a year into the above calculations yields a total EOQ cost of €6,460. Since OC has a more proportionate impact on total EOQ than HC, the reduction of 1.3 orders per year actually results in a reduced total cost, notwithstanding there are 11 more units being provided per order. These nuances with the EOQ model make it useful to note the underlying assumptions with the model and the equation as follows:

- Demand is continuous and constant (i.e. the rate of demand of inventory is constant).
- There are no quantity constraints for either inventory on-order or storage capacity.
- Replenishment is instantaneous.
- No shortages are allowed, i.e. all orders must be fulfilled, as safety stocks are not included in the calculation.

Thus, the basic EOQ model is limited in that it doesn't consider random variations in demand or supply. Its use is therefore preferable[7] when there are good levels of business and logistics certainty, such as:

- ordering truckloads, container loads or other efficient and fixed shipping capacities;
- obtaining quantity discounts from suppliers;
- obeying fixed capacity constraints.

However, a firm's operations, transportation and other order costs, customer demand, supplier lead times and orders for discrete numbers of items, i.e. non-EOQ, affect the basic EOQ model – these factors must be taken into account to reduce any increasing uncertainty. Many amendments to the model have been developed over the last 50 years but deeper consideration of them is beyond the scope of this text. Interested readers are encouraged to seek out these discussions in both texts devoted to inventory[8] and academic journal articles.

The periodic review method sets a fixed point in time where a review is made of inventory on-hand and any inventory in-transit, and then ordering an amount to replenish inventory to a maximum stock level. The critical decision parameters are the fixed review period and the maximum replenishment level. Dividing D by EOQ may help determine an initial review period P in order to take advantage of minimum total costs that the EOQ equation provides. However, this may be modified based on demand and supplier variability – for example, a retailer's review period may be decreased in the last three months of the year due to increased demand for the holiday period.

The maximum replenishment level, sometimes referred to as the target stock level or TSL, is a function of D, P and the supplier's lead time or LT as follows:

$$\text{TSL} = \text{D} \times (\text{LT} + \text{P})$$

In this equation units for D must equal those of LT and P, either weeks or days. Returning to the example given above where D is 120,000 units per year or 329 per day assume P is 2 days and LT is 1 day. Thus, substituting into the equation the appropriate TSL would be $329 \times (1 + 2)$ or 987 maximum. This value corresponds favourably to the EOQ or maximum order of 989 given above and in this example these methods seem roughly equivalent. However, there would now be 183 orders per year when ordering every two days, which is over 60 additional orders per year. The increase in order costs would thus be an additional €3,270 compared with the EOQ calculation.

However, the periodic review method is easier to administer and permits tighter scheduling of deliveries and is therefore preferable[9] for:

- SKUs that are difficult to count and administer or low-cost SKUs that do not warrant detailed monitoring, for example 'C' category items;
- joint orders from common suppliers;
- orders delivered on routine supplier visits or 'milk runs;'
- high-demand items such as perishable food and other fast-moving consumer goods.

There are two common hybrid methods.[10] One is a periodic review with a re-order point or level from the continuous review, fixed-order quantity method. If inventory falls below a designated re-order point or level, an order is placed; however, if inventory on-hand remains above the designated re-order point, no order will be placed until the next period as usual. The other is a re-order point or level and a target stock level from the periodic review method, and is also referred to as a 'min-max' or 'minimax' system. When stock falls below the re-order point, the firm does not order EOQ; rather, it orders an amount that raises current stock to a target level. Thus, the *minimum* is the re-order point while the *maximum* is the target stock level. This particular hybrid method is useful when individual customer orders are large and might take inventory levels well below the re-order point.

One requirement all these methods have in common is an independent demand profile of customers. Large volumes of customers or SKUs will require some form of computer support or automation to perform the various calculations and assist in inventory management decision making. Logistics Example 6.2 discusses how such systems are capable of doing so. However, the determination of accurate independent demand is crucial for calculating various replenishment parameters. One way of determining such demand is the use of forecasting, which we will discuss next.

LOGISTICS EXAMPLE 6.2

Reducing inventory through automation

A new inventory optimisation system has enabled motor distributor Autosdistribution Losch to cut its investment in stock from €3.4 million to €2 million in a period of six months. Losch supplies 22 dealerships in Luxembourg with original parts and accessories for Volkswagen, Audi, Seat and Skoda. Its product range of 900,000 parts and accessories is sourced predominantly from Volkswagen's European central warehouse in Kassel, Germany each night, while Skoda and Seat parts are imported from the Czech Republic and Spain respectively. The 25,000 standard parts that Losch deals in equate to 90 per cent of its annual turnover of €20 million.

For almost 30 years Losch managed its inventory through a system from Volkswagen, which processed data from the in-house ERP system. The manager for the spare parts and accessories department at Losch noted that it took at least three months to identify sales trends with the old system, which was far too late. Losch needed a better understanding of immediate stock needs and consequently had ongoing problems with managing warehouse stock. Additionally, the costs for storage and express deliveries had reached a level which was no longer justifiable. The German software company Inform GmbH provided a new inventory optimisation system that first extracted data from the old system to begin stock optimisation with its 'add*ONE' optimisation product.

Logistics example 6.2 (*cont.*)

Since implementation, the quantity of ordered items has been reduced from 23,000 to 19,500. At the same time stock value declined from €3.4 million to nearly €2 million, which has increased Losch's inventory turnover ratio from 5.9 to 10. Additionally, the service level has improved for the dealerships and is running at 96 per cent, reaching targets set by Volkswagen.

There is only one employee responsible for the overall work flow in original parts and accessories for each of the four automotive brands at Losch – spanning across purchasing, promotions and sales. The automation of the planning process has led to a simplified way of working. Expensive overnight express deliveries of standard parts have become a thing of the past as planners now receive cost-optimised high-volume order recommendations. These orders are then delivered on a daily basis, which is more cost effective and shortens delivery lead times to a maximum of one day, whereas in the past it could have taken up to eight days.

Question

How can information technology and automation assist inventory management?

Source: adapted from 'Inventory optimizer gives big savings for motor distributor,' Logistics Manager Case Study, www.logisticsmanager.com (March 2011).

Forecasting

Forecasting is important for many business aspects, such as marketing research, finance, purchasing and operations. Demand forecasting is particularly important for logistics and SCM as it helps determine appropriate inventory levels. Further, warehouse space and operations are influenced by demand predictions and transportation operations can be scheduled more effectively when forecasts are more accurate. Finally, relationships with suppliers can be more effectively managed with accurate forecasting, leading to supply chain coordination and collaboration.

The selection of the right forecasting technique is important and there are two major types of forecasting methods: qualitative and quantitative. Qualitative or judgemental methods use judgement, intuition, surveys or comparative techniques to produce estimates about the future. Measures are non-quantitative and subjective and are based on 'soft' data. Conversely, quantitative or statistical methods use hard data that can be verified and objectively assessed. There is no single method that is superior in all cases, since each one has different strengths and weaknesses.

It is useful to identify and analyse general characteristics of forecasting situations before choosing a particular method. There are three basic data demand patterns. Horizontal patterns do not change over time, trend patterns linearly and steadily move upwards or downwards, and seasonal patterns repeat themselves in a regular pattern that is predictable over a particular time period. In reality, it is usually necessary to combine the three basic patterns in order to explain data behaviour. Factors influencing forecasting decisions include the planning horizon, nature of demand, cost of forecast preparation, degree of accuracy desirable, amount of available data, market structure or situation characteristics. An example of forecasting decision-making as it affects inventory is provided in Logistics Example 6.3.

LOGISTICS EXAMPLE 6.3

Forecasting and ABC inventory analysis for whisky

A Scottish whisky producer, which we shall call 'WhiskCo', specialises in the production of single malt whiskies and employs about 300 people. It has a market share of around 17 per cent in the United Kingdom, with annual turnover of about £65 million. The brand portfolio of WhiskCo primarily consists of three single malt whisky products. All bottling and warehouse activities are performed at one site in central Scotland. The company also sells its products around the globe; however, its United Kingdom volume is two-thirds of company output.

WhiskCo uses primarily qualitative methods for forecasting, taking previous year's sales, stock on hand and incoming orders as inputs to produce outputs of projected shipments of each item to all customers for the next six months. A member of the forecasting team forecasts shipment quantities by product, customer and month going out six months, thus a rolling horizon is used. WhiskCo's forecasts may be categorised as medium term and while forecasts go out for six months, only forecasts for one or two months affect resource and capacity planning. Consequently, demand prediction is used for tactical decisions.

WhiskCo has a bottom-up approach as forecasts are first made at each product level and then aggregated into an overall forecast. Forecasters predict on the basis of the above inputs and their intuition and experience. Although WhiskCo does not generally perform market surveys to identify opinions and buying intentions of its customers, it occasionally contacts large retail customers such as Sainsbury's, Tesco or Asda regarding their opinion on how successful various sales promotions might be. The previous year's sales figure of a respective forecasted month is used when the forecaster does not have any information of likely demand or sales promotion activity.

There is an exchange of forecast data information between WhiskCo's sales and logistics departments. When the forecast is prepared it is also distributed to various areas inside the organisation so that they can be aware of the next month's forecasted demand and control their respective activities appropriately. Seasonal variations, general market trends, promotional activities and other economic and environmental factors affect product demand and an effort is made to incorporate these factors into forecasts. The pattern of WhiskCo's demand is seasonal. WhiskCo does not measure actual sales but shipments of cases during each month. Shipments have a large peak in November followed by a large decrease in December and January. The Christmas holiday period causes this peak as WhiskCo ships its products to retailers early enough for the season since various sales promotions may be undertaken.

WhiskCo uses a form of average percentage error (APE) to measure accuracy. The measure is calculated for all SKUs and an average is calculated to obtain WhiskCo's overall forecast accuracy. Forecasts of total shipments are also desegregated for analysis of individual product SKUs.

An ABC analysis of the 37 United Kingdom SKUs that are forecasted yielded 4 fast-moving 'A' SKUs, 6 medium-moving 'B' SKUs and 27 slow-moving 'C' SKUs. The 4 fast-moving 'A' SKUs represented 78 per cent of sales and 11 per cent of items shipped during the 12-month period of analysis. These items also constituted almost 20 per cent of shipments. The forecast accuracy error for the 4 fast-moving products averaged about 13 per cent.

WhiskCo places a greater importance on maintaining customer service than on having excess inventory resulting from over-forecasting. Its methodology appears sound, is reasonably accurate and certainly meets its customers' needs.

> **Logistics example 6.3 (cont.)**
>
> **Question**
>
> *What are the advantages and disadvantages of qualitative versus quantitative forecasting?*
>
> Source: David B. Grant, Charoula Karagianni and Mei Li, 'Forecasting and stock obsolescence in whisky production,' *International Journal of Logistics: Research and Applications*, 2006, Vol. 9, No. 3, pp.319–334.

Accuracy has long been considered one of the most important selection criteria for a forecasting technique. However, implementation-related criteria such as ease of use, ease of interpretation and flexibility, and ease of implementation of available data are also important. A forecasting method's accuracy is influenced by the stability of data patterns and the forecasting time horizon. However, all forecasts contain error, which refers to how close the forecast comes to the actual demand and can be measured by its deviation. Deviation indicates the absolute magnitude of the average error while bias indicates the arithmetic magnitude of the average error. Forecast error is defined as actual demand minus forecasted demand, or A(t) minus F(t). Three usual measures of error are absolute percentage error (APE), mean absolute percentage error (MAPE) and mean absolute deviation (MAD). Table 6.2 provides formulae for each measure together with their respective advantages and disadvantages.

Forecast error should be measured as customer service depends on the forecast error distribution; thus it is necessary to estimate the deviation of forecast error when establishing safety stocks of products and appropriate levels of customer service. There are several causes of forecast error: inaccurate data, use of sales information rather than demand statistics, forecast bias, slow speed of response to change, poor assessment of supply capability,

Table 6.2 Comparison of forecast error measures

Measure	Formula	Advantages	Disadvantages
Absolute percentage error (APE)	$APE = \left\| \dfrac{A(t) - F(t)}{A(t)} \right\| \times 100$	Eliminates the cancelling of positive and negative errors.	It does not treat single errors above the actual value any differently from those below it.
Mean absolute percentage error (MAPE)	$MAPE = \sum\limits_{t=1}^{N} \dfrac{(APEt)}{N}$	It allows comparisons among different series. It is more valid when the assumption that severity of error is linearly related to its size cannot be supported.	It is asymmetric, i.e. greater APE results from equal errors above the actual values than from equal errors below the actual values.
Mean absolute deviation (MAD)	$MAD = \dfrac{1}{N} \times \sum\limits_{t=1}^{N} ABS\,[A(t) - F(t)]$	It does not overestimate or underestimate the error, i.e. positive and negative errors do not cancel each other.	MAD weights all errors equally but it can be exponentially weighted towards the most recent data so that calculation of safety stocks becomes more effective.

inclusion of extra demand in the forecast, shortage of data and failure in using available contextual information.

There is mixed evidence regarding the accuracy of qualitative or judgemental forecasting compared with quantitative or statistical/computer-based models. A study[11] of US marketing executives found that firms which used quantitative techniques outperformed firms which used judgemental techniques, particularly as regards forecast error. Firms which used judgemental techniques did not have significant access to information and also operated in uncertain environments, thus they preferred to rely on subjective information to enhance their decision making. However, the greater accuracy achieved from quantitative techniques should provide an impetus for firms to adopt them.

Summary

Many people consider transportation and warehousing as the two key elements in logistics, i.e. the 'Stop' and 'Go' activities. However, the management of inventory is also crucial as stocks comprise myriad raw materials, parts, sub-assemblies and finished products being moved and stored from the point of origin to the point of consumption in the supply chain. The costs to buy and keep stocks are large and affect a firm's profitability. Yet stocking-out of products is also costly as customers may change suppliers in order to ensure continual availability – this situation seriously affects a firm's competitive advantage. Thus, a firm faces an 'inventory conundrum' as it tries to balance various competing interests.

This chapter has considered the nature of inventory and its benefits in providing a buffer between supply and demand as well as the financial impact inventory has on the firm, and qualitative and quantitative inventory management techniques related to how much stock to order and when to order it, i.e. notions related to independent demand. An appreciation of forecasting as it relates to the determination of independent demand was also provided to close the discussion. The next chapter on production and operations management will consider the effect of inventory management for dependent demand as it forms part of the production and operations process, and discuss dependent demand techniques aimed at providing retail stores with full shelves of products to meet independent consumer demand.

DISCUSSION QUESTIONS

1 How important is inventory to a firm in comparison with transportation and warehousing?

2 What benefits does inventory provide to a firm and its customers?

3 Why should a firm care about inventory carrying or holding costs?

4 What are the advantages and disadvantages of the economic order quantity (EOQ) model?

5 What pitfalls must a firm avoid when forecasting independent demand?

Suggested reading

Buxey, Geoff 'Reconstructing inventory management theory,' *International Journal of Operations & Production Management*, 2006, Vol. 25, No. 9, pp.996–1012.

Forrester, Jay W. 'Industrial dynamics,' *Harvard Business Review*, 1958, Vol. 36, No. 4 (July–August), pp.37–66.

Grant, David B., Charoula Karagianni and Mei Li 'Forecasting and stock obsolescence in whisky production,' *International Journal of Logistics: Research and Applications*, 2006, Vol. 9, No. 3, pp.319–334.

Harris, Ford W. 'How many parts to make at once,' *Factory, The Magazine of Management*, 1913, Vol. 10, No. 2 (February), pp.135–136, 152.

Kotzab, Herbert 'Improving supply chain performance by efficient consumer response? A critical comparison of existing ECR approaches,' *Journal of Business & Industrial Marketing*, 1999, Vol. 14, No. 5/6, pp.364–377.

Lee, Hau L., V. Padmanabhan and Seungjin Whang 'Information distortion in a supply chain: The bullwhip effect,' *Management Science*, 1997, Vol. 43, No. 4, pp.546–558.

Makridakis, Spyros G., Steven C. Wheelwright and Rob J. Hyndman *Forecasting: Methods and Applications,* 3rd ed. Chichester: John Wiley & Sons Ltd, 1998.

Sanders, Nada R. and Karl B. Manrodt 'The efficacy of using judgmental versus quantitative forecasting methods in practice,' *Omega*, 2003, Vol. 31, pp.511–522.

Silver, Edward A., David F. Pyke and Rein Peterson *Inventory Management and Production Planning and Scheduling*, 3rd ed. New York: John Wiley & Sons Ltd, 1998.

Slack, Nigel, Stuart Chambers and Robert Johnson *Operations Management,* 6th ed. Harlow: FT Prentice Hall, 2010.

Stank, Theodore P., Patricia J. Daugherty and Chad W. Autry 'Collaborative planning: Supporting automatic replenishment programs,' *Supply Chain Management: An International Journal,* 1999, Vol. 4, No. 2.

Tersine, Richard J. and Michele G. Tersine 'Inventory reduction: Preventive and corrective strategies,' *The International Journal of Logistics Management,* 1990, Vol. 1, No. 2, pp.17–24.

Waters, Donald *Inventory Control and Management,* 2nd ed. Chichester: John Wiley & Sons Ltd, 2003.

Wild, Tony *Best Practice in Inventory Management*, New York: John Wiley & Sons Ltd, 1997.

Zinn, Walter 'Developing heuristics to estimate the impact of postponement on safety stock,' *The International Journal of Logistics Management,* 1990, Vol. 1, No. 2, pp.11–16.

Notes

1 Rosalyn Wilson 'CSCMP's 22nd Annual State of Logistics Report: Navigating through the recovery,' http://cscmp.org/ 2011.
2 This chapter draws on materials from three classic and well-known inventory texts: Tony Wild, *Best Practice in Inventory Management* (New York: John Wiley & Sons Ltd, 1997); Edward A. Silver, David F. Pyke and Rein Peterson, *Inventory Management and Production Planning and Scheduling*, 3rd ed.

(New York: John Wiley & Sons Ltd, 1998); and Donald Waters, *Inventory Control and Management,* 2nd ed. (Chichester: John Wiley & Sons Ltd, 2003).

3 Mary Lu Harding (2006) 'What's the cost of your inventory?' WERCSheet, October, Warehousing Education and Research Council, www.werc.org/.

4 See Jay W. Forrester (1958) 'Industrial dynamics,' *Harvard Business Review*, Vol. 36, No. 4 (July–August), pp.37–66; and Hau L. Lee, V. Padmanabhan and Seungjin Whang (1997) 'Information distortion in a supply chain: The bullwhip effect,' *Management Science*, Vol. 43, No. 4, pp.546–558.

5 Geoff Buxey (2006) 'Reconstructing inventory management theory,' *International Journal of Operations & Production Management*, Vol. 25, No. 9, pp.996–1012.

6 Ford W. Harris (1913), 'How many parts to make at once,' *Factory, The Magazine of Management*, Vol. 10, No. 2 (February), pp.135–136,152.

7 Buxey (2006), pp.999–1000.

8 For additional examples of special-purpose EOQ models and amendments, see Waters (2003), pp. 65–191.

9 Buxey (2006), p.1000.

10 Waters (2003), p.186.

11 Nada R. Sanders and Karl B. Manrodt (2003) 'The efficacy of using judgmental versus quantitative forecasting methods in practice,' *Omega*, Vol. 31, pp.511–522.

Operations and materials management

Introduction

A manufacturing facility or factory represents a 'Stop' node in a supply chain. However, unlike a warehouse or distribution centre, there are more complex operations taking place within a factory that require the coordination of various logistical activities. This situation requires even more logistical effort in a global setting when the factory is not in the country where its products are sold. The introduction of materials into the factory and their release from it require an understanding of the factory's requirements and how those requirements shape logistics and supply chain considerations.

This chapter discusses operations and materials management approaches such as materials requirements planning (MRP), manufacturing resource planning (MRP II), distribution resources planning (DRP) and enterprise resource planning (ERP) that culminate in various web-based platforms. Techniques affecting these approaches include total quality management (TQM), just-in-time (JIT)[1] and lean and agile systems.[2] This discussion will take place in the context of a chapter-long case of Harley-Davidson, Inc., the US-based motorcycle manufacturer (referred to hereafter as Harley).[3]

Harley has been a popular subject for discrete and topical cases studies in various texts over the past 30 years, since its business renaissance in the 1980s that was predicated upon incorporating almost all of the approaches and techniques under consideration in this chapter at one time or another as well as several marketing techniques. Thus, Harley is still a very relevant and useful subject for discussion and for this chapter the entire Harley situation is presented from a broad and cumulative operations and logistics perspective that is not present in other texts.

The background of Harley-Davidson

Harley was founded in 1903 by William S. Harley and Arthur Davidson. Its product line consists primarily of super-heavyweight motorcycles (i.e. engine size larger than 1,000 c.c. and weighing in excess of 500 pounds or 230 kilograms). These motorcycles have traditionally appealed to younger males because of their size and visual features and Harley dominated this market niche for many years, manufacturing out of a single production plant in Milwaukee, Wisconsin. However, it has not always been smooth sailing for the company, particularly in the 1970s when Harley almost went out of business.

In the late 1950s the Japanese entered the US motorcycle market, led by Honda Motor Company, which initially targeted the lightweight motorcycle segment. By the mid-1970s the Japanese had penetrated the super-heavyweight and heavyweight motorcycle markets that had previously belonged almost entirely to Harley. With a corporate takeover by American Machine & Foundry (AMF) in the 1970s and subsequent production increases to meet demand, quality at Harley deteriorated. The Milwaukee plant simply could not produce high-quality products at the rate AMF demanded and the manufacturing equipment was old and unreliable. AMF elected to move motorcycle assembly from Milwaukee to York, Pennsylvania in order to accommodate the production expansion. However, AMF faced labour and union problems and further quality deterioration followed.

Harley dealer complaints of poor quality were ignored and ultimately nearly every motorcycle produced and delivered to the dealer required extensive servicing before it was ready for sale to a customer. Market share eroded quickly from 80 per cent in 1973 to 31 per cent in 1980 and total sales were declining at a time when the overall motorcycle market was growing. AMF eventually put Harley up for sale and in 1981 13 Harley executives, led by chairman Vaughan Beals, consummated a leveraged management buyout. The challenges facing Harley's new owners were:

- Japanese competition which produced a better quality, more up-to-date, reliable, cheaper product;
- a motorcycle market that was beginning to erode due to the economic recession of the day, high interest rates and increased fuel prices;
- a lack of capital for expansion;
- an outdated product that leaked oil, vibrated badly and generally did not meet customer expectations;
- quality problems which led to half of the motorcycles leaving the assembly line missing parts;
- poor customer service by Harley itself and its dealer network, which featured poor locations and facilities, and contempt for non-Harley riders and machinery.

Beals and Harley management studied Japanese production methods, and visited the Honda factory in the US. Harley's goals were clear: improve quality and efficiency, cut costs, lower the per unit break-even point for its products, and regain customers and market share.

What is a manufacturing facility or factory?

A manufacturing facility or factory uses its available resources to produce or convert a number of different inputs from suppliers into outputs for customers. Figure 7.1 shows a schematic for a typical factory. Inputs from suppliers for a Harley motorcycle will include raw materials such as steel and other metals to make frames, bodywork and other components; parts such as tyres, light bulbs and cables; sub-assemblies such as engines and transmissions; and consumables such as cleaning materials and lubricants. The introduction of these inputs to the factory will be through in-bound logistics provided by suppliers, 3PL service providers, or Harley on its own account. (These concepts were discussed in Chapter 4.)

Within the factory Harley would use its various resources to undertake the production or conversion processes. These include physical resources such as land, building and equipment; human resources such as shopfloor workers and management; financial resources such as working capital for operational expenses and long-term capital for investment in equipment or other long-term physical resources or assets; and informational resources such as information technology (IT) and paper-based systems to track customer orders and supplier invoices and to follow factory progress for efficiency and effectiveness.

The outputs of Harley's factory would be finished motorcycles for delivery to customers, in this case Harley's dealer network around the world. Again, this delivery is part of outbound logistics and would be provided by 3PL service providers or Harley itself. This type of factory is representative of Harley's assembly plants in York, Pennsylvania and Kansas City, Missouri.

Harley's York factory, built in 1973, assembles the Touring, Softail and Trike models of motorcycles, as well as limited production, factory-custom motorcycles. It performs a variety of manufacturing operations, making parts such as fuel tanks, frames and fenders. York is the largest Harley manufacturing facility, employing 3,100 people or roughly half the company's production workforce. It covers more than 230 acres and has over 1.5 million square feet under roof. In 1991 Harley opened a $31 million state-of-the-art paint facility at York.

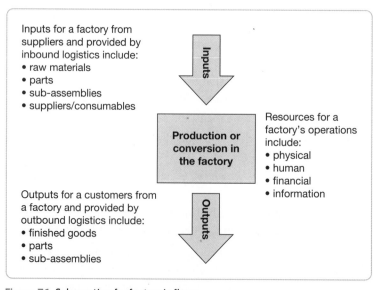

Figure 7.1 Schematic of a factory's flows

The 358,000 square foot Kansas City facility, built in 1998, employs 900 people and produces the Sportster, Dyna and VRSC families of motorcycles from fabrication and finishing through final assembly and shipping to dealerships around the world. The plant has the unique distinction of being the only Harley facility to produce an entire motorcycle, the VRSCA V-Rod, from assembly of the liquid-cooled Revolution powertrain and hydroformed frame to painting and final testing.

An exception to the above factories are Harley's 849,000 square foot facility in Menomonee Falls, Wisconsin (1,020 employees), which produces engines and transmissions, and its 192,000 square foot facility in Tomahawk, Wisconsin (415 employees), that has two separate operations. One operation at Tomahawk manufactures plastic and fibreglass parts, including saddlebags and bodywork, and then paints, assembles and ships these components to York. The operation produces windshields, parts and accessories, as well as components that are used at the Kansas City facility. Thus, the customers for these two facilities are the York and Kansas City factories, and the 250,000 square foot parts and accessories distribution centre opened in 1996 in Franklin, Wisconsin that employs 130 people who process and fill motorcycle part and accessory orders. Inbound and outbound logistics also affect the Menomonee Falls and Tomahawk facilities as well as the Franklin DC. The latter is, of course, representative of a warehouse as discussed in Chapter 5. The issue of spare parts is important for any manufacturer and Logistics Example 7.1 provides an example of this issue.

LOGISTICS EXAMPLE 7.1

Materials management of automotive spare parts

Spare parts and related support have surfaced as major challenges to many firms due to the amount of investment required for this part of the supply chain. Materials management in this area has received little attention until recently. One example is the UK telecommunications company, BT International, which developed a 'Global Spares Initiative' in the mid-2000s to save €80 million a year in reduced inventory and operating costs, a value that doesn't include labour savings. This was accomplished by BT and Alcatel-Lucent of France signing a major managed services contract in 2006 under which Alcatel-Lucent's Services assumed responsibility for the majority of BT's equipment maintenance and spares management contracts. The eight-year contract covers first line maintenance, second, third and fourth line support and spares management and is worth approximately €263 million; BT expects to derive cost savings in excess of €75 million over the lifetime of the contract.

The automotive industry has its own special characteristics, which have so far prevented much action in this area. There is a customer need for rapid response to ensure consumers' vehicles are repaired in a timely manner; however, maintaining minimal stocks and shipping by air freight cannot be justified on a cost basis.

Thus, automakers typically maintain a network of distribution centres across Europe instead of one central facility to ensure fulfilment is made to dealers for repair and service. However, inventory and handling costs are high. Given this problem, some members in the auto spares supply chain are suggesting a shared user approach where automakers share facilities and information systems, and thus costs.

> ### Logistics example 7.1 (*cont.*)
>
> The lack of suitable software and systems is also an issue as most manufacturers have MRP/ERP systems that don't work well with the uncertain demand parameters of after-market sales and support for automotive spares. One suggestion is to break up automotive spare parts into categories and use different logistics strategies and perhaps supply chains for each. However, this would probably entail developing new supply chains and systems. Another suggestion is to outsource the spares supply chain to the parts manufacturers themselves instead of the automaker, although in this case the automakers might find it difficult to give up control.
>
> But an explosion in customer expectations has made automotive spare parts logistics and materials management important. Motorists expect to be mobile for life and competition for their repair and servicing business is heating up as the end of the European Union 'block exemption' sees more competitors entering the marketplace.
>
> #### Question
>
> *How might the automotive sector utilise outsourced or managed services for spare parts and service for consumers?*
>
> *Sources*: adapted from Chris Lewis 'Pain or gain?' *Supply Chain Standard* (formally *Logistics Europe*), 2004, Vol. 12, No. 5, pp.26–31; and 'Alcatel-Lucent wins BT deal,' 5 December 2006, www.lightreading.com/document.asp?doc_id=112050 (accessed 1 October 2011).

Harley has two other major facilities that support the above operations. The company's corporate headquarters is in Milwaukee on Juneau Avenue on a site where the first factory – a wooden shed – was built in 1903 in the backyard of the Davidson family home. Over 1,500 employees work there and in 1994 the site was listed on the National Register of Historic Places by the US government. The 370,000 square foot Willie G. Davidson Product Development Center (PDC) in Wauwautosa, Wisconsin opened in March 1997 to bring together in one location the 1,100 people responsible for new product development, original equipment (OE) engineering, testing, styling and developmental purchasing.

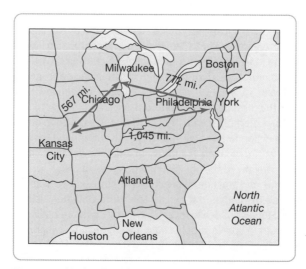

Figure 7.2 Harley-Davidson's factory locations in the US

Figure 7.2 is a map of the US showing the two production facilities of York and Kansas City and the various facilities around the Milwaukee area. The distance in miles from each to the others is also shown and demonstrates the transportation and logistical challenges for Harley in moving materials, parts, sub-assemblies and finished goods among them. These challenges require planning that is supported by the proper information. However, the source document for all operations and materials handling planning is the master production schedule (MPS), which contains a statement of the volume and timing of the products to be produced, together with the bill of materials (BOM), which is a list of the component parts required to make up the product together with information regarding their level in the product structure and the quantities of each component required.

Operations and materials handling planning approaches

Figure 7.3 presents a hierarchical view of the various planning approaches used in operations and materials handling management. The movement from MRP through MRP II and DRP to ERP is dependent upon an increasing integration of information systems and the increasing impact of these approaches on the supply network or indeed supply chain as the impact extends downstream to customers.

MRP enables order requirements to be generated for both internal and external component parts, sub-assemblies and assemblies, and any other procured items. MRP starts with the MPS and BOM and uses them to determine a timetable for gross material requirements. Then stock records or inventory levels, purchasing conditions, work in progress, etc. can be used to calculate net requirements and details of ordering policies. The main result is a schedule for the supply of materials to be ordered and related internal operations.

The characteristics of MRP are:

- it is forward looking and not based on past trends;
- it provides time-phasing of the replenishment process;

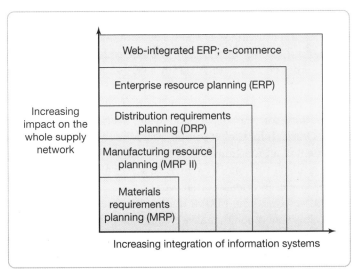

Figure 7.3 From MRP to ERP

Source: adapted from Slack *et al.* (2010, p. 409).

- it takes account of the interrelationships between components and sub-assemblies;
- it is oriented to final product rather than components to maximise the availability of groups of products.

This approach has a number of benefits, particularly relating stocks to known demand. A strength of MRP is that it can be extended from its original function of scheduling materials to scheduling other resources. In principle, it can be used to schedule all activities in an organisation.

MRP is a simple idea, but it is practical only with lots of computing and connected systems. This complexity is its main problem and can result in errors from:

- an inaccurate MPS due to forecasting errors and short-term, unplanned reallocation of resources;
- inaccurate inventory records;
- unreliable lead times from suppliers;
- variability of lead times from internal and external sources.

Another weakness is MRP's reduced flexibility as it is not responsive enough for flexible manufacturing. As a result, MRP can work well in some circumstances, but it should not be considered a universal tool for all organisations. It is only really suitable for certain types of process and is most successful for batch manufacturing.

MRP II is an extension to MRP and involves the integrated planning of materials and resources across the marketing, finance and purchasing functions in an organisation. MRP II was made possible due to advanced computing power that linked these different functions and was a precursor to ERP. Both MRP and MRP II are considered 'push' systems when it comes to material and capacity scheduling and ordering.

DRP is a special case approach suitable for retailers or other organisations such as wholesalers dealing in finished goods, i.e. there are no processing or production requirements. DRP provides a schedule to determine inventory requirements from forecasted or actual demand and receipts of incoming products from the MRP at certain time periods to match needs and coordinate customer-generated buying schedules. While DRP would be well suited to operate Harley's parts and accessories DC, Harley has actually gone one step further and established a web-based extranet system known as H-D.Net where customers meet on the company's website and dealerships execute warranty-claim transactions and parts order entry. In 1987, Harley sold $42 million in parts and accessories, but by 2010 revenue was more than $864 million; thus the new platform was warranted at that time.

ERP is an information system covering all of the business processes of a modern enterprise. It is a software-driven system and the main software suppliers are companies such as SAP, Oracle, Infor Global Solutions and the Sage Group. ERP provides comprehensive management of all functions across the business and integrates all departments and functions onto a single computer system. This serves all the different departments' particular needs and provides information transparency.

ERP evolved from MRP II due to the onset of supply chain management, e-commerce and global operation that have created a need to provide and exchange information directly with other companies and customers. The difference between MRP II and ERP is that MRP II synchronises an organisation's information systems and provides insight into the implications of the MPS and materials plan but focuses only on internal operations. However, ERP has additional capabilities for quality management, field service, human resources, maintenance management, distribution, marketing and supplier management. ERP also interfaces with the organisation's entire supply chain. Thus ERP is essentially the newest generation of MRP/MRP II systems and represents an extended application of MRP principles to the supply chain.

Benefits of ERP systems include:

- visibility throughout the organisation and more sophisticated communication with suppliers, customers and other business partners due to integrated software communication;
- a discipline of forcing process-based changes to make the organisation more efficient;
- a better sense of operational control to enhance continuous improvement;
- the capability of integrating the entire supply chain beyond 'tier 1' customers and suppliers.

ERP depends on trust and information sharing between organisations, yet ERP systems are complex and have many practical problems. The final approach shown in Figure 7.3 is based on web-based ERP, e-commerce and extranet systems that make the flow of information easy to organise and help overcome these disadvantages and take advantage of large third-party, remote servers to access data available via what is termed 'cloud computing' that is usually hosted by the software supplier. These issues will be discussed further in Chapter 8. In summary, although many system suppliers may disagree, ERP is still evolving but has been proved successful at many firms.

Harley's manufacturing strategy is designed to continuously improve product quality and productivity while reducing costs and increasing flexibility to respond to ongoing changes in the marketplace. Harley believes that flexible manufacturing processes and flexible supply chains combined with cost-competitive and flexible labour agreements are the key enablers to respond to customers in a cost-effective manner.

In the 1990s Harley engaged Manugistics, now part of JDA Software, to develop its supply chain software and uses American Software's IBM AS/400-based ERP suite for manufacturing. Harley also uses DataMirror Corporation's transformation server and high-availability suite to move data, such as information on inventory levels, among the AS/400s running its manufacturing systems. The company also uses the software to move warranty and parts information between its main manufacturing system and its web server supporting H-D. Net. Harley is aggressively standardising its IT systems to streamline operations, reduce the expense of supporting multiple products and become more nimble or agile with its IT. A further example of technology and software from SAP is provided in Logistics Example 7.2.

LOGISTICS EXAMPLE 7.2

The use of SAP at Sharp Electronics (Europe)

SAP AG from Germany, founded in 1972, is the world's leading and largest ERP software company. In 2011, it provided services to more than 172,000 customers and more than 12 million users in over 120 countries, including FORTUNE 500 corporations, entrepreneurial start-ups and government agencies, and had more than 30 per cent of the total market for ERP systems. Its SAP R/3 Enterprise, an integrated suite of financial, manufacturing, distribution, logistics, quality control and human resources application systems,

Logistics example 7.2 (*cont.*)

was replaced in 1999 by mySAP.com, which combines e-commerce solutions with SAP's existing ERP applications on the basis of cutting-edge web technology.

Its basic software architecture consists of three main layers:

1 The SAP graphical user interface (GUI), representing the presentation layer.

2 The SAP application layer.

3 The SAP database layer.

Reported experiences in SAP-enabled supply chain re-engineering applications (Al-Mashari and Zairi, 2000) have shown that effective implementation requires establishing the following five core competencies:

1 Change strategy development and deployment.

2 Enterprise-wide project management.

3 Change management techniques and tools.

4 Business process re-engineering integration with IT.

5 Strategic, architectural and technical aspects for SAP installation.

One firm that has enjoyed success with SAP is Sharp Electronics, part of Sharp Corporation of Japan and one of the world's largest and most respected manufacturers of electronics products, including television and audio equipment, document systems, liquid crystal display (LCD) screens, mobile phones and solar cells.

Sharp Europe's ERP software needs are complex: its broad product portfolio includes some of the most technologically advanced consumer electronics in the world, it deals with various retailers in more than a dozen European countries, and it has a workforce that speaks numerous languages. Sharp Europe places a high value on standardisation and ease of use for software applications required to manage all of this complexity. Its relationship with SAP began and it now uses the mySAP enterprise solution.

The common features of mySAP, such as user-adaptable screen layouts, download into Microsoft Excel and decentralised reporting and printing. It helps minimise interfaces between subsidiaries and locations, reduces the need for local development, and simplifies documentation and training. Sharp Europe achieved standardisation of codes, customer groups and other factors, which also enabled it to set up standardised interfaces to other IT systems and to have joint development of add-on functions.

Based on the success of its European group, Sharp has implemented a variety of SAP solutions throughout its global operations. Utilising web services and SAP NetWeaver Process Integration as its enterprise service bus, Sharp consolidated its third-party providers, created standardised web services and adopted a more flexible infrastructure for integration and message processing. Sharp interacts with a variety of customers and partners through multiple channels, including e-commerce, EDI systems and customer care centres.

In early 2007, the Sharp IT team focused on a new approach for its many B2B transactions. It adopted a web services computing model, standardising and consolidating interfaces across many systems and processing scenarios to achieve greater efficiency and flexibility to support new and expanding business demands in a standards-based manner. There were so many different custom and manual processes that consolidating all of these activities into one enterprise solution was a huge win for all involved. Once the primary processes were automated and services enabled, they were able to be consumed within

> **Logistics example 7.2 (*cont.*)**
>
> the SAP portal, by its customer care centre, and in direct B2B transactions. Not only has this led to a much greater level of customer satisfaction and positive user experience, but it has significantly cut down the time it takes to process orders. By eliminating many manual steps, the company has also improved the accuracy and compliance of its orders and all the processes involved.
>
> The major objective of having one platform and integration methodology in place was successfully achieved, and now the focus is on company-wide education and training, raising awareness and gaining experience. Sharp is anticipating SAP's upcoming releases of enabled services to be automatically populated within SAP's Enterprise Services Repository, so when ready, the firm can start using this mechanism to help integrate and manage these services.
>
> **Question**
>
> *How could products from SAP or other information technology companies be used in small and medium-sized enterprises?*
>
> *Sources*: adapted from Majed Al-Mashari and Mohamed Zairi 'Supply chain re-engineering using enterprise resource planning (ERP) systems: An analysis of a SAP R/3 implementation case,' *International Journal of Physical Distribution & Logistics Management*, 2000, Vol. 30, No. 3/4, pp.296–313; Nigel Slack, Stuart Chambers and Robert Johnson (2010) *Operations Management*, 6th ed. Harlow: FT Prentice Hall, p.410; and SAP (2011) www.sap.com/ (accessed 5 August 2011).

Just-in-time (JIT) and total quality management (TQM)

JIT and TQM are independent techniques to improve production, yet given their origins they are symbiotic, particularly in the case of Harley.

JIT organises all activities so that materials and supplies arrive just in time for the manufacturing or conversion process. If such activities occur early or late there is either a waste of resources or poor customer service. In particular, JIT sees stocks as a waste of resources that can be eliminated by proper coordination of supply and demand; in a JIT environment an ideal lot size of stock would be one item. In a broader sense, JIT tries to eliminate all waste in an organisation. This is difficult to achieve and needs a fundamental change in thinking. It recognises fundamental problems and then searches for ways of solving them rather than ways of hiding the symptoms. This demands new relationships with suppliers, customers and employees.

JIT works by pulling materials through a supply chain rather than the traditional MRO/MRO II methods that push them through. Customer demand triggers operations, with a message passed backwards through the supply chain by *kanbans*, a Japanese term signifying a card or record. There are many different forms and ways of using *kanbans*, most usually electronic tags. The overall stock of any item depends on the number of *kanbans* and size of containers used.

Tangible benefits of using JIT include:

- inventory reduction of anywhere from 30–60 per cent;
- reduction in storage space on average of 30 per cent in factories and warehouses;

- productivity improvement between 30–50 per cent;
- improved product and service quality through the elimination of quality inspection at factories, i.e. non-value-adding activities, with costs in scrap reduced from 10 per cent to 6 per cent and a 26 per cent increase in product quality.[4]

JIT cannot be implemented in isolation but depends on associated changes. New relationships with suppliers, customers and employees have been mentioned, but JIT also needs TQM, continuous improvement, devolved decision making and so on. JIT can bring considerable benefits to an organisation, based on the elimination of waste, including stocks of work in progress. However, it is inevitably difficult to introduce and can bring significant problems, including reduced flexibility, reliance on suppliers and problems linking to other systems.

JIT can be extended to other organisations within a supply chain using quick response or efficient customer response in a retail setting for more effective replenishment. This aspect will be discussed in Chapter 8. Regarding inventory management, techniques such as independent demand for economic order quantity discussed in Chapter 6, MRP and JIT need not be used in isolation and there can be benefits in combining the different approaches. An organisation might, for example, use MRP for planning the overall supply of materials and then JIT for controlling the detailed delivery. For example, a cost tradeoff between using EOQ and JIT is shown in Figure 7.4, which is a graphical representation of the cost difference between EOQ and JIT as a function of annual demand. The vertical axis is the cost difference when subtracting the cost under JIT from the cost under EOQ. As demand increases along the horizontal axis, the cost difference between EOQ and JIT widens rapidly until a point where this difference is at its maximum of around $8,000 when demand equals 18,750 units. As annual demand increases beyond this point, the cost advantage of JIT begins to gradually fade until the two costs become equal at a demand level of 75,000 units. For annual demand above this level, EOQ is the more cost-effective alternative.[5]

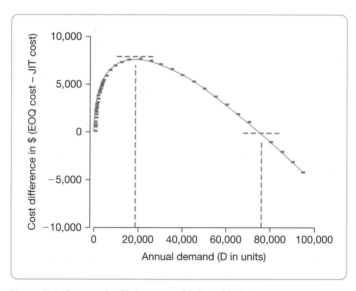

Figure 7.4 Cost tradeoffs between EOQ and JIT

Source: adapted from A comparative analysis of inventory costs of JIT and EOQ purchasing, *International Journal of Physical Distribution & Logistics Management*, Vol. 27, No. 8, pp. 496–504 (Fazel, F. 1997).

Criticisms of JIT are that it merely repositions inventory within the supply chain, increases the vulnerability of production and distribution operations, and increases other logistical costs, mainly transportation. For example, some research has found that JIT replenishment is up to 27 per cent more expensive than conventional replenishment due to higher transport costs, and that around 40 per cent of firms have incurred a transport cost penalty under JIT.[6]

TQM is a philosophy of how to approach the organisation of quality improvement that stresses the 'total' of TQM and focuses on:

- meeting the needs and expectations of customers;
- covering all parts of the organisation;
- including every person in the organisation;
- examining all costs which are related to quality, especially failure costs;
- getting things 'right first time', i.e. designing in quality rather than 'inspecting it in';
- developing the systems and procedures which support quality and improvement;
- developing a continuous process of improvement.[7]

TQM is another concept developed by the Japanese, especially Toyota. TQM 'gurus' who studied this Japanese technique and brought about its acceptance in the US and Europe include W. Edwards Deming (1900–1993) and Joseph M. Juran (1904–2008). Awards such as the Deming Prize, the Malcolm Baldrige National Quality Award and the European Foundation for Quality Management's (EFQM) European Quality Award have helped shape corporate thinking on quality issues. TQM today is conducted under the auspices of the International Standards Organisation's (ISO's) 9000 (2000) standard for quality assurance, which covers aspects of TQM and subjects a registered firm to third-party assessments of quality standards and procedures and regular audits to ensure ongoing compliance.

Implementing TQM has provided significant benefits and improvements for many companies. One example is GSM Primographic in the United Kingdom. GSM specialises in printing onto polycarbonates, plastics and metals, employs 75 people and generates annual turnover of £4.5 million from customers including Creda, BAE Systems, Ford, Jaguar and Rolls-Royce. It has ISO 9000 approved status and has also adopted a 5-S quality implementation programme. The Japanese 5-S practice is considered an important base for successfully implementing TQM; 5-S is the acronym for five Japanese words – *seiri, seiton, seiso, seiketsu* and *shitsuke* – that literally mean organisation, neatness, cleanliness, standardisation and discipline, respectively. GSM has passed stage three, i.e. 'cleaning'. Three out of its four production teams have been trained and cost savings around 2004 stand at £75,000, mainly through sorting out, cleaning up, rationalising space, improving work flow, and reducing job times and raw material.[8]

When a contingent of Harley managers, engineers and union leaders toured the Honda motorcycle assembly plant in Ohio in 1982, what they saw was mind-boggling compared with Harley's facilities. Harley reviewed the three practices Japanese manufacturers were using and set about implementing them across the firm.

JIT

The Japanese were successful in turning inventory 20–30 times a year compared with Harley's 4 times a year. Harley called its programme materials-as-needed (MAN) as it believed in most cases JIT simply pushed inventory back to the suppliers. Its approach reflected a closer working relationship with Harley's suppliers to eliminate this problem. Inventory at Harley spends just 8–10 hours on-hand, making suppliers integral to the success of MAN. Additionally, many Harley products are custom-built so that any delay in sourcing can cause production delays or even halt custom orders.

Harley moved quickly in implementing MAN, which is ideal for a repetitive manufacturing environment. Further, cash flow problems dictated that the company did so. With MAN it was able to eliminate its excessive inventories without drawing further on cash. Once inventories were fully depleted the MAN system eliminated the need for vast expenditures on future inventories. With the new system established, manufactured bikes were often produced and sold before Harley had to pay its suppliers. MAN was such an improvement that the cash flow effects alone were enough to justify its implementation.

Prior to MAN, Harley operated large production runs resulting in the accumulation of partially manufactured inventories. When the next stage of the bike was manufactured Harley would retrieve these assembled parts for further production. Often these parts sat in inventory for months. The net effect was poor quality and high costs of goods sold. Harley management therefore implemented what they termed the 'jelly bean' method of production where the assembly line would produce every model in different colours (hence 'jelly beans') every day. Small production runs were then implemented for each manufactured part, eliminating the mass accumulation of inventories that tended to rust, be lost, get damaged or become obsolete with long production runs.

Unfortunately, when Harley implemented MAN it moved so quickly that it neglected to secure the support and understanding of its staff and middle management personnel. For optimal operation of MAN or JIT, employees should be included in all aspects of the design and implementation. Therefore, Harley experienced productivity gains but not nearly to the extent that it could have achieved if worker acceptance had been sought.

Employee involvement (EI)

Employment involvement enlists the full participation of all employees in solving problems and in controlling quality. Quality circles were established at Harley, with each employee taking responsibility for his/her own work. No longer were quality control specialists responsible for checking other workers' product workmanship but rather individuals were responsible for quality in their stage of production and they could interact with other groups to ensure quality was maintained. For example, assemblers were asked to meet with suppliers to discuss quality problems, material changes and package changes. Department layout changes were discussed with the operators before implementation. Individual process sheets and work content were reviewed with assemblers before line balance changes were made. New equipment was reviewed with assemblers and in some cases they were asked to visit the vendor with the production engineer to participate in preliminary production run before delivery.

Statistical operator control (SOC)

Under SOC, employees were provided with the tools and technical expertise/training necessary to use these tools to accurately measure quality. Harley concluded it needed a SOC method so that plant operators and office employees could communicate with management regarding quality assurance issues and results. Harley turned to the University of Tennessee to train its managers and supervisors, who in turn trained others at Harley-Davidson in statistical analysis and quality improvement.

JIT, EI and SOC are referred to at Harley as the 'productivity triad' because they all must exist and operate with each other to achieve maximum efficiency. Through the implementation of this triad in 1981, Harley was able to accomplish the following within a few years:

- increase inventory turns to 20 times per year from 6 times for engines and 3–5 times for assembled motorcycles;
- reduce defects per assembled motorcycle by 52 per cent;
- reduce work-in-progress fivefold;
- increase engine units per employee by 38 per cent;
- reduce lot quantity sizes from 25 to 1 through mixed-model 'jelly bean' assembly technique;
- reduce break-even by one-third from 53,000 to 32,000 units per year.

Lean, agile and 'leagile'

Two different manufacturing and logistics/supply chain paradigms emerged during the late 1990s: 'lean' and 'agile'. In the United Kingdom the lean paradigm is prevalent at Cardiff Business School's Lean Research Centre, while the agile paradigm has stemmed from the Cranfield University School of Management's Centre for Logistics and Supply Chain Management.

The lean paradigm is based on the principles of lean production in the automotive sector detailed in the book *The Machine that Changed the World*.[9] The idea behind lean is the development of a value stream to identify bottlenecks in order to eliminate all waste, including time, and ensure a level production system. The five principles behind lean are:

1 Specify what creates value from the customers' perspective.
2 Identify the steps necessary to add value at each stage in the production and distribution process, i.e. the 'value stream'.
3 Make products flow smoothly along the value stream.
4 Make only what is demanded by the customer.
5 Strive for perfection, eliminating waste wherever possible.

The use of lean at a metals manufacturer is described in Logistics Example 7.3.

Conversely, the agile paradigm has its origins in principles of postponement that were discussed in Chapter 1. Being agile means using market knowledge and a virtual corporation to exploit profitable opportunities in a volatile marketplace. Characteristics of agility include the following:

- An agile supply chain is market sensitive.
- An agile supply chain is demand driven rather than forecast driven.
- There is significant use of IT to promote sharing of data.
- There is significant sharing of information through '*process integration*'.

LOGISTICS EXAMPLE 7.3

Going lean at UltraFit Manufacturing

Founded in 1982, UltraFit Manufacturing is a North American leader in tube bending and parts manufacturing using carbon steel, stainless steel, aluminium and other alloys, and whose expertise covers a broad range of processes from complex metal bending and forming to welded fabrication and sub-assembly. The finishing processes include end forming, perforating, polishing, heat treatment, plating and coating, fabrications, kitting and custom packaging. UltraFit works with industry-leading companies in the automotive, medical, furniture, recreation and heavy equipment markets and is a source for original equipment, aftermarket and performance exhaust products. The company guides projects from design through manufacturing to delivery, and works closely with customers to achieve the appropriate production system, from small batch runs to a constant supply of quality parts with just-in-time delivery. UltraFit serves its customers across North America from its Toronto, Canada manufacturing facility.

Until the mid-2000s UltraFit was a typical batch manufacturing company where machinery required to complete the process was located in different areas of the plant, e.g. tube bending in the bending department, tube-end sizing in the end finishing department, and welding of brackets and flanges to tubes in the welding department. Long changeover times on tube bending equipment meant the manufacturing department produced parts in batch quantities. In some cases orders were batched together for two-week periods or longer to be run during the same set-up. This practice created a need for higher levels of finished goods inventory to create a safety stock of parts and prevent shortages at shipping, resulting in:

- increased inventory being required;
- more floor space consumed for both finished goods and work in process;
- an inability to meet customer requests for short lead times.

The company initially set out to effect improvements internally, but managing the change generated only limited success and management engaged Lean Manufacturing Solutions, Inc., a Hamilton, Canada-based consulting firm to train UltraFit's teams in lean manufacturing concepts and methodologies and to facilitate the teams throughout the change process. Shopfloor employees and support personnel from scheduling, supervision, engineering and maintenance met to look at processes and break them down into components. They measured and mapped the manufacturing processes and used a video camera to record an actual product changeover on the bender.

Initially, a 'manufacturing cell' was created to comprise bending, end finishing and welding in one location. By eliminating work-in-process inventory created by large batch flows, the company was able to fit the new cellular production layout into the same area and use less floor space. The production line was balanced and moved to a one-piece flow, from 300 individual batch pieces, where downstream operations pulled production through the cell rather than allowing faster operations to work ahead and create inventory traffic jams. Communication improved and the work teams cross-trained each other to facilitate job sharing and rotation throughout the day.

Set-ups are now much faster, at just under 4.5 minutes compared with 39 minutes previously, and more consistent, yielding higher machine utilisation and a reduction in both set-up and production scrap. Lead times were reduced from two weeks to 1.5 hours and parts now travel only 30 feet as opposed to 150 feet in the old set-up. Reduced set-up time also enhances manufacturing flexibility and allows a greater number of different parts to be produced each day. This reduces the need for 'safety stock' inventory and improves responsiveness to customer needs.

These improvements at UltraFit, which also have significant impacts on its entire supply chain, are the result of a company-wide commitment to this project. The company has now obtained ISO 9001:2008 and 14001:2004 certifications, many customer certifications, and has adopted a lean process management philosophy.

Question

How could UltraFit utilise an agile approach in conjunction with its lean strategy?

Sources: adapted from UltraFit Manufacturing, www.ultrafitmanufacturing.com/; and Lean Manufacturing Solutions Inc., www.lmsi.ca/cs.htm#ultrafit (accessed 5 August 2011).

- The creation of '*virtual supply chains*' which are information based rather than inventory based.
- There is an emphasis on maximising product availability and customer service rather than minimising inventory.

In comparison, the lean approach seeks to minimise inventory of components and work-in-progress and to move towards a just-in-time environment wherever possible. Yet firms using an agile approach are meant to respond in shorter time-frames to changes in both volume and variety demanded by customers. Thus, lean works best in high-volume, low-variety and predictable environments while agility is needed in less predictable environments where the demand for variety is high.

While the paradigms appear dichotomous, in reality most organisations probably need both lean and agile logistics and supply chain solutions that suggest using a 'hybrid' strategy. Such a strategy has been developed, as shown in Figure 7.5, and is called 'leagile'. The 'decoupling point' for materials represents the change point from a lean production strategy to an agile production strategy. A well-known example is Benetton's use of delaying the final colour dyeing of garments until market demand information has been received. The information 'decoupling point' represents the point where actual demand or market sales information can assist forecasting efforts within the lean approach of this hybrid solution.

Harley's 'productivity triad' is a hybrid strategy as it is benefiting from lean techniques while being able to customise products as they are built. To be sure, the Harley product is quite simple and consists of really two strategic components: the motorcycle frame and the engine; there are few variants of each. For example, there are different frames for the Touring, Softail, Dyna and Sportster series and two engine variants each for the three former frames and the Sportster frame. Customisation comes in the form of different paint colours and 'accessories' on each bike. Thus, the design of the product lends itself to a degree of manufacturing modularisation,[10] which can take advantage of a 'leagile' strategy.

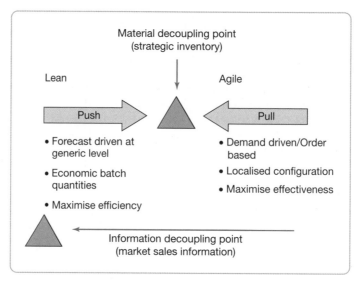

Figure 7.5 A 'hybrid' lean and agile strategy: 'leagile'
Source: adapted from Naylor *et al.* (1999).

The outlook for Harley

In 2010 Harley had worldwide revenue of $4.8 billion from motorcycles and related products, of which motorcycle sales accounted for 75 per cent and sales in the US and Europe accounted for 83 per cent. It had a net profit of $146 million compared with a net loss of $55 million on $4.3 billion revenue in 2009. Harley's performance in 2009 was affected by the global recession and the company thus committed to a combination of restructuring activities designed to reduce administrative costs, eliminate excess capacity and exit non-core business operations.

The distribution facility in Franklin, Wisconsin was scheduled to be closed and distribution operations consolidated through a third-party provider some time in 2011. In addition, certain areas of the York facility were expected to be sold to third parties with sale agreements effective in 2011. In early 2009, the company relocated its previous testing operations in Mesa, Arizona to a new facility in Yucca, Arizona as a first step towards consolidating all three of its testing sites. Beginning in 2010 and continuing into 2011, the motorcycle testing facilities in Talladega, Alabama and Naples, Florida were to be consolidated into the testing facility at Yucca. This ongoing restructuring supports Harley's efforts to become more flexible and cost competitive, allowing it to get the right product at the right time to the customer.

Harley faces substantial tariffs when importing its products into countries like Brazil. To deflect these tariffs it has adopted a postponement strategy and in 1998 opened a new assembly facility in Manaus, Brazil, the first operation outside of the US. This facility is a 'complete knock down' (CKD) assembly plant which will assemble motorcycles for the Indian market from component kits produced by Harley's US plants and its suppliers. Harley ships these component kits and thus delays final assembly until the parts have reached Brazil. This has cut import duties by over 85 per cent. To support its international growth initiatives, Harley has embarked on its second CKD facility in India, which was expected to be operational in 2011.

Summary

The case of Harley-Davidson discussed throughout this chapter has demonstrated what it has achieved by improving its operations, materials management and logistical processes. However, the competitive global marketplace and external environmental factors have forced Harley to go even further in addressing its other business processes in order to remain competitive. Its situation illustrates that while operations, materials management and logistics are cornerstones of any business to ensure the timely provision of quality and relevant products to customers, a strategic outlook is required to stay ahead of any environmental uncertainty, as will be discussed in Chapter 13.

This chapter has covered various aspects of operations and materials handling, such as MRP, MRP II, DRP, ERP, JIT, TQM, lean and agility in the unique factory 'Stop' nodes in the supply chain and discussed their interface with inbound and outbound logistics. One element that was discussed repeatedly was the need for proper information, starting with a master production schedule and bill of materials in an MRP system. The importance of information and various techniques used in logistics and supply chains will be covered in Chapter 8.

DISCUSSION QUESTIONS

1 How important are readily available spare parts to a manufacturer?

2 Compare and contrast the materials requirements planning (MRP) and enterprise resource planning (ERP) approaches.

3 What are the differences between just-in-time (JIT) and total quality management (TQM)?

4 Describe the advantages of the decoupling points in a leagile strategy.

5 What additional techniques discussed in this chapter might Harley-Davidson, Inc. adopt to further improve its business processes?

Suggested reading

Ansari, A. and B. Modarress *Just-in-Time Purchasing*, New York: Free Press, 1990.

Christopher, Martin 'The agile supply chain: Competing in volatile markets,' *Industrial Marketing Management*, 2000, Vol. 29, No. 1, pp.37–44.

Christopher, Martin *Logistics and Supply Chain Management*, 4th ed. Harlow: FT Prentice Hall, 2011.

Fazel, Farzaneh 'A comparative analysis of inventory costs of JIT and EOQ purchasing,' *International Journal of Physical Distribution & Logistics Management*, 1997, Vol. 27, No. 8, pp.496–504.

Foster, S. Thomas *Managing Quality: Integrating the Supply Chain*, Upper Saddle River, NJ: Pearson–Prentice Hall, 2007.

Jones, Daniel T., Peter Hines and Nick Rich 'Lean logistics,' *International Journal of Physical Distribution & Logistics Management*, 1997, Vol. 27, No. 3/4, pp.153–173.

Kotzab, Herbert, David B. Grant and Anders Friis 'Supply chain management implementation and priority strategies in Danish organizations,' *Journal of Business Logistics*, 2006, Vol. 27, No. 2, pp.273–300.

Mikkola, Juliana H. 'Capturing the degree of modularity embedded in product architectures,' *Journal of Product Innovation Management,* 2006, Vol. 23, No. 2, pp.128–146.

Naylor, J. Ben, Mohamed M. Naim and Danny Berry 'Leagility: Integrating the lean and agile manufacturing paradigms in the total supply chain,' *International Journal of Production Economics*, 1999, Vol. 62, pp.107–118.

Reid, Peter C. *Well Made in America*, New York: McGraw-Hill Publishing Company, 1990.

Slack, Nigel, Stuart Chambers and Robert Johnson *Operations Management,* 6th ed. Harlow: FT Prentice Hall, 2010.

Teller, Christoph, Herbert Kotzab and David B. Grant 'Improving the execution of supply chain management in organizations,' *International Journal of Production Economics*, 2011, in press, doi:10.1016/j.ijpe.2011.03.002.

Waters, Donald *Inventory Control and Management,* Chichester: John Wiley & Sons Ltd, 2003.

Womack, James P., Daniel T. Jones and Daniel Roos *The Machine That Changed the World*, London: Simon & Schuster, 2007.

Notes

1 Sources and information for this chapter about these approaches and techniques are adapted from Nigel Slack, Stuart Chambers and Robert Johnson (2010) *Operations Management,* 6th ed. Harlow: FT Prentice Hall; and Donald Waters (2003) *Inventory Control and Management,* Chichester: John Wiley & Sons Ltd.

2 Sources and information for this chapter about these two techniques are adapted from Slack *et al.* (2010); Martin Christopher (2011) *Logistics and Supply Chain Management,* 4th ed. Harlow: FT Prentice Hall, pp.112–116; Daniel T. Jones, Peter Hines and Nick Rich (1997) 'Lean logistics,' *International Journal of Physical Distribution & Logistics Management*, Vol. 27, No. 3/4, pp.153–173; and J. Ben Naylor, Mohamed M. Naim and Danny Berry (1999) 'Leagility: Integrating the lean and agile manufacturing paradigms in the total supply chain,' *International Journal of Production Economics*, Vol. 62, pp.107–118.

3 Sources and information for this chapter about Harley-Davidson are adapted from Peter C. Reid (1990) *Well Made in America*, New York: McGraw-Hill Publishing Company; David B. Grant (1994) *Harley-Davidson: A Case Study of a Corporate Turnaround Using Business Logistics and Marketing*, University of Calgary: Class Teaching Case; Bruce Caldwell (1998) 'Harley shifts into higher gear: Harley-Davidson turns to IT to rev up production and tighten supply chain links,' http://informationweek.com/711/11iuhar.htm (accessed 5 August 2011); and Harley-Davidson, Inc. (2011) www.harley-davidson.com/ (accessed 5 August 2011).

4 A. Ansari and B. Modarress (1990) *Just-in-Time Purchasing*, New York: Free Press.

5 Farzaneh Fazel (1997) 'A comparative analysis of inventory costs of JIT and EOQ purchasing,' *International Journal of Physical Distribution & Logistics Management*, Vol. 27, No. 8, pp.496–504.

6 Ansari and Modarress (1990).

7 Slack *et al.* (2010), p.508.

8 Stephen J. Warwood and Graeme Knowles (2004) 'An investigation into Japanese 5-S practice in UK industry,' *The TQM Magazine,* Vol. 16, No. 5, pp.347–353.

9 See James P. Womack, Daniel T. Jones and Daniel Roos (2007) *The Machine that Changed the World*, London: Simon & Schuster.

10 Juliana H. Mikkola (2006) 'Capturing the degree of modularity embedded in product architectures,' *Journal of Product Innovation Management,* Vol. 23, No. 2, pp.128–146.

Chapter 8

Logistics information technology

Key objectives

- To understand the role of information technology in logistics.
- To further consider warehouse and transportation management systems.
- To describe electronic data interchange and scanning technology.
- To illustrate the concept of cloud computing for logistics applications.
- To explore technology's use in retail replenishment.

Introduction

The role of information technology (IT) applications, also referred to as information and communications technology (ICT), has been briefly discussed for various logistics contexts: e-procurement in Chapter 3, e-tendering and telematics as part of transportation management systems (TMS) in Chapter 4, warehouse automation and warehouse management systems (WMS) in Chapter 5, inventory replenishment in Chapter 6, and a host of applications culminating in enterprise resource planning (ERP) in Chapter 7. Yet IT plays a key role at every stage of the logistics decision-making process and enables managers to make better decisions on the basis of accurate data and information. Several studies of logistics trends in Europe have cited logistics IT systems and electronic commerce or e-commerce as growth areas and keys to competitiveness.[1]

This chapter focuses on broader IT issues and applications supporting logistics and supply chain activities. First it discusses the nature of information and IT systems. It then provides an overview of the main IT systems and applications supporting the management of logistics and supply chain management (SCM) activities using a matrix that segments activities and IT systems. Newly emerging IT such as cloud computing and QR codes issues follow before the chapter concludes with a discussion of retail logistics as it pertains to timely replenishment.

Logistics information technology systems

Data become information only when they are timely and relevant. As discussed in Chapter 1, logistics is focused on providing time and place utility for customers; thus timely information is of the utmost importance. However, if the information is meaningless or confusing then it has no relevance. Thus, data from any logistics IT system must be able to address both these issues before they are appropriate for logistics and supply chain users.

Chapter 7 discussed the two key documents for operations and material handling: the master production schedule (MPS) and the bill of materials (BOM). However, two other important documents are the shipping document or bill of lading and the customer order. If logistics is a flow process comprising 'Stop' and 'Go' activities, then knowledge of what products are coming, where they are, and where they are going is vital to maintain effective (i.e. meet everyone's needs) and efficient (i.e. with respect to time and costs) flow.

The rapid changes that have affected the evolution of logistics and SCM concepts in recent decades have been accompanied by a parallel development in IT systems and applications. The use of IT in the field of logistics has increased over the past 30 years, delivering significant benefits in terms of enabling management to make decisions which have a significant impact on the company's performance. The successful application of IT in logistics depends on the objectives and type of technology being deployed. Direct IT applications for logistics activities include:

- repetitive transactions;
- creating customer orders or making payments through EDI and EPOS;
- creating operations planning systems such as ERP;
- operating computerised routing and vehicle scheduling (CRVS);
- achieving a greater level of systems control;
- performing load and item tracking and tracing, including using RFID;
- supporting strategic decision making;
- automating warehouse operations and monitoring performance.

Regarding the type of technology there are four primary categories of logistics and supply chain solutions:[2]

- *point solutions*, which are used to support the execution of one link or point in the supply chain, e.g. a TMS such as Optrak or a WMS such as Swisslog;
- *'best of breed' solutions*, where two or more existing stand-alone solutions are integrated, usually using middleware technology to connect them and functioning as a conversion or translation layer as well as a consolidator and integrator;
- *enterprise solutions*, which are based on the logic of ERP, as discussed in Chapter 7;
- *extended enterprise solutions* (XES), which refer to the collaborative sharing of information and processes between the partners along the supply chain using the technological underpinnings of ERP and possibly a web-based platform to communicate. This concept is illustrated in Logistics Example 8.1.

LOGISTICS EXAMPLE 8.1

An integrated ERP solution for LOGiCOM

The IT sector argues that if a firm integrates its ERP, SCM and Customer relationship management (CRM) systems then it will have the best of all possible situations. However, a survey by Siebel Systems of its customers found that, on average, 50 systems need to be integrated and 51 per cent of customers need to integrate in excess of 50 systems. This is the real world, with lots of systems and, critically, a large number of existing or 'legacy' systems requiring integration. The reasons for IT system integration can be a merger or acquisition, change of business strategy, company expansion or the addition of suppliers and customers. But the underlying issue is always the need to manage a complex flow of information from a variety of disparate and incompatible systems.

LOGiCOM, an independent pan-European provider of comprehensive logistics services for IT service parts, faced such an issue in 2001 when it was spun off from its parent company, Fujitsu Services (formerly ICL). LOGiCOM serves the needs of original equipment manufacturers (OEMs) and multi-vendor service providers by coordinating all supply chain activities required to source, manage and deliver parts to field service engineers or end-consumers. The company has premises in more than 60 locations across Europe, providing a 365-day, 24-hour operation and distributing to 83 countries worldwide. It handles 50,000 part requests every month and maintains a multi-vendor inventory valued at £50 million.

LOGiCOM rejected the costly option of customising its legacy ERP system in favour of an integration strategy using an integration broker to link new best-of-breed applications into the framework. Instead, it selected SeeBeyond's 'e*Gate Integrator' against other solutions available on the market. Implementation began in March 2001. Cap Gemini Ernst & Young was responsible for developing the integration solution while SeeBeyond's consultants ensured the overall design and architecture were appropriate and that the Integrator was configured and installed correctly. Two interfaces were developed: the parts for service (PAFOS) interface, which operates between LOGiCOM's ERP system and multiple external service delivery systems, and the carrier interface, which has a similar relationship with external carrier systems.

LOGiCOM achieved integration with a major new OEM customer and its maintenance company in July 2001, followed in October 2001 by integration with one of its main third-party carriers, UPS. When the OEM needs spare parts for one of its own customers, it sends a parts request message to LOGiCOM over the internet using the Integrator. This message is routed to the ERP system to automatically allocate stock to the request. The allocated stock is picked and added to a shipping manifest that is automatically transmitted to UPS by the Integrator. The carrier picks up the part at the warehouse and delivers it to the OEM's customer. During transit, the carrier sends frequent track-and-trace information to LOGiCOM, to automatically update the part's request status and feed this information to the OEM through the Integrator. A similar approach is used to manage the collection of failing parts when required by the customer. Normally, all the processes are completed within time periods necessary to achieve the customer's service-level agreement, demonstrating the benefit of real-time supply chain integration.

The LOGiCOM situation illustrates one way to solve an issue of 'legacy' integration in the short term to protect an application investment in the long term. Other benefits of IT integration strategy come from the flexibility a company can portray to potential trading partners and resultant revenue opportunities from those partnerships.

Logistics example 8.1 (*cont.*)

Question

What do you think are the implications of a firm changing its legacy IT systems for its suppliers and customers?

Source: adapted from Ian Howells 'Integrating IT systems: Legacy no problem,' *Logistics & Transport Focus*, 2003, Vol. 5, No. 2, pp.37–40.

Point solutions and functionally focused applications in transport and logistics link planning and control activities. Such applications, often based on sophisticated algorithms, e.g. linear programming, mixed-integer programming or genetic algorithms, include TMS and WMS. The aim of TMS is to optimise the management of product shipping. Five functionalities are typically incorporated in this application: freight payment auditing, transportation planning, carrier performance, trailer loading and vehicle/fleet management. The main benefit associated with using TMS is the capacity of the firm to increase the speed of order processing with a high service level without incurring additional operating costs. Further, TMS allows the automation of the above activities, thus allowing a company's transportation function to manage, instead of reacting to, transportation events and opportunities.

WMS is a software package that enables maximisation of the use of space, equipment and labour. It enables the execution of inventory planning commands, inventory and location control and the management of the flow of warehouse orders and processes on a day-to-day basis. The main benefits relate to reductions in order fulfilment lead time and inventory management. These include improved customer service and quicker turnover of inventory, resulting in substantial potential savings in warehousing operational costs.

The move away from point and 'best-of-breed' solutions towards enterprise and XES solutions in many ways reflects the shift from traditional internally oriented to more integrated process-oriented logistics and SCM models in recent years. Other integrative technologies, in particular EDI and the internet, have enabled upstream and downstream supply chain partners to use common data which facilitates agility as companies can act based on real-time demand rather than be dependent on the distorted and noisy picture that emerges when orders are transmitted from one step to another in an extended chain. It also facilitates higher levels of inventory visibility throughout the supply chain, thereby creating conditions where excessive reliance on stockholding and forecasting can be reduced.

Considering the significant range of technology tools and options available, with complex and varying levels of functionality, it is important to have a picture that facilitates an understanding of the roles of the various technologies that are used in different logistics functions. Figure 8.1 provides a matrix that covers the types of applications for the logistics functions of order and fulfilment, inventory, warehousing and transportation.[3]

It has been built on two dimensions: the scope of the logistics function covered by the information system (horizontal) and the decision-making level in which the system is used (vertical). The horizontal dimension defines the scope of the information and communication system; cross-functional information systems have also been considered as there are many systems on the market that are able to integrate the different applications used at the functional level in one single software package. The vertical dimension denotes the levels within the logistics decision-making process for which an IT system is adopted. Four different

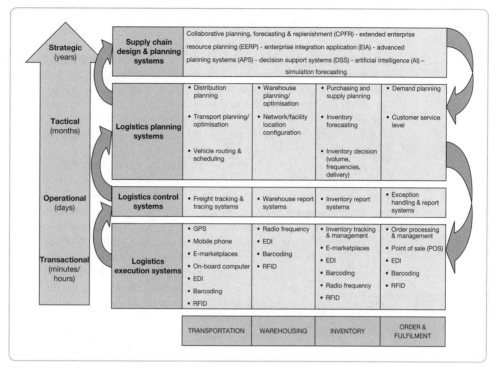

Figure 8.1 ICT systems and logistics applications

Source: Evangelista (2007, p.251).

phases have been identified – strategic, tactical, operational and transactional – according to the different types of problems they are required to solve. Each phase also has a different time-frame, ranging from short term to long term. For example, IT supporting transportation opti-misation and network facilities configuration provides the basis for tactical logistics planning decisions on a monthly basis. Meanwhile, IT applications used in the logistics transactional phase have to provide-real time information about order, inventory, warehouse and transpor-tation management in real time, i.e. by the minute, or daily at the most. Chapter 13 discusses strategic issues and the different phases in strategic planning; see also Logistics Example 8.2.

LOGISTICS EXAMPLE 8.2

Supply chain technology integration in the chemical processing industry

Basell Polyolefins Company is the world's largest producer of polypropylene, a leading supplier of polyethylene and advanced polyolefin products, and a global leader in the development and licensing of polypropylene and polyethylene processes and catalysts. Basell was created in 2000 from subsidiaries of Shell and BASF and its corporate centre is located in Hoofddorp, the Netherlands. The company maintains regional offices in Wilmington, DE, Brussels, Mainz, Germany, São Paulo, Brazil and Hong Kong. It serves more than 4,000 customers in over 120 countries and its largest market segments are

---

flexible packaging, which includes food and soft drinks, consumer products packaging, the automotive industry and the consumer goods industry.

Basell is the global leader in the production of polypropylene, with capacity of more than 8,000 kilo tonnes, including its joint ventures. It is also the seventh largest producer of polyethylene in the world and number one in Europe, with capacity of more than 2,500 kilo tonnes, including its joint ventures. Basell employs 6,600 people worldwide to generate annual turnover of about €6.7 billion.

In such a commoditised market, Basell faces significant challenges in differentiating itself and really adding value in its supply chain. Martin Feuerhahn, Senior Vice President Supply Chain – Europe, says that the company 'recognised from the beginning that only a fully integrated supply chain would allow it to effectively and efficiently deploy its multiple resources'. At Basell, such deployment meant fully integrated order-to-cash and demand-to-supply processes supported by SAP's R3 software system. SAP's APO software is also used for Basell's forecasting, planning, plan execution and product sourcing optimisation.

Feuerhahn believes supply chain integration, for example with customers through vendor managed inventory (VMI) or with logistics service providers via the internet tool 'Basell Connect', is an important prerequisite for an adaptable and responsive supply chain.

The speed with which Basell created one unified company with aligned processes across Europe and sharing a common database is impressive. The SAP systems implementation has provided real visibility over the entire supply chain across different countries and sectors. Connectivity with Basell's supply base, customer base and transport operations already sees over 20 per cent of orders being entered electronically and growing.

Question

What other industry sectors could follow Basell's strategy to enhance their processes and logistics?

Source: adapted from Sam Tulip 'The European Supply Chain Excellence Awards 2003,' *Supply Chain Standard* (formerly *Logistics Europe*), 2003, Vol. 11, No. 10, p.47.

The level at the top of the matrix is referred to as the *supply chain design and planning systems* level. It refers to strategic decisions that go beyond the scope of logistics management to embrace a firm's corporate strategy and the entire supply chain configuration and planning. The time-frame of decisions at this level spans many years and managers need to define target customer segments, types of products to manufacture, the number of production sites to be involved and their location, the type of distribution systems to be adopted, and decisions about vertical integration and outsourcing. IT used at this level is highly analytical as it is focused on analysing rather than gathering information. The main characteristics of IT adopted at this level include collaborative planning (CPFR), extended enterprise planning (EERP), enterprise integration applications (EIA), advanced planning systems (APS) and various decision support systems (DSS), some of which make use of artificial intelligence (AI), simulation and forecasting.

The *logistics planning systems* level focuses on information support to develop and refine logistics activities within a firm. Such systems enable accurate planning for each logistics activity. The main objective is to allocate available resources among the different logistics activities. This level is of particular importance as it provides a critical link between the supply chain decision level and decisions affecting a firm's logistics functions. Typical planning decisions involve time-frames of several months to a year. Information requirements at this level include costs, capacities and demand to assist managers in identifying, evaluating and comparing tactical logistics alternatives. Typical analyses include transport planning or optimisation, vehicle routing and scheduling, warehouse planning or optimisation, network or facility location configuration, purchasing and supply planning, and inventory forecasting. Planning decisions at this level also focus on analysing rather than gathering information.

The *logistics control systems* level is focused on performance measurement and management reporting for each logistics function. Here it is important to identify exceptions that allow the solution for problems related to specific customers or orders. Logistics control systems are focused on both gathering and analysing information.

Logistics execution systems initiate and record individual logistics activities. Such systems aim to execute what has been planned earlier in higher levels and deal with time-frames of typically minutes or hours. At this level IT systems execute and record transactions that include order entry, inventory assignment, order selection, transportation, pricing, invoicing and customer enquiry. This level is information intensive as it requires that information be available for every transaction executed. Logistics execution systems are characterised by formalised rules and a large volume of transactions. For this reason, the emphasis is on system efficiency that means faster processing or higher transaction volume with fewer resources. The typical example in this field is EDI, which has become the transaction system messaging standard in many industries.

Electronic data interchange

As noted above, EDI is the electronic, computer-to-computer transfer of standard business documents between firms. For example, Wal-Mart can collect daily sales data from its electronic point-of-sale scanners for all of its stock keeping units and then send reports each night to a supplier showing its sales by SKU as well as stock levels throughout the Wal-Mart system in order to assist the supplier in making replenishment decisions, especially if they are operating on a vendor managed inventory (VMI) basis.

EDI is usually considered to be electronic business or e-business, which is the use of electronic information technologies to conduct business transactions among buyers, sellers and other trading partners to improve customer service, reduce costs and open new channels to help drive shareholder value; it is a B2B concept. Electronic commerce or e-commerce, meanwhile, is the marketing, selling and buying of products and services on the internet; it is both a business-to-consumer (B2C) and a B2B concept as firms have the ability to use the internet to effect EDI.

An issue with EDI is the multitude of protocols in use today. Some are unique systems created by and for a particular firm. Some standards have been adopted within a certain industry. The American National Standards Institute (ANSI) has proposed the use of the ANSI X12 standard, for use in the US, while the Trade Electronic Data Interchange System (TEDIS) is the standard adopted for use in the EU. While standards such as these are designed to allow communications between different computers, they are only message formats: they do not specify how communications will take place between the trading partners and another networking service is needed to transmit messages between them. Such services also have protocols, such as the Odette file transfer protocol (OFTP), to provide a standardised way for separate computer systems to communicate with each other. OFTP is a high-level protocol and is applied to the way messages are sent rather than the physical communications line across which they travel.

The physical connections are also standardised and are covered by other protocols such as X.25 and TCP/IP. X.25 is a packet switched data network protocol which defines an international recommendation for data exchange as well as control information between a user device or host and a network node. TCP/IP, or Transmission Control Protocol/Internet Protocol, is a suite of communication protocols used to connect hosts on the internet.[4]

Using EDI over the internet is rapidly becoming a reality, with annual growth rates in excess of 50 per cent.[5] After initial software purchase and systems set-up, EDI over the internet is virtually 'free' versus transmission by a third-party value-added network (VAN). EDI over the internet also uses various protocols such as OFTP or HTTP, which is the hypertext transfer protocol everyone is familiar with when using the worldwide web. A key issue for firms using the internet is security. A secure website uses a secured socket layer (SSL) that functions by using a private 'key' to encrypt data that is transferred over the SSL. For example, the UK grocery retailer Tesco integrated its 'Tesco.com' online customer order processing systems using EDI. A customer order received from the website is sent to the computer server at the store nearest to the customer's home and is then assigned to the van that will deliver the goods. It is then sent to a 'picking trolley', a shopping cart with a screen and 'shelf identifier' software that takes a picker to where each item is found. Pickers scan the items they select and the system compares barcode details with the item ordered on the customer's shopping list, sounding an alert if the wrong item is selected. Pickers also inspect expiry dates and check for damage on every item. Once the trolley is loaded, it is sent straight to the van for delivery. Average picking time is 30 seconds per item and a typical order of 64 items could be fulfilled in about 30 minutes. Pickers work during normal store trading hours but usually go around stores when they are not crowded, between 6am and 10am, and 11am and 3pm. Two to three waves of orders are filled per day so an order placed as late as noon could be delivered by 10pm the same day. Tesco's picking-out-of-store approach enabled the rollout of this online service that meets the needs of 'cash-rich' and 'time-poor' customers.[6]

The key to EDI and scanning is the identification of individual SKUs at item level, which is accomplished by use of a barcode. Although there are several forms of barcodes, the most popular standard in Europe is the European Article Numbering (EAN) Uniform Code Council (UCC), with over 1 million firms operating under that system. To obtain a barcode, a firm must register with EAN International to receive an assigned and unique barcode prefix to use with all its products. The firm must then allocate a unique number to each product.

Barcoding can be useful in logistics applications, particularly in track-and-trace situations. Receiving also can be automated, which further contributes to cycle time reduction and data accuracy. These data can automatically be used by the accounts payable department for generating cheques and reconciling invoices with purchase orders and receiving. Thus, barcoding represents a logical extension of the organisation's information systems and a linkage with EDI.

Barcodes are accurate and efficient. Since 1995 they have proved their worth as an enabling technology contributing to manufacturing cost reduction, quality improvement, cycle time reduction and improved profitability. The technology is a passive format, i.e. the firm must seek out the item and scan the barcode. A successor technology, radio frequency identification (RFID), is an active format that is being developed for logistics applications around the world and is discussed further in Logistics Example 8.3.

LOGISTICS EXAMPLE 8.3

The RFID revolution

Radio frequency identification is a technology considered to improve logistics and supply chain management. RFID systems use radio frequencies to provide automatic identification and location of electronic data-carrying devices or 'tags' attached to items and can be either 'active' – the tag is powered by a battery and sends out a radio signal – or 'passive' – must be sought out and read by a mobile scanner.

RFID tags consist of a semiconductor chip with memory-processing capability and a transmitter connected to an antenna. The memory can be configured to read only, write once, read many times or read/write. The tags can be detected by radio frequencies at a remote distance from a reader without the necessity of contact or line of sight. A network or computer information system can process the data received for final application, such as materials handling, inventory replenishment, asset and product tracking, anti-counterfeiting or safety and security functions.

When compared with other auto-identification systems such as barcodes, RFID technology offers additional benefits such as fewer labour requirements, reading speed and multiple reading, read/write capacity and higher security levels.

The cost of RFID tags is still something of a barrier, particularly at individual item level – for example, putting a 5 pence passive tag on a 50 pence tin of beans. Standards are also slow in being developed, although the Auto-ID Center at the Massachusetts Institute of Technology is working towards global harmonisation.

There are some technical issues, one of which pertains to differences in radio-communication UHF radiation limits between Europe and the US. Europe limits are 0.5 watts while US limits are 4 watts. The European limits being 100 times slower than US limits means the readable range in Europe would also be 100 times lower than in the US. Also, an issue in the retailing and warehousing environment relates to the risk of tags being misread due to metal interference.

Question

What other uses can you foresee for RFID technology?

Sources: adapted from Richard Wilding and Tiago Delgado 'The story so far: RFID demystified,' *Logistics & Transport Focus*, 2004, Vol. 6, No. 3, pp.26–31; 'RFID demystified: Supply chain applications,' *Logistics & Transport Focus*, Vol. 6, No. 4, pp.42–48; 'RFID demystified: Company case studies,' *Logistics & Transport Focus*, Vol. 6, No. 5, pp.32–42; and Tim Butcher 'Radio frequency identification: An enabler of agile supply chain decision-making,' *International Journal of Agile Systems and Management*, 2007, Vol. 2, No. 3, pp.305–320.

Quick response (QR) codes

Another new technology started in a B2B environment but currently being adopted in B2C applications is quick response code. A QR code is a specific two-dimensional matrix barcode that is readable by dedicated QR readers, smartphones and, to a less common extent, computers with webcams. The code consists of black modules arranged in a square pattern on a white background. The information encoded may be text, URL or other data.

QR codes were designed in 1994 by the Toyota subsidiary Denso-Wave to allow content to be decoded at high speed. Although initially used for tracking parts in vehicle manufacturing,

QR codes now are used in a much broader context, including both commercial tracking applications and convenience-oriented applications aimed at mobile phone users, termed mobile tagging.

The technology has been embraced and is in use in Japan, the Netherlands and South Korea, but has enjoyed only relatively recent use in the US and North America. One of the largest barriers preventing people from using QR codes is simply awareness of the technology. Smartphones make up 32 per cent of mobile phones owned by adults in the UK. This is significant because as more consumers use smartphones they are discovering QR codes. Google has recently seen an increase in searches about the technology. Although there has been very little research on the use of QR codes in the UK, according to 3GVision the UK was the seventh largest user of mobile barcodes in the world in the fourth quarter of 2010.[7]

In a B2C context QR codes are a really cost-effective way to provide more information and drive consumers online. They are interactive by their very nature and allow engagement to be measured. Brands can gain insight from metrics such as unique user usage, when and where the code was seen and even the duration of the interaction.

QR codes can hold several hundred digits and function even if they are partially damaged. They are also omni-directional, which means they are readable from any direction, ensuring high-speed scanning. Some better smartphones can read a QR code from a distance of about 15 metres. From a technical perspective QR codes have more advantages than other barcodes. Universal product codes (UPCs) have their limitations as they are only capable of storing up to 20 digits and can easily be corrupted. Also, a large part of the successful adoption of UPCs is a result of industry support. However, many firms, including Metro, Tesco, Calvin Klein, eBay and P&G, are leveraging the advantages of QR codes at a B2C level for their brands.

QR barcodes have many disadvantages, which are currently hindering their adoption in the West. One of the largest issues is the standardisation of symbols and a move towards open standards. One of the reasons UPC has been so successful is simply because it is universal. With so many different code versions, from 'QR' to Microsoft's 'Tag', there is no standard reader. Therefore, a consumer has to download multiple readers in order to scan different codes. QR codes or 2D barcodes in general are also easily defrauded when used for payments. By simply taking a photo of the code, it can be reused.

However, the advantages of QR code technology may have advantages for logistics and supply chain situations where UPC and RFID have disadvantages, for example the ease of reading a QR code from a distance versus having to get close to a UPC barcode or RFID tag. It is still early days for this technology, but QR codes are an interesting development with potential.

Cloud computing[8]

The term 'cloud computing' has been used in IT circles for several years now. Cloud computing describes a technological solution that removes the need for a firm to have its own premises-based IT server in favour of a supplied and managed remote service accessible over a high-speed network connection. The firm has access to its data and software over the internet which in most diagrams is shown as a 'cloud' or virtual server.

Cloud based servers are placed in secure, serviced, custom-built locations and have reliable, high-speed, high-bandwidth network connections. Server operating systems, databases and software are installed and maintained by the supplier's staff and data is backed up according to automated schedules as required.

There are several key benefits to the cloud:

- *Cost*: There are significant cost savings due to the removal of the need for expensive inter-branch network connections, company computer servers and support. Secure computing capacity is provided on a rental basis as required with no capital costs, and comprehensive technical support is usually provided as part of the service, thus it has advantages for new firms and small and medium-sized enterprises (SMEs);
- *Speed of access and usability*: The cloud provides elasticity, making it possible to scale-up at pace with minimal waste of time and capital, and even switch applications entirely without a lot of added cost or complexity. This allows firms to enter new markets or launch new services quickly. Further, firms can rapidly implement and operate applications that are secure and inexpensive, while enjoying lower IT maintenance and upgrade costs.
- *Reliability and resilience*: Data from existing in-house stock management systems can be uploaded to the cloud for secure remote access, interrogation and storage;
- *Operational support and upgrades for the servers and network*: Support and upgrades for the servers and network are included in the service and provided by the supplier.

Keyfort Limited, a cloud and IT supplier in Hull, England, has developed a logistics management information system in a cloud application called Keyfort Data Interchange Service (KDIS). KDIS takes data, stores it and then manipulates it to provide reports, analysis and on-demand enquiry responses. Features of KDIS include:

- Integration with existing applications such as a TMS or WMS such that familiar and working in-house systems do not have to be replaced;
- Integration with existing transportation carrier systems;
- Provision of access to carrier brokerage services;
- Transit shipment visibility;
- Production and completion of necessary paperwork;
- A simple but secure interface via Internet browser for staff and trading partners from any web enabled location;
- A management information system with storage capacity for three years of data; and
- System resilience, auto backups and capacity upgrades as part of the service.

While the KDIS 'cloud' system is for use by any firm, Keyfort has also developed a specific, optional application called KeyPOD to improve product traceability across a firm's delivery operations using a driver's 'smartphone'. Using KeyPOD, distribution centres and carriers can work more efficiently together and provide a better service for firms by sharing real-time delivery information as and when it is required.

In summary, the use of mobile technology and cloud computing appears to provide online, real-time benefits for firms, particularly in logistics and supply chain environments where time and reliability are of paramount importance.

IT and retail replenishment

A major concern for retailers is shelf replenishment to ensure on-shelf availability (OSA) and reduce out-of-stocks (OOS) for consumers. The five consumer reactions to an in-store OOS are:

1 Consumers buy the item at another store (store switching).

2 Consumers delay ordering or purchasing the item (postpone purchase at the same store).

3 Consumers do not purchase the item (a lost sale).

4 Consumers substitute the same brand (different size or type).

5 Consumers substitute another brand (brand switching).

About 65 per cent of UK consumers looking for a specific grocery item will adopt one of the first three reactions, thus not buying in that particular store on that occasion if a stock-out occurs. The retailer then incurs a 'lost sale' for that product. ECR Europe has indicated that the cost of lost sales for the entire European grocery sector due to lack of products being available on-shelf is over €4 billion per annum.[9]

Retailers have attempted to solve OOS and increase OSA through a number of IT-driven initiatives: efficient consumer response (ECR) and collaborative planning, forecasting and replenishment in the food sector and quick response in the non-food sector.

The concept of ECR was introduced at the beginning of the 1990s by the US-based Food Marketing Institute (FMI). The objective of ECR is to organise the entire grocery supply chain in a holistic way by implementing strategic alliances between involved actors which ensure a profitable situation for every single member of the chain despite stagnant markets, i.e. a win/win/win situation. Such cooperative management increases total channel performance as compared with managing the channel in an isolated way such as through pure market exchange.[10]

The ECR concept suggests integrating specific business functions between retailers and suppliers and operating the business based on specific processes such as category management, continuous replenishment programmes (CRP), cross docking, efficient unit load (EUL), and standards for item identification and communication in supply chains. Figure 8.2 shows the distinction between supply side and demand side, as well as between processes and standards. Both supply and demand sides include 'involved' departments, e.g. procurement, logistics, marketing and sales, at both retailer and manufacturer levels. Processes and standards represent the content of ECR and the way business should be performed in channels of distribution.

There are three stages of ECR which reflect different levels of interdependence and levels of coordination between the involved members. The first stage, industry ECR, refers to the adaptation of common standards, such as EAN codes, EDI standards and certified pools for master data, in order to gain critical mass. The implementation of specific processes between several channel actors takes place at the next stage. These processes, e.g. cross-docking, are based on implemented standards and norms or network ECR. The final stage is the so-called partnership ECR where more sophisticated collaborative processes, e.g. category management, are executed in dyadic partnerships. This approach includes an implicit logic of having implemented certain standards on a broad level in the total channel. Certain firms then have the capabilities to transform these standards into processes and only selected channel players are able to perform ECR on the highest level.

ECR Europe has identified seven 'levers' that can be used to improve OSA. These are measurement 'levers' which need 'managerial attention' (levers 1 and 2); 'replenishment' and 'in-store execution,' namely merchandising (levers 3 and 4); 'inventory accuracy' (lever 5); and 'promotional management' and 'ordering systems' (levels 6 and 7). In order to address the 'seven levers', certain pre-requisites are required, such as management commitment and a motivated workforce; strong information technology systems, a centralised buying and logistics network infrastructure; and a high degree of intra- and inter-collaboration within the sector.[11]

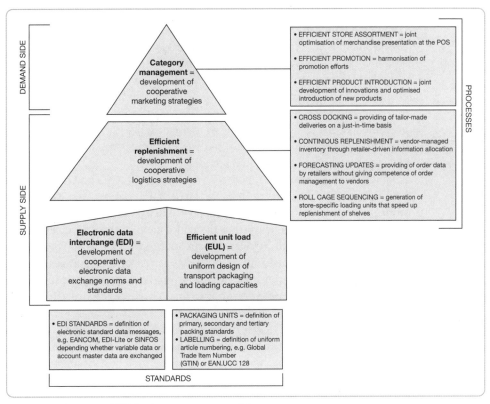

Figure 8.2 A generic ECR business process model

Source: A Model for Structuring Efficient Consumer Response Measures, *International Journal of Retail & Distribution Management*, Vol. 36, No. 8, p. 593 (Aastrup, J., Kotzab, H., Grant, D.B., Teller, C. and Bjerre, M. 2008), International Journal of Retail & Distribution Management by Emerald Group Publishing Limited. Reproduced with permission of Emerald Group Publishing Limited in the format Journal via Copyright Clearance Center. © Emerald Group Publishing Limited all rights reserved.

The UK leads the way in European ECR implementation due to ECR UK being integrated with, and supported by, the UK's IGD, formerly the Institute of Grocery Distribution. Also, in order to improve operational efficiencies, UK grocery retailers have streamlined their supply chains. From centralisation of distribution in the 1980s companies began to integrate primary and secondary distribution to reduce lead times and take inventory out of the retail supply chain. In the 1990s/early 2000s the UK was considered to have one of the most efficient grocery supply chains in the world. And yet, even the UK's use of ECR is not without its flaws regarding collaboration and relationships between suppliers and retailers.[12]

Collaborative planning, forecasting and replenishment is a cross-industry initiative designed to improve supplier, manufacturer and retailer relationships through co-managed planning processes and shared information.[13] Requirements for CPFR include:

- *process model* – how and where forecast collaboration fits into supply chain processes;
- *front-end agreements* – changes to trading partner agreements to support, define and measure collaboration;
- *data sharing* – definition of the data elements to be shared to support collaboration;
- *common metrics* – definition of measures to ensure achievement of objectives of collaboration, e.g. reduce supply chain inventories and increase sales and profits;
- *rule sets* – defines how partners will determine which forecasts require collaboration.

Since the 1998 publication of the CPFR guidelines by the Voluntary Interindustry Commerce Solutions Association (VICS), over 300 companies have implemented the process. Numerous case studies of CPFR projects document OSA improvements of 2–8 per cent accompanied by inventory reductions of 10–40 per cent across the supply chain.

By linking sales and marketing best practices such as category management to supply chain planning and execution processes, CPFR increases availability while reducing inventory, transportation and logistics costs. The experience gained from pilot and production implementations of CPFR has yielded many insights. In 2004, the VICS CPFR committee developed a major revision of the CPFR model to integrate innovations and overcome shortcomings identified in the original process.

Quick response strategies, not to be confused with QR codes above, were developed in the US in the 1980s and also applied in the UK. QR is defined as a consumer-driven business strategy of cooperative planning by supply chain partners using IT and flexible manufacturing to eliminate inefficiencies from the entire supply chain. In essence, raw material suppliers, manufacturers and retailers create long-term relationships to reduce the timescale of manufacturing and distribution processes to respond to changes in demand while also keeping items available on-shelf. Retail buyers book production time but do not finalise product specification until closer to the time of delivery in order to get as close to actual demand as possible.

The objective behind QR was threefold. First, QR was introduced to reduce excess stocks along the supply chain; second, to reduce forecasting risk by making the decision of what and how much to produce and buy closer to the time of consumer purchase; and third, to pass on to consumers some of the savings gained through greater efficiencies. One important similarity between QR and ECR is the use of time in the form of speed to market as a competitive weapon. This strategy involves all of the firm's operations throughout the supply chain, including shorter development times, efficient transportation and delivery using IT, and floor-ready merchandise with price tickets and barcodes already installed.[14]

QR was a good strategy by non-food retailers for improving speed to market by domestic suppliers through mutually beneficial long-term relationships. However, the last decade has seen increased offshore sourcing even for high-fashion goods and the debate has now focused upon a supply chain strategy that best suits this evolving market. For most non-food retailers, particularly fashion and clothing retailers, this has meant having to meet more demanding lead times from more distant markets. IT continues to be important in this context with sourcing, ordering, and tracking and tracing.

Summary

IT systems support all logistical activities, particularly in a global and complex business environment. There are IT applications for every level in the organisation and they are the most involved and costly at a firm's corporate strategy level, which involves collaboration and information sharing across the supply chain. Various platforms and operative technologies, such as ERP, ECR, CPFR, EDI, RFID and cloud computing, offer IT choice to firms, but decision making can be a difficult process.

This chapter has discussed all these issues, but technology marches on rapidly and by the time you are reading this text it is very likely that newer technological applications will already be in use. Thus, vigilance and environmental scanning of IT and logistics issues is vital to ensure a good choice that provides value for money.

The next chapter considers financial aspects and performance for logistics and SCM.

DISCUSSION QUESTIONS

1 Discuss the importance of information technology for logistics and supply chain management.

2 Describe the type of IT used in various logistics functions at the four different decision-making levels.

3 What are the benefits of electronic data interchange (EDI)?

4 What logistics and supply chain applications could benefit from cloud computing?

5 Compare efficient consumer response (ECR), collaborative planning, forecasting and replenishment (CPFR) and quick response (QR) replenishment strategies.

Suggested reading

Aastrup, Jesper, Herbert Kotzab, David B. Grant, Christoph Teller and Mogens Bjerre 'A model for structuring efficient consumer response measures,' *International Journal of Retail & Distribution Management*, 2008, Vol. 36, No. 8, pp.590–606.

Birtwistle, Grete, Noreen Siddiqui and Susan S. Fiorito 'Quick response: Perceptions of UK fashion retailers,' *International Journal of Retail & Distribution Management*, 2003, Vol. 31, No. 2, pp.118–128.

Butcher, Tim 'Radio frequency identification: An enabler of agile supply chain decision-making,' *International Journal of Agile Systems and Management*, 2007, Vol. 2, No. 3, pp.305–320.

Evangelista, Pietro 'Information and communications technology (ICT) applications in transportation and logistics,' in Edward Sweeney (ed.) *Perspectives on Supply Chain Management and Logistics*, Dublin: Blackhall Publishing, 2007, pp.249–264.

Fernie, John and David B. Grant 'On-shelf availability: The case of a UK grocery retailer,' *International Journal of Logistics Management*, 2008, Vol. 19, No. 3, pp.293–308.

Grant, David B. 'The transaction–relationship dichotomy in logistics and supply chain management,' *Supply Chain Forum: An International Journal*, 2005, Vol. 6, No. 2, pp.38–48.

Grant, David B. and John Fernie 'On-shelf availability and out-of-stocks in UK retailing,' in Peter Schnedlitz, Dirk Morschett, Thomas Rudolph, Hans Schramm-Klein and Bernhard Swoboda (eds.) *European Retail Research*, Wiesbaden: Gabler, 2009, Vol. 23, No. 2, pp.51–76.

Grant, David B., Herbert Kotzab and Yuan Xing 'success@tesco.com: Erfolg im Online-Lebensmittelhandel oder "Wie macht das der Tesco?",' in Peter Schnedlitz, Renate Buber, Thomas Reutterer, Arnold Schuh and Christoph Teller (eds.) *Innovationen In Marketing Und Handel*, Vienna: Linde, 2003, pp.203–213.

Howells, Ian 'Integrating IT systems: Legacy no problem,' *Logistics & Transport Focus*, 2003, Vol. 5, No. 2, pp.37–40.

Lim, Don and Prashant C. Palvia 'EDI in strategic supply chain: Impact on customer service,' *International Journal of Information Management,* 2001, Vol. 21, pp.193–211.

Ludwick, David P. and David B. Grant 'Simulation models and quality of service in IP networks – an exploratory investigation,' *Operational Research: An International Journal*, 2002, Vol. 2, No. 1, pp.71–84.

McDonnell, Ronan, John Kenny and Edward Sweeney 'The role of information and communications technology in the supply chain,' in Edward Sweeney (ed.) *Perspectives on Supply Chain Management and Logistics*, Dublin: Blackhall Publishing, 2007, pp.235–248.

Wilding, Richard and Tiago Delgado 'The story so far: RFID demystified,' *Logistics & Transport Focus*, 2004, Vol. 6, No. 3, pp.26–31.

Wilding, Richard and Tiago Delgado 'RFID demystified: Supply chain applications,' *Logistics & Transport Focus*, 2004, Vol. 6, No. 4, pp.42–48.

Wilding, Richard and Tiago Delgado 'RFID demystified: Company case studies,' *Logistics & Transport Focus*, 2004, Vol. 6, No. 5, pp.32–42.

Notes

1 Helmut Baumgarten and Frank Straube (1997) *Towards the 21st Century – Trends and Strategies in European Logistics*, Brussels: European Logistics Association; and Alan C. McKinnon and Mike Forster (2000) *European Logistical and Supply Chain Trends: 1999–2005*, Edinburgh: Heriot-Watt University.

2 Ronan McDonnell, John Kenny and Edward Sweeney (2007) 'The role of information and communications technology in the supply chain,' in Edward Sweeney (ed.) *Perspectives on Supply Chain Management and Logistics*, Dublin: Blackhall Publishing, pp.235–248.

3 This figure and this section are adapted from Pietro Evangelista (2007) 'Information and communications technology (ICT) applications in transportation and logistics,' in Edward Sweeney (ed.) *Perspectives on Supply Chain Management and Logistics*, Dublin: Blackhall Publishing, pp.249–264.

4 David P. Ludwick and David B. Grant (2002) 'Simulation models and quality of service in IP networks – an exploratory investigation,' *Operational Research: An International Journal*, Vol. 2, No. 1, pp.71–84.

5 Don Lim and Prashant C. Palvia (2001) 'EDI in strategic supply chain: Impact on customer service,' *International Journal of Information Management*, Vol. 21, pp.193–211.

6 David B. Grant, Herbert Kotzab and Yuan Xing (2003) 'success@tesco.com: Erfolg im Online-Lebensmittelhandel oder "Wie macht das der Tesco?",' in Peter Schnedlitz, Renate Buber, Thomas Reutterer, Arnold Schuh and Christoph Teller (eds.) *Innovationen In Marketing Und Handel*, Vienna: Linde, pp.203–213.

7 Oliver Williams (2011) 'Why isn't everyone using QR codes?' www.imediaconnection.com/content/28604.asp (accessed 6 August 2011).

8 Adapted from Keyfort Limited (2012) http://www.keyfort.net/, (accessed 10 April 2012).

9 David B. Grant and John Fernie (2009) 'On-shelf availability and out-of-stocks in UK retailing,' in Peter Schnedlitz, Dirk Morschett, Thomas Rudolph, Hans Schramm-Klein and Bernhard Swoboda (eds.) *European Retail Research*, Wiesbaden: Gabler, Vol. 23, No. 2, pp.51–76.

10 Jesper Aastrup, Herbert Kotzab, David B. Grant, Christoph Teller and Mogens Bjerre (2008) 'A model for structuring efficient consumer response measures,' *International Journal of Retail & Distribution Management*, Vol. 36, No. 8, pp.590–606.

11 John Fernie and David B. Grant (2008) 'On-shelf availability: The case of a UK grocery retailer,' *International Journal of Logistics Management*, Vol. 19, No. 3, pp.293–308.

12 David B. Grant (2005) 'The transaction–relationship dichotomy in logistics and supply chain management,' *Supply Chain Forum: An International Journal*, Vol. 6, No. 2, pp.38–48.

13 This section is adapted from the Voluntary Interindustry Commerce Solutions Association (2011) www.vics.org/ (accessed 6 August 2011).

14 Grete Birtwistle, Noreen Siddiqui and Susan S. Fiorito (2003) 'Quick response: Perceptions of UK fashion retailers,' *International Journal of Retail & Distribution Management*, Vol. 31, No. 2, pp.118–128.

Chapter 9

Logistics financial performance

Key objectives

- To understand the role of a firm's performance in logistics.
- To consider the relationship of logistics and supply chain management to economics.
- To introduce several models of logistics performance.
- To describe logistics and supply chain financial performance.
- To explore several techniques for measuring logistics financial performance.

Introduction

An old adage proposes that in business 'you can't manage what you can't measure'. This notion is also applicable to logistics and supply chain management (SCM). Performance measurement systems are therefore important and over the last few decades there has been a transition from traditional, stand-alone performance measures to more sophisticated and balanced ways of measuring logistics and supply chain performance. This transition has been driven by increased complexity and globalisation and an attempt by logistics and supply chain managers and others to increase visibility over areas that are not directly within their control.

Such performance measures have conventionally been orientated around financial and quantifiable measures of cost, time and accuracy. However, firms are now coming under increased scrutiny from customers regarding non-financial measures and governments regarding their compliance with environmental and social responsibility.

This chapter presents and discusses logistics and supply chain performance measurement, and begins by providing an overview of firm performance. Then, the importance of logistics and SCM is reviewed and concepts of economic theory related to them are presented. Some popular models of logistics firm performance are then discussed before the remainder of the chapter considers financial measurement and management of logistics and supply chain activities.

Logistics and supply chain management versus firm performance

As discussed in Chapters 1 and 2, logistics and SCM activities provide time and place utility for customers, that is to say, the right products arrive at the right place at the right time in the right condition and at the right cost. Thus, providing customer satisfaction via these elements is the critical output related to these activities, and logistics and supply chain performance measurement has emerged as one of the major business areas where companies can obtain a competitive advantage. It is a key strategic factor for increasing organisational effectiveness and for better realisation of organisational goals such as enhanced competitiveness, better customer care and profitability. A key feature in the business environment is that supply chains, not companies, compete with one another.[1]

And yet, how does a manager know if the output of customer satisfaction has been achieved through the firm's logistics and supply chain activities? Appropriate performance measures are essential for managing and navigating firms through turbulent and competitive global markets. They allow firms to track progress against their strategy, identify areas of improvement and act as a good benchmark against competitors or industry leaders. The information provided by performance measures allows managers to make the right decisions at the right times.

However, it is important to know what standards should be used with performance measures. Further, should the measure be numerical or quantitative and thus a 'hard' measure, or should it be non-numeric or qualitative and thus a 'soft' measure? Finally, on what basis is the measure compared? For example, is it a ratio of input to output or the difference between value or profit and cost? A useful taxonomy to consider logistic measures, that has been developed by academic researchers Chris Caplice and Yossi Sheffi and presented as Figure 9.1, delineates three basic types of measures: utilisation, productivity and effectiveness.[2]

Utilisation measures are a measure of input use and are usually presented as a ratio of actual input used to a predetermined 'norm' value. For example, logistics and supply chain inputs may be financial (warehouse cost versus total warehouse costs or total logistics costs), assets (truck usage hours versus available hours excluding maintenance), or inventory (inventory turnover ratio discussed in Chapter 6).

Productivity measures are a measure of transformational efficiency and are usually presented as the ratio of an actual output produced to actual inputs consumed. For example, the financial ratio return on investment (ROI) is a measure of net profits after costs compared with total assets, expressed as a percentage.

Effectiveness measures are a measure of the quality of an output and are usually presented as a ratio of actual output achieved to a predetermined 'norm' value. For example, an online retailer might track the percentage of home deliveries made within the two-hour delivery windows specified by customers.

All these types of measures have advantages and disadvantages and thus managers must take care when using them. Appropriate inventory turnover ratios will depend on the type of inventory being measured, for example perishable food goods versus home electronics. A ROI percentage is affected by elements comprising either the numerator (net profit) or denominator (total assets) of the ratio being arbitrarily allocated (overheads), which can lead to gamesmanship. Lastly, the percentage of home deliveries made in a two-hour window may be subject to external factors such as traffic congestion and weather that may not be considered in the percentage calculation. In summary, logistics and supply chain measures are not a 'one-size-fits-all' proposition.

One of the most prevalent issues associated with performance measurement is having too many metrics. Some firms are using hundreds of metrics which are often not aligned

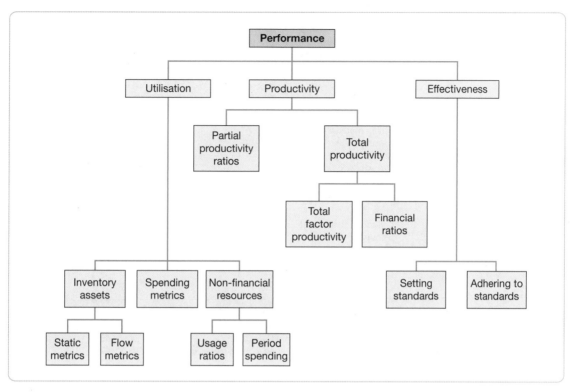

Figure 9.1 Taxonomy of logistics performance measures

Source: A Review and Evaluation of Logistics Metrics, *International Journal of Logistics Management*, Vol. 5, No. 2, p. 20 (Caplice, C. and Sheffi, Y. 1994), International Journal of Logistics Management by Emerald Group Publishing Limited. Reproduced with permission of Emerald Group Publishing Limited in the format Journal via Copyright Clearance Center. © Emerald Group Publishing Limited all rights reserved.

to the firm's strategy.[3] This leads to confusion, often results in 'paralysis by analysis' and presents difficulties in conducting benchmarking exercises. Thus, there is a requirement for a meaningful but parsimonious set of measures. Table 9.1 provides a list of popular logistics performance measures used by firms responding to an academic survey in 2009.[4]

However, how does a manager know if a measure is good, relevant and useful? Caplice and Sheffi[5] have also provided a guide of eight metric or measure criteria to help ascertain

Table 9.1 Performance measures used by firms (percentage of survey respondents)

Effectiveness measures involving trading partner (%)	
Customer complaints	75.6
On-time delivery	78.6
Over/short/damaged	72.3
Returns and allowances	69.1
Order cycle time	62.3
Overall customer satisfaction	60.8
Days sales outstanding	58.7
Forecast accuracy	54.4
Invoice accuracy	52.1
Perfect order fulfilment	39.5
Enquiry response time	29.6
Average	**59.4**

Table 9.1 (*continued*)

Effectiveness measures internal focus (%)	
Inventory count accuracy	85.8
Order fill	80.8
Out of stock	70.5
Line-item fill	68.5
Back orders	64.4
Inventory obsolescence	62.7
Incoming material quality	61.6
Processing accuracy	45.0
Case fill	39.1
Cash/cash cycle time	32.2
Average	**61.1**
Efficiency measures (%)	
Cost	
Outbound freight cost	87.3
Inbound freight cost	68.9
Inventory carrying cost	60.4
Third-party storage cost	58.6
Logistics cost/unit/budget	52.4
Cost to serve	37.4
Average	**60.8**
Productivity	
Finished goods inventory turn	80.2
Orders processed/labour unit	43.3
Product units processed per warehouse labour unit	47.6
Units processed/time unit	37.2
Orders processed/time unit	36.1
Product units processed/transportation unit	21.8
Average	**44.4**
Utilisation	
Space utilisation/capacity	46.5
Equipment downtown	46.0
Equipment utilisation/capacity	40.4
Labour utilisation/capacity	35.8
Average	**42.2**

Source: Logistics performance measurement in the supply chain: a benchmark, *Benchmarking: An International Journal*, Vol. 16, No. 6, pp. 785–798 (Keebler, J.S. and Plank, R.E. 2009), Benchmarking: An International Journal by Emerald Group Publishing Limited. Reproduced with permission of Emerald Group Publishing Limited in the format Journal via Copyright Clearance Center. © Emerald Group Publishing Limited all rights reserved.

appropriate measures, shown in Table 9.2. It is fair to say that not every measure for every firm will meet all eight criteria; however, if a measure meets a majority of them it should stand the firm in good stead.

As many of these popular measures are quantitative and economic, the next section considers the relationship of logistics and SCM to the science of economics.

Logistics, supply chain management and economics

The importance of logistics to the economy

As discussed in Chapter 1, logistics activities have a major economic impact on countries and their societies. Logistics and supply chain costs were in the order of 15–20 per cent of gross

Table 9.2 Eight criteria for good performance metrics

Criterion	Description
Validity	The metric accurately captures the events and activities being measured and controls for any exogenous factors
Robustness	The metric is interpreted similarly by the users, is comparable across time, location and organisations, and is repeatable
Usefulness	The metric is readily understandable by the decision maker and provides a guide for action to be taken
Integration	The metric includes all relevant aspects of the process and promotes coordination across functions and divisions
Economy	The benefits of using the metric outweigh the costs of data collection, analysis and reporting
Compatibility	The metric is compatible with the existing information, material and cashflows and systems in the organisation
Level of detail	The metric provides a sufficient degree of granularity or aggregation for the user
Behavioural soundness	The metric minimises incentives for counterproductive acts or game playing and is presented in a useful form

Source: A Review and Evaluation of Logistics Metrics, *International Journal of Logistics Management*, Vol. 5, No. 2, p. 14 (Caplice, C. and Sheffi, Y. 1994), International Journal of Logistics Management by Emerald Group Publishing Limited. Reproduced with permission of Emerald Group Publishing Limited in the format Journal via Copyright Clearance Center. © Emerald Group Publishing Limited all rights reserved.

domestic product (GDP) in both the US and Europe during the 1970s and 1980s. However, these cost percentages have reduced from these higher levels; in 2010 they accounted for 8.3 per cent of GDP in the US or just over $1.2 trillion. In Europe, they accounted for 7.2 per cent of European GDP across the EU-27 countries, or about €850 billion ($1.2 trillion) in 2009.[6]

Activities of business logistics and SCM can also be understood through reference to existing economic theory. Two predominant approaches used by many researchers and firms in this discipline are transaction cost economics (TCE)[7] and the resource-based view of the firm (RBV).[8]

TCE contains four key concepts of bounded rationality, opportunism, asset specificity and informational asymmetry:

- Bounded rationality suggests that actors, while willing to do so, cannot evaluate accurately all possible decision alternatives to make a rational decision due to physical or other constraints.

- Opportunism considers that actors will exploit a situation to their own advantage. This does not imply that all those involved in transactions act opportunistically all of the time; rather, it recognises that the risk of opportunism is often present.

- Asset specificity arises when one actor to an exchange invests resources specific to that exchange, which have little or no value in an alternative use, and another actor in the exchange acts opportunistically to try to appropriate economic rent from that investment (economic rent being the additional amount over the minimum return the focal partner requires from the specific investment).

- There is a relaxation of the perfect information assumption of neoclassical economic theory; many business exchanges are characterised by incomplete, imperfect or asymmetrical information.

TCE thus takes issue with neoclassical economic theory that describes the firm in technical terms or as a production function where all markets are considered perfectly competitive and firms are materialistic, i.e. utility or profit maximisers, and self-regarding. Essentially, though, TCE describes the firm in organisational terms or as a governance structure where decision makers respond to economic factors or transaction costs within the firm that affect both the structure of the firm and the structure of the industry within which it operates. The increasing division of labour within a supply chain determined by governance mechanisms has been recognised as a means of competitiveness through activities such as strategic sourcing discussed in Chapter 3 or outsourcing discussed in Chapter 4.

The origin of RBV is from Edith Penrose's 1959 book entitled *The Theory of the Growth of the Firm*, which defined a firm as a collection of resources whose growth is limited by its resource endowment. As the nature and range of resources vary from firm to firm, so will their respective resource constraints. RBV suggests that the keys to superior performance are a firm's resources and its capability to convert these resources to provide sustainable competitive advantage.

Resources are referred to as physical, financial, individual and organisational capital attributes for a firm. Resources are necessary inputs for producing a final product or service and form the basis for a firm's profitability. They may be considered both tangible assets such as plants and equipment and intangible assets such as brand names and technological know-how. Resources can also be traded; however, few resources are productive by themselves – they add value only when they are converted into a final product or service.

The dedication of a firm's resources is very much a micro-economic perspective and thus analogous to logistics functional activities, for example how many vehicles a firm should invest in to conduct its transport activities. However, this decision migrates towards a macro-economic or strategic perspective, i.e. towards TCE or a higher-level SCM decision-making context, when the option of outsourcing transport is introduced and the notion of a firm's core competencies is considered. Further, macro-externalities such as government regulation may also affect performance, as illustrated in Logistics Example 9.1. Some models related to economic and other types of performance are presented next.

LOGISTICS EXAMPLE 9.1

Gearing up for lorry road user charging

According to the UK's Chancellor of the Exchequer's 2002 Budget statement, the government's proposed Lorry Road User Charge (LRUC) had a modest and worthy aim: to 'ensure that lorry (truck) operators from overseas pay their fair share towards the cost of using UK roads'. Foreign-registered hauliers would have to pay around 15 pence for every kilometre travelled in the UK, assuming they bought their fuel outside the country, as most currently do. This would raise an extra £39 million annually for the UK Treasury.

But this system of road user charging, which the government was planning to introduce in 2008, would not be applied only to foreign hauliers. All 430,000 lorries registered in the UK with gross weights of over 3.5 tonnes will also be subject to exactly the same charges.

There were significant technical and organisational challenges identified in the proposed system of vehicle tracking and toll collection. This system involved the integration of a range of telematics and communication technologies, including satellite tracking, cellular

Logistics example 9.1 (*cont.*)

telephony, microwave systems and digital tachographs. Registers of vehicles, operators and authorised fitters of tolling equipment were to be compiled and maintained. Separate revenue streams would have to be created for the inward flow of toll income and return flow of fuel rebates.

Even at the outset this proposed system would have been highly complex. To put the complexity of the UK system into context, it is worth comparing it with the German Maut system. In Germany, only vehicles with a gross weight of 12 tonnes or more travelling on autobahns are to be tolled and the level of toll will be fixed. In the UK, all vehicles over 3.5 tonnes are to be charged for their use of all roads at a rate that is likely to be varied by road type and time of day.

It was widely expected that with the introduction of LRUC, vehicle excise duty (VED) would be abolished, but some reports suggested that it would have been retained. Annual taxes on UK lorries in the mid-2000s were £280 million for VED and £3,040 million for fuel tax for a total of £3,320 million. In the absence of any offsetting administrative cost savings, the annual operating cost of LRUC could well have been £700 million or more – five times as much as the extra revenue from foreign hauliers. Internalising this total cost within the LRUC scheme would have added a further 3 pence per kilometre or more to the charge. Alternatively, if the Chancellor was true to his word and did not increase the total tax burden on the UK haulage industry, the Treasury would have had to incur this cost.

The key component in the new charging regime was the on-board unit (OBU) installed in all lorries travelling more than 12,000 kilometers on UK roads each year. This would have determined the lorry's location using GPS, matched that location against a built-in digital map of the UK road network (to determine the class of road) and communicated with a control centre, relaying information about the distance travelled and toll to be charged. One of the ironies of the proposal was that the majority of the foreign trucks entering the UK were travelling less than 12,000 kilometres annually on UK roads. Those vehicles would have been covered by a separate occasional user scheme, which would have required them to use a low-use OBU. After much discussion, public consultation and lobbying by the Freight Transport Association, the Road Haulage Association and others in the late 2000s, the UK government deferred a decision for implementation until 2012.

Question

Given all these parameters and uncertainties, what are the cost and accounting factors that a UK or foreign haulier must consider in preparation for the implementation of LRUC at some point in the future?

Sources: adapted from Alan C. McKinnon, *Lorry Road User Charging: A Review of the UK Government's Proposals*, 2004, Edinburgh: Logistics Research Centre, Heriot-Watt University; and Alan C. McKinnon 'Government plans for lorry road-user charging in the UK: A critique and an alternative,' *Transport Policy*, 2006, Vol. 13, pp.204–216.

Models of logistics performance

There are a number of theories regarding how the concept of performance measurement was first developed. One suggests that modern performance measurement originated in Venice during the 15th century with the invention of double book-keeping in accounting. Others believe it originated during the industrial revolution. Regardless of its sources, performance measurement and management emerged as a field of research in the 1950s when academics and practitioners became interested in the need to measure and the unanticipated consequences of such measurement.

Traditionally, performance measures were oriented around financial metrics such as ROI, return on capital employed, or total profit that record how an organisation has performed in the past, but do not necessarily reflect how it will perform in the future. Thus, traditional financial performance measures worked well previously but are now out of step with the skills and competencies firms are trying to achieve today. Throughout the 1980s and early 1990s several authors suggested various models to manage firm performance. Three of the most popular models – the balanced scorecard that was introduced in Chapter 2,[9] the supply chain operations reference model (SCOR)[10] and the performance prism[11] – are presented briefly below as alternatives for logistics and SCM applications.

The balanced scorecard attempts to reduce confusion and increase clarity in the performance management process by providing managers with a fast but comprehensive view of their business through four key perspectives: financial, customer, internal business, and innovation and learning. It also helps managers focus on a handful of critical measures that are aligned with the business strategy, including both financial and non-financial information. A Bain and Company survey of more than 708 companies on five continents found that the balanced scorecard was used by 62 per cent of responding organisations.[12]

The SCOR model is the product of the Supply Chain Council, an independent not-for-profit corporation with open membership for firms and organisations that are interested in applying and advancing the state-of-the-art in supply chain management systems and practices. SCOR is a process reference model integrating three concepts: business process re-engineering (BPR) and modelling, process mapping and measurement, and performance benchmarking to determine 'best-in-class' practices. The SCOR model is based on five management processes, which are shown in Figure 9.2.

- *Plan* – considers levels of aggregate demand and supply and information sources to meet sourcing, production and delivery requirements.
- *Source* – considers locations and products to procure in order to meet demand.
- *Make* – considers production sites and methods to transform products to a finished state to meet demand.
- *Deliver* – considers channels, inventory deployment and processes that provide finished products to meet demand.
- *Return* – considers locations and processes associated with returning or receiving returned products. These processes extend to post-delivery customer support.

The performance prism shown in Figure 9.3 was developed to addresses the needs and wants of all stakeholders of a firm rather than a sub-set such as employees and shareholders. The performance prism is considered as a second-generation performance measurement framework design, and could be used to enable organisations to select appropriate performance measurements. It consists of five 'facets' of a prism representing five distinct, but logically interlinked, perspectives on performance that have been identified together with five key questions for measurement design:

- *Stakeholder satisfaction* – who are the key stakeholders and what do they want and need?
- *Strategies* – what strategies does the firm have to put in place to satisfy the wants and needs of these key stakeholders?

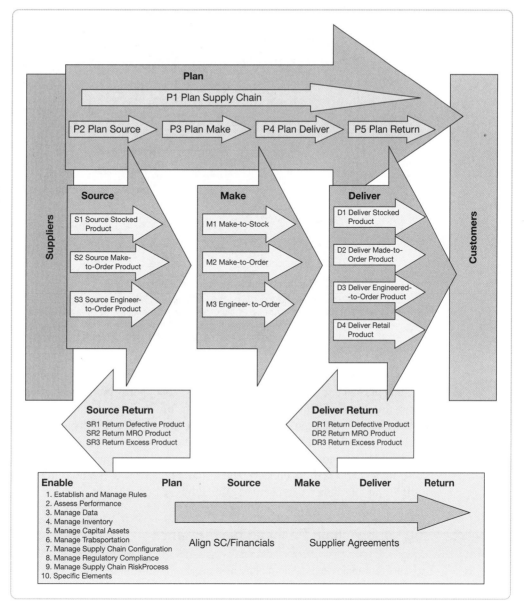

Figure 9.2 Supply chain operations reference model
Source: http://supply-chain.org.

- *Processes* – what critical processes does the firm require if it is to execute these strategies?
- *Capabilities* – what capabilities does the firm need to operate and enhance these processes?
- *Stakeholder contribution* – what contributions does the firm require from its stakeholders if it is to maintain and develop these capabilities?

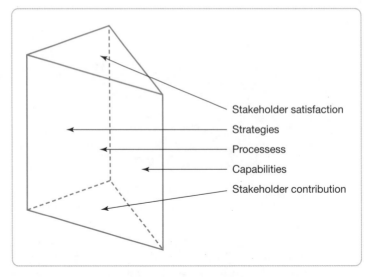

Figure 9.3 The facets of the performance prism

Source: The Performance Prism in Practice, *Measuring Business Excellence*, Vol. 5, No. 2, p. 12 (Neely, A., Adams, C. and Crowe, P. 2001), Measuring Business Excellence by Emerald Group Publishing Limited. Reproduced with permission of Emerald Group Publishing Limited in the format Journal via Copyright Clearance Center. © Emerald Group Publishing Limited all rights reserved.

Thus, the priority of the performance prism is to identify all stakeholders and assess their requirements before deciding on a strategy and a set of performance measures. The authors suggest that like a prism refracting light, the performance prism illustrates the complexity of performance measurement and management. They further argue that while single-dimensional, traditional frameworks pick up elements of this complexity, they have only a single uni-dimensional perspective on performance. Performance is not uni-dimensional and to understand it in its entirety, the authors believe it is essential to view it from the multiple and interlinked perspectives offered by the performance prism.

Logistics and supply chain financial performance

There are four major logistics cost activities: transportation management, warehouse or storage management, inventory management, and information technology and administrative management. A breakdown of these cost allocations for the US and Europe presented in Chapter 1 noted that on average transportation is the largest cost for firms, at 63 per cent in the US and 48 per cent in Europe. However, the combined effect of warehouse and inventory management comprises 32 per cent of costs in the US and 41 per cent in Europe. Much extant research has independently considered these cost centres in order to optimise or minimise discrete activities.

Further, as firms in a supply chain look to add value, end-users or consumers begin to consider total supply chain costs that are reflected in the price of the goods on offer in the market. For example, while it took 20 years for a video cassette recorder (VCR) to fall in price by 90 per cent from £400 to £40, it took only 4 years for a digital video disc (DVD) recorder to fall by the same amount. Thus, firms need to adopt a proper view of costs from 'end to end' in their supply chain since all costs will ultimately be reflected in the price of the finished product in the final marketplace.[13]

However, one of the difficulties in obtaining logistics costs is that they may be grouped under a series of natural accounts instead of by functions to satisfy generally accepted accounting principles (GAAP). The nature of this difficulty is shown in Figure 9.4, which illustrates how various logistics variables interface with the two traditional accounting statements: the balance sheet, which represents the firm's assets, liabilities and shareholders' equity, and the income statement, which represents the firm's sales, expenses and profit.

Some research[14] has reported that the pre-eminent drivers for logistics and SCM initiatives continue to be cost reduction (65 per cent of respondents) and revenue enhancement (25 per cent). Various factors, including logistical and supply chain decisions, affect a

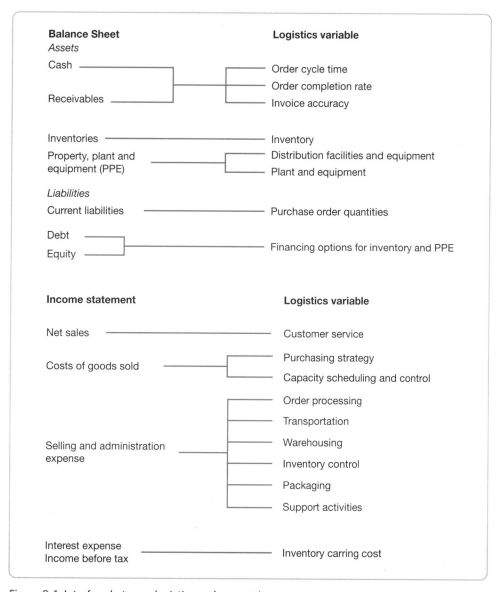

Figure 9.4 Interface between logistics and accounting
Source: adapted from Christopher (2011).

firm's capital structure, risk level, cost structure, profitability and ultimately market value. Thus, logistics and SCM are shifting from a tactical, back-office function to a driver of shareholder value. Logistics Example 9.2 discusses a new approach to understanding how financial performance cuts across internal and outsourced activities.

However, there are relatively few firms that know where to direct their supply chain investments to maximise business results and bottom-line value.[15] Further, there are many criticisms of traditional costing and management accounting regarding retrieving

LOGISTICS EXAMPLE 9.2

Open book accounting adds flexibility and new information

The global market for communication equipment has shown a growing demand for measurement systems that can handle sound and picture signals through digital technology and thus increase transmission capacity. For the last 15 years, LeanTech in Denmark has been an actor in this market, where it manufactures high-quality products for telecoms companies, radio and TV stations all over the world.

In recent years, the company has expanded heavily and turnover has multiplied. Traditionally, LeanTech handled a large part of its production work in-house, but due to a steep increase in activities it started to use suppliers to ensure production capacity relative to demand. Recently, the firm outsourced the whole production department to suppliers. Outsourcing the production meant that suddenly inter-organisational relations became 'highly significant', the logistics manager said. He elaborated the new challenges of the inter-organisational relations: 'The sub-contractors were handling the main part of our production, which meant that flexibility primarily had to come from that side. The whole thing depended on whether we were able to cooperate more closely with the suppliers in an effort to reduce costs and deliver faster.'

An intense debate among managers over how to regain control of production processes was taking place. When production was inside, managers were said to have a direct sense of what was going on in production. After outsourcing, this confidence was lost. As an answer to the frustrations of putting production processes at a distance, the logistics management introduced open book accounting as a medium to control and facilitate production flexibility. Sales forecasts were open to the subcontractors and suppliers' production accounting system information was opened to LeanTech.

The logistics manager stressed: 'By opening the books they learn more about us and we learn more about them, and thereby we could ensure flexibility.' Open book accounting provided the logistics management with access to time and cost information about production processes. All material flows, from delivery of the individual types of components to the final shipment of the product to the customer, had been barcoded. In addition, information about suppliers' cost structures was provided. It included adjustment times for assembling machines, the size of the intermediate product inventory and rate of turnover.

The firm was said to have lost touch with production after it had been outsourced, but this was being restored by the new approach. The logistics manager commented on the open access to time and cost information: 'Before I was quite convinced that we were doing everything we could in order to optimise the production. We were quite close. Everyone knew each other and their responsibility. I think that the system was transparent because we were so close. This transparency was lost when we outsourced the production system. But it was regained with open book accounting. Today, open access to time and cost information at assembly suppliers is the key element in our efforts to improve production flexibility.'

Logistics example 9.2 (cont.)

Open book accounting made it possible to benchmark suppliers and to redesign suppliers' production and distribution processes. Furthermore, the logistics manager pointed out, production planning improved, as the open books gave him an overview of the capacity utilisation at the different suppliers.

Open book accounting made LeanTech an organiser of inter-organisational relations, setting up a form of virtual organisation that used information to coordinate other companies. Open book accounting inscribed a network of companies in terms of productivity, capacity, financial resources, competencies, etc. and it also let the logistics manager play a new role as inter-organisational coordinator between firms.

The insights offered by the open book arrangement into the production processes, which previously were unusual in LeanTech due to a rather informal control system, had other effects than just improving production flexibility. Open book accounting's information about the production process gave the logistics management an unprecedented opportunity to discuss competitive advantage in terms of faster delivery time and competitive prices. The production manager commented: 'Suddenly, we had a whole arsenal of information that disclosed the consequences and problems of decisions made by development and sales engineers in relation to the new market demands. Today, our open book arrangement gives us this opportunity.'

Through open book accounting with the suppliers, the logistics management got access to financial information that disclosed time and cost in production processes. The logistics management used this information to increase production flexibility, but this work took a direction that they had not originally planned. Their efforts became concentrated on development and sales activities as the two action areas.

In all, open book accounting appeared to be a resource in new translations of competitive strategy, which effected development and sales activities and the interpretation of what a technological edge and customisation meant to the firm. The search for flexibility through open book accounting showed up to be a resource for advancing productivity matters in the firm.

Question

Can you think of circumstances where open book accounting would not be appropriate?

Source: adapted from Jan Mouritsen, Allan Hansen and Carsten Ørts Hansen, 'Inter-organizational controls and organizational competencies: Episodes around target cost management/functional analysis and open book accounting,' *Management Accounting Research*, 2001, Vol. 12, pp.221–244.

proper data, and relatively little research that looks at the nature, type and roles of accounting information in the formation, management and functioning of supply chains that would inhibit a manager's ability to collect and analyse such data. This has led to rule-of-thumb techniques such as the Pareto principle or the 80–20 rule being posited as simply decision making.[16]

Within today's business environment of increasingly rampant global competition, mass customisation, product diversification and technological advances, the need for more effective use of financial and non-financial information within firms has become imperative, particularly for logistics and supply chain activities. Some authors have raised notions of customer profitability or product profitability, but again these discussions have focused on aggregate data and have not provided sufficient granularity. Thus, more precise and relevant cost and performance information is needed regarding a firm's processes, activities, products, services and customers. To begin with, the notion of customer value must be considered.

Customer value

Some authors argue that customer value is created when perceptions of benefits received from using and enjoying a product exceed the costs of ownership for the product, as shown in Figure 9.5.[17] Others argue that customer value is provided by Quality (multiplied by Service) divided by Cost (multiplied by Lead Time).[18]

Regardless, competitive and market factors in a firm's business environment stipulate that developing a competitive advantage through the delivery of superior customer value is here to stay. However, there is a question as to whether logistics activities provide real customer value or whether they are, as characterised by Peter Drucker, just 'distribution . . . a cost area and purely a cost area'.[19] One way to consider this proposition is to deconstruct the value paradigm as follows and as shown in Figure 9.6: a customer buys on value where value equals quality relative to price. However, quality includes the two non-price attributes of product and customer service. Quality, price and value are relative and in a logistics or supply chain context the determining and controllable factor is customer service.[20]

Customer service and cost-to-serve

While customer service leading to customer value and satisfaction is an output of logistics and SCM, it nevertheless represents a cost to the firm; thus some form of a cost–service tradeoff is required. Rule-of-thumb techniques such as the Pareto principle or the 80–20 rule have been successfully used; however, there has been a paucity of research into the true cost-to-serve in logistics and SCM activities. This is surprising given that cost-to-serve is considered significant as it facilitates organisational decision making at strategic, tactical and operational levels.

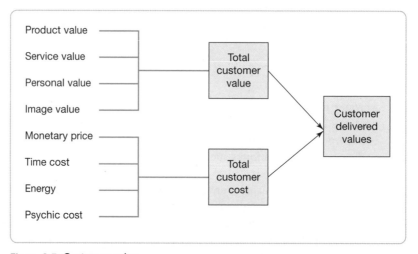

Figure 9.5 Customer value
Source: Kotler (2000).

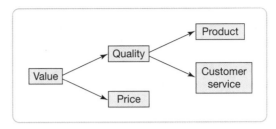

Figure 9.6 Value and customer service
Source: Gale (1994, p.29).

The notion of the cost-to-serve for customers is important for organisational decision making regarding the provision of products and customer service and was identified as one of the key logistics and supply chain trends for the new millennium.[21] However, due to different customer service costs, firms need to consider different customer service strategies for different customers. The question is, how does the firm quantify the cost-to-serve for each customer?

Traditional accounting methods were established on suppositions of stable and predictable markets, long product life cycles and production runs, and a large portion of directly variable costs attributable to total product costs. However, product life cycles have become shorter, markets more fragmented, production more flexible and the amount of direct variable costs is decreasing. Therefore, extant accounting methods provide incongruous information for a firm's decision-making purposes. One solution to this dilemma is the use of activity-based costing, which provides a technique for achieving relevant and granular data.

Activity-based costing (ABC)

Activity-based costing can identify and properly allocate true functional activity costs, and is increasingly being utilised as both an accounting tool and catalyst in decision-making processes. This form of ABC is different from ABC analysis discussed in Chapter 6 to classify different products and inventories. ABC here is considered one technique to provide a firm with financial insights about its activities and as a means of capturing their respective underlying costs as products flow downstream in the supply chain; thus a firm can accomplish a high level of customer service in a cost-effective manner.

The notion behind the ABC concept is that products and services require an organisation to perform activities, which in turn incur costs. Costs can therefore be attributed to cost objects, such as products, customers, service and markets, throughout all activities undertaken to serve customers and based on their proportionate use of an activity. Analysing and orchestrating logistics and SCM using ABC techniques thus appears a sensible and attractive option to determine total costs.

ABC is considered an appropriate alternative to traditional methods. In essence, resources are assigned to activities and activities are then assigned to cost objects based on their use, thus recognising causal relationships of cost objects to activities. ABC therefore determines the costs of cost objects by summing the costs of activities required across the processes of manufacturing a product, providing service or serving the customer. These relationships are represented in Figure 9.7 as a 'cross' wherein activities are in the centre of the cross to indicate their role as a central node of reporting both process and object costs.[22]

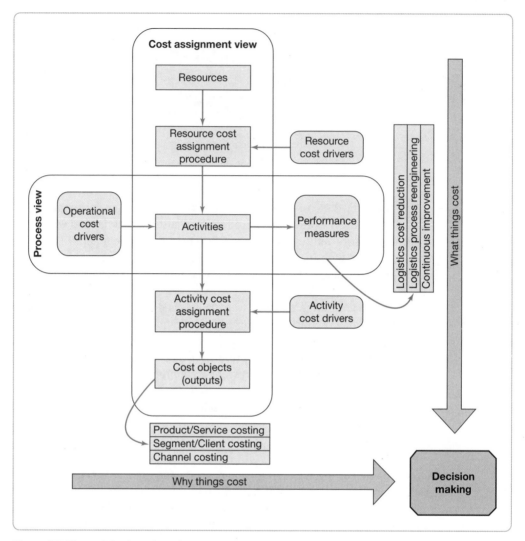

Figure 9.7 The activity-based costing cross

Source: adapted from Pohlen and La Londe (1994).

On the vertical axis, the cost chain includes resources 'consumed' by activities and which in turn are cost objects. On the horizontal axis, the various business processes are viewed as a network of activities that produces the necessary information for costing and performance measures relative to the focal organisation.

The basic implementation steps of ABC in a supply chain environment are summarised from these works and are depicted in Figure 9.8.[23] Examining these steps one by one, the ABC model requires the implementation to begin with the selection of the right team players. In order for an ABC project to be successful, all those who understand and coordinate or perform the activities that consume resources in different departments of the firm need to be present on the ABC team and assist with their knowledge and experience.

Then, this team has to start with a comprehensive understanding of the firm's business resources and activities performed by the majority of its employees. The logistics function of

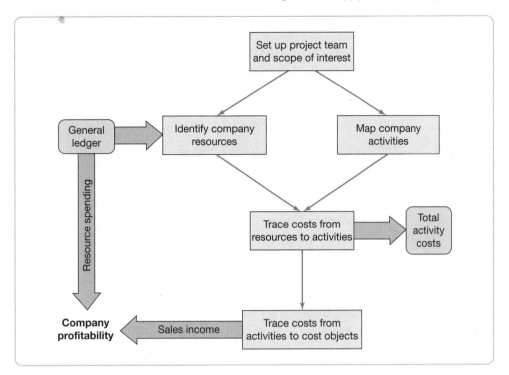

Figure 9.8 Steps in an ABC implementation model

Source: Supply chain costing: an activity-based perspective, *International Journal of Physical Distribution & Logistics Management*, Vol. 31, No. 10, pp. 702–713 (Lin, B., Collins, J. and Su, R.K. 2001).

the firm is to be scrutinised in order to classify the major processes of the company's logistics department. After these processes have been identified, specific resource-consuming business activities within each logistics process have to be distinguished. Breaking down the processes into individual well-defined activities allows for better analysis of the cost of the process.

Next, resource expenses are to be assigned to activities performed by identifying these expenses in the financial system and distributing them to these activities to discover their true costs. A more thorough analysis should separate variable from fixed costs so that the firm has a clear understanding of the costs of individual activities carried out to support certain products and services.

Lastly, it is important to identify the most appropriate cost drivers that reflect the cost of performing each activity and reveal the cause-and-effect relationship between consumption of resources and performance of activities. These cost drivers, although few in types, can produce a wide variety of information and can be divided into unit-level, batch-level, product-level and facility-level activities. The addition of these types enhances the cause-and-effect relationship between resources and their consumption drivers by the activities, providing transparency and understanding of the company's cost structure.

All the foregoing data should be inserted into a software program to be sorted and processed in order to produce the desired outputs. A simple spreadsheet program will suffice and workbook data should be delineated into inputs (allocation of resources to activities) and outputs (results of costs per activity or cost object) in order for the results to be generated automatically. Input spreadsheets will include all the information related to the company in terms of resources, while results spreadsheets should include activity performance based on the different cost concepts of each activity as well as total costs, which summarises all activity costs. However, sophisticated software programs and services exist that will assist firms in dealing with the preponderance of financial data, as discussed in Logistics Example 9.3.

LOGISTICS EXAMPLE 9.3

SAP software helps manage financial and logistics issues

Founded in 1972 in Walldorf, Germany, SAP AG has grown into the leading enterprise software supplier across the globe. It provides collaborative software business solutions for all types of industries in every major market. In 2010 SAP generated sales of €12.5 billion and €1.8 billion profit from its more than 100,000 customers in more than 120 countries. It is the world's largest inter-enterprise software company and the world's third-largest independent software supplier overall.

Two of its most popular software product suites are 'mySAP ERP', which contains modules for accounting, financial reporting, performance management and corporate governance, and 'mySAP SCM', which contains modules for planning and execution capabilities for managing enterprise operations, as well as coordination and collaboration technology to extend those operations beyond corporate boundaries.

An example of one product that can benefit a specific industrial sector is the oil and gas accounting suite. When oil companies such as BP, Royal Dutch Shell and Norway's Statoil explore and develop oil reserves in the North Sea, they tend to do so on a joint-venture or shared basis regarding costs and resultant revenues. One firm is the managing partner or contractor and is responsible for operations related to production, suppliers, customers and so on. The joint venture also has a silent partner in government: the national government where the oil field is located takes a percentage royalty on all oil and gas production revenue. The managing partner also does all the accounting for the joint venture, including allocating costs and revenues, paying the other joint-venture partners and billing them if capital expenditures need to be done, such as servicing or re-working the well, and ensuring the government royalties are paid.

SAP has developed SAP PSA and SAP JVA to meet the requirements of upstream oil and gas companies involved in production-sharing contracts (PSCs) and joint-venture accounting respectively. SAP PSA enables the managing partner to effectively manage PSCs, plan budgets and project expected financial results. By using SAP PSA and JVA together, the cost data (maintained in SAP JVA accounting ledgers) can be used as the source cost data in SAP PSA, providing consistent accounting.

SAP PSA automates the following processes: recording and classifying costs, allocating production to government royalty and contractor, calculating profit shares and entitlements, and reporting results for use by the joint-venture partners and government.

SAP RLM for remote logistics management keeps an oil company's offshore production facilities in the North Sea supplied by seamlessly integrating remote logistics with all other logistics processes. The oil company can stock materials onshore, offshore, or both. SAP RLM can automatically convert stock transfer requests, created at the remote location, into stock transport orders or purchase requisitions at an onshore base plant.

Besides this suite of products for upstream oil and gas exploration companies, SAP provides products to downstream operations for commodity sales, bulk transportation and inventory management of hydrocarbon products and to service station operations for convenience retailing, fuels management, site and headquarters management, and business analysis and reporting.

Direct product profitability

Direct product profitability (DPP) is another method of allocating logistics costs that has become popular in the retail sector. The process behind DPP is to identify all attributable costs accruing to a product, including logistics costs. To make this process practical, products will probably need to be grouped together in categories. Table 9.3 shows a generic income statement determination of DPP.

The DPP process attempts to convert fixed logistics costs into direct costs associated with a product or product category. The result is that DPP should provide better information about which products or product groups contribute most to a firm's profitability. All supply chain members, including retailers, distributors and suppliers, need to be conscious of and appreciate the effect of a product or product group's DPP as it moves their particular logistics system so as to seek to influence it favourably. But, as discussed above, the need for proper cost data is an important factor to undertake DPP analysis, and the question arises again of how and where to source the correct cost data for DPP calculations.

Cash-to-cash cycle

The cash-to-cash (C2C) cycle concept has emerged as a new metric for supply chain management and it is important from both supply chain and financial perspectives.[24] The most commonly accepted definition is inventory days of supply plus accounts receivable or a

Table 9.3 Determination of direct product profitability (DPP)

	Sales		Y
–	Direct product costs or cost of goods sold	X	
=	**Gross product profit or margin**		Y
–	Logistics related costs:		
	Transportation costs	X	
	Warehousing costs	X	
	Inventory costs	X	
	Sourcing or procurement costs	X	
	Operation support costs	X	
	Invoicing and collection costs	X	
	Retail costs	X	
–	Overheads directly attributable to product	X	
=	**Direct product profit**		Y

Source: adapted from Christopher, 2011.

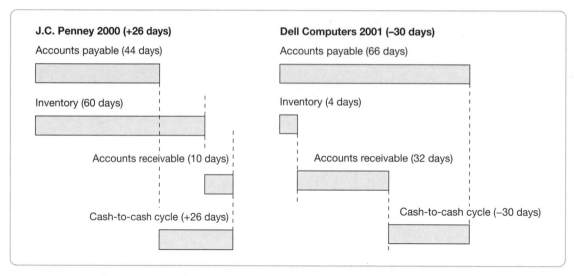

Figure 9.9 The cash-to-cash cycle illustrated

Source: Cash-to-cash: the new supply chain management metric, *International Journal of Physical Distribution & Logistics Management*, Vol. 32, No. 4, p. 290 (Farris, M.T. and Hutchinson, P.D. 2002), International Journal of Physical Distribution and Logistics Management by Emerald Group Publishing Limited. Reproduced with permission of Emerald Group Publishing Limited in the format Journal via Copyright Clearance Center. © Emerald Group Publishing Limited all rights reserved.

firm's average collection period less accounts payable or a firm's average age of accounts payable. The C2C cycle can thus be influenced by reducing inventory, obtaining better credit terms with suppliers and/or reducing payment terms for customers. Figure 9.9 shows the application of C2C to two firms, J.C. Penney and Dell Computers. In the case of Penney, the C2C cycle is +26 days. That is, they have to wait 26 days from when they pay their accounts payable to their supplier before their customer pays them. In the case of Dell, the C2C cycle is −30 days. That is, they have the customer's payment 30 days before they have to pay their accounts payable to their supplier.

The C2C cycle and resultant metric is important from both an accounting and a logistics and SCM perspective. For accounting purposes the metric can be used to help measure firm liquidity, i.e. how quickly it can liquidate assets to pay its account payables and firm valuation, i.e. a shorter cash conversion cycle results in a higher present value of cash flows generated by the company's assets, thereby increasing the firm's value. For logistics and supply chain activities the metric serves a measurement bridging the procurement and sales processes and helping identify the use of inventory.

One criticism, however, would relate to a firm's management fixating on trying to achieve a negative cycle where they are in receipt of cash from customers before having to pay their suppliers. This notion has been considered[25] using 'other people's money' and a logical question to ask is whether Dell is in the computer business or is simply a bank that manufactures computers.

Summary

Logistics and supply chain performance has primarily been examined from a quantitative and financial perspective for several decades. However, the number and type of measures span a wide range of efficiency and effectiveness metrics that are both quantitative and qualitative. A firm needs to understand both types of measures in order to generate customer value and competitive advantage.

This chapter has presented an introduction to some measures, models and financial applications in logistics and SCM. A managerial approach to broad, important concepts was provided and thus this chapter resisted the temptation to turn the discussion into an accounting treatise. Instead, it opted to show the interfaces between logistics and SCM and the financial world. The next chapter also examines another interface of logistics and SCM, but with human resources.

DISCUSSION QUESTIONS

1 Compare the three basic types of firm performance measures: utilisation, productivity and effectiveness. How would you rank these measures and why?

2 Define transaction cost economics (TCE) and the resource-based view (RBV) of the firm, and discuss their relative merits.

3 What is customer value? Is it important for logistics and supply chains?

4 Describe the elements of activity-based costing (ABC).

5 Evaluate the use of the cash-to-cash (C2C) cycle for global logistics operations.

Suggested reading

Caplice, Chris and Yossi Sheffi 'A review and evaluation of logistics metrics,' *International Journal of Logistics Management*, 1994, Vol. 5, No. 2, pp.11–28.

Christopher, Martin and John Gattorna 'Supply chain management cost and value-based pricing,' *Industrial Marketing Management*, 2005, Vol. 34, pp.115–116.

Coase, Ronald H. 'The nature of the firm', *Economica*, 1937, Vol. 4, No. 16, pp.386–405.

Farris, M. Theodore and Paul D. Hutchison 'Cash-to-cash: The new supply chain management metric,' *International Journal of Physical Distribution & Logistics Management*, 2002, Vol. 32, No. 4, pp.288–298.

Gomm, Moritz L. 'Supply chain finance: Applying finance theory to supply chain management to enhance finance in supply chains,' *International Journal of Logistics: Research and Applications*, 2010, Vol. 13, No. 2, pp.133–142.

Hofman, Debra 'Getting to world-class supply chain measurement,' *Supply Chain Management Review*, 2006, Vol. 10, No. 7, pp. 18–24.

Huan, Samuel H., Sunil K. Sheoran and Ge Wang 'A review and analysis of supply chain operations reference (SCOR) model,' *Supply Chain Management: An International Journal*, 2004, Vol. 9, No. 1, pp.23–29.

Kaplan, Robert S. and David P. Norton, 'The balanced scorecard – measures that drive performance', *Harvard Business Review*, 1992, Vol. 70 (January), pp.71–79.

Keebler, James S. and Richard E. Plank 'Logistics performance measurement in the supply chain: A benchmark,' *Benchmarking: An International Journal*, 2009, Vol. 16, No. 6, pp.785–798.

Lin, Binshan, James Collins and Rober K. Su 'Supply chain costing: An activity-based perspective,' *International Journal of Physical Distribution & Logistics Management*, 2001, Vol. 31, No. 10, pp.702–713.

McKinnon, Alan C. 'Government plans for lorry road-user charging in the UK: A critique and an alternative,' *Transport Policy*, 2006, Vol. 13, pp.204–216.

Mouritsen, Jan, Allan Hansen and Carsten Ørts Hansen, 'Inter-organizational controls and organizational competencies: Episodes around target cost management/functional analysis and open book accounting,' *Management Accounting Research*, 2001, Vol. 12, pp.221–244.

Neely, Andy, Chris Adams and Paul Crowe 'The performance prism in practice,' *Measuring Business Excellence*, 2001, Vol. 5, No. 2, pp.6–12.

Penrose, Edith *The Theory of the Growth of the Firm,* 4th ed. Oxford University Press, 2009.

Pohlen, Terence L. and Bernard J. La Londe 'Implementing activity-based costing (ABC) in logistics,' *Journal of Business Logistics*, 1994, Vol. 15, No. 2, pp.1–23.

Rutner, Stephen M. and C. John Langley 'Logistics value: Definition, process and measurement,' *International Journal of Logistics Management*, 2000, Vol. 11, No. 2, pp.73–82.

Williamson, Oliver E. *The Mechanisms of Governance*, Oxford University Press, 1999.

Notes

1 Martin Christopher, *Logistics and Supply Chain Management,* 4th ed. Harlow: FT Prentice Hall, 2011.
2 Chris Caplice and Yossi Sheffi, 'A review and evaluation of logistics metrics,' *International Journal of Logistics Management*, 1994, Vol. 5, No. 2, pp.11–28.
3 Debra Hofman, 'Getting to world-class supply chain measurement,' *Supply Chain Management Review*, 2006, Vol. 10, No. 7, pp.18–24.
4 James S. Keebler and Richard E. Plank, 'Logistics performance measurement in the supply chain: A benchmark,' *Benchmarking: An International Journal*, 2009, Vol. 16, No. 6, pp.785–798.
5 Caplice and Sheffi, 1994.
6 Sources: Rosalyn Wilson 'CSCMP's 22nd Annual State of Logistics Report: Navigating through the recovery,' http://cscmp.org/ 2011.
7 More on transaction cost economics theory can be found in Ronald H. Coase, 'The nature of the firm,' *Economica*, 1937, Vol. 4, No. 16, pp.386–405; and Oliver E. Williamson, *The Mechanisms of Governance*, Oxford University Press, 1999.
8 More on the resource-based view of the firm can be found in Edith Penrose, *The Theory of the Growth of the Firm,* 4th ed. Oxford University Press, 2009.
9 Robert S. Kaplan and David P. Norton, 'The balanced scorecard – measures that drive performance,' *Harvard Business Review*, 1992, Vol. 70 (January), pp.71–79.
10 For further information on the SCOR model see http://supply-chain.org and Samuel H. Huan, Sunil K. Sheoran and Ge Wang 'A review and analysis of supply chain operations reference (SCOR) model,' *Supply Chain Management: An International Journal*, 2004, Vol. 9, No. 1, pp.23–29.
11 Andy Neely, Chris Adams and Paul Crowe 'The performance prism in practice,' *Measuring Business Excellence*, 2001, Vol. 5, No. 2, pp.6–12.
12 K.B. Hendricks, L.J. Menor and C.I. Wiedman, 'The balanced scorecard: To adopt or not to adopt?' *Ivey Business Journal Online*, 2004, November/December, 1–9, www.ivey.uwo.ca.
13 Martin Christopher and John Gattorna 'Supply chain management cost and value-based pricing,' *Industrial Marketing Management*, 2005, Vol. 34, pp.115–116.

14 Moritz L. Gomm, 'Supply chain finance: Applying finance theory to supply chain management to enhance finance in supply chains,' *International Journal of Logistics: Research and Applications*, 2010, Vol. 13, No. 2, pp.133–142.

15 Ibid.

16 Christopher (2011).

17 Philip Kotler, *Marketing Management: The Millennium Edition,* 20th ed. Upper Saddle River, NJ: Prentice Hall, 2000.

18 Christopher (2011).

19 Stephen M. Rutner and C. John Langley 'Logistics value: Definition, process and measurement,' *International Journal of Logistics Management*, 2000, Vol. 11, No. 2, pp.73–82.

20 Bradley T. Gale, *Managing Customer Value,* New York: The Free Press, 1994.

21 Donald J. Bowersox, David J. Closs and Theodore P. Stank 'Ten mega-trends that will revolutionize supply chain logistics,' *Journal of Business Logistics*, 2000, Vol. 21, No. 2, pp.1–16.

22 Terence L. Pohlen and Bernard J. La Londe 'Implementing activity-based costing (ABC) in logistics,' *Journal of Business Logistics*, 1994, Vol. 15, No. 2, pp.1–23.

23 Binshan Lin, James Collins and Rober K. Su 'Supply chain costing: An activity-based perspective,' *International Journal of Physical Distribution & Logistics Management*, 2001, Vol. 31, No. 10, pp.702–713.

24 M. Theodore Farris and Paul D. Hutchison 'Cash-to-cash: The new supply chain management metric,' *International Journal of Physical Distribution & Logistics Management*, 2002, Vol. 32, No. 4, pp.288–298.

25 Ibid.

Chapter 10

Human resources and logistics

Key objectives

- To describe organisation in logistics and supply chains.
- To consider different types of organisational structures.
- To discuss the importance of human resources in logistics.
- To consider the role of knowledge workers in today's work environments.
- To explore human resources and technology and gender issues in logistics.

Introduction

The preceding chapters had themes of organisation and collaboration running through them. These themes have been discussed in the context of external organisations such as suppliers and customers, but that is only one aspect for a firm. While the organisation of a supply chain is a macro-activity where a firm must work in concert with other external organisations to achieve supply chain objectives, the organisation of a firm, including its human resources, is a micro-activity where elements of the firm must work in concert to achieve the firm's corporate and human resources objectives.

This chapter first provides an overview of supply chain organisation and governance, the macro perspective, and a firm's organisation and governance, the micro perspective. It then examines issues of human resources in the firm in general and in logistics and supply chain management in particular, including changes to human resources in the form of interactions with technology and gender.

Organisation of the supply chain

Supply chain management is considered a primary driver of performance and customer service, and a firm's supply chain consists of multiple business partners across many countries. A significant commitment of finite resources (e.g. human resources, capital, time) is necessary to manage supply chain relationships, thus strategy decisions aimed at maximising performance cannot be made for a single relationship to the exclusion of others. Rather, SCM necessitates a manager's understanding of the unique needs of each relationship and the effective management of multiple relationships simultaneously.[1]

However, managing and governing these multiple relationships can be difficult. Figure 10.1 shows a hypothetical supply chain consisting of nine partners. Most discussions of supply chain networks centre on a 'focal firm' that has many suppliers and customers represented by the eight relationships in the figure. However, the issue of governance, i.e. 'who is in charge of the supply chain', is almost indeterminate given possible myriad other relationships. An example of this is provided in Figure 10.1 for supplier S1, which supplies to customers C1–C4 and has relationships with its three fellow suppliers, S2–S4. Any attempt to draw similar relationships for the other seven firms would render the figure unreadable but would illustrate the complexities involved.

A conventional view[2] of a marketing channel is that of a vertically coordinated system of exchange, i.e. one in which channel strategy is devised and coordinated by a channel captain. A channel captain is usually the most dominant member of the channel and their role is to provide the necessary channel leadership and governance. However, in global and complex supply chains different structures and governance processes are required. Governance refers to the formal and informal rules of exchange between partners in inter-organisational settings such as supply chains. There are several governance models based on perspectives of power dependence, transaction cost analysis and agency theory. Underlying these perspectives is the assumption that inter-organisational governance is accomplished through compliance with hierarchical authority and/or differential power.

By developing appropriate governance across relationships a firm can maximise overall performance, e.g. efficiency and productivity. Further, effective management of supply chain relationships depends on the ability of managers to appropriately 'fit' elements with environmental opportunities and threats. Fit is defined as the degree to which the needs, demands, goals, objectives and/or structures of one component are consistent with the same of another component.

Relationships are also governed by cooperation founded on an element of social exchange, that is, relational norms. Relational norms are a sub-set of norms directed

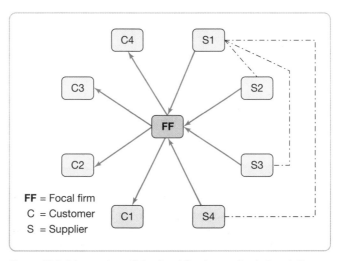

FF = Focal firm
C = Customer
S = Supplier

Figure 10.1 Macro view of the focal firm's supply chain relations

towards maintaining a relationship between partners and curtailing behaviour promoting goals of the individual partners. Relational norms are important as they set forth the scope of permissible limits on relationship behaviour. Within inter-organisational exchange relationships, relational norms have been found to be a key governance mechanism. Relational norms are different from other norms because of their bilateral nature. Adjustments under bilateral governance are based on processes of mutual adjustments, in which partners are prepared to show flexibility and will negotiate adjustments as environmental events unfold.

However, exchange partners in a global supply chain have norm expectations founded on national cultural characteristics and thus a derived relational norm between two exchange partners is embedded with cultural norm expectation artefacts. A global supply chain also requires spatial or geographic attributes to be considered. As a supply chain is concerned with coordinating the movement and storage of physical items, geographic dispersion characteristics of the supply chain – the geographic scope of suppliers' locations, production facilities, distributors and customers in the supply chain – also relate to how the supply chain is governed.

There are three reasons for including geographic dispersion as a dimension of supply chain structure. First, it influences how tasks are allocated within the focal firm. Second, the extent to which the supply chain is either concentrated or dispersed geographically most likely has a significant effect on the decision-making authority and coordination within the focal firm. Finally, the idea of geographic dispersion reflects recent trends towards the location of production facilities in different markets throughout the world.

While some research has been conducted on relational norm governance strategies, there is much to learn about establishing different relational norms to govern global supply chain relations and how managers can and should work towards establishing relational norm strategies across partners simultaneously. Consequently, the study of relational norm governance strategies in SCM as well as SCM macro-organisation structures remains an important and ongoing area of enquiry.

Organisation of the firm

The organisational structure of the firm is an important part of strategy. Chapter 13 discusses corporate strategy in more detail, but this section considers issues directly affecting organisational structure and design. The management activities essential for strategy are:

- *planning* – defining goals, establishing strategy and developing sub-plans to coordinate activities;
- *organising* – determining what needs to be done, how and when it will be done, and who will do it;
- *leading* – directing and motivating all involved parties and resolving conflicts;
- *controlling* – monitoring activities to ensure they are accomplished as planned.[3]

An appropriate organisational structure is required to ensure these activities are successful as an inappropriate structure may well be inefficient and ineffective. An example is the information technology-enabled process reengineering implemented for the Holland Supply Bank (HSB), a Dutch flower sales intermediary. The Netherlands leads the world in producing and distributing cut flowers and potted plants, with a global market share of over 50 per cent and annual sales from the seven Dutch flower auctions exceeding €2.2 billion. These auctions are large events, with about 2,000 buyers conducting 50,000 transactions daily with growers at auction sites almost 750,000 square metres in size. The seven auctions use the traditional 'Dutch auction' method for determining price where a clock hand starting at a high price drops until a buyer stops the clock to bid for a lot at the price determined by the clock hand.

Logistically, an auction site acts as a central hub for transferring products from sellers to buyers. However, the weaknesses of this approach are multiple handling and repackaging of products that incur higher costs and damage. Two flower auctions sought to solve these structural weaknesses by creating HSB to mediate purchases by large customers. Prices, lot sizes and product and delivery specifications are set by contract and electronic data interchange is used to communicate orders and coordinate settlements and delivery. The logistical benefits include fewer logistics activities at the auction site as growers can directly and efficiently transfer products in bulk to buyers with no repackaging costs.[4]

An organisational structure is the manner in which a firm arranges or rearranges itself and an organisation chart is used to display this structure. The chart contains a vertical dimension, in which the organisation is considered to be either a tall or a flat structure, and a horizontal dimension, in which an organisation is considered to be either wide or narrow. Figure 10.2 shows example organisation charts for these two structures.

The vertical dimension lays out who is in charge of whom and who makes the decisions inside the organisation. It represents a hierarchy of authority within a firm and also details the span of control, which refers to the number of people who can report to

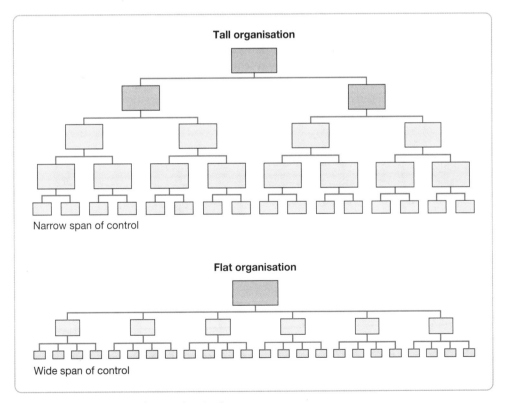

Figure 10.2 Organisational span of control
Source: adapted from Fontaine (2007).

a single manager inside the hierarchy. The upper chart in the figure is a tall organisation with five levels – in a larger organisation there will probably be more levels. Managers in a tall organisation tend to have a narrow span of control due to the numerous levels, which means there may be no more than five or six people reporting to any one individual.

The horizontal dimension of an organisation addresses the division and assignment of tasks and functions across various departments within the organisation. The lower chart in the figure represents a flat organisation. The flat structure results from having fewer levels; there are three in this case. In a flat organisational structure managers tend to have a wide span of control because there are fewer levels, so there could be as many as ten or twelve people reporting to any one individual.

Other general organisational issues include centralised and decentralised decision making, formalisation, and hierarchy of authority. Centralised decision making refers to a business model where decisions are directed to the top of the organisation, while decentralised decision making tends to push the decisions down to the lowest levels, which can be a good thing. A benefit of decentralised decision making is that those individuals at lower levels in the organisation best know the firm's processes and are in a better position to respond to external and internal drivers and make decisions to control those drivers. Formalisation is the degree to which an organisation tends to document its processes, rules and regulations. Hierarchy of authority relates to who is in charge of which elements and who reports to whom, and has implications for the division of labour as many tasks are divided and distributed across the organisation.

The three most common organisational types are a functional structure, a divisional structure and a matrix structure. The functional structure, shown in Figure 10.3, is by far the most popular organisational structure as probably 65–75 per cent of firms use it. The functional structure represents how most organisations align themselves into various departments, for example production, marketing, logistics, accounting, etc.

Decision making in a functional structure occurs at the top and thus there is more upper management control in the organisation. A functional structure also fosters stability and efficiency as employees know what their role is and as a group they all use similar processes so it is an effective way of operating that can achieve economies of scale.

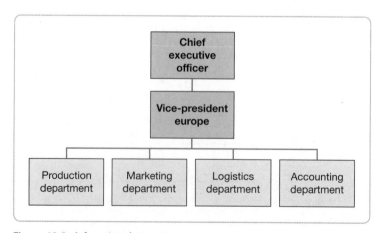

Figure 10.3 A functional structure

Source: adapted from Fontaine (2007).

Disadvantages of the functional structure include poor communication and conflict between departments. A great deal of literature on functional structures is focused on the effect of what is called the functional 'silo', where an organisation has very thick walls so that various departments are isolated from each other and employees of those departments don't think in terms of company-wide teamwork.

Michael Porter proposed three competitive strategies for organisations to pursue to meet their overall corporate objectives:[5]

- *cost leadership* – where an organisation focuses on those factors that will help it achieve and maintain a low-cost position in its industry;
- *differentiation* – where an organisation creates a unique image or value for a product or service;
- *focus* – where an organisation takes actions to compete in a particular industry segment or 'niche' that can be based on a variety of criteria, including customers, products and geography.

Organisations must develop complementary and specific functional area strategies to implement any or a combination of these competitive strategies. However, some research has shown that organisations performing well in one functional area also tend to be good performers in other functional areas; thus customers can and should expect overall firm excellence rather than compensating tradeoffs between functional areas.[6] Nevertheless, process integration across functional areas can still be a source of competitive advantage for better performing organisations and logistics can act as a bridge for such cross-functional integration.

The divisional structure shown in Figure 10.4 is concerned with placing groups of people with similar abilities where they are needed all across the organisation. For example, under a functional structure, you would expect to find logisticians only in the accounting department, but under a divisional structure you may find logisticians in different divisions of the same company, in separate logistics departments dedicated to separate product lines.

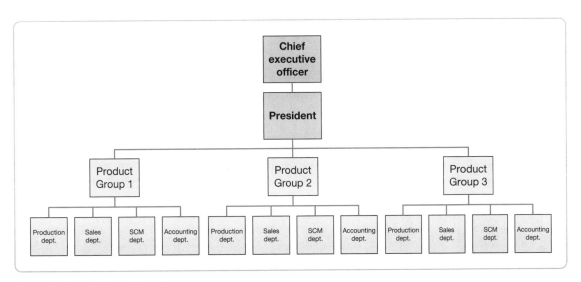

Figure 10.4 A divisional structure

Source: adapted from Fontaine (2007).

The advantage of the divisional structure lies in the coordination of functions within the separate divisions. Behind any single product, market or geographic group is one person who is in charge of all the functions within the division. This improves the ability of a firm to respond to customer issues because there is more accountability – everyone in a given division reports to a single individual at the top of the division rather than to a department supervisor. This arrangement also helps to develop managerial and executive skills as people working in a divisional structure are exposed to all of the other functions, unlike the 'siloing' effect seen in a straight functional structure.

The disadvantage of the divisional structure lies in redundant efforts and resources due to multiple departments performing essentially the same tasks across the organisation, which is inefficient on many levels. Within the divisional structure there is also a reduction in specialisation and occupational skills, not to mention a high probability of in-house competition between the various divisions.

The matrix structure shown in Figure 10.5 for a US motorcycle division such as Harley-Davidson, discussed in Chapter 7, incorporates elements of both functional and divisional structures and yet does not operate like either. The structures in Figure 10.5 are easily identifiable: the illustration depicts a single division of a large firm that contains elements of a functional structure comprised of a production department, a legal department, an engineering department and an accounting department. There are also three projects cutting across all departments horizontally: projects alpha, beta and gamma.

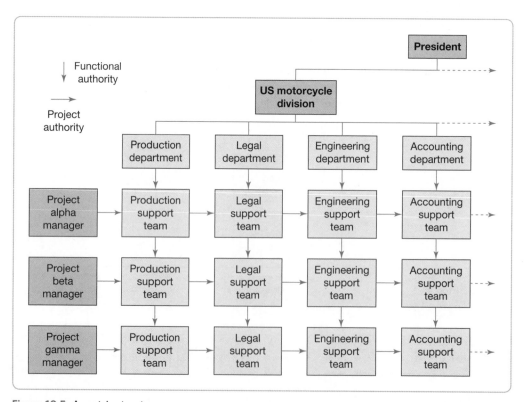

Figure 10.5 A matrix structure

Source: adapted from Fontaine (2007).

Each project that passes through the functional structure of this division will be allocated its own production, legal, engineering and accounting support teams. The manager for each project has no staff and must assemble them from the functional areas of the organisation in order to see the project through from conception to completion. In other words, the project manager must borrow staffing from each department. The challenge is that each department has a finite number of staff and the demands of each project are not equal – so one project may require more staffing than the others. Accordingly, there will be competition among them for staffing.

The advantage of the matrix structure is that it is extremely efficient, particularly when resources are scarce. This structure is a good way to ensure that expensive specialists are busy and using their skills on the most critical portions of a project for the good of the organisation. It also allows an organisation to begin projects quickly as there is no need to hire staff from outside – staff are readily available. The matrix structure helps develop cross-functional skills in employees as they are dealing with many different types of projects, working with and learning from many other participants with a diversity of skill sets. It also increases employee involvement because the project managers seldom possess all the necessary technical and functional knowledge; they rely on the expertise of the 'borrowed' staff to make more decisions at a technical level.

The main disadvantage of the matrix structure is that employees may become frustrated and confused with the chain of command in these hastily assembled support teams. There may also be conflicts between project and department managers concerning deadlines and priorities.

Human resources in logistics

Professor Hans-Christian Pfohl, Head of the Research and Development Committee for the European Logistics Association (ELA), wrote:

> Business is people. At the end of the day, the success or failure of a business depends on management's ability to harness the willing participation and creativity of people. Most of the actions taken to implement the SCM concept are of top-down character ... Engaging people's motivation and empowerment at all levels is a necessary complement to big one-time steps of innovation to improve performance ... Using this premise, it is rewarding to study the extent of the human capital contribution for meeting ongoing challenges.[7]

There are four primary human resource policy areas – staffing, training, compensation and evaluation of employees.[8] Some firms carefully screen for individuals with high educational attainment, excellent interpersonal, technical and communication skills, and a strong work ethic. For example, the Ritz-Carlton uses a selection process that combines interviews that determine a person's natural talents and abilities with skills assessment tests for the particular job. In contrast, Cisco Systems requires job applicants to complete 5–10 face-to-face interviews. There may also be government or legislative issues affecting staffing – see Logistics Example 10.1.

Some firms provide extensive initial training on a wide range of topics and follow up with continuous on-the-job training and mentoring. For example, Disney's Polynesian Resort has developed a training programme, Magic of Polynesia, to facilitate employee understanding

LOGISTICS EXAMPLE 10.1

EU Working Time Directive affects freight transport

In March 2005 the European Union's (EU) Working Time Directive (WTD) 93/104/EC came into effect. The main feature of the Directive was that allowable hours of work per week in EU countries were reduced from 55 to 48 in order to prevent abuse of workers by employers.

From a logistics perspective, truck drivers can work up to 60 hours a week providing the average does not exceed 48 over a four-month period. Self-employed drivers were exempt until 2009; their inclusion was affirmed by a vote in the European Parliament in June 2010. However, various organisations believe the WTD has serious implications for long-haul freight transport across Europe and into Asia and Africa.

The UK government puts the extra cost of the WTD at more than £1 billion a year, while members of the UK Freight Transport Association believe it will require them to recruit another 44,000 drivers and leave customers facing larger transport bills. A Lex Transfleet *Report on Freight Transport 2003* determined the WTD could add £18 on every UK family's monthly shopping bill, based on 4,000 tonne kilometres of freight carried each year for every man, woman and child.

The Freight Transport Association believes it won some flexibility by designating periods when drivers are 'queueing' to load or unload or are held up on the road to be treated as non-working periods. However, the UK Transport and General Workers Union disputes that interpretation, arguing there can't be a situation where drivers say they aren't working because they are stuck on the M25 (London circular motorway) due to a ferry dispute.

In the meantime, employers are reorganising drivers' working schedules so they spend their time driving rather than loading or unloading to avoid breaching the 48-hour limit. However, the real effects of the WTD have still not been calculated.

Question

Do you think the WTD legislation is good or bad for logistics?

Sources: adapted from Roland Gribben (2005) 'EU rules threaten chaos on the roads,' www.telegraph.co.uk (accessed 17 February 2005); and Lex Transfleet (2003) 'Press Release 1 April 2003.

and commitment to the business and its values. Conversely, many organisations provide minimal initial training, few ongoing development programmes and poorly implemented, on-the-job training.

Compensation systems vary widely, with some firms assuming a leading approach offering high pay and benefits, while others follow a laggard approach offering lower pay and little or no benefits. For example, Charles Schwab has taken the position that in order to provide outstanding customer service, employees must also be treated well. This translates into Schwab employees with five years of service being eligible for four-week paid sabbaticals that can be combined with vacation time. Employees at Cisco Systems can earn on-the-spot bonuses of up to $2,000 for exceptional performance.

Evaluation and feedback procedures also differ significantly between firms. Some firms evaluate employees infrequently and provide feedback primarily in terms of job quantity, while others focus more on job quality and provide frequent and specific behavioural feedback. For example, at General Electric some managers annually receive 3–4 formal reviews and feedback about their performance in addition to feedback regarding their progress towards achieving agreed-upon promotion goals. Communication is vital, as shown by DHL's unique approach to driving around to talk to employees, as discussed in Logistics Example 10.2.

LOGISTICS EXAMPLE 10.2

Internal organisational communication: driving the message home to employees

Informed and satisfied employees are arguably the linchpin within any successful organisation. However, one of the most effective ways to ensure that is arguably one of the least practised. Communication is the key to employee engagement. Defined as an exchange of information, good internal communication requires a two-way process and is a vital means of addressing staff. Internal communication helps employees to understand a firm's vision, values and culture and on maintaining open lines of communication is one of the most effective ways to build strong relationships and forge a sense of fulfilment. The logistics sector is one area where a solid internal communications strategy is essential. With members of staff located all over the world, in different places at different times, internal engagement is essential to ensure that messages are communicated, expectations are met and interaction is achieved at all levels.

Strategically, the inherent message and tone of the communication are important for the receiving audience. In the logistics sector it is important that the message is consistent so everyone receives the same communication, irrespective of their whereabouts or position within the firm. Delivering the key points in an uncomplicated and clear format is essential to ensure that messages are absorbed properly and not diluted or modified as they are discussed. The way these points are conveyed can have either a positive or negative impact, regardless of the core presentation content, so it is important to strike a balance between representing the hard truth and keeping employees' interests at heart. As firms that have mastered the art of good internal communications will know, avoiding manipulative or ambiguous messaging is key to building trust in senior management and leaders.

Timeliness is also key, particularly in the fast-moving transport industry. One of the worst communications mistakes that any firm can make is telling the public about its intentions before informing its employees. As soon as information is confirmed it is essential that details are disseminated around the firm and employees hear the news first. This creates a sense of appreciation and that all-important sense of worth. Lastly, it is also important to cater for wide-ranging cultural differences that may exist among employees in an internal communications plan, particularly in the logistics sector; where employees are based all over the world, content and messaging need to be culturally sensitive from the outset and aligned throughout the process.

With a suitable strategy in place, the next stage is implementation. Although simpler to do, it is important to ensure that the structure and tools are selected correctly to suit the audience. Within the logistics sector, the structure of the programme needs to be bottom-up rather than downward or horizontal. A programme that focuses solely on top management will not achieve the overall aims of the campaign as it is likely these employees are already well informed.

Logistics example 10.2 (*cont.*)

The operative tools complete the final piece in the internal communications process. Firms need to develop and maintain a number of diverse channels that meet the needs of their stakeholders and allow effective communication to take place. While traditional written methods are still considered effective, new, more interactive channels have entered into the mix that broaden the campaign's reach and satisfy an ever-diversifying audience. Holding events is one way of doing this. Taking people out of their 'day jobs' and creating a dynamic experience breaks the traditional. One logistics organisation that has done this well is DHL.

In 2007 DHL launched an internal multi-country initiative programme for its emerging markets region. The objective was to expose the company's latest initiatives to the workforce in this region and inspire each employee. DHL and Maverick Events Worldwide took a completely fresh approach that would redefine the way the company addressed its staff. A Formula-1-style fold-out vehicle was transformed into an innovative mobile communication unit that could literally drive the programme to employees based anywhere in Russia, the Middle East or South Africa. The vehicle allowed Maverick to spread the message to a substantial percentage of the DHL workforce in or around the workplace. During the first few months of the campaign, the vehicle travelled to over 5,600 employees and covered a distance of more than 8,000 miles. The programme has been so successful that a replica version of the Formula 1 truck that folds away into just 21 cases and can be transported by land, air and sea has been created for remote areas that are beyond the truck's reach. Even lighter versions are being rolled out to suit smaller countries and offices.

Question

What are potential barriers to effective communication inside a firm?

Sources: adapted from Rob Evans 'Internal communication: A logistical nightmare?' *Logistics and Transport Focus*, 2008, Vol. 10, No. 9, pp.24–27; and Maverick Advertising and Design Ltd (2011) www.mavad.co.uk/#/home/ (accessed 7 August 2011).

Logistics skills[9]

It has been suggested that senior-level logistics managers need to be proficient in three skill categories: management skills, business skills and logistics skills, in order of importance. A consensus view across studies of supply chain managers appears to be that they regard themselves as 'managers first and logisticians second' and require skills and competencies sets that comprise both general management skills and competencies and specific logistics/supply chain skills and competencies.

SCM implies a 'horizontal' organisational orientation rather than a 'vertical' one. The implication is that the management development process must focus on a holistic view of the way in which customer value is created and delivered. This in turn suggests the need to develop an awareness of how interfaces in a supply chain need to be managed and how actions taken in one area might affect the performance of the whole. Thus, there is a need for a greater level of 'cross-training' across functional boundaries such that the supply chain manager of the future will require a 'T-shaped' skills profile in Figure 10.6. The idea here is that as well as bringing specific logistics management skills to the job (the vertical bar), supply chain managers need to have a wide understanding of related areas such as business process engineering, asset management and activity-based costing (the horizontal bar).

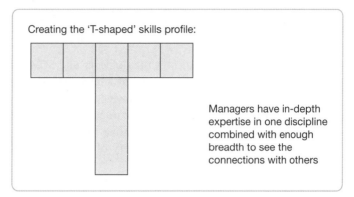

Figure 10.6 Cross-functional skills profile

Source: Management development and the supply chain manager of the future, *International Journal of Logistics Management*, Vol. 16, No. 2, p. 181 (Mangan, J. and Christopher, M. 2005), International Journal of Logistics Management by Emerald Group Publishing Limited. Reproduced with permission of Emerald Group Publishing Limited in the format Journal via Copyright Clearance Center. © Emerald Group Publishing Limited all rights reserved.

There are seven major business transformations which have significant implications for SCM skills profiles, as shown in Table 10.1. These transformations are mapped against both their direct impact on the supply chain and the skills which would be required as a result. This framework comprises both management skills and competencies and logistics/SCM skills and competencies. These skills requirements for supply chain managers are wide and varied, perhaps more so than might be the case with other categories of managers, with an emphasis in particular on what could be described as interpersonal and communications skills.

Table 10.1 Business transformations and implications for management skills

Business transformation	Leading to	Skills required
From supplier- to customer-centric	The design of customer-driven supply chains	Market understanding, customer insight
From push to pull	Higher levels of agility and flexibility	Management of complexity and change
From inventory to information	Capturing and sharing information on real demand	Information systems and information technology expertise
From transactions to relationships	Focus on service and responsiveness as the basis for customer retention	Ability to define, measure and manage service requirements by market segment
From 'trucks and sheds' to end-to-end pipeline management	A wider definition of supply chain cost	Understanding of the 'cost-to-serve' and time-based performance indicators
From functions to processes	The creation of cross-functional teams focused on value creation	Specific functional excellence with cross-functional understanding. Team working capabilities
From standalone competition to network rivalry	More collaborative working with supply chain partners	Relationship management and win-win orientation

Source: Management development and the supply chain manager of the future, *International Journal of Logistics Management*, Vol. 16, No. 2, p. 181 (Mangan, J. and Christopher, M. 2005), International Journal of Logistics Management by Emerald Group Publishing Limited. Reproduced with permission of Emerald Group Publishing Limited in the format Journal via Copyright Clearance Center. © Emerald Group Publishing Limited all rights reserved.

A shift in roles to knowledge work

The foregoing discussion indicates that logistics and SCM human resources, especially at management level, require new forms of knowledge. There has been a shift in thinking about the role of workers towards a knowledge base, particularly in the Western or North Atlantic nations of North America and Europe, fostered by Peter Drucker's book *The Post-Capitalist Society*.[10] This view is in contrast to that of Edith Penrose, who reformulated familiar cost functions used in the theory of the firm to develop a resource-based view (RBV) in the late 1950s.

Penrose argued that as average costs are increased by adjustments in the rate of output, changing the rate of output also dislocates the allocation of resources, particularly human resources. She further argued that employees are usually the most productive when they repeat the same routines; when their work is repetitive, productivity may improve as a result of learning on the job. As a firm grows, the internal division of labour has to change and this forces people to change their roles. Their previous learning of job-specific skills becomes obsolete as they return to the start of the 'learning curve' in their new job.[11]

Drucker's thesis is that society has undergone three evolutions in the concept of knowledge and related applications since the mid-1700s. The first evolution was the 'industrial revolution' where knowledge was applied to *tools, processes and products* (1750–1880); for example, the steam engine which provided a change in manufacturing processes. This 'revolution' led to the definition of two social classes – proletariat and bourgeois – and the development of Marxist and communist thinking. This evolution demonstrated the first need for 'societal logistics' to transport people and feed them as they moved from agricultural communities to expanding cities and fostered theoretical work on marketing and distribution by academics such as Arch Shaw and Louis Weld in Kent and Flint's Era 1, referred to in Chapter 1.

In the second evolution, knowledge was applied to the *study of work* (1880–1945) and included Frederick Taylor's famous principles of scientific management brought about by his 'time-motion' studies of factory workers. Taylor's work had an impact on the set-up of factories, workplace locations and activities, training and productivity. This 'productivity revolution' led to the proletariat becoming bourgeois and accounted for the disenchantment of Marxism and most forms of centrally planned communism as sustainable economic systems.[12] The productivity of manual workers was deemed to have achieved maximum efficiency and productivity (see Penrose, above) and from a logistics perspective was responsible for much of our current thoughts and practice on sourcing and wider supply chain issues, such as outsourcing, 'offshoring' and 'nearshoring', as discussed in Chapters 3 and 4. In other words, not much true manufacturing is done in the North Atlantic countries any more.

The last evolution relates to the application of *management knowledge* from 1945 onwards in a 'management revolution'. The US 'GI Bill of Rights' for education after the Second World War developed more trained managers in the workforce, changes in the control over the means of production, i.e. between supply chain participants, and changes in the ownership of the means of production, i.e. by firms and nations. The significance of this 'revolution' is that two new 'classes' of workers have emerged: knowledge and service workers. However, a caveat here is that this analysis applies to the North Atlantic countries and may not be applicable to many other countries around the world.

Knowledge workers are considered those who research, use and disseminate knowledge in work, for example managers, investment bankers and academics. The economic challenge regarding these workers involves determining their *productivity*. In this current era of recession that many experts believed was caused by poor banking practices, how can society evaluate the productivity, or lack of it, behind investment bankers' actions and the internal 'bonus culture' that follows such actions?

Service workers are those who undertake and provide the front-line services that support the North Atlantic countries' economies, for example staff in restaurants, retail and leisure. The social challenge regarding these workers involves ensuring their *dignity*. Many people do not consider service work rewarding despite its necessity. For example, many students think of undertaking a career in fast-food retailing as a hard endeavour and uninteresting, i.e. it is only 'McJobs' and should be no more than a last resort. However, many major fast-food chains offer salaries, benefits and promotional opportunities on a par with other major firms and there are many logistics and supply chain challenges of receiving supplies, converting them into products for sale and consumption, and dealing with much varied and independent consumer demand.

This last 'revolution' focusing on managerial issues has led to deeper 'scientific analyses' within organisations, particularly regarding the increasing adoption of technology. The interface between humans and technology will be discussed next.

Human resources and technology

The increasing use of technology, for example automation and computerisation, is reducing human intervention in many aspects of logistics, particularly the physical handling of products, and thus has important implications for job design. However, equilibrium should be achieved between the 'social system' or people and the 'technical system' to gain optimal process performance.

A knowledge worker is someone who knows more about his or her job than anyone else in the organisation, and is autonomous, project-oriented and holds the tacit knowledge required for problem solving, creativity, strategic flexibility and market responsiveness.[13] Knowledge workers are thus adaptive in decision-making situations and able to make quick responses.

Technology, meanwhile, leads to increased process standardisation, reduced human intervention and error, and improves process velocity, accuracy and precision (i.e. quality control) and dependability, and is thus better for productivity, as noted by Edith Penrose. Various process improvement techniques due to technology include just-in-time (JIT), total quality management (TQM) using techniques such as enterprise resources planning (ERP), collaborative planning, forecasting and replenishment (CPFR), and transport and warehouse management systems (TMS/WMS), discussed in previous chapters, and new technologies such as radio frequency identification (RFID) and 'pick-to-voice' or 'pick-to-light' operator assistance systems. An example of one such system is given in Logistics Example 10.3.

While each has its advantages, there are tradeoffs required between people and technology in terms of cost and flexibility. Table 10.2 provides a list of issues surrounding these tradeoffs. In summary, there is an argument that using human resources is more akin to agile processes while technology works best in lean scenarios.

LOGISTICS EXAMPLE 10.3

Implementing pick-to-voice technology in warehousing

Pick-to-voice (PTV) technology has revolutionised the use of labour in warehouse and distribution centres. DC workers can dramatically affect an organisation's profitability – they can operate very efficiently or waste time, make mistakes and make wrong decisions. PTV technology is part of a process termed dynamic workforce optimisation (DWO), which is a people-centric solution to the challenges of labour use in the DC to improve floor logistics and maximise the contribution of the front-line workforce.

PTV is a computer-aided warehouse data-capture technology that instructs an operator as to what items to pick from which storage or pick face location. The operator then confirms what has been picked, either verbally or by scanning a barcode at the pick location. These data are communicated to a warehouse management system (WMS), which in turn transmits the next pick to be executed by the operator. The PTV hardware consists of an earpiece to receive pick instructions, a microphone and/or barcode scanner to confirm the pick, and a mini-computer that communicates with the WMS, the data being transferred wirelessly between them. The data transmitted between the PTV and the WMS enable effective and accurate performance metrics via the collection of real-time data. These real-time data aid instantaneous decision support and prioritisation of tasks following certain events, such as pick errors.

Other advantages of PTV include improved productivity from increased pick rates, throughput and fill rates; reduced error, wastage and supply costs; improved process safety, control and visibility; enhanced operator satisfaction; and minimal operator training. It also removes language barriers by being multilingual and does not require written instructions or responses. These features enable employers to hire non-native speaking and non-literate operators, which potentially can reduce labour costs, for example by employing migrant workers from lower-cost economies.

However, several disadvantages have also been noted, including the inability of computerised voice software to recognise uninterrupted interactions or commands; high infrastructure costs for WMS interfaces and wireless technology; operator confusion as they are 'blind' to the overall pick list and cannot anticipate or maximise order arrangements; and issues of 'dehumanising' operators via wearable technologies, which might increase warehouse staff turnover resulting from operator physical ailments such as repetitive strain and hearing injuries or from a lack of fulfilment in their work.

PTV is nevertheless a widely adopted innovation and the idea of DWO goes further than that and focuses on everything a DC worker does regarding floor logistics and leverages the fact that the worker is always in constant, real-time communication. For example, a worker can advise the system of blocked aisles and coordination issues between workers who finish tasks at different times, and identify why certain exception situations occur. So while voice technology emphasises picking and data capture, the benefits come when it is strategically used, thus taking DC workers to new levels of effectiveness.

Question

Could PTV work for other picking situations such as consumers buying groceries?

Sources: adapted from Steven Gerrard 'Optimising floor logistics,' *Logistics Manager*, 2003, November, pp.36–39; and David B. Grant and Tim Butcher 'Implementing pick-to-voice technology in warehousing,' *Proceedings of the 15th Annual Logistics Research Network (LRN) Conference*, 2011, University of Southampton, e-proceedings.

Table 10.2 Human versus technology

Humans	Technology	
● Labour costs are highest capital costs	● High initial startup costs	
● Cost is continually rising with inflation	● Long payback periods	Cost
● Trend towards outsourcing (someone else's problem) and offshoring (cheaper labour)	● Tangible short-term benefits (e.g. faster, more accurate processing)	
● Offer flexible, bespoke processes	● Offers standardised processes	
● Offer dexterity	● Offers repeatable processes	Flexibility
● Offer 'workarounds' or compensation for process inefficiencies	● Requires modularity to become flexible	
Suited to agile processes?	*Suited to lean processes?*	

The interaction between human and technological resources might best be addressed by invoking the application of social-technical systems (STS).[14] STS looks to obtain joint optimisation of the technical and social systems and provide a quality of work life through employee participation in system design and the use of semi-autonomous work groups, and is illustrated in Figure 10.7.

Retail replenishment: an example[15]

Store operations represent a large share of costs in the retail supply chain. Labour is the second largest cost factor in retailing and most retail workers are employed at store level; thus store handling accounts for about half of retail operation costs. Despite the increasing use of technology at store level as discussed in Chapter 8, most in-store logistics operations are still performed manually and rely on human labour. The way these human resources are managed therefore impacts a retailer's performance. As managerial systems need store-level input, the interaction of employees with these systems strongly influences their outcome.

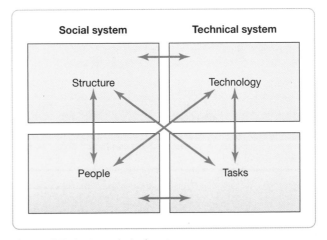

Figure 10.7 Socio-technical systems

Source: adapted from Bostrom and Heinen (1977a, p.25).

The interaction between employees and systems in the retail replenishment process comprises four main tasks of the in-store logistics operation: ordering (shop floor and central allocation), data accuracy (checks and quality), physical replenishment of products (replenishment schedules and triggers) and inventory management (back of store and shelf management). The requirements towards these interactions at shop floor operations can differ between the four areas depending on the individual requirements of the retail concept, and, different concepts can exist within one firm. Also, different categories within a store can be managed in individual ways.

The amount of interaction and the impact on performance of this interaction are thus important in the store replenishment process. Figure 10.8 illustrates a typology of how employees interact or communicate with systems and the extent to which employees can impact or influence the systems and data. The four types of retailers according to their categories shown in the resultant matrix are as follows:

- *Operations focus.* The operations focus retailer designs its replenishment system in a rather centralised and standardised way. Replenishment is managed to achieve efficient processing for a high throughput of products. Employees concentrate on achieving a high throughput of customers through the standardised process, instead of taking much time for every individual customer and its needs. Interaction between employees and systems is frequent. Unusual and time-consuming issues are passed to the next management level to be dealt with.

- *Store-based retailing.* The store-based retailer gives a lot of decision making to shop floor employees as local knowledge and judgement are essential for store operations. The store employees need to interact with the system often and can adjust data and orders according to their store's specific needs.

- *Customer care focus.* At the customer care focus retailer, interaction with the customer and not the systems is at the centre of employees' attention. The replenishment system is designed in a way that the employees do not need to interact with it often but can if need be for customer orders. In case a customer has a particular request, the employee can use the system to learn whether he can help the customer and place orders on the system.

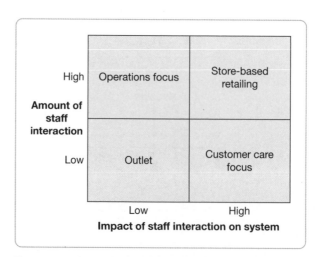

Figure 10.8 Replenishment interaction typology
Source: Trautrims *et al.* (2011).

● *Outlet.* The employees hardly interact with the replenishment system at an outlet retailer. They replenish to shelf what is delivered to the store and have little or no say in what these products are. Correspondingly, they cannot see which products are coming to the store or order products for customers. A bargain or discount retailer is an example for such a replenishment system. The way promotions are often run at some retailers, where inventory is pushed into stores, follows such an approach.

Gender issues in logistics

An important human resource issue in logistics for this next decade is gender, i.e. more female involvement in logistics and supply chain activities. Many people consider that the logistics and supply chain professions and related careers are for men only and findings from two recent surveys[16] show that females are very under-represented in these domains:

● Only 21 per cent of the workforce is female in a majority of companies operating in the logistics and supply chain sector.

● This statistic is significantly lower at management level, with only 10 per cent of staff being female.

● Regarding salary and benefits, females are paid 23 per cent less than their male counterparts.

Further, old habits die hard, with half of survey respondents still believing that working in logistics is harder for women than for men and that women need to show higher performance in order to receive the same amount of appreciation. Yet despite these findings almost 75 per cent of the logistics and supply chain professionals surveyed believe that opportunities for women for building a sound professional career in logistics are better today than they have ever been. Aspects of being a logistics professional that female respondents liked best include the utilisation of different areas of expertise and a fast-paced environment.

Respondents believe that future requirements will include a high level of IT skills. They also stressed the importance of having a mentor at some point in their careers who provided assistance in the form of advice, guidance, moral support, constructive criticism, understanding politics, networking and help finding a job. This finding is not surprising when less than 30 per cent of logistics professionals surveyed believe that schools and universities and industry are supportive in promoting this industry to women.

There have been several initiatives to address gender imbalances in the UK. An example of women addressing them directly is the Women in Logistics UK association designed to provide networking and mentoring opportunities, which has more than 400 members.[17] There are similar associations in the US and Canada.[18]

In an industrial context the British Armed Forces provide opportunities for women to join the military in transport or other logistics capacities which support activities in peacetime, e.g. emergency response to floods, or in operational theatres such as Bosnia or Afghanistan.[19] Military driver training is undertaken at the Defence School of Transport (DST), a 740-acre site in the East Riding of Yorkshire that has 17 miles of road and 16 miles of cross-country terrain. More than 550 female recruits from all service branches – Royal Air Force, Royal Navy and the Army – annually attend courses at the DST. The DST maintains a close liaison with the government's Department for Transport and Skills for Logistics group of the Sector Skills Council.

Finally, an example of addressing gender issues from an academic perspective was the *EMPATHY Net-Works Project* in 2006–2007 hosted at the University of Hull's Business School in conjunction with its Logistics Institute, and which was part-funded by the European Social Fund.[20] The overall aim of the project was to increase representation of women in the logistics and supply chain (LaSC) industries in the Hull and Humber region by raising awareness of LaSC industries and opportunities and equipping women to enter LaSC industries through a taught programme and a mentoring programme providing support and guidance from women managers working in industry. The project aimed to encourage women to pursue careers in the LaSC industries and to raise the skill levels of women so that they might take advantage of the opportunities provided in the new employment and high-growth areas of these industries.

The project outcomes were positive: 60 students were recruited onto the project over 4 cohorts and 52 of them successfully completed the taught programme (6 students withdrew as they had gained employment) while 2 students only signed up for mentoring. There were significant changes in participants' employment status from when they enrolled on the project to when they had completed the programme. Examples of typical career outcomes included employment in a local authority planning department, as a sales and marketing coordinator at a local transport company, and as a claims administrator at a South African logistics company, as well as work experience at a local humanitarian aid organisation.

Summary

The organisation of a firm's activities has three distinct and fundamental stages: the overall organisation with its various partners in its supply chain, its internal organisation as to structure and design, and its organisation of its human resources, particularly as they interact with technology. The recurrent themes of collaboration, coordination and communication are essential for all three stages. Additionally, firms must recognise that employees today are more likely to be knowledge workers and thus their job design with respect to skills and their interactions with technology require more sophisticated thought and application, including considering how agile and lean strategies may be used with people and technology respectively, and the application of socio-technical systems theory. Finally, an example of such issues in retail replenishment and a discussion of gender issues in logistics rounded off this chapter.

The next chapter considers global aspects of logistics and supply chain management.

DISCUSSION QUESTIONS

1 How should logistics and supply chain management be organised?

2 Describe the different types of organisational structures.

3 What are the benefits of electronic data interchange (EDI)?

4 Are human resources in logistics and supply chains knowledge workers, and why?

5 Do you think that the logistics sector is leading other sectors regarding gender issues?

Suggested reading

Achrol, Ravi S. and Michael J. Etzel 'The structure of reseller goals and performance in marketing channels,' *Journal of the Academy of Marketing Science*, 2003, Vol. 31, No. 2, pp.146–163.

Bostrom, Robert P. and J. Stephen Heinen 'MIS problems and failures: A socio-technical perspective: Part I,' *MIS Quarterly*, 1977a, Vol. 1, No. 3, pp. 17–32.

Bostrom, Robert P. and J. Stephen Heinen 'MIS problems and failures: A socio-technical perspective: Part II', *MIS Quarterly*, 1977b, Vol. 1, No. 4, pp. 11–28.

Butcher, Tim 'Supply chain knowledge work: Should we restructure the workforce for improved agility?' *International Journal of Agile Systems and Management*, 2007, Vol. 2, No. 4, pp.376–392.

Drucker, Peter *The Post-Capitalist Society*, New York: HarperCollins, 1993.

Griffith, David A. and Matthew B. Myers 'The performance implications of strategic fit of relational norm governance strategies in global supply chain relationships,' *Journal of International Business Studies*, 2005, Vol. 36, pp.254–269.

Kambil, Ajit and Eric van Heck 'Reengineering the Dutch flower auctions: A framework for analyzing exchange organizations,' *Information Systems Research*, 1998, Vol. 9, No. 1, pp.1–12.

Koechlin, Cecilia Loureiro and Barbara Allan 'What is it? Approaches to developing shared meaning about the logistics and supply chain industries: Lessons from the EMPATHY Net-Works project,' *International Journal of Logistics: Research and Applications*, 2008, Vol. 11, No. 5, pp.381–392.

Mangan, John and Martin Christopher 'Management development and the supply chain manager of the future,' *International Journal of Logistics Management*, 2005, Vol. 16, No. 2, pp.178–191.

McAfee, R. Bruce, Myron Glassman and Earl D. Honeycutt 'The effects of culture and human resource management policies on supply chain management strategy,' *Journal of Business Logistics*, 2002, Vol. 23, No. 1, pp.1–18.

Morash, Edward A., Cornelia Dröge and Shawnee Vickery 'Boundary spanning interfaces between logistics, production, marketing and new product development,' *International Journal of Physical Distribution & Logistics Management*, 1996, Vol. 26, No. 8, pp.43–62.

Penrose, Edith *The Theory of the Growth of the Firm,* 4th ed. Oxford University Press, 2009.

Porter, Michael E. *Competitive Strategy,* New York: Free Press, 1980.

Notes

1 This section is derived from David A. Griffith and Matthew B. Myers (2005) 'The performance implications of strategic fit of relational norm governance strategies in global supply chain relationships,' *Journal of International Business Studies*, Vol. 36, pp.254–269.

2 Ravi S. Achrol and Michael J. Etzel (2003) 'The structure of reseller goals and performance in marketing channels,' *Journal of the Academy of Marketing Science*, Vol. 31, No. 2, pp.146–163.

3 Craig W. Fontaine (2007) 'Organisational structure: A critical factor for organizational effectiveness and employee satisfaction,' *Human Resource Management Knowledge Base*, Boston: Northeastern University College of Business Administration.

4 Ajit Kambil and Eric van Heck (1998) 'Reengineering the Dutch flower auctions: A framework for analyzing exchange organizations,' *Information Systems Research*, Vol. 9, No. 1, pp.1–12.

5   Michael E. Porter (1980) *Competitive Strategy*, New York: Free Press.

6   Edward A. Morash, Cornelia Dröge and Shawnee Vickery (1996) 'Boundary spanning interfaces between logistics, production, marketing and new product development,' *International Journal of Physical Distribution & Logistics Management*, Vol. 26, No. 8, p.54.

7   European Logistics Association and Kurt Salmon Associates, *Success Factor PEOPLE in Distribution Quality in Logistics*, Brussels: European Logistics Association, 2004, Preface.

8   This section is derived from R. Bruce McAfee, Myron Glassman and Earl D. Honeycutt (2002) 'The effects of culture and human resource management policies on supply chain management strategy,' *Journal of Business Logistics*, Vol. 23, No. 1, pp.1–18.

9   This section is derived from John Mangan and Martin Christopher (2005) 'Management development and the supply chain manager of the future,' *International Journal of Logistics Management*, Vol. 16, No. 2, pp.178–191.

10 This section is derived from Peter Drucker (1993) *The Post-Capitalist Society*, New York: HarperCollins.

11 Edith Penrose (2009) *The Theory of the Growth of the Firm*, 4th ed. Oxford University Press.

12 For an interesting treatise on this subject see Francis Spufford (2010) *Red Plenty*, London: Faber & Faber.

13 Tim Butcher (2007) 'Supply chain knowledge work: Should we restructure the workforce for improved agility?' *International Journal of Agile Systems and Management*, Vol. 2, No. 4, pp.376–392.

14 Robert P. Bostrom and J. Stephen Heinen (1977a) 'MIS problems and failures: A socio-technical perspective: Part I,' *MIS Quarterly*, Vol. 1, No. 3, pp. 17–32; and (1977b) 'MIS problems and failures: A socio-technical perspective: Part II,' *MIS Quarterly*, Vol. 1, No. 4, pp. 11–28.

15 This section is derived from Alexander Trautrims, David B. Grant and Chee Wong (2011) 'Investigating human and systems interactions in store replenishment operations,' *Proceedings of the 15th Annual Logistics Research Network (LRN) Conference*, University of Southampton, e-proceedings.

16 Martha C. Cooper, John Santosa and Angelina Burgos-Dominguez (2007) *Career Patterns for Women in Logistics*, Lombard, IL: Council of Supply Chain Management Professionals and Europhia Consulting (2008) 'Women in Logistics,' *Global Supply Chain Human Resource Research 2008*, Europhia Consulting: Singapore.

17 Ruth Waring (2009) 'Happy birthday, women in logistics UK!' *Logistics and Transport Focus*, Vol. 11, No. 10, pp.24–26.

18 See www.womenandlogistics.com/ and www.womeninlogistics.com/ for the US and Canada respectively.

19 Squadron Leader Leigh Wilson (2007) 'Jobs for the girls: Women and extreme logistics,' *Logistics and Transport Focus*, Vol. 9, No. 8, pp.12–14.

20 Adapted from Barbara Allan, Jane Craig, Cecilia Loureiro Koechlin and Hannah Robinson (2007) *EMPATHY Net-Works E-mentoring Project Report*, University of Hull Business School; and Cecilia Loureiro Koechlin and Barbara Allan (2008) 'What is it? Approaches to developing shared meaning about the logistics and supply chain industries: Lessons from the EMPATHY Net-Works project,' *International Journal of Logistics: Research and Applications*, Vol. 11, No. 5, pp.381–392.

Chapter 11

Global logistics

Key objectives

- To understand the nature of international and global trade.
- To consider how and why to go global.
- To describe features of international and global logistics.
- To explore international logistics documentation and terms of trade.
- To discuss logistics characteristics in various international markets.

Introduction

One of the key trends discussed in Chapter 1 was the globalisation of the world economy. Factors such as the advent of container shipping and computing power, the removal of tariff barriers, and the move to outsourcing manufacturing and services to other countries have all contributed to an increase in global trade. This trend has had a significant effect on logistics activities over the past 20 years, in addition to the container phenomenon, and will continue to do so in coming decades. This chapter considers international and global logistics in the context of this trend.

First, the increase in trade and its inherent factors are presented, followed by a discussion of the nature of global logistics and supply chain activities. Then, operational and financial aspects of global business are considered, and finally the logistics characteristics of certain key countries are presented.

The nature of international and global trade

What is the difference between international and global business? The two terms are used interchangeably in many cases, but it is useful to define them in order to understand the distinction. *Collins English Dictionary* defines international as 'concerning or involving two or more nations or nationalities'[1] and global as 'covering, influencing or relating to the whole world'.[2] Thus, firms may be considered international if they conduct business in only a few 'host' countries outside their own 'home' country. However, aggregate economic and trade statistics usually do not make this distinction and so these terms have to be considered as synonymous when examining such information. Global activities undertaken by many firms has continued apace – Table 11.1 identifies the world's 20 largest corporations as well as their sales and 'home' country of origin, notwithstanding that their markets and facilities may be scattered around the world.

With the exception of the US-based retailer Wal-Mart and a few state-owned industries, these top 20 corporations are primarily oil and gas producers or automobile manufacturers. However, Wal-Mart led all corporations in the world in 2011 with sales of US$418 billion, which represents 0.7 per cent of the world's gross domestic product (GDP) and a yearly spend of almost US$60 for every one of the almost 7 billion people on earth! Put another way, during every minute of every day in 2011 Wal-Mart generated more than $797,000 in sales and $31,180 in profit in its 8,416 stores across the globe. Over $100 billion of sales (25 per cent) were in international markets where Wal-Mart has 4,112 stores.[3] Wal-Mart's cost of sales, or purchase of goods for resale, was $305 billion (73 per cent) and many of these goods are sourced and manufactured in other countries and are thus dependent on global logistics activities to bring them to market.

Table 11.1 The world's twenty largest corporations by revenue in 2011

Rank	Company	Country	Industry	2010–11 Revenue US$ millions	2010–11 Profit US$ millions
1	Wal-Mart Stores	US	General Merchandisers	418,952	16,389
2	Royal Dutch Shell Group	UK/Netherlands	Petroleum refining	373,260	20,412
3	Exxon Mobil	US	Petroleum refining	341,578	30,460
4	BP	UK	Petroleum refining	300,439	−3,761
5	Sinopec	China	Petrochemical	284,741	10,894
6	PetroChina	China	Petroleum refining	222,333	21,240
7	Toyota Motor	Japan	Motor vehicles	202,775	2,241
8	Chevron	US	Petroleum refining	189,607	19,024
9	Total	France	Petroleum refining	188,054	14,151
10	ConocoPhillips	US	Petroleum refining	176,906	11,358
11	Volkswagen	Germany	Motor vehicles	169,846	9,150
12	General Electric	US	General Industries	149,060	11,620
13	Samsung Electronics	South Korea	Technology Hardware and Equipment	137,930	14,093
14	General Motors	US	Motor vehicles	135,592	6,172
15	Eni	Italy	Petroleum refining	132,348	8,458
16	Daimler	Germany	Motor vehicles	130,872	6,021
17	Ford Motor	US	Motor vehicles	128,954	6,561
18	Petrobras	Brazil	Petroleum refining	128,478	21,198
19	Hewlett-Packard	US	Technology Hardware and Equipment	125,682	8,761
20	E On	Germany	Gas, Water and Multi-utilities	124,315	7,835

Source: Financial Times Global 500 2011, http://media.ft.com/cms/33558890-98d4-11e0-bd66-00144feab49a.pdf

Global and international trade has increased significantly since the end of the Second World War, with merchandise exports growing by a factor of 3,300 per cent, as shown in Figure 11.1. This increase has outstripped GDP growth, due in large part to more globalised production processes and trade in parts and components, greater economic integration, and the deepening and widening of global supply chains.[4]

These three factors represent some of the major issues for the dramatic changes in logistics activities. Relocating production facilities from a home country to a host country will incur extra costs and efforts; however, firms will anticipate that these costs are outweighed by potential savings and other benefits in production processes such as reduced labour. Greater economic integration includes reductions in tariff and trade barriers, and may even include the host country establishing special free-trade zones for various home countries to use. Lastly, deeper and wider supply chains involve more participants in the supply chain, thereby adding complexity, as well as increasing the number of storage or 'Stop' nodes and length of transport or 'Go' distances and time.

A firm must develop a global supply chain or network that satisfies its particular needs in those markets. For example, supply chains in developing countries are often characterised by large numbers of smaller intermediaries, such as wholesalers, supplying large numbers of small retailers; poor and inefficient transport and storage infrastructure; large and unskilled labour pools; and a lack of supply chain support systems. Yet despite these challenges there are also many good reasons for firms to do business outside their own country.

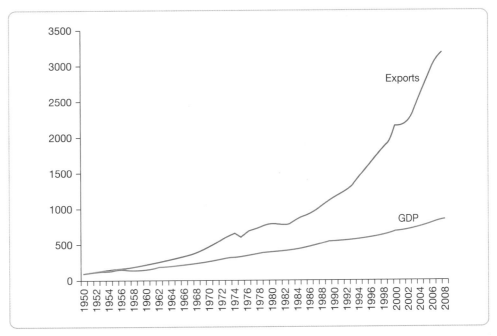

Figure 11.1 Indices for world economic growth in GDP and world merchandise exports in volumes (1950=100)

Source: UNCTAD (2009, p.7).

The why and how of going global

There are two primary ways firm can do business internationally: marketing or selling into a host market, or sourcing or obtaining supplies from another country. From a marketing or selling perspective there are several advantages for firms in entering international markets:[5]

1 Products in the home market that have reached the maturity stage in the product life cycle may be at the introductory stage in a host market.

2 Increased competition in the home market may not be as intense in a host country.

3 Excess production capacity at home may be sold in international markets.

4 Geographical diversification as part of a corporate strategy may yield additional sales and market share.

5 The potential and population size within the host market may significantly increase a firm's business activities.

There are several ways to enter an international market, as shown in Figure 11.2. A firm may initially license a host country firm to manufacture its products and pay a royalty for each unit manufactured or sold. Over time, the firm may export its own products for resale in the host market through an agent or distributor. The next step would entail a firm packaging or assembling products in the host country either in its own facilities or in a joint venture with a firm in the host country. Finally, a firm can enter a host market fully via foreign direct investment (FDI) where it locates a production plant or other facilities in the host country to conduct its business there.

As Figure 11.2 shows, as a firm moves from licensing to FDI over time it increases its involvement in the host country. This involvement may increase costs to set up facilities

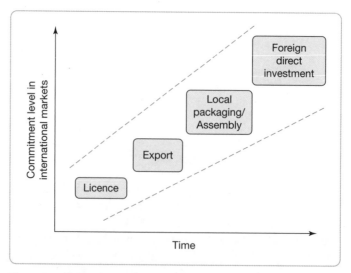

Figure 11.2 Entry into international markets
Source: adapted from Paliwoda and Thomas (1998, p.27).

and infrastructure as well as introduce associated risks such as cost changes due to currency fluctuations, uncertain labour markets in the host country, political instability of the host country and possible expropriation of assets if the host country's view towards FDI changes. However, the potential for business growth is attractive – see Logistics Example 11.1.

Firms can reduce or mitigate such risks by doing an environmental assessment of the host country. Two popular models for doing so in international markets include the SLEPT dimensions of social and cultural, legal, economic, political and technological, and the 4C factors of corporations, countries, currency and competitors.[6]

From a sourcing or import perspective, firms face similar issues and risks but must also address issues of customs or import documentation and duties.[7] Firms tend to source

LOGISTICS EXAMPLE 11.1

The growth of DHL in China

The German logistics service provider DHL announced in September 2011 that it would set up 5 more branch offices and open another 20 sales offices across China by 2015 to increase its coverage to 30 per cent of the nation's third-tier cities. DHL will spread to the central and western regions of the country because many industries are moving to these areas. 'Growth in central and western regions of China is in keeping with the government plan, and it is definitely the key priority,' according to Steve Huang, CEO of DHL Global Forwarding China.

DHL has already set up 39 branches and 26 sales offices nationwide and it plans to have 90 branches and sales offices in China by 2015; its total investment in China has so far reached $30 million.

DHL has recently opened five branch offices in line with the geographical shift in the nation's industry from the coastal areas of the Yangtze River Delta and the Pearl River Delta to the central and western regions. Foreign investment in central and western regions is being strongly encouraged by the national and provincial governments and FDI to central and western regions surged by 27.6 per cent year-on-year in 2010, compared with 15.8 per cent year-on-year in the eastern regions. The location of new branches and offices will be established according to demand.

DHL is looking beyond Beijing and Shanghai, and tapping into China's existing infrastructure in these inland markets enables the company to make its multimodal solutions that much more comprehensive. DHL customers can now not just opt for a combination of rail, road, sea and air transport with different transit times and costs but with different origins and destinations.

In the first half of 2011. China's logistics sector grew steadily, with revenue reaching 74.7 trillion yuan, up 13.7 per cent year-on-year, according to figures released by the China Federation of Logistics and Purchasing.

Question

How could the recent recession affect prospects for logistics service providers in China, including DHL?

Sources: 'Expansion of DHL and FedEx in China: Good examples of opportunity in a growing economy,' *Logistics & Transport Focus*, 2004, Vol. 6, No. 5 (June), p.63; and Wang Ying 'DHL expands service in West, Central China,' China Daily, www.chinadaily.com.cn/business/2011-09/21/content_13746165.htm (accessed 30 September 2011).

from countries that meet their needs for cost primarily but also delivery and quality. This phenomenon of international sourcing has two interesting geographical aspects to it:

- *off-shoring*: where goods are manufactured or sourced in a host country some distance away from the home country, for example a European firm sourcing from China;
- *near-shoring*: where goods are manufactured or sourced in a host country at a near distance to the home country, for example a US firm sourcing from Costa Rica.

A recent consultancy report on off-shoring noted that a substantial number of major US companies sourcing internationally have either made changes or were planning to make changes in their supply chains to source closer to home.[8] These changes were being driven by considerations other than price, such as supply chain resiliency and responsiveness. More than 75 per cent of respondents to the consultant's survey were sourcing internationally and China was the most frequent supplier country (22 per cent), followed by other Asian countries (16 per cent), Western Europe (14 per cent), Canada (12 per cent) and Mexico (9 per cent). The vast majority of respondents (79 per cent) benefited from lower costs, but other benefits included increased production capacity (24 per cent), improved logistics for accessing international markets (22 per cent), access to technology or equipment (18 per cent), access to intellectual property and ideas (11 per cent) and improved quality (11 per cent). Nearly one-quarter (24 per cent) of respondents noted higher overall off-shoring, while almost half of respondents (47 per cent) considered off-shoring as neutral or detrimental to their firm's return on investment.

Other elements regarding sourcing are related to corporate social responsibility and ethical sourcing. Much has been written about foreign labour 'sweat shops' where employees, including young children, work long hours for very little pay in unsafe conditions.[9] Firms nowadays are exercising more care that their foreign suppliers adhere to good business practices. Further, there is a natural environment aspect to sourcing abroad. The concept of environmental purchasing for a firm includes a set of purchasing policies held, actions taken and relationships formed in response to concerns associated with the natural environment. These concerns relate to the acquisition of raw materials, including supplier selection, evaluation and development; suppliers' operations; inbound distribution; packaging; recycling; reuse; resource reduction; and final disposal of the firm's products.[10]

An example of a company that is pursuing sustainable objectives is the French Group KINDY, positioned in the sock and underwear segments of the garment sector. The company has improved its ICT connections with its suppliers by using EDI, has optimised the fill-rate of its vehicles, is recycling carton packages and is moving on to resource-sharing initiatives with suppliers and customers, especially in the field of waste collection. Through more effective coordination with other members in its supply chain, it is both reducing production costs, thereby lowering energy consumption and procurement costs, and subsequently increasing its responsiveness to changing needs in the market.[11]

Features of international and global logistics activities

Trade intermediaries

There are several types of trade intermediaries that can assist firms in exporting and importing goods, including arranging necessary transportation and storage.

Export management companies (EMCs) provide export support services such as marketing products in host markets and providing trade finance expertise and credit capabilities. However, the export firm will deal directly with the host buyer and will also have to arrange the logistics activities. Conversely, *export trading companies* (ETCs) buy goods from firms in the home market for export to other countries. Using an ETC reduces the financial risk involved with exporting, although there may be a financial risk associated with the creditworthiness of the ETC.

An *international freight forwarder* is a transaction-based service contracted to manage export or import needs of a firm regarding transportation, storage, customs clearance and documentation. A firm might use the services of both an EMC and a freight forwarder to ensure a smooth and efficient business transaction.

Non-vessel-operating common carriers (NVOCCs) are shipping consolidators who secure cargo from many shippers and consolidate this cargo into full container loads. They thus act as shipping carriers and accept all responsibility for documentation; however, they are not able to clear customs and firms would require the services of a *customs broker* to attend to this task. NVOCCs may also provide ocean shipping for freight forwarders.

Containerisation

Much of the increase in international trade and globalisation is due to the development and use of standard shipping containers.[12] A standard container is considered to be 8 feet high by 8 feet wide by 20 feet long, and such a container is commonly referred to as a 20-foot equivalent unit (TEU). Containers also come in other lengths, with the second most popular style being 40 feet long. Figure 11.3 shows several types of TEU containers: a standard box container for normal goods, a refrigerated container for perishable goods and a tank container frame housing a storage tank.

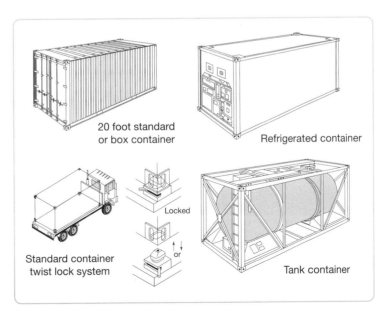

Figure 11.3 Types of containers

Sources: www.azs-bn.de/cms/index.php/en/service/types-of-containers and www.nzta. govt.nz/resources/roadcode/heavy-vehicle-road-code/gfx.

Containers have corner castings that form a unique twist lock system when used with a standardised rotating connector. The twist lock system, also shown in Figure 11.3, allows containers to be securely attached to trucks and flatbed railcars or to one another when stacked in storage or during transport on a container ship, and to container cranes and self-lifting vehicles when the container is moved.

Global container trade has increased on average 5 per cent per year over the past 20 years, as shown in Figure 11.4, and at its peak in the mid-2000s comprised 350 million TEUs a year. The rapid decline of container use in 2008 and 2009 to a low of 60 million TEU was due to the worldwide economic downturn. However, the market is recovering and in 2010 approached 200 million TEU.

World trade flows

Since most global trade takes place using ocean shipping for either bulk or container goods, global trade flows are important in terms of shipping and port capacities. Figure 11.5 shows forecast annual container trade flows in 2015 according to the Danish conglomerate A.P. Møller – Maersk Group, which runs one of the largest liner shipping companies in the world.[13] The forecast indicates that container traffic will be 42 million TEU between Asia and Europe and 31 million TEU between Asia and North America. Interestingly, there are 45 million TEU forecast for Intra-Asia, which probably reflects trade between Asian countries related to sub-contracting manufacturing and providing logistics services such as consolidation for other marketplaces.

Figure 11.5 also indicates there will be bottlenecks in port capacity to handle increased container traffic in 2015. The Maersk Group has led the shipping sector in building large vessels that can carry up to 12,000 or more TEU. However, such large ships may not be able

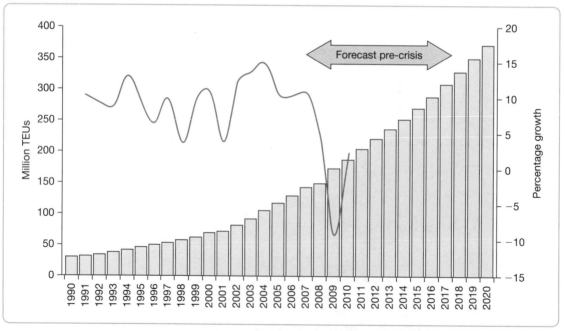

Figure 11.4 Global container trade 1990–2020 (TEU and percentage change)
Source: UNCTAD (2009, p.25).

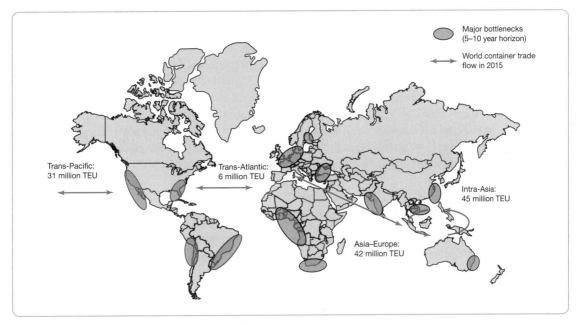

Figure 11.5 World container trade flows by 2015
Source: Maersk Line (2008).

to go through the Panama or Suez Canals and thus take longer to reach their destinations and many ports around the world do not have ship berths or handling equipment sufficient to attend to these behemoths. One solution to this problem is the concept of port-centric logistics,[14] where a few large ports such as Shanghai, Singapore, Rotterdam and Los Angeles act as hubs for the very large ships, i.e. greater than 12,000 TEU, to offload their cargo. Subsequently, consolidated loads are put onto smaller feeder ships and transported to smaller ports such as the Humber ports complex discussed in Chapter 4, or despatched via rail or road from the large port complex.

International trade documentation

International trade documentation takes several forms and can be complex.[15] Following is a sample of common export documents.

Air freight shipments require *airway bills*, which can never be made in directly negotiable form and are shipper-specific, for example Fed-Ex, UPS or DHL.

A *bill of lading* is a contract between the owner of the goods and the carrier. For vessels, there are two types: a straight bill of lading, which is non-negotiable, and a negotiable or shipper's order bill of lading. The latter can be bought, sold or traded while the goods are in transit. The customer usually needs an original as proof of ownership to take possession of the goods.

A *commercial invoice* is a bill for the goods from the seller to the buyer. These invoices are often used by governments to determine the true value of goods when assessing customs duties. Governments that use the commercial invoice to control imports will often specify its form, content, number of copies required, language to be used and other characteristics.

An *export packing list* is considerably more detailed and informative than a standard domestic packing list. It lists seller, buyer, shipper, invoice number, date of shipment, mode of transport, carrier, and itemises quantity, description, the type of package, such as a box, crate, drum, or carton, the quantity of packages, total net and gross weight in kilograms, package marks, and dimensions, if appropriate.

The *electronic export information* (EEI) form or *shippers export declaration* (SED) is the most common of all export documents. It is required for all shipments above certain levels of value and for shipments of any value requiring an export licence.

A *certificate of origin* is required by some countries for all or only certain products. In many cases, a statement of origin printed on a company letterhead will suffice. An exporter should verify whether a certificate of origin is required with the buyer and/or an experienced shipper/freight forwarder.

International trade finance

International trade finance relies on the use of a documentary letter of credit (LC), which is a written undertaking given by a bank on behalf of an importer to pay an exporter a given sum of money within a specified time, providing that the exporter presents documents which comply with the terms laid down in the LC. Letters of credit can be for any amount, in any freely traded currency, and subject to the presentation of compliant documents may be payable at sight, which means as soon as a compliant set of documents is presented to the paying bank or after a specified term, for example at 30, 60, 90 or 180 days of sight or the bill of lading date. If the documents are not presented exactly as specified in the LC, payment will not be made unless the importer gives their authority to waive or amend the specified condition.[16]

A fundamental principle of LCs is that banks deal with documents and not with the goods to which the documents refer. For example, if the importer is not happy with the quality of the goods but the documents comply with the terms and conditions of the LC, the importer's bank is obliged to pay the exporter. Thus, an LC's terms and conditions would need to specify various and relevant business terms to be truly effective.

A revocable LC can be cancelled or amended by the applicant or the opening bank without prior notice to the exporter. With an irrevocable LC the issuing bank gives its irrevocable undertaking to pay if all the terms of the LC are met. The issuing bank can amend or cancel its undertaking only if all parties to the LC consent to the change.

Incoterms[17]

The terms of international trade are required to be included on the actual shipping and export documents and note which party, buyer or seller, has responsibility at the various stages of delivery, which party bears what risks, when ownership changes hands from seller to buyer, and which party pays for the various elements of transportation and storage. Such terms have been designed by the International Chamber of Commerce (ICC) and are known as Incoterms. The latest version, Incoterms 2010, is the eighth revision since inception in 1936. The 11 terms have now been placed into 2 categories and are expressed in the terms of sale by a 3-letter abbreviation followed by a named location and the designated year of the Incoterms definition being used.

One category is deliveries by any mode of transport (sea, road, air and rail); the seven related Incoterms may also be used where there is no maritime transport at all:

- *EXW*. Ex-Works (. . . named place). Origin should be identified as factory, plant and so forth. The seller's only responsibility is to make the goods available at the seller's premises and the seller bears the costs and risks until the buyer is obligated to take delivery. The buyer pays for the documents, must take delivery of the shipment when specified, and must pay for any export taxes.

- *FCA*. Free Carrier (. . . named place). This term has been designed to meet the requirements of multimodal transport, such as container or roll-on, roll-off traffic by trailers and ferries. It is based on the same name principle as FOB except the seller fulfils its obligations when the goods are delivered to the custody of the carrier at the named place.

- *CPT*. Carriage Paid to (. . . named port of destination). The seller pays the freight for the carriage of the goods to the named destination. The risk of loss or damage to the goods and any cost increases transfers from the seller to the buyer when the goods have been delivered to the custody of the first carrier, and not at the ship's rail.

- *CIP*. Carriage and Insurance Paid to (. . . named port of destination). This term is the same as CPT but with an additional requirement that the seller has to procure transport insurance against the risk of loss or damage to the goods during the carriage.

- *DAP*. Delivered at Place (. . . named place). The seller delivers the goods when they are placed at the disposal of the buyer on the arriving means of transport ready for unloading at the named place of destination and bears the responsibility and risks to deliver the goods to the named place. The seller is required to clear the goods for export and they incur unloading costs at the place of destination; they are not entitled to recover any such costs unless previously agreed.

- *DAT*. Delivered at Terminal (. . . named terminal of destination). The seller delivers when the goods, once unloaded from the arriving means of transport, are placed at the disposal of the buyer at a named terminal at the named port or place of destination. The term 'terminal' includes quays, warehouses, container yard or road, rail or air terminals. The seller is responsible for the costs and risks to bring the goods to the point specified in the contract including export clearance.

- *DDP*. Delivered Duty Paid (. . . named place of destination). DDP represents the seller's maximum obligation and notes that the seller bears all risks and all costs until the goods are delivered. This term can be used irrespective of the mode of transport.

The four Incoterms in the other category are related to deliveries by sea or inland waterways:

- *FAS*. Free Alongside Ship (. . . named port of shipment). Similar to FOB but certain additional port charges for the seller may apply. The buyer is responsible for loss or damage while the goods are on a lighter (small barge) or within reach of the loading device. Loading costs are the responsibility of the buyer.

- *FOB*. Free on Board (. . . named port of shipment). The goods are placed on board a ship by the seller at a port of shipment named in the sales agreement. The risk of loss of or damage to the goods is transferred to the buyer when the goods pass over the ship's rail (i.e. off the dock and placed on the ship). The seller pays the cost of loading the goods.

- *CFR*. Cost and Freight (. . . named port of destination). The price quoted includes all transportation to the point of destination. The seller pays export taxes and similar fees. The buyer pays the cost of certificates of origin, consular invoices, or other documents required for importation into the buyer's country. The seller must prove these, but at the buyer's expense. The buyer is responsible for all insurance from the point of vessel loading.

- *CIF*. Cost, Insurance and Freight (. . . named port of destination). The price quoted includes the cost of goods, transportation and marine insurance. The seller pays all taxes or fees, as well as marine and war risk insurance. The buyer pays for any certificates or consular documents required for importation. Although the seller pays for insurance, the buyer assumes all risk after the seller has delivered the goods to the carrier.

Two examples of the correct usage of Incoterms are EXW, [Kuala Lumpur, Incoterms 2010] and DDP, [Frankfurt Schmidt GmbH Warehouse 4, Incoterms 2010].

Logistics characteristics in international markets

Table 11.2 shows GDP and estimated growth rates for various countries and regions in the world. It is important to note that GDP values are based on official foreign currency exchange rates and thus may be different from values published elsewhere; however, this notation allows direct comparison among countries. The negative growth rates are of course a reflection of the economic recession affecting the world in 2008 and 2009. The three major geographic regions that account for the bulk of world economic activity and international trade are, in order of size: the 27 member states of the European Union (EU) with 29.9 per cent of world GDP, the North American Free Trade Association (NAFTA) countries of the US, Canada and Mexico with 28.6 per cent, and the two Western Pacific Rim countries of China and Japan with 17.5 per cent. However, two other countries are also worthy of independent discussion as they are considered rapidly developing economies: Brazil in the Mercosur region with 2.7 per cent of world GDP and India with 2.1 per cent.

Table 11.2 Comparison of gross domestic product (GDP) among global regions (2009)

Group	Country	GDP at official exchange rates ($US millions)	Proportion of world GDP	Growth rate (est.)
World		58,150,000	100.0%	−0.7%
European region	European Union (EU-27)	16,240,000	27.9%	−4.1%
	Turkey	615,300		−5.6%
	Switzerland	494,600		−1.5%
	Norway	383,000		−1.5%
	Iceland	12,130		−6.5%
	Total	17,745,030	30.5%	
	Russia	1,255,000	2.2%	−7.9%
	Ukraine	116,200	0.2%	−15.0%
North America	United States	14,280,000	24.6%	−2.6%
	Canada	1,336,000	2.3%	−2.5%
	Mexico	1,017,000	1.7%	−6.5%
	Total	16,630,000	28.6%	
Mercosur	Brazil	1,574,000	2.7%	−0.2%
	Argentina	310,100		−2.8%

Table 11.2 (continued)

Group	Country	GDP at official exchange rates ($US millions)	Proportion of world GDP	Growth rate (est.)
	Uruguay	31,530		1.9%
	Paraguay	14,670		−3.4%
	Total	1,930,300	3.3%	
Pacific Rim	China (including Hong Kong)	5,119,700	8.8%	9.1%
	Japan	5,068,000	8.7%	−5.3%
ASEAN 10	Indonesia	534,400		4.5%
	Thailand	263,900		−2.2%
	Philippines	161,000		0.9%
	Malaysia	191,500		−1.7%
	Vietnam	92,440		5.3%
	Singapore	177,100		−1.3%
	Myanmar (Burma)	27,550		1.8%
	Cambodia	10,800		−1.5%
	Laos	5,598		6.5%
	Brunei Darussalam	10,550		0.5%
	Total	1,474,838	2.5%	
Other	South Korea	832,500	1.4%	0.2%
	Australia	997,200	1.7%	1.3%
	New Zealand	117,800	0.2%	−1.6%
	Taiwan	379,000	0.7%	−1.9%
	India	1,236,000	2.1%	7.4%

Source: Compiled from Central Intelligence Agency World Factbook, www.cia.gov/library/publications/the-world-factbook/index.html, updated 16 November 2010.

World Bank Logistics Performance Index[18]

One way of examining the logistics performance of various countries is with the World Bank's Logistics Performance Index (LPI), a multidimensional assessment of logistics performance rated on a scale from one (worst) to five (best). The LPI and its indicators are a joint venture of the World Bank, logistics service providers and academic partners, and the second edition was published in 2010. The 2010 LPI uses more than 5,000 individual country assessments made by nearly 1,000 international freight forwarders and provides a snapshot of selected performance indicators, including time, cost, and reliability of import and export supply chains, infrastructure quality, performance of core services, and the friendliness of trade clearance procedures. The 2010 LPI and its indicators encapsulate the first-hand knowledge of movers of international trade (data for it were collected during the economic turmoil of 2009).

Table 11.3 provides LPI scores for the top 25 countries in the world together with a few other selected countries. Germany is ranked first with an LPI score of 4.11, followed closely by Singapore at 4.09, Sweden at 4.08 and the Netherlands at 4.07. The LPI represents a good benchmark of logistics performance across various countries and is very relevant for helping identify priorities for government agencies planning to implement logistics reform agendas in cooperation with private stakeholders.

The European Union[19]

An interesting dilemma in a European context is, what is 'international' to a firm in Europe, i.e. is France an international market for Germany and vice versa? The Maastricht Treaty in

Table 11.3 World Bank Logistics Performance Index 2010

Economy	Rank	Score	% of highest performer
Germany	1	4.11	100.0
Singapore	2	4.09	99.2
Sweden	3	4.08	98.8
Netherlands	4	4.07	98.5
Luxembourg	5	3.98	95.7
Switzerland	6	3.97	95.5
Japan	7	3.97	95.2
United Kingdom	8	3.95	94.9
Belgium	9	3.94	94.5
Norway	10	3.93	94.2
Ireland	11	3.89	92.9
Finland	12	3.89	92.6
Hong Kong SAR, China	13	3.88	92.4
Canada	14	3.87	92.3
United States	15	3.86	91.7
Denmark	16	3.85	91.4
France	17	3.84	91.3
Australia	18	3.84	91.2
Austria	19	3.76	88.7
Taiwan, China	20	3.71	86.9
New Zealand	21	3.65	85.0
Italy	22	3.64	84.9
Korea, Rep.	23	3.64	84.7
United Arab Emirates	24	3.63	84.5
Spain	25	3.63	84.3
China	27	3.49	79.9
Brazil	41	3.20	70.6
India	47	3.12	67.9

Source: The World Bank International Trade Department, Connecting to Compete 2010: Trade Logistics in the Global Economy, http://siteresources.worldbank.org/INTTLF/Resources/LPI2010_for_web.pdf, viii.

1991 established the European Union and created concepts of harmonised trade, standards and laws, the abolition of borders and the four freedoms – freedom of movement of persons, goods, service and capital. This indicates that an EU country dealing with another EU country might consider them part of their domestic market.

However, the reality 20 years after the event is somewhat different. The four freedoms are still subject to national protectionist behaviour; not every EU member has adopted the euro common currency or the Schengen Agreement regarding free movement of people across international borders; and national corporate tax rates still differ, ranging from 28 per cent in Sweden and Finland to 41.7 per cent in France and 43.6–56.7 per cent in Germany.[20] Trade between individual EU member states is considered international in this book such that following discussions on international strategies and issues will apply to individual EU member states. However, it should be borne in mind that the EU situation may be different in some circumstances and contexts and that associated trade might be considered domestic in nature.

The EU-27 states are Austria, Belgium, Bulgaria, Cyprus, Czech Republic, Denmark, Estonia, Finland, France, Germany, Greece, Hungary, Ireland, Italy, Latvia, Lithuania, Luxembourg, Malta, the Netherlands, Poland, Portugal, Romania, Slovakia, Slovenia, Spain, Sweden and the United Kingdom. The EU-27, with a population of almost 500 million people, has the largest GDP of any region in the world at US$16.2 billion.

Logistics systems in Europe are characterised more by political change associated with EU enlargement than by geographic features. However, as a result of uniform regulations, transport, storage, packaging and administrative jobs are becoming considerably more efficient. The transport networks are very well developed but average shipping distances have grown in the wake of this enlargement.

The current economic heart of Europe is the 'Golden Triangle' with vertexes in the English midlands, eastern Germany and southern France. Most production and consumption take place within that area and are therefore of major logistics importance. This area contains major distribution centres to supply European customers or secondary warehouses. However, the vertexes of this 'triangle' will undoubtedly shift eastwards as the 12 accession countries become more fully integrated into the EU.

The creation of a common European market and the introduction of the euro as a common currency across many member states have caused major changes in Europe. While geographic conditions have remained largely the same in the past 15 years, changes in the logistics sector have generated increased efficiency in shipping, packaging and labelling due primarily to the reduction of customs processing and technological improvements throughout Europe and not just in individual countries. As a result, order processing, inventory management, warehousing and IT technology are being further centralised and firms are tending to set up European distribution centres (EDCs) and move away from having national distribution centres (NDCs) in several countries.

In geographic terms, the Strait of Gibraltar is particularly important for Europe. The Strait is located between Spain on the north and Morocco in the south. It connects the Mediterranean and the Atlantic. Around 300 trade ships pass through it every day, making it one of the world's most heavily travelled water routes. The ambition of Morocco to become a major logistics hub, as discussed in Logistics Example 11.2, may affect such shipping flows in future.

LOGISTICS EXAMPLE 11.2

Logistics in the Maghreb: the Port of Casablanca

The three Maghreb countries of Tunisia, Algeria and Morocco, formerly known as French North Africa, have hitherto not been significant players in global logistics. Tunisia's LPI ranking in 2010 was 61 (60 in 2007) with a score of 2.84, while Algeria's was 130 (140 in 2007) with a score of 2.36. Morocco did not participate fully in the 2010 LPI survey and was ranked 94 in 2007, but it is moving forward rapidly in its economic and logistics development while political issues and turmoil dominated and distracted its two Maghreb neighbours in 2010–2011.

Morocco's primary trade links are with the European Union and will continue to be so in the near future. Strategically situated with both Atlantic and Mediterranean coastlines, Morocco has a strong, low-cost manufacturing base and is an efficient agricultural producer for the EU as well as other African neighbours. Historically a market dominated by phosphate rock mining, food processing, leather goods, textiles, construction and tourism, the country's focus is changing with new entrants from the high-tech and automotive sectors now investing in the country. Today, Morocco is one of the fastest growing economies in Africa and has been identified as an off-shore production hub for consumers within Europe.

Logistics example 11.2 (*cont.*)

Key logistics issues in Morocco over the last decade included underdeveloped infra-structure and customers indicating that suppliers needed to improve their performance on product quality and availability or lack of delays; price was usually less of a concern. However, Morocco has launched a new National Scheme as part of its sectoral develop-ment strategy to improve the Moroccan logistics sector's competitiveness. The National Scheme, which will be carried out in partnership with the private sector, will see investment of more than €10 billion by 2030 and provides for constructing 70 facilities in 18 Moroccan cities, mainly in the coastal cities of the Mediterranean and the Atlantic. It is expected that the implementation of these will lead to a reduction of the logistics costs from the current 20 per cent to 15 per cent of GDP.

Greater Casablanca is the driving force behind the Moroccan economy. According to the Casablanca Regional Investment Centre it represents 44 per cent of the industrial work-force in Morocco, 48 per cent of its domestic investment, and 35 per cent of the country's companies are located there. The Port of Casablanca, operated by Marsa Maroc, handles about one-third of all Moroccan port trade, handling over 35 million tonnes in 2009, com-prised primarily of 13.6 million tonnes of bulk liquids, almost 9 million tonnes of dry bulk, and over 6 million tonnes in more than 430,000 containers. However, growth in port-side handling and storage are geographically constrained due to urban development butting up against the port facilities.

As part of the 2030 plan, Marsa Maroc will look to expand its integrating freight forwarding services from 'port to door', improve the quality of its service and industrial performance, and develop partnerships with private-sector industrial firms. These objec-tives will be realised as Marsa Maroc will be participating in the deployment of Multi-Flow Logistics Zones (*Zones Logistique Multi-Flux*) under the National Scheme. As a result, by 2015 607 hectares across the greater Casablanca region should be upgraded to better respond to the growing need for organised logistics, and 978 hectares by 2030.

Question

Can you identify any other areas in the developing world that could provide infrastructure competition to North America and Europe?

Sources: adapted from Theodore O. Ahlers and Karim Ghellab *La Logistique du Commerce et la Compétitivité du Maroc*, Paris: Banque Modiale and Maroc Ministère de l'Equipment et du Transport, 2006; Hassan Benabderrazik, 'Opportunities for logistics improvements through Maghreb integration,' in G.C. Hufbauer and C. Brunel (eds.) *Maghreb Regional and Global Integration: A dream to be fulfilled*, Washington, DC: Peterson Institute for International Economics, 2008, pp.139–148; Karim Beqqali, *CB Richard Ellis Market View: Morocco*, 2010, www.cbre.ma.; and interview with Rachid Hadi, Directeur d'Exploitation au Port de Casablanca et Membre de Directoire de Marsa Maroc.

European-wide transport networks have grown because of deregulation of shipments, optimal route scheduling and the development of national services. In recent years, the largest growth in transport volume has been achieved by freight transport on roads, closely followed by sea freight; total European freight volumes in 2007 from all sources were 4.3 trillion tonne kilometres. There are more than 3.8 million kilometres of roads in the EU-27 countries but only 175,000 kilometres of rail track. The share of freight transport by road transport was almost 2 trillion tonne kilometres, followed closely by sea transport (ocean and coastal waterway shipping) with 1.5 trillion tonne kilometres. Rail transport accounted for almost 500 billion tonne kilometres but has hardly gained any market share across Europe during the last decade.

Outsourcing of logistics activities is widespread in Europe and gaining in popularity. Many firms no longer view logistics as a part of their core business and hire specialised logistics service providers to do the job. As a result many firms have already outsourced parts of the standard logistics services such as shipping, trans-shipping and storage. Added to this development are increasing numbers of high-quality logistics service and contract logistics providers. The share of contract logistics in total revenue of European logistics service providers rose 58 per cent in 2006 and it is estimated that annual growth rates of contract logistics will be 10–15 per cent over the next 4–5 years. The largest logistics service providers in Europe include DHL, Maersk, Schenker, TNT and Kühne & Nagel.

The largest logistics markets in Europe are Germany and France, followed by Great Britain, Italy and Spain. One of the biggest changes in recent years has been the erection of EDCs as opposed to NDCs. On one hand, bigger markets can be served with them. On the other, an improved network and a uniformly coordinated, European-wide strategy could create cost and service improvements. European distribution locations have evolved as clusters with about 25 primary logistics clusters and more or less 60 secondary logistics clusters. At least four locations operate as global logistics clusters: London, Paris, Frankfurt (Rhine–Main) and Randstad Holland (with an extension to Rhine–Ruhr and Northeastern France). A long-established cluster agglomeration is in the Benelux region and along the Rhine.

At present Germany has the highest logistics market take-up of warehousing space in Europe with over 3 million square metres, followed by France and the UK that average about 2.5 million square metres each. The three main markets add up to 70–75 per cent of the total warehousing take-up in Europe while long-established logistics and trading platforms, the Netherlands and Belgium, follow with a market share of 10–15 per cent. Spain and Italy come next, but their take-up market share is comparatively low. The Central European countries of Poland, Hungary and the Czech Republic have emergent logistics clusters that now take a market share of 5–10 per cent. More than 90 per cent of the take-up in the agglomerations is renting while owner-occupiers still dominate the market in the rest of Europe. Transport, traffic and storage firms are renting the largest amount of space (40–60 per cent), followed by trade (30–40 per cent) and industrial firms (10–20 per cent). The rising significance of the logistics sector is reflected in its share of the overall take-up, which has doubled in the last decade.[21]

North America[22]

The North American Free Trade Association signed in January 1994 brought together the economies of Canada, the United States and Mexico. By 2009, the flow of trade among the NAFTA members was over US$1 trillion. Exports from Mexico and Canada to the United States were $568 billion while exports from the United States to Mexico and Canada were $452 billion. Two-way trade between Canada and Mexico amounted to only about $22 billion. Also, since NAFTA was enacted, US FDI in Mexico and Canada has more than tripled to $349 billion while Mexican and Canadian FDI in the US has grown to US $219 billion. This increased trade has had significant impacts on logistics infrastructure and practices.

The North American continent is vast in terms of geographic area: it is over 4,000 miles wide and 4,500 miles deep and comprises an area of more than 9.3 million square miles. However, its population is only about 530 million people and it thus has a density of 57 people per square mile; this density is half Europe's of 134 people per square mile. Thus, the movement of goods across the continent is critical. Trade in North America is dominated by road, rail and ocean, which account for 85 per cent of total trade. Trade by air cargo is less than 4 per cent of total trade value and only 1 per cent of total cargo weight from all modes. However, more than half the world's volume in tonne kilometres is performed at North American hubs, including Memphis, Tennessee (home of FedEx), Louisville, Kentucky (home of UPS), Los Angeles and New York.

The grid-like US interstate highway system enacted by President Eisenhower in the 1950s has provided the road infrastructure required for efficient and large movements of goods – across North America there are almost 588,000 miles of very good highway and freeway systems, more than 445,000 miles located in the US. There are over 6 million commercial freight vehicles in North America, with 5.4 million domiciled in the US.

North American railroads operate over 173,000 miles of track and there is a high level of geographical specialisation, with big rail carriers servicing large regional markets. Rail carriers have multilateral agreements with shipping companies to provide intermodal services at major rail, road and port gateways. Chicago, which is located at the junction of eastern, western and Canadian rail networks, is the largest centre in North America and handles 10 million TEUs a year. Intermodal services are primarily container on flat car (COFC) and truck trailer on flat car (TOFC) and are provided at around 206 facilities in the inland market.

Five major port clusters in North America – Vancouver–Portland, San Francisco–Los Angeles, New York–New Jersey, Charleston–Jacksonville and Palm Beach–Port Everglades – handle 55 per cent of all container volumes. The success of these clusters is due to capital investment in container handling facilities and access to major roads and rails for onward distribution. Most container import volumes accrue to major retailers; in 2008 the top five importers were Wal-Mart (700,000 TEU), Target (450,000), Home Depot (300,000), Sears Holding (220,000) and Dole Food (210,000). Further waterway transportation is available on inland systems such as the Mississippi and Missouri river systems and the St Lawrence Seaway and Great Lakes system between Canada and the US.

The Pacific Rim

This discussion of the Pacific Rim will refer to those countries on the western side of the Pacific Ocean: China, Japan, the ASEAN 10 countries, South Korea, Australia, New Zealand and Taiwan. The eastern Pacific Rim comprises the three NAFTA countries; countries in Central and South America and areas are discussed elsewhere in this chapter. The western Pacific Rim region's economy enjoyed almost US$14 trillion GDP in 2010 (see Table 11.2). However, the two largest players in the region are China and Japan, which generate 73 per cent of that GDP, and they will be the focus of discussions in the next two sections.

On a general level, firms doing business in the Pacific Rim region, including importing or exporting products, sourcing raw materials and undertaking logistics activities, will find many differences in economies, politics and culture that greatly influence their business activities. The region has a number of immense problems but provides significant opportunities for firms.

China[23]

China, including Hong Kong, is the largest economy in the world after the US, with US$5.12 trillion GDP in 2010, surpassing Japan into second place. Its average growth rate from its transformation into a market economy in 1978 to 2010 was over 9 per cent per year and this boom shows little sign of abating. China excluding Hong Kong is ranked 27 in the World Bank LPI index with a score of 3.49, while the Hong Kong special administrative region (SAR) is ranked 13 with a score of 3.88. China's annual spend on logistics activities of $352 billion is 21 per cent of GDP and is twice as high as the US and European countries.

The Chinese government controls the planning and operations of logistics infrastructure, energy and resources, market entry and administrative regulation, taxations and incentive policies for logistics and supply chain activities. Consequently, dealing with the government and its agencies can be time and resource consuming. However, benefits to persistent organisations can be meaningful. For example, the China Communications and Transport Association (CCTA) developed a link with the United Kingdom's Chartered Institute of Logistics and Transport (CILT) to deliver CILT qualifications to Chinese logisticians. This was important for the 29th Olympic Games held in Beijing in 2008. It is estimated that logistics services worth approximately 42 billion Chinese yuan or US$5 billion were used during the Games. Several large multinational logistics services providers, including DHL and UPS, met this demand along with Chinese firms.

China's transport infrastructure is vast. It has 1.87 million kilometres of roads but only 1 per cent of that includes national roads or multi-lane highways. There are 74 kilometres of railroad that handle 1.9 billion tonne kilometres of freight each year. Almost 2.2 million tonnes of air freight go through China's 135 airports for a total of 5.8 billion tonne kilometres. Lastly, China has many of the largest seaports in the world, including Shanghai, Ningbo, Guangzhou, Tianjin, Qingdao, Dalian and Shenzhen, that have collective throughput of over 1.6 billion tonnes of cargo and over 47 million TEU of containers.

While the Chinese logistics situation is changing rapidly, there are still challenges in outsourcing and third-party logistics, logistics skills, infrastructure and property, and the development of private firms from state-owned entities.

Japan[24]

Japan is now the third-place economic powerhouse in the world after being surpassed by China. Japan's GDP is US$5.1 billion and it ranks seventh on the World Bank LPI index with a score of 3.97. The majority of Japan's 127 million population live on the four major islands of Hokkaido, Honshu, Kyushu and Shikoku and a group of smaller islands that collectively is the same size as the state of California. Of these, the island of Honshu contains all the major cities and most of the population of Japan.

The Japanese distribution system is complex and somewhat inefficient due to the government's propensity to encourage and support small enterprises and family-owned retailers. Logistics costs in Japan are high due to its traditional transportation structure that relies on trucks handling over 90 per cent of logistics volumes in tonne kilometres over its 1.2 million kilometres of highways. Rail transport, by contrast, is only 4 per cent of logistics volume and 1 per cent of weight over the 24,000 kilometres of railroad lines. Similarly, air freight is only 0.2 per cent of logistics volumes and weight.

Japan has led the world for several decades with its JIT manufacturing expertise, its TQM techniques, and collaboration with suppliers and customers. These features of its manufacturing environment have led to Japanese physical distribution being characterised by small-lot, high-frequency conveyance. Also, the adoption of Western business models for convenience stores and door-to-door parcel deliveries has helped reduce inefficiencies. Further opportunities for improving this situation include the use of enhanced ICT to improve information flow and reduce inventories, congestion, energy consumption and pollution.

India[25]

India enjoyed more than US$1.2 trillion GDP in 2010 and its economy grows by almost 8 per cent per year (see Table 11.2). Indian industry spends 12 per cent of its GDP on logistics and India is ranked 47 on the World Bank LPI index with a score of 3.12. The Indian logistics environment comprises road transport companies, railways, air freight companies, intermodal transport providers, ports and shipping companies, as well as 3PL companies. Their performance is critically dependent on the state of the Indian logistics infrastructure.

India has a road network totalling 3.3 million kilometres of road length. Express and national highways constitute only 2 per cent of this road length but carry nearly 40 per cent of all road freight. The overall quality of roads is poor, resulting in slow transport speeds, increased wear and tear of vehicles, and high accident rates. The Indian government has initiated a National Highway Development Programme and is spending about $4.5 billion annually on road networks.

The Indian trucking industry is entirely privately owned, with 77 per cent of truck owners possessing 5 or fewer trucks and only 6 per cent possessing more than 20 vehicles. The intensity of truck competition has led to low freight rates and there are also a number of intermediaries, such as broker and booking agents, which have an important role in facilitating road freight movements.

The Indian railways network is state owned and is the second largest railroad system in the world, covering 63,465 kilometres and handling 382 million tonnes of freight every year. The cost of using the rail network is high due to handling requirements and the time and cost of arranging pick-up and drop-off of consignment to and from railway facilities. This results in the slow average speed of freight movement and low average wagon turnaround time, which are major concerns for Indian logisticians. The number of employees is also high at 1.6 million, or about 25 employees for every kilometre of track.

There are 12 major seaports under the control of the Indian government and 187 minor ports under state jurisdiction along India's 7,517 kilometres of coastline. Total volumes at all Indian ports is about 720 million tonnes a year, with the major ports handling about 520 million tonnes, or 72 per cent of total trade. The facility and infrastructure of Indian ports are rated low by global standards, primarily on account of lack of storage space and outdated handling equipment. Most Indian seaports are inefficient in loading and unloading operations, with the result that ships spend more time there, which increases costs for a shipper by 10–20 per cent.

The 15 international and 110 domestic airports handle 570,000 tonnes of domestic cargo and 1.15 million tonnes of international cargo, which is low in terms of world standards. To make air cargo more attractive and efficient, the Indian government has initiated the introduction of an 'open sky' policy, integrated cargo management systems at the four metropolitan airports, and provision of centres for perishable cargo.

All the above factors related to transport infrastructure have adversely affected the logistics network in the country both in terms of lead-time and costs. Further, there is a logistics skills gap and complex distribution system network that exacerbate matters. Nevertheless, the noted policy changes are expected to bring about a positive change in the Indian logistics environment. This provides vast opportunities for companies offering logistics services in the country so Indian organisations will be able to reduce logistics costs by using third-party logistics services for enhanced supply chain efficiencies.

Brazil[26]

The Mercosur region was created by Argentina, Brazil, Paraguay and Uruguay in March 1991 with the signing of the Treaty of Asuncion. Bolivia, Chile, Colombia, Ecuador and Peru are associate members; they can join free-trade agreements but remain outside the bloc's customs union. Mercosur tariff policies regulate imports and exports and the bloc can arbitrate in trade disputes among its members. In the longer term, Mercosur aims to create a continent-wide free-trade area, and the creation of a Mercosur development bank has been mooted. The combined GDPs of the Mercosur nations accounted for about 3.3 per cent of the world's economic output in 2010 (see Table 11.2).

Brazil is Mercosur's economic giant with US$1.57 trillion GDP in 2010 but is similar to India as it is ranked only 41 on the World Bank LPI index with a score of 3.20. It depends on its 1.7 kilometre highway system for 60 per cent of the total tonne kilometres moved in the country. Most of the good road infrastructure is located in the southeast of the country where the major cities such as Rio de Janeiro and São Paulo are located.

Brazil has 1.4 million cargo transportation vehicles, of which about 50 per cent are owned by self-employed truck drivers. Its railways are only about 30,000 kilometres in size but handle 128 billion tonne kilometre cargo units (TKUs) per year or about 24 per cent of the country's total, and 85 per cent of these movements are related to exports.

Brazil has 7,367 kilometres of coastline on the Atlantic Ocean, with 36 public ports. Privately, there are 3 ports and 42 terminals. The ports handle more than 620 million tonnes of cargo every year and productivity at container ports increased from 8–15 containers per hour in 1995 to over 40 containers per hour by the mid-2000s. Air cargo transport is still underdeveloped and comprises only 0.1 per cent of total TKUs; however 68 per cent of the largest Brazilian companies involved in import and export use airborne cargo.

Summary

Globalisation has become the norm for businesses across the globe. Firms are achieving economies of scale through sourcing and manufacturing in foreign or host countries, and enhanced global logistics functions and procedures have assisted that growth over the past 30 years, particularly the development of standard shipping containers to safely and efficiently move goods and computerisation to enhance international orders and track global shipments.

Yet challenges remain for firms wishing to 'go global', including the prolonged and worldwide economic recession that took force in 2008, concerns about ethical sourcing from foreign manufacturers, and a growing sympathy for the wider natural environment that is affected by outsourcing or off-shoring. The importance of these challenges may grow in the coming decade as we come to understand more about the wider economic and natural environment.

This chapter has considered the reasons for conducting international and global business and the primary characteristics involved in doing so. It then considered the logistical challenges of globalisation, including processes, terms of trade and international finance. Lastly, the logistical features of several global regions were discussed to provide an appreciation of the major customers and suppliers in today's global marketplace.

The next chapter on reverse and sustainable logistics continues the discussion about the impact of logistics on the natural environment, and vice versa.

DISCUSSION QUESTIONS

1 Discuss the advantages and disadvantages of the four international market-entry modes.

2 Describe the different trade flows and how you think they may change during the next 20 years.

3 Explain the different types of trade documentation and the letter of credit as the primary method of international trade finance.

4 Explain the various Incoterms and provide an example of each.

5 Assess Europe, North America, China and India in terms of their logistics characteristics and capabilities.

Suggested reading

Browne, Michael, Julian Allen and Allan Woodburn 'Developments in Western European logistics strategies,' in Donald Waters (ed.) *Global Logistics: New Directions in Supply Chain Management,* 6th ed. London: Kogan Page, 2010, pp.420–442.

Carter, Craig R., Rahul Kale and Curtis M. Grimm 'Environmental purchasing and firm performance: An empirical investigation,' *Transportation Research Part E*, 2000, Vol. 36, pp.219–228.

Centro de Estudos em Logística of COPPEAD Management Institute, Federal University of Rio de Janeiro, *CSCMP Global Perspectives: Brazil*, 2007, http://cscmp.org.

Kitamura, Toshiyuki *CSCMP Global Perspectives: Japan*, 2006, http://cscmp.org.

Levinson, Mark *The Box: How the Shipping Container Made the World Smaller and the World Economy Bigger*, Princeton University Press, 2006.

Mangan, John, Chandra Lalwani and Brian Fynes 'Port-centric logistics,' *International Journal of Logistics Management*, 2008, Vol. 19, No. 1, pp.29–41.

Paliwoda, Stanley and Michael Thomas *International Marketing*, 3rd ed. Oxford: Butterworth-Heinemann, 1998.

Rodriquez, Jean-Paul and Marcus Hesse 'North American logistics,' in Donald Waters (ed.) *Global Logistics: New Directions in Supply Chain Management,* 6th ed. London: Kogan Page, 2010, pp.477–504.

Shah, Janat and Suresh D.N. *CSCMP Global Perspectives: India*, 2009, http://cscmp.org.

Stone, Marilyn A. and John B. McCall *International Strategic Marketing: A European Perspective*, London: Routledge, 2004.

Wang, Charles Gouwen *CSCMP Global Perspectives: China*, 2006, http://cscmp.org.

Wang James 'Logistics in China,' in Donald Waters (ed.) *Global Logistics: New Directions in Supply Chain Management* 6th ed. Kogan Page: London, 2010, pp.443–457.

Zsidisin, George A. and Sue P. Siferd 'Environmental purchasing: A framework for theory development,' *European Journal of Purchasing & Supply Management*, 2001, Vol. 7, pp.61–73.

Notes

1. *Collins English Dictionary: Millennium (4th) Edition*, Glasgow: HarperCollins, 1998, p.802.
2. Ibid, p.652.
3. *Wal-Mart 2010 Annual Report*, http://cdn.walmartstores.com/sites/AnnualReport/2010/PDF/WMT_2010AR_FINAL.pdf.
4. United Nations Conference on Trade and Development (UNCTAD) *Review of Maritime Transport 2009*, www.unctad.org/en/docs/rmt2009_en.pdf.
5. Stanley Paliwoda and Michael Thomas, *International Marketing,* 3rd ed. Oxford: Butterworth-Heinemann, 1998, pp.15–17.
6. Paliwoda and Thomas, p.42.
7. See European Union Eurostat at http://epp.eurostat.ec.europa.eu/portal/page/portal/european_business/special_sbs_topics/international_sourcing.
8. World Trade 100 – The Benchmark for Global Supply Chain Business, *International Sourcing: Offshore or Nearshore?* 2009, www.worldtrademag.com/Articles/Feature_Article/BNP_GUID_9-5-2006_A_10000000000000581811.
9. See for example Naomi Klein, *No Logo*, Toronto: Knopf, 2000.
10. See George A. Zsidisin and Sue P. Siferd, 'Environmental purchasing: A framework for theory development,' *European Journal of Purchasing & Supply Management*, 2001, Vol. 7, pp.61–73; and Craig R. Carter, Rahul Kale and Curtis M. Grimm, 'Environmental purchasing and firm performance: An empirical investigation,' *Transportation Research Part E*, 2000, Vol. 36, pp.219–228.
11. See www.kindy.com.
12. For a history of the container see Mark Levinson, *The Box: How the Shipping Container Made the World Smaller and the World Economy Bigger*, Princeton University Press, 2006.
13. Eivind Kolding, 'Challenges and opportunities,' *Presentation at the 25th German Logistics Congress*, October 2008, Berlin.
14. John Mangan, Chandra Lalwani and Brian Fynes, 'Port-centric logistics,' *International Journal of Logistics Management*, 2008, Vol. 19, No. 1, pp.29–41.
15. See htttp://export.gov/logistics/eg_main_018121.asp.
16. See Barclays Corporate Trade Tutorials at www.business.barclays.co.uk/BRC1/jsp/brccontrol?task-artic legroup&site=bbb&value=3408&menu=2837.
17. See the International Chamber of Commerce at www.iccwbo.org/incoterms/.
18. The World Bank International Trade Department, *Connecting to Compete 2010: Trade Logistics in the Global Economy*, http://siteresources.worldbank.org/INTTLF/Resources/LPI2010_for_web.pdf.
19. The material in this section is adapted from Michael Browne, Julian Allen and Allan Woodburn, 'Developments in Western European logistics strategies,' in D. Waters (ed.) *Global Logistics: New Directions in Supply Chain Management,* 6th ed. London: Kogan Page, 2010, pp.420–442; A.T. Kearney and European Logistics Association, 'Supply chain excellence amidst the global economic crisis,' *6th European A.T. Kearney/ELA Logistics Study 2008/2009*, Brussels: ELA, 2009; and DHL 'Discover logistics,' 2011, www.dhl-discoverlogistics.com/cms/en/course/trends/europe/europe_west.jsp.
20. Paliwoda and Thomas, pp.392–441; and Marilyn A. Stone and John B. McCall, *International Strategic Marketing: A European Perspective*, London: Routledge, 2004, pp.48–82.
21. Dieter W. Rebitzer, 'The European logistics market,' *Europe Real Estate Yearbook*, 2007, pp.112–117.
22. The material in this section is adapted from Jean-Paul Rodriquez and Marcus Hesse, 'North American logistics,' in D. Waters (ed.) *Global Logistics: New Directions in Supply Chain Management,* 6th ed. London: Kogan Page, 2010, pp.477–504; and *CSCMP's 21st Annual State of Logistics Report*, 2010, http://cscmp.org.

23 The material in this section is adapted from James Wang, 'Logistics in China,' in D. Waters (ed.) *Global Logistics: New Directions in Supply Chain Management,* 6th ed. London: Kogan Page, 2010, pp.443–457; and Charles Gouwen Wang, *CSCMP Global Perspectives: China,* 2006, http://cscmp.org.

24 The material in this section is adapted from Toshiyuki Kitamura, *CSCMP Global Perspectives: Japan,* 2006, http://cscmp.org.

25 The material in this section is adapted from Janat Shah and Suresh D.N., *CSCMP Global Perspectives: India,* 2009, http://cscmp.org.

26 The material in this section is adapted from Centro de Estudos em Logística of COPPEAD Management Institute, Federal University of Rio de Janeiro, *CSCMP Global Perspectives: Brazil,* 2007, http://cscmp.org.

Chapter 12

Reverse and sustainable logistics

Key objectives

- To understand the relationship of logistics and sustainability.
- To consider reverse logistics and product recovery management.
- To examine the science behind environmental sustainability.
- To illustrate the concept of a product life cycle assessment.
- To investigate sustainable logistics in transportation and storage.

Introduction

Issues surrounding the environment and climate change have come to the fore over the last two decades since an article appeared in a 1995 issue of *Nature* documenting a large seasonal disappearance of ozone from the earth's atmosphere over Antarctica. This finding galvanised the scientific community and triggered a sequence of events that dramatically raised the profile of the environment and climate change around the world.

The logistics and supply chain management community is not immune to these events, and efforts to recycle materials and packaging in a reverse logistics process have received considerable attention for several decades. However, an early piece of research by Stefanie Böge in 1995, entitled 'The well-travelled yogurt pot', was one of the first discussions regarding the impact of 'food miles' on consumer products and also quantified the environmental impact of transport. Böge determined that transport intensity to deliver 150 gram yogurt pots across German supply chains meant that 24 fully packed trucks each had to travel 1,005 kilometres to distribution centres, collectively using over 10,200 litres of diesel fuel in the process.[1]

Since then the environmental agenda has grown substantially and there has been much recent activity considering not only reverse logistics but also green or sustainable logistics and supply chain management. This activity will continue to grow as governments and environmental organisations increase their efforts in ensuring that the planet's future environmental needs are met and sustainable. So while this is one of several future trends identified in Chapter 1, it is considered significantly important to warrant its own separate chapter in this text. This chapter thus considers reverse and sustainable logistics in light of their increasing significance in today's business environment. First, reverse logistics and product recovery management are discussed in the context of best-practice recycling. Then, the science of sustainability is presented briefly to set the stage for the application of this concept to green or sustainable logistics and supply chain management. Particular focus is given to sustainable transport and warehousing in concert with the 'Stop' and 'Go' nature of this text and in recognition of their respective impacts on the environment.

Reverse logistics and product recovery management

Reverse logistics, while not a new concept, is a growing area in logistics management.[2] Reverse logistics encompasses all of the activities in the CSCMP definition of logistics provided in Chapter 1, but the difference is that reverse logistics attends to these activities as they occur in the opposite direction. Thus, reverse logistics can be defined as:

> the process of planning, implementing, and controlling the efficient, cost effective flow of raw materials, in-process inventory, finished goods and related information from the point of consumption to the point of origin for the purpose of recapturing value or proper disposal.[3]

Essentially, reverse logistics is the process of moving goods from their point of consumption or use to the appropriate link upstream in the supply chain for the purpose of capturing any residual value through re-manufacturing or refurbishing, or for proper disposal. Thus, reverse logistics management represents a systematic business model ... to profitably close the loop on the supply chain.[4]

If goods or materials are not sent 'backwards' or upstream in the supply chain then an activity is probably not a reverse logistics activity. Reverse logistics also includes processing returned merchandise due to damage, seasonal inventory, re-stock, salvage, recalls and excess inventory. Key management elements in reverse logistics include:

- *gatekeeping* to screen defective and unwarranted returned merchandise at the entry point into the reverse logistics process;
- *short disposition cycle times* related to return product decisions, movement and processing to avert a lengthy ageing process on returns;
- *reverse logistics information systems* to properly track returns and measure disposition cycle times and vendor performance;
- *central return centres* or processing facilities dedicated to handling returns quickly and efficiently;
- *zero returns* policies that avoid accepting any physical returns and instead set maximum values of returned products that are payable to customers;
- *re-manufacture and refurbishment* of products that has five categories: repair, refurbishing and re-manufacturing to recondition or upgrade products, and cannibalisation and recycling to use or dispose of products;
- *asset recovery* classifies and disposes returned goods, surplus, obsolete, scrap, waste and excess material products, and other assets to maximise returns to the owner and minimise costs and liabilities associated with disposition;

- *negotiation* of the value of returned material without any pricing guidelines. This task is often performed by specialist third parties who advise the primary participants in the supply chain who are working to transfer ownership of the material back to the original source;

- *financial management* policies to properly handle accounting and reconciliation issues related to returned products;

- *outsourcing* reverse product flow to outsourced reverse logistics suppliers who can be used as a benchmark to help determine what and how reverse activities should be performed, and how much those activities should cost.

Benefits to firms practising reverse logistics management include cost reductions, added-value for customers and proper compliance with legislative regulations. Critical success factors for reverse logistics programmes to capture the key elements above include:

- *management and control* by mapping or flow charting the reverse logistics process through the firm, developing an environmental management system, educating customers, employees, suppliers and other supply chain members, and developing partnerships to achieve reverse logistics goals and economies of scale;

- *measurement* by adopting full product life cycle and end-of-product life costing as they relate to reverse logistics activities and the product supply chain;

- *finance* to properly allocate sufficient resources for reverse logistics activities and environmental initiatives.[5]

Reverse and green or sustainable logistics come together as a result of regulation and legislation such as the EU Waste Electrical and Electronic Equipment (WEEE) Directive introduced and adopted into EU law in 2005. The directive is designed to reduce the amount of WEEE, of which there was some 915,000 tonnes across Europe at the beginning of the millennium, and increase levels of refurbishment and recycling by requiring EU member states to force producers and retailers to take responsibility for the return and reverse logistics of such products.[6]

The need to consider reverse and green logistics has also seen the growth of third-party reverse logistics providers who assist companies to meet new guidelines and enhance their business opportunities. For example, the Caledonian Alloys Group Ltd[7] is a world leader in the management of nickel and cobalt base 'superalloy' and titanium alloy recycling for the aerospace, land-based turbine and chemical industries. The company transforms revert – excess or decommissioned alloy material or parts arising from high-performance component manufacture – through a rigorous cleaning and grading process into material that can be re-melted to produce new nickel, cobalt or titanium alloys. Caledonian Alloys is accredited with all major vacuum and high-temperature melters worldwide and supplies fully processed nickel and titanium revert material to them as well as purchasing revert material from a wide range of industrial customers throughout the world. The company also provides tailored revert management services to customers to enable them to optimise the use and value of their own revert material.

Reverse logistics forms part of what is known as closed-loop supply chain management and has gained in importance as an environmental, profitable and sustainable business strategy. One aspect of reverse logistics within closed-loop SCM is the product recovery management (PRM) of all used and discarded products, components and materials for which a manufacturer is responsible.[8] While the ideas of recycling and PRM have been in use for more than 30 years, there are still many challenges regarding the influence of PRM on production, operations and logistics management, particularly in supply chains that involve the consumer or end-user as a participant actor and for fast-moving consumer goods. FMCG products such as disposable razors or plastic bottle packaging for cleaners and detergents are difficult to recover and re-use, or even recycle, without some form of consumer incentive in today's 'disposable society' with 'cash-rich and time-poor' consumers. However, some FMCG products such as 'disposable' cameras may lend themselves more readily to PRM techniques and become 're-usable' cameras, as discussed in Logistics Example 12.1.

LOGISTICS EXAMPLE 12.1

Product recovery management of Fujifilm's QuickSnap camera

Fujifilm's QuickSnap popular single-use camera has been designed to use various techniques of product recovery management; it cannot be re-used or re-sold without undergoing some form of PRM due to its design characteristics. Waste management is almost non-existent in the QuickSnap 'inverse manufacturing system' as an almost 100 per cent recycling rate can be achieved, even with components such as packaging for the product. By comparison, over 65 per cent of Kodak's single-use cameras returned to them are recycled. However, unlike Fujifilm, which uses dedicated retailers for product returns, Kodak takes back cameras from any retailer.

Fujifilm launched single-use cameras in 1986 under the brand name QuickSnap after market research determined that a growing segment of Japanese consumers wanted to take pictures only on an occasional basis. QuickSnap quickly became a popular consumer convenience product and 1 million cameras were sold in its first six months in the marketplace. Subsequently, the market expanded dramatically and more than 60 million cameras were sold in 1995. Although the original launching price was around US$10, current selling prices range from $7–15 depending on product features such as zoom lens, waterproof body or high-resolution films.

At the beginning of the 1990s several stakeholder groups attacked the product's disposable nature, which resulted in a negative impact on the brand's image and sales. Consumers began to refer to QuickSnap as 'disposables' or 'throwaways' and the media reported environmental groups' concern regarding their wastefulness. In response to those environmental pressures and as part of its corporate and social responsibility posture, Fujifilm initiated a voluntary take-back programme and began recycling the cameras by utilising a highly developed and original recycling programme. In doing so it established one of the first, fully integrated closed-loop or reverse logistics systems for FMCG products and has since negated much of the poor environmental image of the QuickSnap product. Fujifilm calls its reverse system an 'inverse manufacturing system' and in 2006 this system was awarded the Inverse Manufacturing Grand Prize, which publicly recognises achievements from companies over the past ten years for developing various types of inverse (circulatory) production techniques.

The QuickSnap product concept and structure had two advantages that smoothed the way to recycling. First, the QuickSnap is categorised not as a camera but as 'film' in industrial product classification and the silver and chemical base utilised in films already had recycling targets and measures that Fujifilm could draw upon. It was important to re-use high-priced silver from an economic point of view and that also justified the expense of developing an efficient reverse logistics system. Second, the number of parts utilised in the QuickSnap camera was designed to be as low as possible and cardboard was utilised for the outer package. These two features allowed the easy development of product modularisation and unitisation. QuickSnap cameras are composed of six units: main body, lens, flash, switch, rear cover and front cover. Generally, when a functional change is needed the new function is incorporated into all units except for the main body and flash units.

There are two main reasons for the QuickSnap modular design, according to Fujifilm's manufacturing engineering department. First, it is desirable that products have an easy-to-disassemble structure in order to be re-used or recycled. Second, quality inspection and testing can be conducted specifically on the unit or modular design. Decomposing the product into several units is determined not only from the standpoint of recycling or re-use but also by a balance of various conditions such as design appeal or production costs. The QuickSnap unit structure has been changed only slightly since 1992 and only to correspond to customer needs.

Currently, all QuickSnap products include recycled or reused parts. Accordingly, QuickSnap is considered to be a product that represents recycle-based manufacturing. This recycle-based manufacturing loop facilitates a balance between forecast accuracy and the ability of manufacturing to adjust production to meet current demands. Fujifilm's inverse manufacturing system allows for both processes, production and recycling, to be carried out in the same facilities. The QuickSnap disassembling process is carried out in reverse order of the new product assembling process and is compatible with the recycling and decomposing processes. For example, one machine which is used only to set the rear unit into the main unit can also take the rear unit off the main unit. This means that other machines can also be utilised for the recycling or disassembly process when demand fluctuates and thus efficiency of the inverse manufacturing system is enhanced.

Fujifilm's environmental report notes that the economic impact from QuickSnap recovery within the company amounts to some 1.7 billion yen a year. Further, the environmental economic impact outside the company, i.e. reductions in sulphur dioxide, carbon dioxide and volatile organic compounds, is about 47.2 billion yen. These calculations are consistent with guidelines from the Ministry of the Environment, government of Japan and were vetted and approved by third-party organisations.

There has been a trend towards environmental outsourcing whereby many companies leave a part of the recycling and re-use process to external processors, but the QuickSnap inverse manufacturing system is a truly closed-loop system as only Fujifilm manages it. Fujifilm does not outsource any part of its recycling and re-use processes for strategic reasons as it considers that its self-sustaining PRM process brings out the primary value of its products most effectively and efficiently.

Question

What other products and categories would lend themselves to this sort of product recovery management?

Sources: adapted from David B. Grant and Ruth Banomyong, 'Design of closed-loop supply chain and product recovery management for fast-moving consumer goods: The case of a single-use camera,' *Asia Pacific Journal of Marketing & Logistics*, 2010, Vol. 22, No. 2, pp.233–246; 'Fujifilm Sustainability Report,' 2007, www.fujifilm.com/pdf/about/sustainability; 'Fujifilm Product Information Bulletin: FujiColor QuickSnap Superia,' 2009, www.fujifilm.com/products/quicksnap/pdf/quicksnap_superia.pdf; and R. Canan Savaskan, Shantanu Bhattacharya and Luk N. Van Wassenhove, 'Closed-loop supply chain models with product remanufacturing,' *Management Science*, 2004, Vol. 50, No. 2, pp.239–252.

There are three categories of activities for consumer-returned products in a reverse logistics supply chain: direct re-use or re-sale without any re-processing, PRM activities, and waste management or disposal. These activities are presented in an example supply chain shown in Figure 12.1.[9]

Each PRM option involves the collection of used products and components and their subsequent re-processing and re-distribution. The main difference between each option is the type of re-processing involved. The purpose of repair is to bring used products up to working condition and usually requires only limited product disassembly and re-assembly. Refurbishing brings used products up to a specified quality, but quality standards are less precise than those of new products. After disassembling used products into discrete modules, critical modules are separated and inspected, then fixed or replaced as required.

Remanufacturing means bringing used products up to the specified quality standard of new products and is thus more rigorous than refurbishing. Used products are completely disassembled into discrete modules and are extensively inspected. Depleted or outdated modules are replaced with new ones. Repairable components and modules are fixed and extensively checked. Approved parts are sub-assembled into modules and subsequently assembled into remanufactured products.

Cannibalisation involves selective disassembly of used products and inspection of potentially reusable parts. However, cannibalisation re-uses a smaller proportion of used modules in contrast with a large number of used products re-used during the repair, refurbishing and

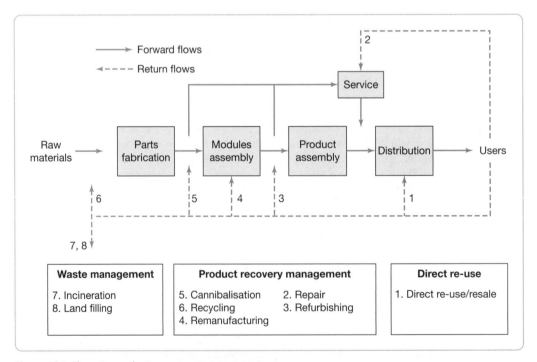

Figure 12.1 Flows in product recovery management

Source: Design of Closed-Loop Supply Chain and Product Recovery Management for Fast-Moving Consumer Goods: The Case of a Single-Use Camera, *Asia Pacific Journal of Marketing & Logistics*, Vol. 22, No. 2, p. 234 (Grant, D.B. and Banomyong, R. 2010), Asia Pacific Journal of Marketing and Logistics by Emerald Group Publishing Limited. Reproduced with permission of Emerald Group Publishing Limited in the format Journal via Copyright Clearance Center. © Emerald Group Publishing Limited all rights reserved.

remanufacturing processes. Their quality level and the process in which they will be re-used will determine the selection of cannibalised parts.

Although the purpose of these product recovery options is to retain the functionality of used products and parts as much as possible, the purpose of recycling is to re-use materials from the used products. Much of a product's functionality is lost in the recycling process. Materials can be re-used in the production of original products if materials quality is maintained and recycling occurs when used products are disassembled into parts, divided into material groups, and the separated materials are re-used in the production of new parts. However, contamination makes primary material impure and reduces its recycling value. For example, mixed resins introduced into a plastic recycling process can lead to the separation of resins, bubbling, lack of coherence, or damage to the extruder. Contaminants such as oil or paper within the plastic recycling process may become dangerous (fire and explosions). Maintaining the purity of recyclable products considerably increases costs, therefore material standardisation is crucial for manufacturers who recycle used plastic product parts themselves. Material standardisation allows manufacturers to recycle plastic materials cheaply and easily during the recycling process and this will result in the reduction of new resin use and its subsequent environmental impact.

Modular production is one measure that eases disassembly and re-assembly by decreasing product complexity, lowering the number of parts used in products and raising the interchangeability and commonality of components. This measure uses generic modules that are interchangeable in a number of different finished products and can contribute to more efficient product differentiation in response to customer orders. Modularity also allows for rapid and easy final modification in the distribution channel.

However, there are some key issues in the reverse logistics flow process outside PRM concerns that include:

- uncertainty regarding quality or condition and quantities;
- uncertainty regarding the timing of material receipt as return forecasting is even more difficult than demand forecasting;
- uncertainty in aspects of consumer behaviour, for example will the consumer initiate a return or simply dispose of products, consumer acceptance of recovered and refurbished products, and the price offered and value placed by the consumer on the reverse logistics is somewhat unclear;
- uncertainty in the total number of origin and collection points (there may also be a delay in the uplift of returned products as time is not as critical as in the forward supply chain);
- clarity of information, traceability and visibility and a lack of security for products;
- poor packaging and small consignment sizes of returned products;
- necessary inspection and separation of returned products that are also labour-intensive activities;
- the next stage in the reverse logistics chain is not always clear.

In consideration of the foregoing and the definition of reverse logistics presented at the beginning of this chapter, the key management decision issues in this area are:

- what type of materials can be sent upstream in the supply chain;
- how various responsibilities of supply chain participants are defined;
- what is reasonably possible to recover, recycle or reuse;
- how economic and ecological value is determined in this entire process.

But reverse logistics is not only about recovering or recycling product materials, re-using containers, recycling packaging materials, or re-designing packaging to use fewer materials. These activities, while important, are part of the realm of green or sustainable logistics, which also encompasses a reduction of energy use and pollution emissions from all logistical and supply chain activities, primarily in the 'Stop' and 'Go' activities of warehousing and transportation. Further, issues about product design and packaging, as illustrated in Logistics Example 12.2, are important in the forward logistics flow. A discussion about the science of the environment is provided next to set the context for sustainable logistics and supply chain management.

LOGISTICS EXAMPLE 12.2

Green logistics and packaging at NKL

Coop NKL BA is a Norwegian food cooperative and since 2002 has been a 20 per cent co-owner of the Nordic cooperative Coop Norden AB together with Kooperativa Förbundet, Sweden (42 per cent) and FDB, Denmark (38 per cent). Norden's vision is for a better, more secure everyday life through profitable shops owned by members. It sees its future as being the Scandinavian retail business with the greatest geographical coverage and thus the best route for suppliers to reach Scandinavian customers. This strategy enables Norden to quickly and responsively implement joint activities, product ranges and agreements across national borders.

NKL, together with its Norden partners, believes reverse and 'green' logistics provides it with a competitive advantage in the difficult Nordic marketplace. NKL's initiatives in being a 'green' retailer provided a 220 per cent increase of environmental product sales in the late 1990s. It used 1.5 million re-usable containers for fruits and vegetables and increased rail transport use from 50 per cent to 60 per cent, which led to reduced costs, improved order cycle times and reduced pollutants and energy wastage. Overall, the Norden group in 2003 sold 93,800 tonnes of eco-labelled/organic foods and used 2,350 tonnes of recycled plastic and 17,600 tonnes of recycled cardboard in its terminals and warehouses.

Packaging design has played an important role at NKL, which has sought to improve under-utilised transportation and warehouse capacity, handling and damage problems, and reduce extra work due to returns and co-distribution problems. For example, the company developed a new consumer and retail package for a potato flakes snack food in conjunction with the manufacturer Nestlé and NKL's retailers. The packaging supply chain project realised total savings of 800,000 Norwegian kroner (NOK) or about €97,000 per year, of which retailers saved 375,000 NOK and NKL saved the balance on warehouse and transportation costs.

Question

Are you aware of your local retailers' reverse or green logistics initiatives and if so, what are they?

Sources: adapted from James R. Stock, *Development and Implementation of Reverse Logistics Programs,* Oak Brook, IL: Council of Logistics Management, 1998; and Coop NKL BA website, http://coop.no/.

The science behind a sustainable environment

Climate change and the need to reduce greenhouse gas emissions is one of the greatest long-term challenges facing the world today. It is continually being discussed by the media and at international conferences, and major reports are issued regularly on the steps to combat climate change by organisations such as the Intergovernmental Panel on Climate Change (IPCC).

Climatic observations over the past 150 years have shown that temperatures at the earth's surface have risen globally, with important regional variations. Most of the observed increase in global average temperatures since the mid-20th century is considered to be due to an observed increase in greenhouse gas concentrations.[10] The six major greenhouse gases are:[11]

- carbon dioxide (CO_2)
- methane (CH_4)
- nitrous oxides (N_2O)
- hydrofluorocarbons (HFC)
- perfluorocarbons (PFC)
- sulphur hexafluoride (SF_6).

Carbon dioxide is the most significant of these greenhouse gases and is the main contributor to global warming. Concern about environmental issues due to increased greenhouse gases, such as pollution, traffic congestion, global warming, disposal and the clean-up of hazardous materials, has led to a number of environmental laws and EU directives that affect logistics systems design and strategies.

Table 12.1 shows the ten countries emitting the most carbon dioxide in 2009 according to the US Energy Information Administration.[12] China and the US are the two largest emitters at 7.7 and 5.4 billion tonnes respectively, while Russia, India and Japan are all between 1–1.6 billion tonnes each. China (13.3 per cent), India (8.7 per cent), South Korea (1.2 per cent) and Iran (3.2 per cent) increased emissions over 2008, although the other eight countries decreased emissions anywhere from 7.0–9.7 per cent. How many of these decreases are related to measures to reduce emissions or the result of the severe economic

Table 12.1 Carbon dioxide emissions in 2009

Rank	Country	Million tonnes 2009	Change from 2008
1	China	7,711	+13.3%
2	United States	5,425	−7.0%
3	India	1,602	+8.7%
4	Russia	1,572	−7.4%
5	Japan	1,098	−9.7%
6	Germany	766	−7.0%
7	Canada	541	−9.6%
8	South Korea	528	+1.2%
9	Iran	527	+3.2%
10	United Kingdom	520	−7.8%

Source: Eyewitness: An atlas of pollution; the world in carbon dioxide emissions, *The Guardian*, 31/01/2011, p. 18 (Harvey, F.), Fiona Harvey Copyright Guardian News & Media Ltd 2011.

recession in 2008–2009 is unknown. Overall, though, total global emissions fell by only 0.1 per cent and thus may not be in accord with global agreements.

In 1997, the Kyoto Agreement legally bound industrialised nations to reduce emissions of greenhouse gases, particularly carbon dioxide, to an average of 5.2 per cent below 1990 baseline levels by 2012.[13] The aim of this legislation as well as various climate change bills in the EU and UK is to maintain global carbon dioxide levels below 450 parts per million and limit the temperature rise to no more than 2 degrees Celsius by 2100. The UK government has committed to reduce greenhouse gas emissions to at least 12.5 per cent below baseline by the same date and has also set a tougher long-term goal of reducing carbon dioxide emissions by 80 per cent by the year 2050. This dramatic decrease compared with the rise in emissions over the last several decades is shown in Figure 12.2.

Environmental issues are considered one part of a wider corporate social responsibility perspective that has been represented in various forms of John Elkington's 'Triple Bottom Line' (TBL) of profits, people and planet.[14] The TBL posits that firms should focus not only on the maximisation of shareholder wealth or economic value that they create in economies but also on the environmental and social value that they add – or possibly destroy – in order to achieve long-term environmental security and egalitarian living standards for all human beings.

It thus becomes intuitively obvious that a firm's environmental or 'green' agenda will contain an additional 'green' aspect: the 'colour of money' from achieving cost reductions through energy and emissions savings. Thus, like any other business decision a firm will make, an environmental agenda will be subject to its own cost–benefit tradeoffs. But, how can a firm calculate all true and total costs and benefits? The overriding method proposed

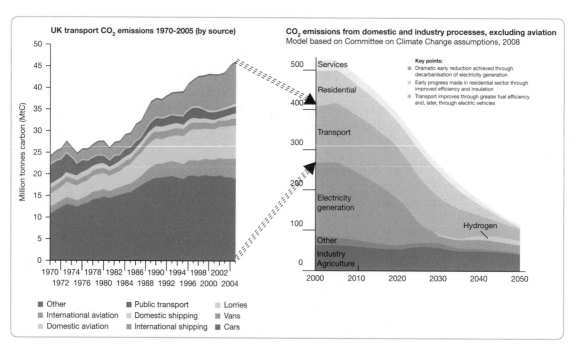

Figure 12.2 UK actual increases and proposed decreases in carbon dioxide emissions

Sources: Commission for Integrated Transport (2007) and *The Guardian*, 01/12/2008, http://image.guardian.co.uk/sys-files/Guardian/documents/2008/12/01/CO2_EMISSIONS_0212.pdf, Copyright Guardian News & Media Ltd 2008.

for environmental performance measurement is the life cycle assessment (LCA), which is a 'cradle-to-grave' approach for assessing industrial systems. The LCA approach begins with the gathering of raw materials from the earth to create products and ends at the point when all materials are returned to the earth. LCA evaluates all stages of a product's life cycle from the perspective that they are interdependent, meaning that one stage leads to the next.

LCA also enables the estimation of cumulative environmental impacts resulting from all stages in the product life cycle, often including impacts not considered in more traditional analyses – for example, raw material extraction, material transportation and ultimate product disposal. By including the impacts throughout the product life cycle, LCA provides a comprehensive view of the environmental aspects of the product or process and a more accurate picture of the true environmental tradeoffs in product and process selection.[15]

The International Organization for Standardization (ISO) 14000 series of standards for environmental management systems formalises LCA components and allows firms to establish an environmental management system (EMS). According to ISO 14040, LCA consists of four phases, as presented in Figure 12.3:[16]

1 Goal and scope definition.

2 Inventory analysis.

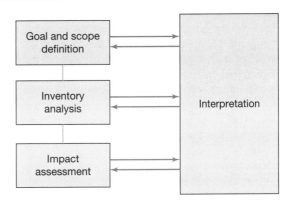

Goal and scope definition: the product(s) or service(s) to be assessed are defined, a functional basis for comparison is chosen and the required level of detail is defined.

Inventory analysis: the energy carriers and raw materials, the emissions to atmosphere, water and soil, and different type of land use are quantified for each process, then combined in the process flow chart and related to the functional basis.

Impact assessment: the effects of the resource use and emissions processed are grouped and quantified into a limited number of impact categories which may then be weighted for importance.

Interpretation: the results are reported in the most informative way possible and the need and opportunities to reduce the impact of the product(s) or service(s) on the environment are systematically evaluated.

Figure 12.3 Phases of life cycle assessment ISO 14040

Source: UNEP (2003, p.2).

3 Impact assessment.

4 Interpretation.

These phases are not simply followed in a single sequence, this is an iterative process, in which subsequent iterations can achieve increasing levels of detail from screening LCA to full LCA, or lead to changes in the first phase prompted by the results of the last phase. LCA has proven to be a valuable tool to document and analyse environmental considerations of product and service systems that need to be part of decision making towards sustainability and ISO 14040 provides a general framework for LCA. However, LCA is not without flaws; currently it does not accommodate externalities, which are discussed in Logistics Example 12.3.

LOGISTICS EXAMPLE 12.3

Determining external environmental costs of freight transport

Freight transport 'internal' costs, often referred to as market or private costs, are the costs borne directly by transport operators. These costs consist of operating costs and capital investments in facilities and vehicles, rail stock, airplanes and/or ships which eventually need to be replaced. Operating costs are closely related to the level of transport activity and include fuel, labour, repair and maintenance, infrastructure charges, taxes, insurance and depreciation.

However, the adverse impacts of freight transport also impose 'external' costs which are borne not by those who generate the freight traffic but by society as a whole. Hence, externalities are not normally taken into account in the decisions made by freight transport users. External costs relate to the negative effects of air pollution and greenhouse gas emissions, infrastructure, noise, accidents and congestion related to freight transport. It is proposed that environmental and congestion costs should be recovered through taxation; application of a full 'polluter pays principle' would require taxes paid by freight transport operators to cover their allocated infrastructure, as well as their environmental and congestion costs.

Internalisation measures aim to do so by increasing the price of transport services in proportion to all the relevant social and environmental costs generated. Therefore, placing an appropriate value on external costs of freight traffic is fundamental to their internalisation. The UK's Department for Transport (DfT) and Department for Environment, Food and Rural Affairs (Defra) have examined these issues during the last decade regarding road freight transport and it is estimated that total external costs in the UK are £6.7 billion, £7.1 billion and £7.7 billion using low-, medium- and high-emission cost values respectively.

The heaviest articulated vehicles with gross vehicle weights of over 33 tonnes carry 72 per cent of all road tonne kilometres but are responsible for only around 47 per cent of all external costs of road freight transport. Conversely, rigid vehicles in all gross vehicle weight categories account for 48 per cent of total external costs while carrying only 24 per cent of total tonne kilometres. These differing proportions show how larger and heavier trucks have lower external costs per t-km, assuming loading factors and empty running figures at normal levels.

Overall, 40 per cent of the total external costs are attributable to congestion (£2.9–3.1 billion), 23 per cent to infrastructure (£1.5–1.8 billion), 19 per cent to traffic accidents (£1.3–1.4 billion), 15 per cent to air pollution and greenhouse gas emissions (£1.0–1.2 billion) and only 2 per cent to noise (£134–154 million).

Logistics example 12.3 (*cont.*)

At a European level, according to the European Environmental Agency (EEA), distance-related charges including fuel taxes and infrastructure charges levied on road freight transport are still below minimum estimates of marginal external cost in all EU nations. The average value of the full external cost of road freight traffic was estimated to be €0.26 per truck kilometre. More than 80 per cent of these external costs in Europe were related to accidents, climate change and air pollution. Noise and congestion were also included in the calculation and were a substantial proportion of external costs in urban areas. According to EEA estimates, taxes levied on vehicle operators in the UK internalised around 88 per cent of external costs of road freight transport, a higher proportion than in any other EU country. At the other extreme, countries such as Poland, Greece and Luxembourg internalised only about 30 per cent of the external costs arising from road freight transport.

Awareness of the full costs of freight transport services, including both internal and external costs, should help firms plan, manage and change their logistics activities to achieve long-term sustainability. Changes may involve a greater use of alternative and more environmentally friendly transport modes, more localised sourcing, improved utilisation, and even some relaxation of current just-in-time scheduling. Further, if higher freight costs associated with internalisation are passed along the supply chain, the purchasing behaviour of final consumers may become more sensitive to the environmental impact of distribution operations that keep them supplied with goods and services.

From a global shipping perspective there are substantial factors which are difficult to assess as well as mitigate. A move towards sustainable shipping will require ships with lower emissions, environmental training for crews and management, and ongoing reports on performance. The world's merchant ships generated 2.7 per cent of total carbon dioxide emissions in 2009, or some 870 million tonnes. This value is an increase of 85 per cent since 1990 and it is estimated that by 2020 these ships will generate 6 per cent of global carbon dioxide emissions. However, who will have responsibility to collect taxes to offset such external costs when a ship is on the high seas?

Similarly, ports and surrounding areas will have to develop a strong environmental outlook and a public and ecological health approach. It has been estimated that 70 per cent of shipping emissions occur within 400 kilometres of land; thus ships contribute significant pollution in coastal communities. Shipping-related particulate matter (PM) emissions are considered to cause 60,000 cardiopulmonary and lung cancer deaths annually, with most deaths occurring near coastlines in Europe, East Asia and South Asia. With the expected growth in shipping activity, the annual mortalities could increase by 40 per cent by 2012.

Mortality and health benefits in many regions globally could be realised from policy action to mitigate ship emissions of PM formed during engine combustion and gaseous exhaust pollutants. Policy discussions aimed at reducing ship emissions are currently focused on two concerns: geospatial aspects of policy implementation and compliance, for example uniform global standards versus requirements for designated control areas, and the benefits and costs of various emission-reduction strategies, for example fuel switching versus after-treatment technologies or operational changes.

The Port of Long Beach in Los Angeles has proven to be a leader in addressing such issues. It has developed an environmental management policy 'committed to managing resources and conducting Port developments in both an environmentally and fiscally responsible manner'. Some of the Port's initiatives include investing $40 million to test new ideas, using shore power by installing shoreline electrical extension cords, using electric

> **Logistics example 12.3** (*cont.*)
>
> hauling trucks capable of carrying 60,000 pounds at 40 miles per hour, and using diesel–electric hybrid tug boats.
>
> What these various examples demonstrate is that environmental issues in logistics and supply chain management extend beyond the usual factors regarding transportation and warehousing and include wider societal impacts that should be considered in any environmental assessment.
>
> **Question**
>
> *How easy will it be for governments to assess and charge firms for external environmental costs?*
>
> *Sources:* adapted from Maja Piecyk, Alan McKinnon and Julian Allen, 'Evaluating and internalizing the environmental costs of logistics,' in Alan McKinnon, Sharon Cullinane, Michael Browne and Anthony Whiteing (eds.) *Green Logistics: Improving the Environmental Sustainability of Logistics*, London: Kogan Page, 2010, pp.68–97; Christine Loh, 'Port cities: The sustainability challenge,' *The Annual Peter Thompson Lecture*, University of Hull, 28 October 2009; and James J. Corbett, James J. Winebrake, Erin H. Green, Prasad Kasibhatla, Veroniks Eyring and Axel Laurer, 'Mortality from ship emissions: A global assessment,' *Environmental Science & Technology*, 2007, Vol. 41, No. 24, pp.8512–8518.

Green or sustainable logistics and supply chains

Sajed Abukhader and Gunilla Jönson posed two interesting questions in an academic article in 2004:[17]

1 What is the impact of logistics on the environment?

2 What is the impact of the environment on logistics?

The impact of logistics on the environment is the easier question to answer, but the second question is a bit more difficult to conceptualise. However, an example should illustrate their point. Cotton does not grow naturally in many countries in northern latitudes. Thus, if people living in northern European countries or Canada desire cotton clothing or other cotton goods, then some form of logistics activity such as transport and/or warehousing will be required to bring cotton to their respective market. The main issue here is whether the cotton should be in the form of raw materials or finished goods. The answer to that issue will depend on the design of the particular logistical system and supply chain.

Abukhader and Jönson also argued there are three 'themes' regarding green or sustainable logistics and supply chain management:

1 Reverse logistics.

2 Assessment of emissions.

3 The 'greening' of logistical activities and supply chains.

The first two themes have been discussed above and the third will be the point of departure for the remainder of this chapter. It only remains to note a final point by Abukhader and Jönson that when they wrote their article there was little use of life cycle assessment in logistics and supply chain management and little consideration of environmental impacts beyond cost–benefit analysis. That situation has improved and is rapidly expanding, but it is important to remember that the sustainability agenda in general and its application to logistics and supply chain management in particular are still fairly recent and underdeveloped.

The 'greening' of logistics activities and supply chains means ensuring that these activities are environmentally friendly and not wasteful, and particularly focus on reducing carbon emissions across the entire supply chain. Although logistics activities comprise many aspects, as discussed in previous chapters, the two primary and significant activities that impact the environment are the 'Stop' and 'Go' activities of storage and transportation. While manufacturing is considered a 'Stop' point in the supply chain and also has a significant environmental impact through the production process, its consideration is beyond the scope of this text. Readers are encouraged to seek out good texts on operations management for a full appreciation of environmental issues in that context.[18]

Transportation and storage in a wider environmental context

How do transportation and storage activities compare with other activities in society with respect to their environmental impact? Both are users of energy, for example fuel and electricity, and both produce carbon dioxide emissions as a result of using this energy. About 75–80 per cent of a firm's carbon dioxide 'footprint' can be attributed to logistics and transport activity and with the transport sector contributing to one-third of all carbon emissions; thus it is not surprising that non-energy companies are beginning to assess the energy consumption of their supply chains as a way to reduce their overall carbon emissions.[19]

The World Economic Forum estimates that logistics and transport activity account for 2,800 mega-tonnes of carbon dioxide emissions annually, or about 6 per cent of the total 50,000 mega-tonnes produced by human activity.[20] Figure 12.4 shows the emissions breakdown within logistics and transport activity and road freight contributes about 60 per cent of the total.

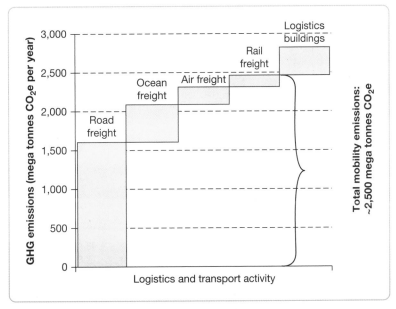

Figure 12.4 Emissions share per logistics activity

Source: World Economic Forum (2009, p.8).

The UK's domestic carbon dioxide emissions, excluding international aviation and shipping, are generated from four main sectors, as shown in Figure 12.5: the energy supply sector (ca. 39 per cent), all modes in the transport sector (ca. 23 per cent), the industrial sector including manufacturing, retailing, service and warehousing (ca. 18 per cent), and the residential sector (ca. 15 per cent).[21]

Examining the transport sector in more detail, private automobiles are the primary source of carbon dioxide emissions (54 per cent), followed by heavy goods trucks or lorries (22 per cent) and vans (13 per cent). Thus, in the UK, truck and van transportation accounts for just over 8 per cent of total carbon dioxide emissions. This is consistent with worldwide estimations of 8 per cent for transport; warehousing and goods handling worldwide are estimated to add about 4 per cent to that total.[22]

On the energy-input side, vehicle engines are becoming more efficient in terms of fuel use and emissions and there are ongoing efforts to consider alternative fuels such as biodiesel or bioethanol, hydrogen, natural gas or liquid petroleum gas, and electricity.[23] However, these developments are still in their infancy and have their own environmental impacts. For example, the growth of crops for biofuels requires the use of arable land, which displaces the growing of crops for food. A response to that situation might see famers cultivating more forests and grasslands for food production, thus possibly negating the positive effects of greenhouse gas emissions reductions from using biofuels.

The UK's total transportation emissions have risen 11 per cent from the Kyoto baseline of 1990 – faster than any other sector, despite efficiencies in fuel use and emissions. This situation is due primarily to the growth in freight transport activity and is again consistent

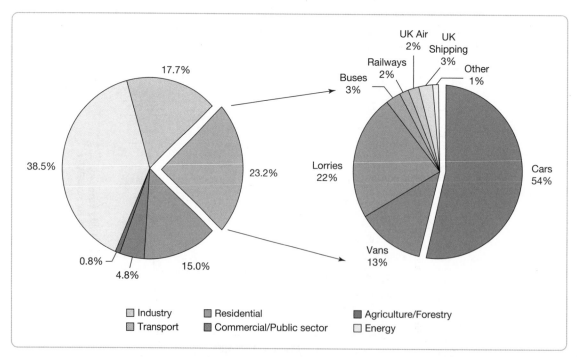

Figure 12.5 UK carbon dioxide emissions by sector and transport sector carbon dioxide emissions by source (excluding international aviation and shipping)

Source: adapted from Commission for Integrated Transport (2007, pp.20–22).

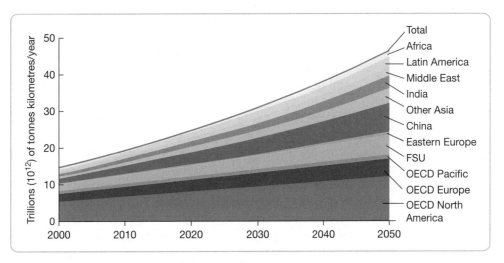

Figure 12.6 Freight transport growth forecasts by region
Source: World Business Council for Sustainable Development (2007, p.6).

with predicted growth in freight transport, particularly road freight, all over the globe, as shown in Figure 12.6.[24]

Turning to warehousing as one aspect of the industrial sector, the World Business Council for Sustainable Development notes that buildings account for 40 per cent of worldwide energy use.[25] Initiatives to increase the efficiency of building in using energy and reducing emissions have been developed by the Leadership in Energy and Environmental Design certification programme (LEED) in the US and the Building Research Establishment Environmental Assessment Method (BREEAM) in the UK.[26] LEED accreditation has five categories: indoor environment quality including lighting, materials and resources used in construction, energy and atmosphere, including electricity use, sustainable sites and water efficiency. The ultimate goal for a sustainable building is a net-zero operation where a building uses little or no outside energy or resources, for example by generating its own electricity through solar power, recycling and re-using waste water.

Suggestions for greening logistics and the supply chain

The World Economic Forum has argued that a collaborative responsibility for 'greening' the supply chain rests with three groups: logistics and transport service providers, shippers and buyers as recipients of such services, and both government and non-government policy makers.[27] Opportunity and challenge areas and specific recommendations for these three groups are as follows.

Transportation, vehicles and infrastructure networks

Logistics and transport service providers should increase the industry-wide adoption of new technologies, fuels and associated processes by implementing where there is a positive business case, deploy network reviews of large closed networks to ensure efficient hierarchies and nodal structures, and look to integrate optimisation efforts across multiple networks, for example integrating their own and customers' networks into one model. They should enable further collaboration between multiple shippers and/or between carriers to make greater use of co-loading opportunities.

Shippers and buyers should build environmental performance indicators into the contracting process with logistics service providers, particularly around carbon emissions, and work with consumers to better support their understanding of carbon footprints and labelling where appropriate and make recycling easier and more resource efficient.

Policy makers should promote further expansion of integrated flow-management schemes for congested roads and make specific, point investments in congested nodes or sections of infrastructure – around congested road junctions, ports and rail junctions.

Logistics and transport service providers should look to switch to more environmentally friendly modes within their own networks, for example in the large closed networks operated by postal operators, parcel carriers and pallet networks. Shippers and buyers should support efforts to make mode switches across supply chains and begin to 'de-speed' the supply chain, allowing economic order quantities to rise and delivery frequencies to fall. This will, of course, have an impact on stockholding and inventory carrying costs.

Another example of 'de-speeding' the supply chain example is the concept of slow-steaming for ocean shipping (see Figure 12.7).[28] A decrease in container ship speed from 22 knots per hour to 20 knots will reduce carbon dioxide emissions by 17 per cent; however, the average journey time of the ship from Asia to Europe would increase from 35 to 42 days.

Policy makers should actively promote mode switches to rail, short sea and inland waterways and consider re-opening idle rail lines, waterways and port facilities with government support.

Green buildings

Logistics and transport service providers should encourage wider industry commitment to improve existing facilities through the retro-fitting of green technologies, via individual

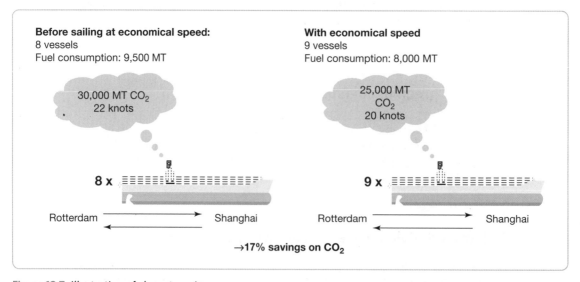

Before sailing at economical speed:
8 vessels
Fuel consumption: 9,500 MT

30,000 MT CO_2
22 knots

8 x

Rotterdam → Shanghai

With economical speed
9 vessels
Fuel consumption: 8,000 MT

25,000 MT CO_2
20 knots

9 x

Rotterdam → Shanghai

→17% savings on CO_2

Figure 12.7 Illustration of slow-steaming
Source: Maersk Line (2008).

and/or sector-wide actions, and work towards industry-wide commitments to boost investment into new building technologies, and develop new offerings around recycling and waste management, working collaboratively with customers. Policy makers should encourage industry to commit to improvements, which consider the boundaries of possibilities with current and future technologies, through individual and sector-wide actions.

Sourcing, product and packaging design

By determining the source of supply, delivery location and many supply chain characteristics for products, shippers and buyers of products lock in much of the carbon emissions associated with supply chains. They determine how much carbon is designed into a product through raw material selection, the carbon intensity of the production process, the length and speed of the supply chain, and (at least partly) the carbon characteristics of the use phase. Shippers and buyers can take decisions which actively drive positive change up and down the supply chain.

Shippers and buyers should agree additional standards and targets around light-weight packaging and seek cross-industry agreements on modularisation of transit packaging materials. They should also develop sustainable sourcing policies that consider the carbon impact of primary production, manufacturing and re-work activities, and integrate carbon emissions impact into the business case for near-shoring projects.

Administrative issues

Logistics and transport service providers should develop carbon offsetting solutions for own operations and clients as part of a balanced suite of business offerings. Policy makers should work with them to develop universal carbon measurement and reporting standards, build an open carbon trading system, and review tax regimes to remove counterproductive incentives, and support efforts to move towards further carbon labelling. Further, they should ensure that the full cost of carbon is reflected in energy tariffs across all geographies and all modes of transport.

Summary

Some reverse logistics and supply chain activities have been in place for a number of years. But they are becoming more important, as are other environmental and sustainable issues in logistics and supply chain management due to the significant impact that logistics and supply chain activities have on the natural environment. Such issues must be addressed in order to ensure economic and environmental sustainability. This area is growing rapidly and many initiatives are under way to increase efficiencies in energy use and emissions. However, there are tradeoffs between a sustainable supply chain and current practices involving just-in-time techniques and time compression.

This chapter has presented an introduction to concepts and current thought and practice on reverse logistics and supply chains, and green and sustainable logistics and supply chain management. The next and final chapter provides a holistic overview of logistics management through a discussion of logistics and supply chain strategy.

DISCUSSION QUESTIONS

1 Discuss the reverse logistics or product recovery management process required for a laptop computer.

2 What are the key external barriers to effective reverse logistics and product recovery management?

3 How would you apply the life cycle assessment (LCA) concept to a new automobile?

4 Explain what is meant by the effect of logistics on the environment and the effect of the environment on logistics.

5 What are the key enablers of a green supply chain?

Suggested reading

Abukhader, Sajed M. and Gunilla Jönson 'Logistics and the environment: Is it an established subject?' *International Journal of Logistics: Research and Applications*, 2004, Vol. 7, No. 2, pp.137–149.

Anono 'Climate change 2007, the physical science basis,' *Working Group 1 Contribution to the Fourth Assessment Report of the Intergovernmental Panel on Climate Change*, Cambridge University Press, 2007.

Böge, Stefanie 'The well-travelled yogurt pot: Lessons for new freight transport policies and regional production,' *World Transport Policy & Practice*, 1995, Vol. 1, No. 1, pp.7–11.

Commission for Integrated Transport, *Transport and Climate Change: Advice to Government from the Commission for Integrated Transport*, London: Commission for Integrated Transport, 2007.

Elkington, John 'Towards the sustainable corporation: Win-win-win business strategies for sustainable development,' *California Management Review*, 1994, Vol. 36, No. 2, pp.90–100.

Grant, David B. and Ruth Banomyong 'Design of closed-loop supply chain and product recovery management for fast-moving consumer goods: The case of a single-use camera,' *Asia Pacific Journal of Marketing & Logistics*, 2010, Vol. 22, No. 2, pp.233–246.

McKinnon, Alan, Sharon Cullinane, Michael Browne and Anthony Whiteing (eds.) *Green Logistics: Improving the Environmental Sustainability of Logistics*, London: Kogan Page, 2010.

Rogers, Dale S. and Ronald S. Tibben-Lembke *Going Backwards: Reverse Trends and Practices*, University of Nevada-Reno: Reverse Logistics Executive Council, 1998.

Shaw, Sarah, David B. Grant and John Mangan, 'Developing environmental supply chain performance measures,' *Benchmarking: An International Journal*, 2010, Vol. 17, No. 3, pp.320–339.

Stock, James R. *Development and Implementation of Reverse Logistics Programs*, Oak Brook, IL: Council of Logistics Management, 1998.

Thierry, Martijn, Marc Salomon, Jo Van Nunen and Luk N. Van Wassenhove 'Strategic issues in product recovery management,' *California Management Review*, 1995, Vol. 37, No. 2, pp.114–135.

World Economic Forum *Supply Chain Decarbonization: The role of logistics and transport in reducing supply chain carbon emissions*, Geneva: World Economic Forum, 2009.

Notes

1 Stefanie Böge, 'The well-travelled yogurt pot: Lessons for new freight transport policies and regional production,' *World Transport Policy & Practice*, 1995, Vol.1, No. 1, pp.7–11.

2 This section is adapted from Dale S. Rogers and Ronald S. Tibben-Lembke, *Going Backwards: Reverse Trends and Practices,* University of Nevada-Reno: Reverse Logistics Executive Council, 1998; and James R. Stock, *Development and Implementation of Reverse Logistics Programs*, Oak Brook, IL: Council of Logistics Management, 1998.

3 Rogers and Tibben-Lembke, 1998, p.2.

4 Stock, 1998, p.20.

5 Stock, 1998, pp. 9–10.

6 Gordon Scott, 'WEEE developments: Who will be accountable?' *Logistics & Transport Focus*, Vol. 7, No. 2 (March 2005), pp.30–33; and 'Working out WEEE,' *Logistics & Transport Focus*, Vol. 7, No. 2 (March 2005), p.34.

7 See the Caledonian Alloys Group Ltd website at www.caledonianalloys.com/.

8 Martijn Thierry, Marc Salomon, Jo Van Nunen and Luk N. Van Wassenhove, 'Strategic issues in product recovery management,' *California Management Review*, 1995, Vol. 37, No. 2, pp.114–135.

9 David B. Grant and Ruth Banomyong, 'Design of closed-loop supply chain and product recovery management for fast-moving consumer goods: The case of a single-use camera,' *Asia Pacific Journal of Marketing & Logistics*, 2010, Vol. 22, No. 2, pp.233–246.

10 For further details about the science of the environment see 'Climate change 2007, the physical science basis,' *Working Group 1 Contribution to the Fourth Assessment Report of the Intergovernmental Panel on Climate Change,* Cambridge University Press, 2007.

11 Sarah Shaw, David B. Grant and John Mangan, 'Developing environmental supply chain performance measures,' *Benchmarking: An International Journal*, 2010, Vol. 17, No. 3, pp.320–339.

12 Fiona Harvey, 'Eyewitness: An atlas of pollution; the world in carbon dioxide emissions,' *The Guardian*, 31 January 2011, pp.18–19.

13 Shaw *et al.*, 2010.

14 John Elkington, 'Towards the sustainable corporation: Win-win-win business strategies for sustainable development,' *California Management Review*, 1994, Vol. 36, No. 2, pp.90–100.

15 For more detail about life cycle assessment see Mary Ann Curran, 'Life cycle assessment: Principles and practice,' *EPA/600/R-06/060*, Cincinnati, OH: US Environmental Protection Agency, 2006, www.epa.gov/nrmrl/lcaccess/pdfs/600r06060.pdf.

16 United Nations Environment Programme, 'Evaluation of environmental impacts in life cycle assessment,' Paris: UNEP, 2003, www.unep.org/.

17 Sajed M. Abukhader and Gunilla Jönson, 'Logistics and the environment: Is it an established subject?' *International Journal of Logistics: Research and Applications*, 2004, Vol. 7, No. 2, pp.137–149.

18 A good example of such a text is Nigel Slack, Stuart Chambers and Robert Johnston, *Operations Management,* 6th ed. Harlow: FT Prentice Hall, 2010.

19 Shaw *et al.*, 2010.

20 World Economic Forum, *Supply Chain Decarbonization: The role of logistics and transport in reducing supply chain carbon emissions*, Geneva: World Economic Forum, 2009.

21 Commission for Integrated Transport, *Transport and Climate Change: Advice to Government from the Commission for Integrated Transport*, London: Commission for Integrated Transport, 2007.

22 Alan McKinnon, 'Environmental sustainability,' in Alan McKinnon, Sharon Cullinane, Michael Browne and Anthony Whiteing (eds.) *Green Logistics: Improving the Environmental Sustainability of Logistics*, London: Kogan Page, 2010, pp.3–30.

23 Sharon Cullinane and Julia Edwards, 'Benefits and costs of switching to alternative fuels,' in Alan McKinnon, Sharon Cullinane, Michael Browne and Anthony Whiteing (eds.) *Green Logistics: Improving the Environmental Sustainability of Logistics*, London: Kogan Page, 2010, pp.306–321.

24 World Business Council for Sustainable Development, *Mobility for Development*, 2007, www.wbcsd.org.

25 World Business Council for Sustainable Development, *Energy Efficiency in Buildings: Business realities and opportunities*, 2007, www.wbcsd.org.

26 Clive Marchant, 'Reducing the environmental impact of warehousing,' in Alan McKinnon, Sharon Cullinane, Michael Browne and Anthony Whiteing (eds.) *Green Logistics: Improving the Environmental Sustainability of Logistics*, London: Kogan Page, 2010, pp.167–192.

27 World Economic Forum, 2009, pp.29–31.

28 Eivind Kolding, 'Challenges and opportunities,' *Presentation at the 25th German Logistics Congress*, October 2008, Berlin.

Chapter 13

Logistics strategy

Key objectives

- To understand the nature and language of corporate strategy.
- To consider the strategic planning process.
- To explore the development of logistics strategy.
- To link logistics and corporate strategy.
- To consider logistics and supply chain risk and resilience as it affects strategy.

Introduction

The American economist and Nobel laureate Milton Friedman repeatedly said that the sole purpose of a business is to generate profits for its shareholders.[1] While simple and a fair reflection of the driving force behind a free-market economy, this view does not consider the complexities behind modern-day global business activities among many different types of economies. Firms need to develop more far-reaching goals and an appropriate strategy or strategies for achieving them. Concepts of business or corporate strategy have existed and been discussed for many decades and most firms today are using some form of strategy to plan, operate and control their business activities.[2]

Strategy is also important for logistics and supply chain activities, which are also increasingly becoming global and sensitive to the environment, as discussed in the last two chapters. While fitting within a firm's overall strategy, there are nuances applicable to logistics and supply chain management that need to be considered by a firm's management. This chapter on strategy discusses such issues and is thus a capstone for this book by providing an overview of strategy, its integration in the logistics and supply chain domain, and how strategy affects and impacts various issues discussed in this book's previous chapters.

This chapter begins by discussing the nature of business strategy in general, including developing a strategic plan, before considering strategy as it relates to logistics activities in particular. While a great deal of strategic thought is given to creating and maximising opportunities for firms, strategy also considers the possibility of risks to the business and how to mitigate such risks. Accordingly, this chapter will conclude with a discussion of risk as it may impact logistics activities and supply chains.

What is business strategy?

Business strategy is defined as:

> the direction and scope of an organisation over the long term: which achieves advantage for the organisation through its configuration of resources within a changing environment, to meet the needs of markets and fulfil stakeholder expectations.[3]

This definition uses the word stakeholder as opposed to shareholder, in contrast with Friedman's view above. Strategic thinking in the 21st century considers that a firm must consider the needs of all relevant stakeholders, i.e. anyone who has an interest in the success of the firm, which include not only shareholders but also suppliers, customers, the government, local citizens where a firm's plant or warehouse may be located, and so on. The definition also contains several elements that encompass three hierarchical levels of strategy:

- an overall *corporate strategy* that is long term in scope and outlook, e.g. five years or more. This strategy represents the overall purpose of the firm to meet expectations of stakeholders;

- individual strategies for *strategic business units* (SBUs), which are independently operated in particular markets to meet those market needs. These strategies are more medium term in nature, e.g. from one to three years;

- *operational strategies* concerned with ongoing and day-to-day operations or products using a firm's resources, processes and skills, in other words its core competencies. Operational strategies are very much short term, e.g. less than one year at the most.

The language of strategy

Like all business disciplines, strategy has its own language, i.e. vocabulary and terms, and the important items applicable for this chapter are as follows:[4]

- *Mission*: the overriding purpose of the firm that is generally in line with values or expectations of stakeholders; the terms goal and vision are also used.

- *Objective*: the quantification or more precise statement of the firm's mission or goal.

- *Strategies*: represent the long-term direction of a firm in concert with the definition of strategy.

- *Core competencies*: represent the resources, processes or skills unique to a firm that provide its 'competitive advantage' in the marketplace.[5]

As an example of these terms being used in a logistics and supply chain context, the 2010 annual report of the French logistics service provider Norbert Dentressangle SA[6] contains the following strategic language:

- *Mission*:

> Norbert Dentressangle [aims to position] our company as a global supply chain leader within the next ten years … to win over new territories, in terms of both services and geographical regions …

- *Objective*: In 2010 Norbert Dentressangle undertook

  rigorous management of balance sheet items ... these operational performances helped reinforce our company's financial position, which included significantly reducing our net financial debt ...

- *Strategies*:

  The company undertook a major strategic shift [in 2010] for its future development, which is that of globalisation ... [and] the gradual integration, by means of internal and external growth, firstly of the two areas of expertise in Europe – transport and logistics – followed by a third area of expertise, the launch of our freight forwarding activity, which has made our company truly international ...

- *Core competencies*:

  Our company is anchored in strong cultural values ... commitment, reactivity, responsibility, thoroughness, innovation and calculated risk-taking ... which have been developed throughout its entire history ... our business relies on the trade of goods, which represents a growth market [calling] for rigorous execution and productivity management ... we provide personal and dependable responses to the challenges faced by our customers and the community as a whole ...

The above statements from Norbert Dentressangle demonstrate how firms can articulate their strategic positions for stakeholders and other interested parties.

Strategic planning

Strategic planning is the process by which firms develop their corporate, SBU and operational strategies and plans. This process:

- forces a firm to critically evaluate its situation in light of current and future trends in its business environment;
- prompts a firm to determine its strengths and weaknesses;
- brings about an evaluation of external opportunities and threats;
- encourages a firm to develop or adapt its strategy in light of its situation;
- stimulates the achievement of the firm's strategic goals;
- assists the firm's search for competitive advantage.

These parts of the process provide benefits towards the firm's strategic success. However, there are costs involved in undertaking strategic planning, an obvious one being the direct opportunity cost of planning; staff time and other resources are required for this process. Further, there are indirect political and other governance costs as managers of SBUs and departments fight for their fair share of resources in the planning process.

Figure 13.1 shows the three elements related to a firm's strategic planning: an analysis of its current situation, the implementation of its strategic choices, and its control and feedback mechanisms to ensure its strategy is working successfully.

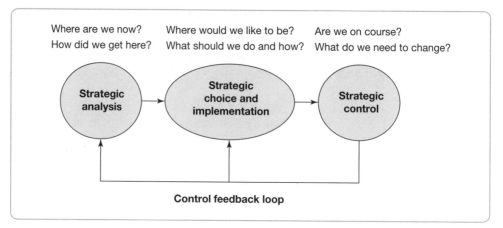

Figure 13.1 Elements of strategic planning

Strategic analysis

The analysis of a firm's current situation answers the questions 'where are we now?' and 'how did we get here?'. This analysis considers not only the situation at the firm but also its external environment. There are several tools for undertaking this analysis, but two of the most popular are the SWOT and PEST. The factors in a SWOT analysis are Strengths, Weaknesses, Opportunities and Threats, shown in Figure 13.2.

Strengths and weaknesses are internal to the firm, i.e. its micro-environment, and are thus controllable by it. Opportunities and threats are external to the firm and are thus uncontrollable by it. Through its strategy a firm should try to convert weaknesses into strengths and threats into opportunities. Further, a firm should try to match its strengths to the opportunities before it.

Returning to the example of Norbert Dentressangle, the company recognised that two of its weaknesses were in not being global and not having a freight forwarding service to aid its logistics and transport efforts. The threat of its competitors taking away business due

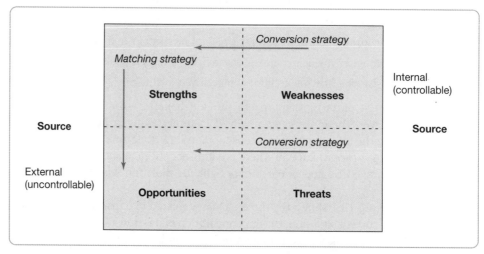

Figure 13.2 SWOT analysis

to their global presence and service offerings led Norbert Dentressangle to convert these weaknesses by establishing a freight forwarding service and thus a global presence of its own that allows it to match its strengths to the global opportunities in the logistics services marketplace.

To assess its internal strengths and weaknesses a firm can audit its activities or benchmark itself to other firms. Several techniques for firm self-analysis have been discussed in previous chapters, such as service and quality tools including benchmarking, the SCOR model and the balanced scorecard in Chapter 2, and financial analysis models, such as ABC analysis, direct product profitability and the cash-to-cash cycle in Chapter 9.

PEST analysis considers those factors in the firm's external or macro-environment over which it has little or no control, i.e. they underlie the opportunity and threat factors in the SWOT analysis. These factors consist of Political, environment and legal factors; Economic and market factors; Social and demographic factors, and Technological and change factors. A PEST analysis is used to summarise and evaluate the impact on the firm of important influences in its external environment. For example, the growth in the global economy during the early and mid-2000s presented tremendous opportunities for logistics service providers such as DHL, which acquired a number of competitors. However, the global recession that began in 2008 and continued for several years afterwards has seen worldwide demand for shipping decrease by about 20 per cent and this has had an effect on logistic service providers (LSPs) within global supply chains. A discussion of latter influences, which are elements of risk, follows later in this chapter.

Strategic choice and implementation

The implementation of a strategy answers the questions 'where would we like to be?' and 'what should we do and how?'. These questions relate to making choices from the options that may be generated during the planning process. Again for example, Norbert Dentressangle chose to establish a freight forwarding service to enhance its global opportunities. However, an alternative would have been not to do so.

All firms will have a choice to 'do nothing' or 'stand still', i.e. they will take no course of action at all. This choice provides a baseline for firms to consider what their future position will be if no action is taken. Most firms will wish to grow and expand their presence in their markets and so this choice is seldom selected. However, given certain conditions in the external environment, such as the global recession commencing in 2008, the selection of this choice might very well be appropriate to prevent a firm taking any unnecessary risks.

There are several models for strategic growth that firms can adopt to generate feasible strategic options. Two well-known models include the Boston Consulting Group (BCG) portfolio growth matrix shown in Figure 13.3 and the Ansoff market–product portfolio matrix shown in Figure 13.4.[7]

The BCG matrix considers a firm's relative market share for its SBUs or products together with potential market growth rate and is based on marketing concepts of a product life cycle and the attractiveness of products in the market.[8] The four quadrants in the matrix are entitled Stars, Cash Cows, Problem Children (or Question Marks) and Dogs.

Stars are those SBUs or products in a high growth rate market where the firm has a relatively high market share compared with competitors. The suggested strategy for Stars is to build sales and/or market share by investing to maintain and/or increase its market leadership position.

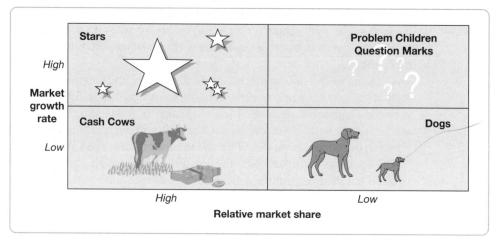

Figure 13.3 Boston Consulting Group portfolio growth matrix

Sources: adapted from Kotler (2000) and Stern and Deimler (2006).

Cash Cows are those SBUs or products in a low growth rate market where the firm has a relatively high market share compared with competitors. Thus, with little chance for any market growth, the suggested strategy is to metaphorically 'milk' the Cash Cows, i.e. the firm should try to hold onto its sales and/or market share. The excess cash generated can then be allocated to Stars, selected Problem Children and/or used for new product development (NPD).

Problem Children are those SBUs or products in a high growth rate market where the firm has a relatively low market share compared with competitors. They thus pose problems for the firm regarding an appropriate strategy to increase market share. The suggested approach here is to build market share selectively for those Problem Children that show the potential to increase market share. This can be done by investing resources and focusing on definable niche product markets. Otherwise, the firm should divest the rest of its Problem Children portfolio.

Dogs are those SBUs or products in a low growth rate market where the firm has a relatively low market share compared with competitors. They may be considered an

| | **Markets** | |
	Existing	*New/related*
Existing **Products**	Market penetration or expansion	Market development
New/related	Product development	Diversification

Figure 13.4 The Ansoff market–product portfolio matrix

Source: adapted from Kotler (2000).

inappropriate use of resources given their return to the firm and thus the suggested strategy is to divest them.

The BCG matrix has stood the test of time over the last 40 years, with many firms achieving strategic success by using it along with other tools and techniques. However, there is some criticism of its basic tenets that firms should consider when using it. For example, does market growth really equal market attractiveness? What is the cost of building market share? And are the matrix's notions of interdependence too simplistic? Further, there are environmental factors that may underlie a firm's choices and ultimately its decisions. For example, which SBUs or products are the real Stars and what is the true length of their product and/or service life cycle? What will a competitor's reaction be to the firm's various decisions? And, as identified above, which Problem Children should receive investment or be divested?

The Ansoff matrix[9], developed by Igor Ansoff in an article in the *Harvard Business Review* in 1957, looks at various product and market strategies. When a firm enters an existing market with its existing products or services it is using a market penetration or expansion strategy. This strategy is usually achieved by taking market share away from competitors; however, other ways to penetrate a market include finding new customers for products or getting current customers to use more products.

When a firm introduces new or related products in its existing markets it is pursuing a product development strategy. Since a firm already sells products in these markets, a suggested strategy would be to develop additional or complementary products for these markets. Even if such new products are not necessarily new to the market, they remain new to the firm.

A market development strategy is when a firm introduces its existing products into new markets where it does not operate. These products can be targeted to different customer segments within its current geographic marketplace or to customers in new geographic locations.

A firm that introduces new products into entirely new markets has chosen a strategy of diversification. When companies have no industry or market experience this strategy is called unrelated diversification. Related diversification is when a firm stays in a market with which it has some familiarity. These brand new products may also be created in an attempt to leverage the firm's brand name.

Much of the previous discussion has focused on a firm's market share. A firm's position in its marketplace will also affect its strategy. There are four basic types of actors in a marketplace based on their market share.[10] A market Leader has the largest percentage share in a marketplace, usually 35–40 per cent or more, and has to be concerned with defending its position from rivals. A market Challenger is the next largest firm, with a share of 20–30 per cent, and is a 'runner-up' wanting 'more of the action' from the Leader and thus a Challenger is concerned with taking away share from the Leader. A market Follower is a runner-up who is satisfied with its lot due to its relative resources or expertise, and thus is not interested in 'rocking the boat' and will pursue a maintenance strategy. Lastly, a market Nicher has a small share, 10 per cent or less, but serves small segments not served by others, with possibly niche products or a niche service offering.

Further, Michael Porter[11] considered that a firm's position and movement within its competitive industry depended upon the bargaining power of suppliers and/or customers and the threat of new entrants to the market and/or products substitutes. His suggested approaches for firms based on these forces include providing low-cost leadership, i.e. producing a product at the lowest cost relative to its competitors, and/or differentiation, i.e. creating products that are unique and valued in the market.

Strategic control

Strategic control answers the questions 'are we on course?' and 'what do we need to change?'. The purpose of control is to evaluate the results of the strategic planning process so that corrective action can be taken if performance does not match objectives. This evaluative and corrective action is shown as a feedback loop in Figure 13.1.

The firm's plan will include suitable performance measures discussed in Chapter 9 for the various goals and strategies that are set, for example key performance indicators (KPIs) or critical success factors (CSFs). The measures are monitored and if there is any deviation from the goals and strategies, both positive and negative, the firm can assess the cause of the deviation or whether there is a mismatch and take appropriate corrective action.

In summary, the entire strategic planning process is shown in Figure 13.5 and encompasses the foregoing sections. The process includes consideration of an overall strategy at the corporate and/or SBU level as well as operational strategies and plans. A firm can review and alter its strategy at any time; however, it is likely that such action will occur during usual strategic planning cycles unless there is a significant deviation from the plan. This can be done at any level since there are both strategic and operational control considerations.

Logistics and corporate strategy

The importance of logistics in a global economy and its strategic role in providing a competitive advantage for firms was discussed in Chapters 1 and 11. A further example is presented in Logistics Example 13.1. Michael Porter's well-known treatise on the 'value chain'[12] noted that inbound and outbound logistics are primary activities in an individual firm's value chain, along with operations, marketing and sales, and service. He argued that secondary activities of a firm's infrastructure – human resource management, information technology and procurement – are necessary only to provide support to the primary activities.

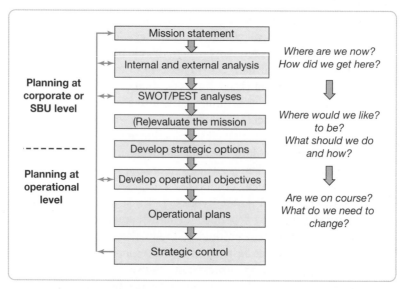

Figure 13.5 The strategic planning process

LOGISTICS EXAMPLE 13.1

Global e-commerce and supply chain strategies for Unilever

Unilever is one of the world's largest consumer products companies, producing an extensive range of foods, home products and personal care items. Its sales in 2010 were over €44 billion in around 180 countries, with more than 2 billion customers using a Unilever product every day, including well-known brands such as Knorr and Lipton in food, Surf laundry detergent, Cif cleaner and Dove soap. Historically, Unilever has grown through a series of acquisitions, which means that the company has inherited a large number of disparate business and technology systems all over the world. The problem it faced was knitting these systems together in order to facilitate communications along the company's many supply chains.

Operating various EDI standards and value-added networks around the world, the company found that it was both complex and expensive to run so many different systems in diverse locations. Unilever realised it had to become more effective at dealing with its trading partners and that installing an electronic exchange would make perfect sense for the company.

In order to increase revenue and maximise competitive advantage, Unilever wanted to achieve much closer collaboration with all sections of its value chain, consisting of customers, suppliers and trading exchanges. This strategy would enable Unilever to manage internal data transfer at a regional and global level across its entire product portfolio, and would also provide an external route or gateway to its customers across the world.

Unilever looked at a broad range of suppliers before deciding to work with IBM for this project. Working closely together the two companies developed and implemented a powerful cross-enterprise web-based collaboration platform, the Unilever Private Exchange. The centralised platform addresses two major areas: first, it provides a common data infrastructure for Unilever's global operations to communicate internally, and second, it enhances the company's relationships with all trading partners that make up the supply chain.

The Exchange enables the company to improve efficiency, reach new markets and enhance the traditional EDI approach. The technology gives Unilever much more visibility across the enterprise and enables far greater collaboration with suppliers. Central to the collaboration platform is IBM's Websphere Integration suite and in particular the trading gateway. The global hub, or switch, is based in North America, with five regional hubs across the world. A key feature is Websphere's ability to enable the Exchange to deal with different communication protocols from the disparate systems run by the various Unilever companies.

The Unilever Private Exchange not only facilitates the company's internal applications, such as SAP, but is also expected to help in transforming and simplifying Unilever's business by enabling the company to get products to market faster and react quickly to changing market conditions. Unilever expects to make significant operational savings, grow revenue and raise productivity levels.

The Unilever Private Exchange first went live in several parts of Unilever's business, mainly in North America, with the company integrating its key customers and suppliers in the process. It was further rolled out worldwide and Unilever has since developed a phased global supply chain change programme. Unilever launched the programme across Europe and Asia first in early 2010 and has since created a new business unit, the Unilever Americas Supply Chain Company, which became operational in late 2011. This initiative brings together common systems and processes across all of Unilever's supply chain operations to deliver better service to its customers and consumers around the world.

Logistics example 13.1 (*cont.*)

Finally, business services account for nearly half of Unilever's indirect costs and it launched Enterprise Support (ES) in 2010 as its global shared services organisation to also benefit from economies of scale and qualitative improvements similar to the supply chain. ES brings together the HR, IT, finance, workplace and information management support services and has already secured new global contracts with providers such as BT, Vodafone and Accenture as part of a drive towards better services for less.

Question

What impact do you think internet-based information and business flows will have on future logistics activities?

Sources: adapted from 'A private function,' *Supply Chain Standard* (formerly *Logistics Europe*), 2003, Vol. 11, No. 6 (July), pp.26–28; and www.unilever.co.uk/ (accessed 20 July 2011).

While there is some debate about the importance and classification of all these activities there is no question that a firm's logistical activities are important to its success. Logistics Example 13.2 illustrates how successful firms understand that importance. What, then, are the different logistics and supply chain strategies that a firm can pursue and how do they relate to its overall corporate strategy?

LOGISTICS EXAMPLE 13.2

The strategic importance of logistics in grocery retailing

Tesco plc is the UK's leading grocery chain and recorded profit before tax of more than £3.5 billion on over £67 billion of sales worldwide in 2010. Tesco's share of the UK grocery retail market is about 31 per cent; thus it accounts for £1 of every £3 spent on groceries in UK retail stores.

Tesco's growth over the past 30 years has been based largely on its strategy to take control of its supply chain and improve its logistics functions. As a result of various strategic initiatives Tesco has been able to pursue a volume-led domestic strategy to reduce operating costs and cut prices for consumers, and in 1997 it established a four-part growth strategy: core UK business, non-food, retailing services and international.

The logistics and supply chain initiatives that have fostered this success are centralisation, composite distribution and vertical collaboration. In the mid-1970s Tesco operated a direct-to-store delivery where suppliers and manufacturers delivered 'as and when' they chose, making product volumes and quality inconsistent. Further, store managers developed their own relationships with suppliers and manufacturers that made central control and standardisation difficult.

Tesco adopted a centrally controlled and physically centralised distribution service in 1980 that provides delivery to stores within a 48-hour lead time. Integral with this service was massive investment in new primary consolidation and regional distribution centres (RDCs), IT, handling systems and working practices that allowed faster inventory turnover to achieve such decreased lead times. Centralisation allowed Tesco to increase its number of stores in the UK from a little over 500 with an average size of just over 9,800 square feet in 1980 to 2,482 stores with an average size of about 35,485 square feet in 2010.

Composite distribution is an extension to centralisation that enables temperature-controlled products (ambient or fresh, chilled and frozen) to be distributed through one system of multi-temperature RDCs and vehicles. Benefits include lower inventory levels from daily deliveries of composite product groups, improvement in quality delivered to the stores with less wastage, and increased productivity through economies of scale and enhanced equipment use.

Tesco's vertical collaboration includes information sharing, electronic trading and collaborative improvements with suppliers. Tesco improved store scanning of products and introduced sales-based ordering with its suppliers over the Tesco Information Exchange (TIE), an internet-based data-exchange system. Tesco also adopted category management and introduced a 'continuous replenishment' system in the late 1990s.

Coupled with continuous replenishment is 'primary distribution', whereby Tesco orders from all suppliers more than once a day and takes responsibility for the delivery of orders to either a primary consolidation centre or an RDC. Store orders are assembled as the stock arrives rather than being held pending batched orders and 'flowed through' by cross docking. Tesco considers primary distribution to be a strategic change in goods flow and about achieving continuous and efficient flows and not a pricing policy. However, cost reduction is a key driver as primary distribution, also referred to as 'factory gate pricing', separates out transportation costs from the purchase price and puts them under Tesco's control. Tesco spends almost £3 billion a year on its supply chain costs from the suppliers' factories through to on-shelf, in-store. About 20 per cent of these costs are attributable to primary distribution.

In 2004 Tesco began the rollout of its Secure Supply Chain initiative tracking high-value and high-shrink or theft products through its supply chain into stores using radio frequency identification (RFID) tags to drive improvements in on-shelf availability and help reduce shrink. Suppliers tag product cases at source, enabling Tesco to track them throughout the supply chain from origin to shelf.

Lastly, as part of Tesco's commitment to carbon reduction, it set up a Knowledge Hub in 2010 to share knowledge and expertise more widely across its supply chain. The Hub consists of an electronic space to share best practice with suppliers on a daily basis to help them to invest in carbon-reduction strategies. Tesco had over 150 members of the Hub in 2010–2011 and aimed to increase membership to 300 in 2011–2012.

The strategic changes Tesco has introduced to its logistics functions and supply chain management over the last quarter-century have enabled it to develop into one of the most sophisticated and efficient distribution systems in the world and have afforded it a key advantage over its rivals in terms of growth and profitability.

Question

How will suppliers have to strategically react to retail initiatives such as primary distribution, efficient consumer response (ECR) and quick response (QR)?

Sources: adapted from David Smith and Leigh Sparks, 'Logistics in Tesco: Past, present and future,' pp.101–120 and 'Temperature-controlled supply chains,' pp.121–137, in John Fernie and Leigh Sparks (eds.) *Logistics and Retail Management*, 2nd ed. London: Kogan Page, 2004; The Institute of Grocery Distribution, *Retail Logistics*, Watford: Institute of Grocery Distribution, 2004, pp.211–229; James Hall, 'Tesco increases market share,' www.telegraph.co.uk/ (accessed 10 December 2010); and www.tescoplc.co.uk (accessed 10 July 2011).

A history of logistics strategy

While logistics strategies in the military and in business have always existed, for example the campaigns of Alexander the Great or the caravan trade routes in Asia thousands of years ago, the nuances of business logistics strategy have been investigated by academics only since the late 1960s. Chapter 2 discussed the relationship between logistics and marketing, but an initial strategic focus for logistics, or physical distribution as it was known then, was provided by the late Donald Bowersox, writing in the *Journal of Marketing* in 1969.[13] Bowersox, in discussing the relationship of physical distribution to marketing, proposed that:

> In a strategic context, the central or focal point of physical distribution is the corporate commitment to inventory. Individual products are properly viewed as a combination of form, time, place, and possession utilities. The product has little value until form is placed in a temporal and spatial context which will provide the opportunity to enjoy the physical and psychological attributes related to possession. If a firm does not consistently meet the requirements of time and place closure, it has nothing to sell. On the other hand, if a firm does not efficiently meet the requirements of time and place closure, profits and return-on-investment are placed in jeopardy. Excessive inventory stockpiles can compensate for errors in basic system design and may even overcome poor administration of physical distribution activities.
>
> The proper objective in inventory commitment is to deploy the minimum quantities consistent with specified delivery capabilities and management's willingness to underwrite total cost expenditures. To achieve these managerially specified goals the inventory allocation must be integrated within a system of facility locations, transportation capability, and a communications network. The capacity of such a system is measured in terms of the dual standards of total cost and customer service.[14]

This proposition introduced many of the notions we now have regarding logistics: various product utilities, total cost and cost tradeoffs particularly for inventory allocation, and the separation of time and space in the logistics function. Following on from this discussion a typology was presented by Bowersox and Patricia Daugherty in the late 1980s that put forward three important elements in a logistics strategy: process, market, and information or channel.[15]

A process strategy is concerned with the management of traditional logistics activities with a primary goal of controlling costs, i.e. it is an efficiency strategy. A market strategy is concerned with the management of selected traditional logistics activities across business units with the goal of reducing complexity faced by customers, i.e. it is an effectiveness strategy. An information or channel strategy is concerned with bringing together a diverse group of traditional – and other activities – managed as a system, with the goal of achieving inter-organisational coordination and collaboration through the channel, i.e. it is a strategy for dealing with wider supply chain issues.

Several other studies have investigated this typology[16] and one recent study[17] by Michael McGinnis, Jonathan Kohn and John Spillan, that synthesised and tested the findings from these earlier investigations, concluded that the three typology elements continue to 'capture the essence of logistics' role in achieving organizational effectiveness'.[18] They suggested that the typology provides a framework that enables firms to better understand their context within overall organisational strategy and that their findings provide a perspective of logistics' dynamics and its role in strategy.

> For example, a firm that faces strong competition in cost and responsiveness would probably need a logistics strategy that is 'intense.' This would be especially true if logistics cost containment

and coordination are sources of competitive advantage. However, if a firm's source of competitive advantage is based on technological dominance, product features, exceptional brand acceptance, or exceptional cost advantages, then a 'passive' logistics strategy could be appropriate.[19]

They also found that the percentage of 'intense' logistics strategies increased over the last 20 years while the percentage of 'passive' logistics strategies declined, thus demonstrating that logistics' importance in overall organisational strategy has increased during that period.

Linking logistics strategy with corporate strategy

How, then, can a firm make use of this typology and link its logistics strategy to its corporate strategy? One way is by using the framework illustrated in Figure 13.6.[20] The authors of the framework argue that logistics has in the past been considered a narrowly defined functional activity concerned with tasks such as transportation, warehousing, inventory, and materials management, and that a new concept, the 'logistics environment', must also be considered. Changes in logistics capabilities, technologies and management techniques have allowed logistics to become a primary mechanism for integrating and coordinating activities across stages of a supply chain. Thus, as firms become less hierarchical they become more dispersed and as customers become more demanding a firm's logistics can provide a coordinating role that will provide it with a competitive advantage.

The range of available choices in these areas of logistics comprises the industry's logistics environment. The logistics capabilities or competences of a firm must change to reflect changes in its logistics environment. For example, if air transportation to deliver time-sensitive products to customers is the norm in an industry, it is likely that any firm serving that market must use air transportation to remain competitive.

This framework links a firm's strategy, structure and logistics capabilities and their influence on performance within the constraints of its industry's competitive and logistics environments. There are three principal elements in this framework:

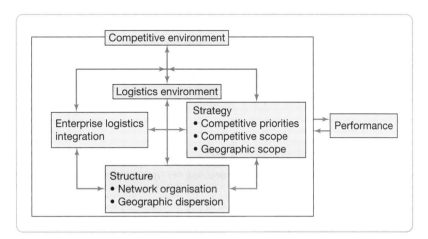

Figure 13.6 A proposed logistics, strategy and structure framework

Source: Logistics, strategy and structure: a conceptual framework, *International Journal of Physical Distribution & Logistics Management*, Vol. 29, No. 4, p. 39 (Stock, G.N., Greis, N.P. and Kasarda, J.D. 1999), International Journal of Physical Distribution and Logistics Management by Emerald Group Publishing Limited. Reproduced with permission of Emerald Group Publishing Limited in the format Journal via Copyright Clearance Center. © Emerald Group Publishing Limited all rights reserved.

- *strategy choices* comprising competitive priorities and scope as well as geographic scope;
- *structure choices* comprising how a firm organises its business network and is dispersed geographically;
- *enterprise logistics integration choices* comprising the integration of logistics activities, such as transportation, warehousing, inventory management and information, both within and across firm boundaries.

The degree of fit among these three choice elements will affect a firm's performance, i.e. various combinations of strategy structure and enterprise logistics integration choices will result in higher firm performance than other combinations.

The concept of 'integrated logistics' was first recognised by an A.T. Kearney study which recognised that benefits, especially cost benefits, would be realised by firms operating their logistics processes as an integrated system rather than by optimising functional sub-systems. This systems approach within the firm, introduced in Chapter 1, has been an underlying premise of current logistics management, thought and practice.

An example of an integrated approach that highlights some tradeoffs between strategic and/or SBU and operational level decisions is shown in Table 13.1.[21] At a purely strategic level, the most common logistical tradeoffs include whether to centralise or decentralise inventories, i.e. warehouse location, as discussed in Chapter 5; whether or not to outsource logistic activities, as discussed in Chapter 4; and whether to adopt lean or agile strategies, as discussed in Chapter 7.[22]

Recent studies by Kearney in Europe have also noted an increase in the complexity of logistics and supply chain environments that necessitates a better appreciation of strategic planning by logistics professionals. They defined four types of complexity in such environments: (1) market-facing with regards to product development and channel selection; (2) internal operating decisions and practices; (3) external factors such as competitors and government; and (4) organisational factors such as corporate governance, IT and cross-functional capabilities.[23]

Kearney believes firms need to take a proactive role in the strategic logistics planning process and differentiate their activities from a uniform and 'predictable' model to more responsive models in order to handle increasing complexity, which is yet another strategic

Table 13.1 Logistical activity and strategic level decision matrix

Activity	Strategic and/or SBU level	Operational level
Transportation	<ul><li>Selecting transport modes</li><li>Redrawing depot delivery areas</li></ul>	<ul><li>Load planning</li></ul>
Inventory management	<ul><li>Selecting the type of replenishment system</li><li>Adjusting safety stock levels</li></ul>	<ul><li>Order fulfilment</li></ul>
Warehousing	<ul><li>Selecting the number, size and location of warehouses</li></ul>	<ul><li>Order picking</li></ul>
Information technology and processing	<ul><li>Selecting order-entry systems, e.g. internet</li><li>Establishing a temporary channel for promotional offers</li></ul>	<ul><li>Processing of orders</li><li>Invoicing</li></ul>

Source: adapted from Ballou (1992).

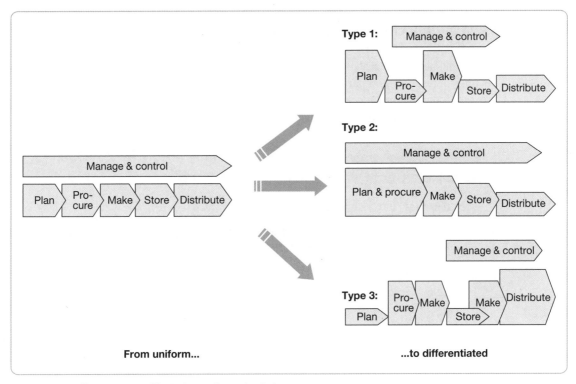

Figure 13.7 Differentiation of logistics and supply chains

Source: adapted from European Logistics Association and A.T. Kearney (2004, p.29).

tool for firms to consider. Figure 13.7 is an example of how firms can do so and synthesises the lean and agile practices discussed in Chapter 7.

The Type 1 model focuses on a lean and efficient operation that is dominated by making products. The Type 2 model focuses on supplying complex products to specific requirements with long lead times, which requires collaborative planning with supply chain partners. The Type 3 model focuses on maximising efficiency to meet customer demands in terms of volume and mix, thus requiring flexibility and late configuration of finished goods.[24]

Finally, as firms move towards a more supply chain orientation, a recent study[25] found a clear hierarchy of antecedents and provided recommendations to firms and managers intent on commencing SCM and thus SCM partnerships. These hierarchical recommendations are for firms to: (1) develop their own internal SCM capabilities; then (2) work with external partners, both downstream (customers) and upstream (suppliers), on developing joint SCM capabilities; before (3) adopting SCM-related processes and thereby achieving successful SCM execution or implementation and thereby adopting a supply chain orientation.

As noted earlier in this chapter, as firms move beyond their national geographic boundaries and into more extensive supply chain relationships with many partners, risks to the firm increase and thus must also be considered within an overall corporate strategy. The next section considers the nature of risk and risk mitigation strategies.

Logistics and supply chain risk and resilience

Risk is defined as the probability that a particular adverse event occurs during a stated period of time, or results from a particular challenge.[26] This notion of an adverse event connotes a detrimental consequence and society is usually concerned with such consequences from a 'downside risk'. An example of such an adverse consequence is presented in Logistics Example 13.3.

LOGISTICS EXAMPLE 13.3

An 'un-merry' Christmas

The turmoil and logistical problems Sony faced in getting stocks of its best-selling mini-PlayStation 2 (PS2) game consoles into stores for Christmas 2004 might even be worthy of its own computer game. Having failed to provide enough by sea, Sony hired Russian Antonov AN24 cargo planes to airlift PS2s directly from China to the United Kingdom because many stores had sold out of that year's 'must have' gaming product.

David Wilson, a spokesman for Sony, said that supplies would be back on track by mid-December. The problem began when a Russian-owned oil tanker got stuck in the Suez Canal in early November 2004. The tanker held up 100 ships, including Sony's Christmas shipment, which was bound from China with thousands of PS2s destined for the UK market. The closure of the 120-mile-long waterway for more than a day was the first in 37 years. But Sony admitted that delays apart, it had also underestimated demand for the new game. The new and lighter version proved so popular that factories were unable to keep up with the demand worldwide. Some parents, desperate not to disappoint their children, turned to the internet auction site eBay where bid prices were far higher than the retail price.

The Russian cargo planes, with capacity for about 40,000 PS2s, were landing at least twice a week at Stansted and Gatwick airports near London. The times of the flights and the deliveries were a tightly guarded secret for fear that trucks could be hijacked by criminals eager to cash in on the Europe-wide shortage.

The PS2 sold at a rate of 70,000 a week in the UK until the end of November 2004 when stocks were depleted and there were only 20,000 sold. During the first week of December that figure was down to 6,000. Mr Wilson said: 'The issue we had was that people couldn't get them because of two weeks worth of pent-up demand. As soon as the games were getting into stores they were being snapped up. By mid-December there should be enough stocks to meet demand in the next two weeks which could be way over the 70,000-a-week sales reported in November.' The Sony spokesman admitted that there may be potential for a new game involving tankers, cargo planes and other forms of transport. But he added: 'It takes two years from a concept to a game going on sale. I think we will have sorted out our supply problems by then.'

The PS2 has been one of Sony's best-selling products, with cumulative sales worldwide exceeding 150 million consoles and over 1.5 billion games at the beginning of 2011.

Question

You are a consultant hired by Sony to examine its supply chain to prevent this situation from happening in the future. How would you face this challenge?

Sources: adapted from Valerie Elliott, 'Merry Christmas, your Playstation 2 is stuck in Suez,' *The Times*, 9 December 2004, p.9; and 'Playstation®2 Sales Reach 150 Million Units Worldwide,' www.scei.co.jp/corporate/release/110214_e.html (accessed 15 July 2011).

Risk is a probability in a statistical theory sense and therefore obeys all formal laws of combining probabilities. For example, if there is a 3 per cent chance that a container ship will sink at sea, there is a 97 per cent chance that the ship will arrive at all its destinations in good order. Thus, the probability that the ship will be lost is 3 per cent and a numerical measure of the expected loss associated with this adverse event can be calculated by multiplying the total costs associated with the loss, e.g. cargo, the ship, the crew, etc. by the 3 per cent probability.

An expected loss is often expressed in terms such as costs in dollars, pounds or euros or the loss in expected years of life or productivity, and is needed for any cost–benefit or risk–benefit analyses. A benefit analysis introduces an ethical dimension to risk: a profit (or loss) is considered a 'reward' (or 'cost') for risk taking in business.

Most businesses in the Western world utilise the teleological approach to ethics based on egoism and utilitarianism, i.e. they are concerned with the consequences of an action. A deontological approach, meanwhile, which stems from the philosophy of Immanuel Kant, is concerned less with consequences of an act and more with the intentions or rationale of an act. Events in certain sectors in the 2000s, such as banking, energy and the media, have focused on the often unethical behaviour of individuals and firms. This debate is outside the scope of this book, but it is also important to the logistics and supply chain domain and therefore worthy of comment for the reader's consideration.

Assuming, then, that there is adherence to probabilistic expected value calculations and proper ethical behaviour, there are three rules for risk management:

1 Maximising positive expected value.

2 Avoiding catastrophe.

3 Ignoring remote possibilities.

However, to undertake any strategic risk assessments a firm needs to know how vulnerable it is to risk, i.e. is it at risk and likely to incur loss or damage, and how resilient it is after an adverse event, i.e. what is its ability to return to its original or desired state after being disturbed?

There are many examples of logistics and supply chain adverse risk events during the last 10–15 years, including infrastructure failures leading to transport accidents and collapsed buildings, contaminated and dangerous products entering the food and toy supply chains, diseases in livestock and humans, terrorist attacks against many nations, and natural disasters such as earthquakes and floods. Given the increase in these events, some of which are outside a firm's control, possible drivers of logistics and supply chain risk include:

- leaner supply chains with reduced numbers of suppliers;

- a decrease in supply chain lead or order cycle times and the use of just-in-time practices;

- the globalisation of sourcing and supply and increased transport links;

- centralised production and distribution at one location;

- an increasing trend towards outsourcing.

Factors in logistics and supply chain risk that must go into any risk assessment or cost–benefit analysis include:

- the nature of the risk: physical, financial/regulatory, external;

- the scale of the potential threat: interruption of operations, short-term sales loss, damage to reputation, bankruptcy;

- the scope of the risk: company-specific versus industry-wide;
- the probability of occurrence;
- whether there can be accidental or deliberate damage.

Further, the firm must be able to continue, i.e. be resilient, while it deals with a risk event. The Business Continuity Institute (BCI) defines business continuity management and planning as 'the process of anticipating incidents which will affect critical functions and activities of the firm and ensuring that response to any incident in a planned and rehearsed manner', i.e. while the firm continues or recovers.[27] However, when the BCI surveyed firms in the mid-2000s regarding business continuity planning, 25 per cent of those surveyed were aware that supply chain disruptions could affect their firm but none had any business continuity plans in place.

Figure 13.8 shows one approach to considering logistics and supply chain risk at four different levels and approaches the supply chain from an idealised integrated end-to-end supply chain management perspective:[28]

- Level 1 is the firm's internal processes or value stream.
- Level 2 is the firm's assets and infrastructure dependencies.
- Level 3 is the firm's contractual relationships and inter-organisational networks.
- Level 4 is the firm's external environment.

Levels 2–4 introduce progressively increased sources of risk that can cause disruption, undermine the firm's efforts to optimise efficiency and effectiveness, are less controllable, and ultimately threaten the firm's business continuity.

Once a firm determines its logistics and supply chain risks and their probabilities and its vulnerability and resilience to these risks, it can then go about deriving various risk mitigation and business continuity strategies. Such strategies include:

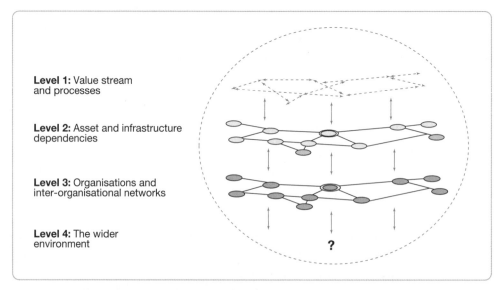

Level 1: Value stream
and processes

Level 2: Asset and infrastructure
dependencies

Level 3: Organisations and
inter-organisational networks

Level 4: The wider
environment

Figure 13.8 Different hierarchical levels of risk

Source: adapted from Drivers of supply chain vulnerability: an integrated framework, *International Journal of Physical Distribution & Logistics Management*, Vol. 35, No. 4, p. 218 (Peck, H. 2005).

- diversification by multiple sourcing for supplies and products;
- having parallel in-house and outsourced systems;
- stockpiling inventory as a buffer;
- having redundancy by building in extra capacity;
- taking out insurance against loss from supply chain disruption.[29]

While these strategies will help mitigate risk, they also increase costs to the firm. However, the alternative of suffering huge losses, eroding customer confidence and negatively affecting an established brand may very well outweigh such costs.

Summary

This chapter has discussed concepts of corporate and logistics and supply chain strategy; these concepts and their associated techniques and tools provide an overview of how firms may undertake strategic planning. Clearly, there is no 'one-size-fits-all' strategy applicable to every firm; thus firms must adopt a logical approach to the planning process. Also, changes in logistics activities and supply chain management such as globalisation, outsourcing and time compression bring increased risk to firms. As this new millennium takes shape there will be much change in the logistics and supply chain domain.

The goal of this book is to provide an overview into the exciting and dynamic domain of logistics and related concepts. The growth of logistics, and latterly supply chain management, has increased their visibility in corporate and political domains as well as in society in general. Such growth is set to continue at a rapid pace and the profession will need eager and talented young people to take it forward. It is hoped that this book has stimulated the reader such that he or she will seek out the many challenging opportunities in the logistics and supply chain management profession.

DISCUSSION QUESTIONS

1 Why is corporate strategy important for any firm?
2 Describe the strategic planning process.
3 Compare and contrast the Boston Consulting Group and Ansoff matrices.
4 How does logistics strategy link to corporate strategy?
5 What can firms do to mitigate the effects of logistics and supply chain risk?

Suggested reading

Ansell, Jake and Frank Wharton (eds.) *Risk: Analysis, Assessment and Management*, Chichester: John Wiley & Sons, 1992.

Bowersox, Donald J. 'Physical distribution development, current status, and potential,' *Journal of Marketing*, 1969, Vol. 38, No. 1, pp.63–70.

Bowersox, Donald J. and Patricia J. Daugherty 'Emerging patterns of logistical organization,' *Journal of Business Logistics*, 1987, Vol. 8, No. 1, pp.46–60.

Clinton, Steven T. and David J. Closs 'Logistics strategy: Does it exist?' *Journal of Business Logistics*, 1997, Vol. 18, No. 1, pp.19–44.

Friedman, Milton *An Economist's Protest: Columns in Political Economy*, Glen Ridge, NY: Thomas Horton and Company, 1972.

Hamel, Gary and C.K. Prahalad 'The core competence of the corporation,' *Harvard Business Review*, 1990, Vol. 68, No. 3, pp.79–91.

Johnson, Gerry and Kevan Scholes *Exploring Corporate Strategy,* 5th ed. Harlow: FT Prentice Hall, 1999.

Kotler, Philip *Marketing Management: The Millennium Edition,* 20th ed. Upper Saddle River, NJ: Prentice Hall, 2000.

Kotzab, Herbert, Christoph Teller, David B. Grant and Leigh Sparks 'Antecedents for the adoption and execution of supply chain management,' *Supply Chain Management: An International Journal*, 2011, Vol. 16, No. 4, pp.231–245.

McGinnis, Michael A., Jonathan W. Kohn and John E. Spillan 'A longitudinal study of logistics strategy: 1990–2008,' *Journal of Business Logistics*, 2010, Vol. 31, No. 1, pp.217–235.

Peck, Helen 'Drivers of supply chain vulnerability: An integrated framework,' *International Journal of Physical Distribution & Logistics Management*, 2005, Vol. 35, No. 4, pp.210–232.

Porter, Michael *Competitive Strategy: Techniques for Analyzing Industries and Competitors*, New York: Free Press, 1980.

Porter, Michael *Competitive Advantage: Creating and Sustaining Superior Performance*, New York: Free Press, 1985.

Sheffi, Yossi 'Supply chain management under the threat of international terrorism,' *The International Journal of Logistics Management*, 2001, Vol. 12, No. 2, pp.1–11.

Stern, Carl W. and Michael S. Deimler (eds.) *The Boston Consulting Group on Strategy: Classic Concepts and New Perspectives,* New York: John Wiley & Sons, 2006.

Stock, Gregory N., Noel P. Greis and John D. Kasarda 'Logistics, strategy and structure: A conceptual framework,' *International Journal of Physical Distribution & Logistics Management*, 1999, Vol. 29, No. 4, pp.37–52.

Wanke, Peter F. and Walter Zinn 'Strategic logistics decision making,' *International Journal of Physical Distribution & Logistics Management*, 2004, Vol. 34, No. 6, pp.466–478.

Notes

1 This view of Milton Friedman was succinctly articulated in a column for *The New York Times Magazine* in 1970, which can be found, along with other commentaries, in Milton Friedman (1972) *An Economist's Protest: Columns in Political Economy*, Glen Ridge, NJ: Thomas Horton and Company, pp.177–184.

2 For further reading on general corporate strategy see Gerry Johnson and Kevan Scholes (1999) *Exploring Corporate Strategy,* 5th ed. Harlow: FT Prentice Hall and Michael Porter (1980) *Competitive Strategy: Techniques for Analyzing Industries and Competitors* and (1985) *Competitive Advantage: Creating and Sustaining Superior Performance*, New York: Free Press.

3 Johnson and Scholes (1999) p.10.

4 This section draws upon vocabulary and terms in Chapter 1 of Johnson and Scholes (1999) *Exploring Corporate Strategy,* 5th ed.

5 For further reading on core competencies in a firm see Gary Hamel and C.K. Prahalad (1990) 'The core competence of the corporation,' *Harvard Business Review*, Vol. 68, No. 3, pp.79–91.

6 Source: www.norbert-dentressangle.com (accessed 15 July 2011).

7 This section is adapted from Philip Kotler *Marketing Management: The Millennium Edition,* 20th ed. Upper Saddle River, NJ: Prentice Hall, 2000.

8 For further discussion about the BCG matrix see www.bcg.com/ and Carl W. Stern and Michael S. Deimler (eds.) (2006) *The Boston Consulting Group on Strategy: Classic Concepts and New Perspectives,* New York: John Wiley & Sons.

9 See www.ansoffmatrix.com/.

10 Kotler (2000).

11 Michael Porter (1980).

12 Michael Porter (1985).

13 Donald J. Bowersox (1969) 'Physical distribution development, current status, and potential,' *Journal of Marketing*, Vol. 38, No. 1, pp.63–70.

14 Bowersox (1969) p.66.

15 Donald J. Bowersox and Patricia J. Daugherty (1987) 'Emerging patterns of logistical organization,' *Journal of Business Logistics*, Vol. 8, No. 1, pp.46–60.

16 See for example Steven T. Clinton and David J. Closs (1997) 'Logistics strategy: Does it exist?' *Journal of Business Logistics*, Vol. 18, No. 1, pp.19–44; Gregory N. Stock, Noel P. Greis and John D. Kasarda (1999) 'Logistics, strategy and structure: A conceptual framework,' *International Journal of Physical Distribution & Logistics Management*, Vol. 29, No. 4, pp.37–52; and Peter F. Wanke and Walter Zinn (2004) 'Strategic logistics decision making,' *International Journal of Physical Distribution & Logistics Management*, Vol. 34, No. 6, pp.466–478.

17 Michael A. McGinnis, Jonathan W. Kohn and John E. Spillan (2010) 'A longitudinal study of logistics strategy: 1990–2008,' *Journal of Business Logistics*, Vol. 31, No. 1, pp.217–235.

18 McGinnis *et al.* (2010) p.232.

19 McGinnis *et al.* (2010) p.233.

20 Stock *et al.* (1999) p.39.

21 Ronald H. Ballou (1992) *Business Logistics Management,* 3rd ed. Upper Saddle River, NJ: Prentice Hall.

22 Wanke and Zinn (2004).

23 European Logistics Association and A.T. Kearney (2004) *Differentiation for Performance: Excellence in Logistics 2004*, Hamburg: Deutscher Verkehrs-Verlag GmbH, pp.14–30.

24 European Logistics Association and A.T. Kearney (2004) *Differentiation for Performance*, pp.28–30.

25 Herbert Kotzab, Christoph Teller, David B. Grant and Leigh Sparks (2011) 'Antecedents for the adoption and execution of supply chain management,' *Supply Chain Management: An International Journal*, Vol. 16, No. 4, pp.231–245.

26 This section on risk draws on Jake Ansell and Frank Wharton (eds.) (1992) *Risk: Analysis, Assessment and Management*, Chichester: John Wiley & Sons; Yossi Sheffi (2001) 'Supply chain management under the threat of international terrorism,' *The International Journal of Logistics Management*, Vol. 12, No. 2, pp.1–11; and Helen Peck (2005) 'Drivers of supply chain vulnerability: An integrated framework,' *International Journal of Physical Distribution & Logistics Management*, Vol. 35, No. 4, pp.210–232.

27 See www.thebci.org (accessed 25 June 2011).

28 Peck (2005) p.218.

29 Sheffi (2001).

Glossary

This glossary contains key terms discussed in this book and is derived from a master glossary provided online by the Council of Supply Chain Management Professionals at **http://cscmp. org/digital/glossary/glossary.asp**. The assistance of the CSCMP in permitting the creation of this glossary is gratefully acknowledged.

ABC analysis A method of classifying inventory items relative to their impact on total control. ABC typically uses movement and cost data to calculate the value of stock usage over the prior period, and uses the result as an element in ranking items under an 80–20 Pareto rule for cycle counting purposes. The group is divided into classes called A, B and C (and sometimes D), with the A group representing the highest value with 10–20 per cent by number of items. The B, C and D (if used) groups are each lower values but typically higher populations. Items with higher usage value (the 20 per cent) are counted more frequently. Specific bars to be used in setting ABC levels will vary by organisation as they will impact the financial control applied to inventory and the level of effort spent counting. See also *Pareto principle or 80–20 rule.*

activity-based costing (ABC) A discipline focusing on the management of activities within business processes as the route to continuously improve both the value received by customers and the profit earned in providing that value. ABC analysis in this context is a methodology that measures the cost and performance of cost objects, activities and resources.

adjustable pallet racking The most widely used storage system for all palletised and non-palletised loads. Single-or double-sided runs of racking are separated by wide aisles which can be sized to suit existing forklift trucks.

advanced planning systems (APS) Refers to a manufacturing management process by which raw materials and production capacity are optimally allocated to meet demand. APS is especially well suited to environments where simpler planning methods cannot adequately address complex tradeoffs between competing priorities.

agility The ability to rapidly and cost-effectively adapt to market changes with no significant negative impact on quality or dependability.

anticipatory stock Extra stocks of inventory which are being held above known requirement in order to accommodate trends or promotions. May also be used to hedge against risk of supply problems.

artificial intelligence (AI) The understanding and computerisation of the human thought process.

backhaul The portion of a transport trip, typically associated with trucking, that is incurred when returning a vehicle to its point of origin. Ideally the carrier will find some sort of freight to carry back; if the trip is empty it is called deadhead.

balanced scorecard A strategic performance management tool used for measuring whether the smaller-scale operational activities of a company are aligned with its larger-scale objectives in terms of vision and strategy. By focusing not only on financial outcomes but also on the operational, marketing and developmental inputs to these, the balanced scorecard helps provide a more comprehensive view of a business, which in turn helps organisations act in their best long-term interests.

barcode A symbol consisting of a series of printed bars representing values. A system of optical character reading, scanning and tracking of units by reading a series of printed bars for translation into a numeric or alphanumeric identification code. A popular example is the UPC code used on retail packaging.

benchmarking A process of comparing performance against the practices of other leading companies for the purpose of improving performance. Companies also benchmark internally by tracking and comparing current with past performance.

bill of material (BOM) A structured list of all the materials or parts and quantities needed to produce a particular finished product, assembly, sub-assembly or manufactured part, whether purchased or not.

blanket purchase orders A long-term commitment to a supplier for material against which short-term releases will be generated to satisfy requirements. Often blanket orders cover only one item with pre-determined delivery dates.

block stacking A storage method which uses no formal racking or shelves to contain the products. Items to be stored (pallets, cases or cartons) are stacked upwards from the floor surface to whatever height is practical.

bonded warehouses Warehouses where goods are stored until import duties or tariffs are paid.

bullwhip effect An observed phenomenon in forecast-driven distribution channels. The oscillating demand magnification upstream of a supply chain is reminiscent of a cracking whip. The concept has its roots in J. Forrester's *Industrial Dynamics* (1958) and thus it is also known as the Forrester Effect.

cabotage Where a carrier from one European Union country is allowed to perform domestic transportation in another EU country.

capital budget A budget that contains budgets for capital expenditures on long-term assets or investments such as plant, property and equipment.

cash-to-cash (C2C) cycle The time it takes for cash to flow back into a company after it has been spent for raw materials.

category management The management of product categories as strategic business units. The practice empowers a category manager with full responsibility for the assortment decisions, inventory levels, shelf-space allocation, promotions and buying. With this authority and responsibility, the category manager is able to judge more accurately the consumer buying patterns, product sales and market trends of that category.

centre-of-gravity approach A supply chain planning methodology for locating distribution centres at approximately the location representing the minimum transportation costs between the plants, the distribution centres and the markets.

channel power The amount of business power a member of a channel of distribution can hold or exert over other channel members.

channels A method whereby a company dispenses its product, such as a retail or distribution channel, call centre or web-based electronic storefront.

cloud computing An emerging computing paradigm where data and services reside in massively scalable data centres and can be ubiquitously accessed from any connected devices over the internet.

collaborative planning, forecasting and replenishment (CPFR) A collaboration process whereby trading partners can jointly plan key logistics and supply chain activities from production and delivery of raw materials to production and delivery of final products to end-customers. Collaboration encompasses business planning, sales forecasting and all operations required to replenish raw materials and finished goods.

common carrier A carrier that provides transportation to the public and does not offer special treatment to any one party and is regulated as to the rates charged, the liability assumed and the service provided.

compatibility Refers to whether goods stored in a warehouse are compatible for storage purposes.

complementarity Refers to whether goods stored in a warehouse are ordered together and are there for complementary storage purposes.

computerised routing and vehicle scheduling (CRVS) Software to determine how a shipment could move efficiently between origin and destination. Routing information includes designation of carrier(s) involved, actual route of carrier and estimated time enroute.

container A 'box', typically 10–40 feet long, which is used primarily for ocean freight shipments. For travel to and from ports, containers are loaded onto truck trailers or on railroad flatcars; the latter are known as containers on flatcars (COFC).

continuous replenishment (CR) The practice of partnering between distribution channel members that changes the traditional replenishment process from distributor-generated purchase orders, based on economic order quantities, to the replenishment of products based on actual and forecasted product demand.

contract warehousing A variation of public warehousing where the warehouse provider and customer have an arrangement that might see customised services and facilities within the warehouse on a shared cost and risk basis.

core competency A specific factor that a business sees as being central to the way it, or its employees, works. A core competency can take various forms, including technical/subject matter know-how, a reliable process and/or close relationships with customers and suppliers. It may also include product development or culture, such as employee dedication.

cost of lost sales The forgone profit or cost associated with a product stock-out.

cost-to-serve A chain of activities required to get a company's products or services into its customers' stores and onto their shelves. This includes order taking, picking and freighting the order, arranging promotions by sales reps, processing credits and merchandising the product.

cost tradeoff analysis The inter-relationship among system variables indicates that a change in one variable has cost impact upon other variables. A cost reduction in one variable may be at the expense of increased cost for another.

cross-docking A distribution system in which merchandise received at the warehouse or distribution centre is not put away but instead is readied for shipment to retail stores. Cross-docking requires close synchronisation of all inbound and outbound shipment movements.

customer order cycle The elapsed time between when a customer places an order and the customer receives the order. Also known as order cycle time or lead time.

customer satisfaction Represents a customer's overall assessment of all elements in the marketing and sales process when purchasing goods or services.

customer service Activities between the buyer and seller that enhance or facilitate the sale or use of the seller's products or services.

customer value The benefit or utility enjoyed by a customer for a product or service minus the cost to acquire and/or maintain the product or service.

cycle stock The average level of normal stock used during operations.

data analysis Advanced analysis of data by mathematical or statistical means to provide management with information for strategic and operational decision making.

data processing The ability to transform raw data into a more useful form by relatively straightforward conversion.

data retrieval The ability to recall data in its raw form conveniently and quickly.

decision-making unit (DMU) In purchasing or procurement, a group of decision makers and decision influencers who combine to make acquisition decisions.

decision support system (DSS) Software that speeds access and simplifies data analysis, queries, etc. within a database management system.

decoupling point The point in a supply chain representing a change from a lean strategy to an agile strategy for both materials and information.

decoupling stock Stock held to decouple production of the stock from its consumption.

dedicated storage A warehouse storage technique where goods are placed in a permanent location within a warehouse. Although this method often requires more storage space than a randomised storage method, it is used in manual labour situations where employee performance improves as they learn each product's location.

direct product profitability (DPP) Calculation of the net profit contribution attributable to a specific product or product line.

direct store delivery Process of shipping direct from a manufacturer's plant or distribution centre to the customer's retail store, thus bypassing the customer's distribution centre.

direct trains A form of combined transport by members of the International Union of Combined Road–Rail Transport Companies (UIRR) where trains operate non-stop between two points.

discrepancy of assortment A discrepancy between what assortment of goods a customer requires and the assortment a manufacturer has on hand or in production. A channel intermediary will adjust this discrepancy by performing various functions such as sorting out, accumulating, allocating and assorting.

distribution centre (DC) The warehouse facility which holds inventory from manufacturing pending distribution to the appropriate stores.

distribution resources planning A system of determining demands for inventory at distribution centres and consolidating demand information in reverse as input to the production and materials system and extended into planning the key resources contained in a distribution system: warehouse space, workforce, money, trucks, freight cars, etc.

divisional structure Organisational structure based on discrete divisions such as geographic regions.

drive-in or drive-through racking Racking where forklift trucks may enter one side (drive-in) or both sides (drive-through) to place pallets.

economic order quantity (EOQ) An inventory model that determines how much to order by determining the amount that will meet customer service levels while minimising total ordering and holding costs.

effectiveness A measure of the quality of an output compared with a pre-determined norm.

efficiency See *productivity*.

efficient consumer response (ECR) A demand-driven replenishment system designed to link all parties in the grocery logistics channel to create a massive flow-through distribution network. Replenishment is based upon consumer demand and point-of-sale information.

electronic data interchange (EDI) Inter-company, computer-to-computer transmission of business information in a standard format. An EDI transmission consists only of business data, not any accompanying verbiage or free-form messages.

electronic or e-procurement The purchase and procurement of goods and services through electronic ordering.

electronic point of sale (EPOS) Retail information technology system to scan and record sales of goods. The EPOS information also allows inventory records to be updated and replacement orders initiated.

employee involvement (EI) The process of involving employees in operations decisions during the production stage for enhanced productivity and quality.

enterprise integration applications (EIA) A computer term for the tools and techniques used in linking ERP and other enterprise systems, which is also known as middleware. Called enterprise application integration (EAI) in some contexts.

enterprise resource planning (ERP) A class of software for planning and managing 'enterprise wide' the resources needed to take customer orders, ship them, account for them and replenish all needed goods according to customer orders and forecasts. Often includes electronic commerce with suppliers.

ethical sourcing The use of ethical standards, i.e. promoting values such as trust, good behaviour, fairness and/or kindness when sourcing and purchasing materials and supplies, particularly from developing nations.

European distribution centre (EDC) One DC to serve all of the European market.

exporting A term used to describe products produced in one country that are sold in another.

extended enterprise resource planning (EERP) The collaborative sharing of information and processes between supply chain partners using ERP and the internet to communicate.

fill rate The percentage of order items that the picking operation actually fills within a given period of time.

finished goods inventory Products completely manufactured, packaged, stored and ready for distribution.

fixed-order interval Within the economic order quantity model, a point in time where the EOQ is ordered based on the level of inventory on hand.

fixed-order point Within a company's inventory policy, a point in time that is a fixed interval, such as one or two weeks, where an amount of inventory is ordered based on an upper level of inventory the company wants to maintain.

forecast error The difference between the actual value and the forecasted value.

forecasting An estimate of future demand. A forecast can be constructed using quantitative methods, qualitative methods or a combination of methods, and it can be based on extrinsic (external) or intrinsic (internal) factors. Various forecasting techniques attempt to predict one or more of the four components of demand: cyclical, random, seasonal and trend.

foreign direct investment (FDI) Direct corporate ownership of a foreign business subsidiary.

for-hire carrier A carrier that provides transportation service to the public on a fee basis.

form utility A value created in a product by the process of creating it in the right form that customers require. Manufacturing provides form utility.

Forrester Effect See *bullwhip effect*.

framework agreement A purchasing agreement between EU governments and public-sector suppliers to establish terms and conditions for all public-sector purchasing in the EU.

free trade zone (FTZ) An area in a country where goods may enter without attracting any duties or taxes until they are removed for use or sale.

freight forwarders Companies that provide logistics services as an intermediary between the shipper and the carrier, typically on international shipments.

fulfilment The act of fulfilling a customer order. Fulfilment includes order management, picking, packaging and shipping.

functional structure An organisational structure where each functional group is operated independent of other groups within the organisation. Each group is referred to as a silo.

green logistics The concept of introducing an environmental or ecological approach to the usual economic approach in logistics management. An example would be an initiative to reduce vehicle emissions in freight transport.

gross domestic product (GDP) The total market value of all final goods and services produced in a country in a given year, equal to total consumer, investment and government spending, plus the value of exports, minus the value of imports.

import quotas Limitations on the amount of goods that can enter a country.

importing Bringing goods into one country that are produced in another country.

Incoterms International terms of sale developed by the International Chamber of Commerce to define sellers' and buyers' responsibilities.

independent versus dependent demand An independent demand item is one that can be produced independently of the demand for its raw materials, for example finished goods. Conversely, dependent demand items are the raw materials or components used in a finished good that are dependent on customer demand for the finished good to be required or introduced in the production process.

integrated logistics management A comprehensive, system-wide view of the entire supply chain as a single process, from raw materials supply through to finished goods distribution. All functions that make up the supply chain are managed as a single entity rather than managing individual functions separately.

intermodal marketing company (IMC) An intermediary that sells intermodal services to shippers.

inventory carrying or holding costs One of the elements comprising a company's total supply chain management costs. These costs consist of opportunity cost of capital, storage and material-handling costs, and loss due to obsolescence, damage and/or pilferage.

inventory turnover ratio The cost of goods sold divided by the average level of inventory on hand. This ratio measures how many times a company's inventory has been sold during a period of time. Operationally, inventory turns are measured as total throughput divided by average level of inventory for a given period; how many times a year the average inventory for a firm changes over or is sold.

judgemental forecasting A method of forecasting that uses people's skills, knowledge and judgement rather than more formal analysis.

just-in-time (JIT) An inventory control system that controls material flow into assembly and manufacturing plants by coordinating demand and supply to the point where desired materials arrive just in time for use. Developed by the automobile industry, it refers to shipping goods in smaller, more frequent lots. See also *kanban* and *Toyota production system*.

kanban Japanese word for visible record. Loosely translated means card, billboard or sign. Popularised by Toyota Corporation, it uses standard containers or lot sizes to deliver needed parts to the assembly line just in time for use. See also *just-in-time* and *Toyota production system*.

lead logistics partner (LLP) An organisation that organises other third-party logistics partners for outsourcing of logistics functions. An LLP serves as the client's primary supply chain management provider, defining processes and managing the provision and integration of logistics services through its own organisation and those of its sub-contractors.

lead time See *customer order cycle*.

leagile A hybrid strategy incorporating both lean and agile techniques. See also *decoupling point*.

lean A business management philosophy that considers the expenditure of resources for any goal other than the creation of value for the end-customer to be wasteful and thus a target for elimination.

letter of credit An international business document that assures the seller that payment will be made by the bank issuing the letter of credit upon fulfilment of the sales agreement.

licensing Involves agreements that allow a firm in one country (the licensee) to use the manufacturing, processing, trademark, know-how, technical assistance, merchandising knowledge or some other skill provided by the licenser located in another country.

life-cycle analysis A financial and performance analysis of a product's life cycle, from production and sale to final disposal.

life-cycle assessment (LCA) An assessment of a product's environmental impact during its usable life and through disposal. See also *life-cycle analysis*.

life-cycle cost (LCC) In cost accounting, a product's life cycle is the period that starts with the initial product conceptualisation and ends with the withdrawal of the product from the marketplace and final disposition. A product life cycle is characterised by certain defined stages, including research, development, introduction, maturity, decline and abandonment. Life-cycle cost is the accumulated costs incurred by a product during these stages.

logistics management As defined by CSCMP, that part of supply chain management that plans, implements and controls the efficient, effective forward and reverse flow and storage of goods, services and related information between the point of origin and the point of consumption in order to meet customers' requirements. Logistics management activities typically include inbound and outbound transportation management, fleet management, warehousing, materials handling, order fulfilment, logistics network design, inventory management, supply/demand planning and management of third-party logistics services providers. To varying degrees, the logistics function also includes sourcing and procurement, production planning and scheduling, packaging and assembly, and customer service. It is involved in all levels of planning and execution-strategic, operational and tactical. Logistics management is an integrating function which coordinates and optimises all logistics activities, as well as integrating logistics activities with other functions, including marketing, sales, manufacturing, finance and information technology.

logistics mission statement An overriding objective of a company as to what business it is in and its logistics strategy, for example it will outsource all of its logistics activities.

logistics strategic planning The process of planning logistics strategy within a company.

manufacturing resource planning (MRP II) A method for the effective planning of all resources of a manufacturing company. It is made up of a variety of processes, each linked together: business planning, production planning (sales and operations planning), master production scheduling, material requirements planning, capacity requirements planning, and the execution support systems for capacity and material.

market-positioned strategy A warehouse location strategy whereby a warehouse is located close to the market it serves.

marketing concept A concept developed in the early 1960s that argues that companies should create products or service to meet customers' needs, but at a profit.

master production schedule (MPS) The master-level or top-level schedule used to set the production plan in a manufacturing facility.

materials management The movement and management of materials and products from procurement from suppliers (inbound logistics) through to the production process.

materials requirements planning (MRP) A decision-making methodology used to determine the timing and quantities of materials to purchase.

matrix structure An organisational structure in which two (or more) channels of command, budget responsibility and performance measurement exist simultaneously.

min-max or minimax A replenishment and inventory management system that sets a minimum inventory level, used to trigger a re-order when the available plus incoming receipt total is less than the minimum. The amount of the order is the difference between the calculated (less than minimum) inventory and a pre-defined maximum. Min-max systems are typically not time-phased.

national distribution centre (NDC) One DC to serve an entire national market.

operational strategy An annual plan that details operations, anticipated revenues and associated costs for the forthcoming year.

order cycle time See *customer order cycle*.

order picking The function of gathering the items associated with an order from their storage locations in order to make them available to be included in production processes or to customers.

outsourcing To utilise a third-party provider to perform logistics services previously performed in-house.

own-account carrier A company that transports its own goods and supplies in its own equipment.

pallet The platform which cartons are stacked on and then used for shipment or movement as a group. Pallets may be made of wood or composite materials. Some pallets have electronic tracking tags (RFID) and most are recycled in some manner.

pallet live racking A single-or multi-level structural storage system that is utilised to support high stacking of single items or palletised loads.

Pareto principle or 80–20 rule The principle suggests that most effects come from relatively few causes; that is, 80 per cent of the effects (or sales or costs) come from 20 per cent of the possible causes (or items). See also *ABC analysis*.

pick to light A system which consists of lights and LED displays for each pick location. The system uses software to light the next pick and display the quantity to pick.

pick to voice A system which guides users such as warehouse personnel via voice commands through a portable communication device.

piggyback Terminology used to describe a truck trailer being transported on a railroad flatcar.

place utility A value created in a product by changing its location. Transportation creates place utility.

point-of-sale (POS) The time and place at which a sale occurs, such as a cash register in a retail operation, or the order confirmation screen in an online session. Supply chain partners are interested in capturing data at the POS because it is a true record of the sale rather than being derived from other information such as inventory movement.

popularity Refers to the order popularity of goods stored in a warehouse which may see such goods stored near shipping and receiving docks for cost and handling efficiency.

possession utility The value created by marketing's effort to increase the desire to possess a good or benefit from a service.

postponement A strategy to delay final activities such as assembly, production or packaging until the latest possible time to eliminate excess inventory in the form of finished goods which may be packaged in a variety of configurations. This is the opposite of speculation.

private warehouses Warehouses owned and operated by a company for its own goods and products.

procurement The business functions of procurement planning, purchasing, inventory control, traffic, receiving, incoming inspection and salvage operations.

product recovery management (PRM) An aspect of reverse logistics where a manufacturer recovers all used and discarded products, components and materials for which the manufacturer is responsible.

production-positioned strategy A warehouse location strategy whereby a warehouse is located close to where the goods or products are produced.

productivity A measure of efficiency of resource utilisation; defined as the sum of the outputs divided by the sum of the inputs.

public warehouse Warehouse owned and operated by a third party who rents or leases the warehouse or storage space to others.

pull versus push systems If a company produces products to a forecast in anticipation of customer demand then it is 'pushing' its inventory. Conversely, if a company waits to produce its products until a customer demands them, the customer is 'pulling' the inventory.

purchasing The functions associated with the actual buying of goods and services required by a company.

quick response (QR) A strategy widely adopted by general merchandise retailers and manufacturers to reduce retail out-of-stocks, forced markdowns and operating expenses. These goals are accomplished through shipping accuracy and reduced response time. QR is a partnership strategy in which suppliers and retailers work together to respond more rapidly to the consumer by sharing point-of-sale scan data, enabling both to forecast replenishment needs.

quick-response code (QR code) A specific two-dimensional matrix barcode that is readable by dedicated QR readers, smartphones and, to a less common extent, computers with webcams.

racking The activity of placing materials onto a rack. May also refer to hardware which is used to build racks.

radio frequency identification (RFID) The use of radio frequency technology including RFID tags and tag readers to identify objects. Objects may include virtually anything physical, such as equipment, pallets of stock or even individual units of product. RFID tags can be active or passive. Active tags contain a power source and emit a signal constantly. Passive tags receive power from the radio waves sent by the scanner/reader.

randomised storage A warehouse storage technique in which goods are placed in any space that is empty when they arrive at the warehouse. Although this method requires the use of a locator file to identify part locations, it often requires less storage space than a dedicated storage method.

regional distribution centre (RDC) One DC to serve a regional market.

replenishment The process of replacing or replenishing stocks that have been used in the production process or sold to customers and consumers.

resilience The ability of a system to return to its original or desired state after being disturbed.

resource-based view (RBV) Views a firm as a collection of resources – physical, financial, individual and organisational capital – whose key to superior performance is the capability to convert these resources to provide sustainable competitive advantage.

return on investment (ROI) A financial performance measure where profit is divided by total assets or investment in a company. ROI represents the ratio of profit provided by all assets in the company.

reverse logistics A specialised segment of logistics focusing on the movement and management of products and resources after the sale and after delivery to the customer. Includes product returns for repair and/or credit.

risk The probability that a particular adverse event occurs during a stated period of time, or results from a particular challenge.

roll-on, roll-off (Ro-Ro) A type of ship designed to permit cargo to be driven on at origin and off at destination; used extensively for the movement of automobiles but also for trucks in short-seas shipping circumstances.

safety stock The stock a firm holds above normal needs as a buffer against delays in receipt of supply or changes in customer demand.

socio-technical systems (STS) These look to provide joint optimisation of technical and social systems in a firm and provide a quality of work life through employee participation in system design and the use of semi-autonomous work groups.

sortation Separating items (parcels, boxes, cartons, parts, etc.) according to their intended destination within a plant or for transit.

span of control Refers to the number of people who can report to a single manager inside an organisational hierarchy.

speculation A strategy of producing finished goods well in advance of their introduction in the marketplace in order to reduce uncertainty over demand. This is the opposite of postponement.

statistical operator control (SOC) A technique where operators use visual means to measure and plot process and product variation. Results are used to adjust variables and maintain product quality.

stock All the goods and materials that are stored by an organisation until they are needed.

stock keeping unit (SKU) A category of unit with unique combination of form, fit and function (i.e. unique components held in stock).

strategic plan Looking 1–5 years into the future and designing a logistical system (or systems) to meet the needs of the various businesses in which a company is involved.

strategy A specific action to achieve an objective.

supplier appraisal A firm's procedures to assess and verify that a supplier operates, maintains, improves and documents effective procedures that relate to the customer's requirements. Such requirements can include cost, quality, delivery, flexibility, maintenance, safety, and ISO quality and environmental standards.

supplier development Where a supplier and customer make dedicated investments in their relationship and create various bonds where the customer takes the lead in setting performance improvement targets for the supplier.

supply chain Links many companies together starting with unprocessed raw materials and ending with the final customer using the finished goods and consists of the material and informational interchanges in the chain for a particular product or service.

supply chain management (SCM) As defined by CSCMP, encompasses the planning and management of all activities involved in sourcing and procurement, conversion, and all logistics management activities, and includes coordination and collaboration with channel partners, which can be suppliers, intermediaries, third-party service providers and customers.

supply chain operations reference (SCOR) A model developed by the Supply Chain Council, built around six major processes: plan, source, make, deliver, return and enable. The aim of the SCOR is to provide a standardised method of measuring supply chain performance and to use a common set of metrics to benchmark against other organisations.

systems approach A concept that considers all functions or activities in a system need to be understood in terms of how they affect or are affected by other elements they interact with in the system.

tactical plan The process of developing a set of tactical plans (e.g. production plan, sales plan, marketing plan and so on). Two approaches to tactical planning exist for linking tactical plans to strategic plans – production planning, and sales and operations planning.

third-party logistics (3PL) service provider A firm which provides multiple logistics services for use by customers. Preferably, these services are integrated or 'bundled' together by the provider. These firms facilitate the movement of parts and materials from suppliers to manufacturers, and finished products from manufacturers to distributors and retailers. Among the services they provide are transportation, warehousing, cross-docking, inventory management, packaging and freight forwarding. Also called a logistics service provider (LSP).

time utility A value created in a product by having the product available at the time desired. Transportation and warehousing create time utility.

total cost analysis A decision-making approach that considers minimisation of total costs and recognises the inter-relationship among system variables such as transportation, warehousing, inventory and customer service.

total cost concept A concept that states the costs of all logistics activities need to be considered in total to effectively manage logistics processes. Total cost analysis is the tool used in this concept.

total cost of ownership (TCO) Total cost of a computer asset throughout its life cycle, from acquisition to disposal. TCO is the combined hard and soft costs of owning networked information assets. 'Hard' costs include items such as the purchase price of the asset, implementation fees, upgrades, maintenance contracts, support contracts and disposal costs, licence fees that may or may not be upfront or charged annually. These costs are considered 'hard costs' because they are tangible and easily accounted for.

total quality management (TQM) A management approach where managers constantly communicate with organisational stakeholders to emphasise the importance of continuous quality improvement.

Toyota production system (TPS) A system of automotive production developed by Toyota to speed up the production process, improve quality and reduce waste. See also *kanban* and *just-in-time*.

trailer on flatcar (TOFC) Transport of truck trailers with their loads on specially designed rail-cars. See also *piggyback*.

transaction cost economics (TCE) Describes a firm in organisational terms or as a governance structure where decision makers respond to economic factors or transaction costs within the firm that affect both the structure of the firm and the structure of the industry within which it operates.

transport management system (TMS) A computer system designed to provide optimised transportation management in various modes along with associated activities, including managing shipping units, labour planning and building, shipment scheduling through inbound, outbound, intra-company shipments, documentation management (especially when international shipping is involved) and third-party logistics management.

transportation brokers Companies that provide services to both shippers and carriers by arranging and coordinating transportation of products.

turnover ratio Measures how many times a company's inventory has been sold (turned over) during a period of time. The cost of goods sold divided by the average level of inventory on hand. Operationally, inventory turns are measured as total throughput divided by average level of inventory for a given period; how many times a year the average inventory for a firm changes over or is sold.

unitisation In warehousing, the consolidation of several units into larger units for fewer handlings.

utilisation A measure of input use and usually presented as a ratio of actual input used to a pre-determined norm value.

value-added networks (VANs) A company that acts as a clearing-house for electronic transactions between trading partners. Receives EDI transmissions from sending trading partners and holds them in a 'mailbox' until retrieved by the receiving partners.

value analysis A method to determine how features of a product or service relate to cost, functionality, appeal and utility to a customer (i.e. engineering value analysis).

value-of-service pricing Pricing according to the value of the product being transported; third-degree price discrimination; demand-oriented pricing; charging what the traffic will bear.

vehicle telematics Systems integrate telecommunications and informatics and are used for a number of purposes, including collecting road tolls, managing road usage, tracking fleet vehicle locations, recovering stolen vehicles, providing automatic collision notification and providing location-driven driver information services.

Vendor-managed inventory (VMI) The practice of retailers making suppliers responsible for determining order size and timing, usually based on receipt of retail POS and inventory data. Its goal is to increase retail inventory turns and reduce stock-outs. It may or may not involve consignment of inventory (supplier ownership of the inventory located at the customer).

very large crude carrier (VLCC) Large crude oil supertanker of between 200,000 and 300,000 dead weight tons (DWT) in size. Tankers that exceed 300,000 DWT are known as ultra large crude carriers (ULCCs).

warehouse Storage place for products. Principal warehouse activities include receipt of product, storage, shipment and order picking.

warehouse management system (WMS) System used in effectively managing warehouse business processes and direct warehouse activities, including receiving, put-away, picking, shipping and inventory cycle counts. Includes support of radio frequency communications, allowing real-time data transfer between the system and warehouse personnel. Also maximises space and minimises material handling by automating put-away processes.

warehousing The storing (holding) of goods in a warehouse.

work-in-process (WIP) inventory Parts and sub-assemblies in the process of becoming completed finished goods. Work in process generally includes all of the material, labour and overhead charged against a production order which has not been absorbed back into inventory through receipt of completed products.

Index